U0798037

2006
中国农产品价格调查年鉴

CHINA YEARBOOK OF AGRICULTURAL PRICE SURVEY

国家统计局农村社会经济调查司 编
Department of Rural Survey, National Bureau of Statistics of China

中国统计出版社
China Statistics Press

(京)新登字 041 号

图书在版编目（CIP）数据

中国农产品价格调查年鉴. 2006
/ 国家统计局农村社会经济调查司编.
- 北京：中国统计出版社，2006. 7
ISBN 7-5037-5023-5

Ⅰ. 中…
Ⅱ. 国…
Ⅲ. 农产品 - 价格 - 统计资料 - 中国 -2006- 年鉴
Ⅳ. F323.7-54

中国版本图书馆 CIP 数据核字（2006）第 049070 号

中国农产品价格调查年鉴— 2006

作　　者 / 国家统计局农村社会经济调查司编
责任编辑 / 姚　立
E-mail /cbsebs@stats.gov.cn
封面设计 / 艺编广告 • 张　冰
出版发行 / 中国统计出版社
通信地址 / 北京市西城区月坛南街 75 号
邮政编码 /100826
办公地址 / 北京市丰台区西三环南路甲 6 号
电　　话 / 邮购 (010) 63376907　书店(010)68783172
印　　刷 / 河北天普润印刷厂
经　　销 / 新华书店
开　　本 /880 × 1230 毫米　1/16
字　　数 / 450 千字
印　　张 /17.75
印　　数 /1 — 1800 册
版　　别 /2006 年 7 月第 1 版
版　　次 /2006 年 7 月第 1 次印刷
书　　号 /ISBN 7-5037-5023-5/F • 2345
定　　价 / 88. 00 元

《中国农产品价格调查年鉴—2006》
编辑委员会

CHINA YEARBOOK OF AGRICULTURAL PRICE SURVEY—2006

EDITORIAL BOARD AND STAFF

前　言

一、本书编辑目的与作用

伴随我国市场经济体制的建立与完善，农村经济运行市场化步伐加快，市场机制在农产品流通与贸易中的基础作用日益显现，宏观决策和社会公众对农产品价格信息的需求与日俱增。为了适应这一新的形势，国家统计局农村社会经济调查系统发挥自身优势，逐步建立起完整的农产品价格调查体系，对农产品生产和流通全过程进行密集跟踪调查，全方位把握农产品价格走势，深入透视农产品生产、贸易和消费环节的分配关系和利益格局。汇编这些价格数据的目的就是为了充分发挥农产品价格信息在分析研究我国农产品供给与需求、农产品市场竞争与产业结构调整、农民收入与居民消费等方面的独特作用，更好地服务于各级党政领导的“三农”决策，服务于社会主义新农村建设，服务于关注农产品价格问题的研究机构和各界社会公众。

二、本书编辑的主要内容与资料调查方法

本书的内容主要包括我国农产品生产价格、集贸市场价格、批发市场价格和国际市场农产品价格信息四部分。农产品生产价格是农产品生产者农户和农场直接出售其产品时实际获得的单位产品价格，它是农产品集贸市场价格、批发价格和消费价格形成的基础和前提。农产品生产价格调查采用随机抽样的方法抽选调查网点，实行抽样调查。全国共抽选31000个农业生产经营单位，其中农户占90.5%，农场占9.5%。调查内容涉及农林牧渔四个大类，十五个中类三十个小类600种农产品。农产品集贸市场价格调查是对全国200个农产品主产县（市）36种农产品进行的集贸市场价格调查，旨在反映我国农产品主产区大宗农产品的交易价格和价格走势。批发市场价格调查是对全国100家大中型农产品批发市场150种农产品进行的批发价格调查，旨

在收集批发价格资料，准确把握全国主要农产品价格走势和供求状况。国际市场农产品价格资料主要来源于芝加哥和纽约商品交易所交易信息以及美国农业部农业统计局的月度价格报告。

三、特别说明

本书重点收录2005年农产品价格调查资料，同时编发了2000年以来全国主要农产品的价格数据。生产价格指数以上年或上年同期价格为100。农产品集贸市场价格单位统一为元/公斤，价格数据保留两位小数。集贸市场价格走势分为环比和同比两个系列，环比以上月或上季度价格为100，同比以上年同月或同期价格为100。

为了及时反映全国农产品价格走势，我们将定期出版《中国农产品价格调查年鉴》。由于农产品价格调查和指数编制是一项全新的工作，限于我们的经验和水平，书中疏漏在所难免，不妥之处敬请读者批评指正。

编　者

2006年5月

Preface

I. Purpose of Compiling this Book

Along with the establishment and development of market economy in China, the market-oriented development of rural economy has been accelerated, the fundamental role of market mechanism has gradually manifested itself in circulation and trade of agricultural products, and the government and general public have more demand for the information on price of agricultural products. so as to meet the needs of macro-economic decision-making and the public understanding.

In order to fit in with this new situation, the National Bureau of Statistics of China set up a systematic survey on price of agricultural products through its rural socio-economic survey system to follow the track of whole process of the production and circulation of agricultural products, keep abreast of the change trend of the price of agricultural products in an all-round way, and thoroughly understand the distribution relations and interest pattern among the production, trade and consumption links. The purpose of compiling price data is to bring the unique role of the information on price of agricultural products into full play in analyzing and studying the supply and demand of agricultural products, market competition of agricultural products and readjustment of industrial structure, income of farmers and the consumption of residents, etc., in order to provide good service to the governments at different levels for decisions on the issues of agriculture, rural areas and farmers, and to provide good services to the research institutes and the general public of different circles, which pay close attention to the issues of the price of agricultural products.

II. Content of This Book and Method of Survey

This book includes mainly four parts of information on agricultural products: (1) producer price, (2) retail price at free market, (3) wholesale price, (4) price at international market. Producer price of agricultural products refers to the farmers and agricultural producers to sell their products directly at the actual unit price. It is the base and prerequisite for forming retail price at free market, wholesale price and consumer price. The sample survey is conducted on producer price. The sample units are selected at random. A total of 31000 units engaged in agricultural production and management have been selected in the whole country, in which the agricultural households account for 90.5% and the farms account for 9.5%. The survey covers crop planting, forestry, animal husbandry and fishery with 15 divisions, 30 groups and 600 products. The survey on the price at free market covers price of 36 agricultural products in 200 major producing counties and cities. It is conducted for the purpose of reflecting the trading price of agricultural products of large amount in major producing areas and the change trend of the price. The survey on wholesale price is the survey on 150 agricultural products at 100 large and medium sized wholesale markets in the city. It is conducted to reflect the fluctuation of price of major agricultural products at the wholesale market and the relationship between supply and demand of such products. The data on the price of agricultural products at the international market are compiled according to the trading information at the Chicago Board of Trade, the New York Board of Trade (NYBOT) and NASS/USDA.

III. Special Notes

Except the data on price of agricultural products in 2005, this book has also compiled and released the data on price of major agricultural products in China since 2000. The price in the previous year or the price in the same period in the previous year is taken as 100 while calculating the producer price index. The price unit of agricultural products at free market is unified as yuan/kg and two decimals are kept. The data on fluctuation of the price of agricultural products at free market are classified into two kinds, namely the chain index and the fixed base index. The chain index takes the price of previous month or quarter as 100 while the fixed base index takes the price of same month or same period in previous year as 100.

In order to reflect the change trend of the price of agricultural products in China, the China Yearbook of Agricultural Price Survey is published periodically. As the survey on price of agricultural products and the compilation of the price index are a great challenge to us because of our limited experience and knowledge, errors will inevitably be made in this book. Comments and corrections from readers are highly appreciated.

The Editor
Beijing
May 2006

目录

第三部分 农产品集贸市场价格
Part III Prices of the Agricultural Products at the Rural Market Fairs

第四部分 农产品批发市场价格
Part Ⅳ Prices of the Agricultural Products at the Wholesale Market

第五部分 国际市场农产品价格
Part Ⅴ Prices of the Agricultural Products At the International Market

1

“十五”期间我国农产品价格回升的特点与影响

Characteristics and Effects of the Rise of Price of Agricultural products in the 10th Five-Year Plan Period

“十五”期间我国农产品价格回升的特点与影响

以入世为契机，“十五”期间国家大力推进农村市场体系建设，相继出台粮棉购销市场化改革的重大政策措施，农产品流通与贸易的市场经济环境日趋完善，价格对农产品生产、流通与消费的调节和引导作用增强。伴随国内市场大宗农产品供求形势的变化，“十五”期间我国农产品价格强劲回升，2005年全国农产品生产价格比2000年上涨23.1%，其中粮食价格上涨35.2%，对我国粮食增产、农民增收做出了重要贡献。

一、“十五”时期我国农产品价格走势

（一）农产品价格强劲回升

“十五”期间，我国农产品价格走出“九五”时期持续下跌的困境，从温和上扬到强势回升，整体呈现逐年上升态势（见图1）。从环比指数看，农产品生产价格[①]除2002年比上年下降0.3%外，其他各年均在上升。2001、2003和2005年生产价格分别比上年上涨3.1%、4.4%和1.4%，2004年涨幅最大，上涨13.1%。与2000年相比，2005年农产品生产价格上涨23.1%，“十五”期间年均上涨4.2%，是改革开放以来我国农产品价格上涨幅度较大的时期，这与“九五”期间的下降行情形成强烈对比。尽管如此，“十五”末全国农产品生产价格总水平仍比1995年低4.7%。

（二）粮食价格接近历史高位

受1999～2003年粮食连年减产、供求关系趋紧和国家实施粮食最低收购价政策的影响，“十五”期间我国粮食价格呈震荡上行态势（见图2）。2002和2005年我国粮食生产价格分别比上年小幅下降3.8%和0.9%，2001、2003和2004年粮食价格分别比上年上涨7.6%、4.5%和26.2%。“十五”时期全国各年度粮食生产价格均高于2000年水平，2004年比2000年上涨36.5%，为“十五”时期粮食生产价格最高年份，仅比1996年的历史最高价位[②]低6.5%。“十五”期间全国粮食生产价格年均上涨6.2%，2005年粮食价格比2000年上涨23%，粮价总水平整体步入“合理的粮价”区间，亿万农民特别是粮食主产区农民从中受益匪浅，这是国家宏观调控政策来之不易的积极成果。

（三）棉花价格大幅波动

“十五”时期我国棉花价格大起大落，波动剧烈。从年度价格走势看，2001和2002年棉花生产价格分别比上年上涨6.7%和3.4%；2003年急剧攀升，上涨幅度达35.3%；2004年急转直下，下跌幅度达20.5%；2005年比上年回升11.8%。受国内棉花需求增长加快的影响，“十五”时期我国棉花价格总水平比“九五”上涨8.8%；各年度棉花价格也都高于“九五”末2000年的价位，2003年比2000年上涨49.2%，为“九五”以来棉花生产价格最高年份。“十五”期间全国棉花生产价格年均上涨5.8%，2005年棉花价格分别比1995和2000年上涨2.6%和32.7%。

（四）油料价格先扬后抑

“十五”时期我国油料生产价格走势呈S形，2001和2005年全国油料生产价格分别比上年下降10%和8.7%，而2002、2003和2004年则分别比上年上涨4.8%、19.4%和16.6%。除2001年外，“十五”时期各年度油料价格指数均高于2000年水平，2004年为“九五”以来油料生产价格最高年份，比1995和2000年分别上涨3.1%和31.3%。“十五”时期油料价格年均上涨3.7%，2005年油料价格比2000年上涨20%。

（五）畜产品价格平稳回升

---

① 农产品生产价格（Farm gate price）是指农产品生产者农户和农场直接出售其产品时实际获得的单位产品价格。生产价格既是影响农民农业收入的重要因素，又是构成流通环节的批发价格、零售价格和居民消费价格的基础。

② 改革开放以来我国农产品价格历经四次较大幅度上涨，其中以1990～1995年的上涨幅度最大，主要粮食品种价格分别于1995年和1996年涨至最高价位，1996年为1978年以来粮价最高年份。

“十五”时期我国畜产品价格逐年上升。从环比价格指数看，2004 年受粮食价格大幅上涨、饲养成本上升的影响，畜产品生产价格指数上涨幅度达 11.1%，其余年份的价格涨幅都在 5%以下。“十五”时期畜产品价格年均上涨 3.4%，2005 年畜产品生产价格比 2000 年上涨 18.4%。

(六)渔业产品价格先抑后扬

“十五”时期我国水产品价格先抑后扬。2001 和 2002 年水产品价格环比指数略降，分别比上年下降 1.4%和 4.1%；2003～2005 年生产价格持续上涨，涨幅分别为 0.3%、10.2% 和 4.7%。与 2000 年相比，2001～2003 年水产品生产价格指数分别下降 1.4%、5.5%和 5.2%；2004 和 2005 年生产价格指数上涨 4.5%和 9.4%。

二、“十五”时期我国农产品价格变化的特点

(一)农产品价格大幅震荡

波动频繁、震荡幅度大是“十五”时期我国农产品价格变化的特点，粮价大幅上涨更是“十五”时期农产品价格波动的突出特点。2004 年全国粮食生产价格比上年上涨 26.2%，其中谷物上涨 28.1%，稻谷、小麦价格分别上涨 36.3%和 31.2%，大豆价格上涨 20.2%，主要粮食品种价格上涨幅度之大远远超出市场预期。从年度价格走势看，“十五”期间棉花价格波动最为频繁。2003 年棉价急剧攀升，涨幅高达 35.3%；2004 年急转直下，下跌幅度达 20.5%；2005 年回升 11.8%。水果、蔬菜等鲜活农产品价格的季节性波动同样引起各界关注。

(二)农产品价格上涨属恢复性回升

改革开放以来，我国农产品价格历经四次大幅上涨，其中尤以“八五”期间的农产品价格上涨时间最长、涨幅最大，主要农产品价格最终在 1996 年达到历史最高价位。“十五”时期的农产品价格上涨是在供求关系发生变化的形势下，对 1997～2000 年农产品市场低迷、价格持续下跌的纠正，属于恢复性上涨。2005 年全国农产品生产价格分别比 1995 和 1996 年低 4.7%和 8.5%，粮食、棉花、油料和畜产品价格分别比 1996 年低 7.4%、0.5%、2.5% 和 8.2%，渔业产品价格比 1996 年低 12.4%。

(三)价格形成机制向市场化迈进

“十五”期间我国农产品购销市场化改革全面深化，市场供求日益成为农产品价格走势的决定因素。从棉花流通体制改革来看，早在 1999 年棉花购销价格就已全面放开，政府仅公布棉花收购指导价；2001 年为打破行业垄断和地区封锁，又放开了对棉花收购主体的限制，凡符合条件的企业均可从事棉花收购，实现了多渠道经营和有序竞争。粮食流通体制改革在“十五”时期也取得重大进展，2004 年全面放开粮食收购市场，国家仅对短缺的重点粮食品种在主产区实行最低收购价。

由此可见，“十五”期间农产品价格回升主要是由于市场供给偏紧所致，市场机制在农产品价格形成中起着基础性作用，这与前三次主要由政府调价主导的农产品上涨完全不同，市场供求变化是本轮价格上涨的主导因素。

(四)国际市场的影响加深

随着经济全球化和我国对外开放的深化，国内市场与国际市场的联系与互动日益加强。“十五”期间，我国农产品对外贸易规模快速增长，比“九五”增长 71%，其中出口增长 47.5%，进口增长 105.8%。“十五”时期我国农业外贸依存度为 18.2%，比“九五”提高 4.2 个百分点，反映了我国农产品国际贸易对国内市场供求的影响加深。随国际市场对国内农产品生产、流通的影响扩大，国内农产品价格走势也日益受到国际因素的影响。

“十五”时期粮食、棉花和油料等土地密集型农产品进口弥补了国内产需缺口，对调节国内供求平衡发挥了重要作用。2004 年我国粮食净进口 482 亿斤，占当年产量的 5.1%；2005 年粮食净进口 429 亿斤，占当年产量 4.4%。“十五”中后期大豆进口量连年超过国内产量，2003、2004 和 2005 年分别进口大豆 415 亿斤、405 亿斤和 532 亿斤，分别高于当年大豆产量 107 亿斤、57 亿斤和 205 亿斤，大豆消费量的 50%以上源于进口，国内市场大豆价格走势与国际市场行情日趋吻合。

三、“十五”时期我国农产品价格回升的积极影响

(一)有利于挖掘生产潜力，扩大农作物播种面积

“十五”前半期，我国农产品价格总体低迷，农作物总播种面积由 2000 年的 23.5 亿亩下降到 2003 年的 22.9 亿亩，下降 5828 万亩。2000～2003 年粮食播种面积减少 1.4 亿亩，其中稻谷减少 5100 万亩，小麦减少 6900 万亩。播种面积的减

少主要是由于农产品价格多年低迷，生产效益下降甚至种地赔本，农民生产积极性降低，农民降低复种面积甚至撂荒部分耕地，导致总播种面积下降。受2003年三季度开始粮食价格大幅上涨的影响，2004年农作物总播种面积比2003增加1700万亩，粮食播种面积增加3294万亩，其中稻谷增加2800万亩，玉米增加2067万亩，大豆面积增加414万亩。

(二)有利于增加农业生产投入，推广先进实用技术

"十五"期间农民农业生产投入增幅总体高于农产品价格上涨幅度。2001年农产品价格上涨3.1%，刺激农业生产投入增长7.2%；2004年农产品价格上涨13.1%，农业生产投入费用增长24.2%。"十五"时期，我国良种覆盖率超过95%。平原地区基本告别"牛耕人收"的传统耕作方式，农业机械设备得到广泛使用。截至2004年底，我国农用机械总动力已达6403亿瓦，比2000年增长21.8%。与2000年相比，2004年我国有效灌溉面积增长1.2%，化肥施用量、农用塑料薄膜使用量分别增长11.8%和25.8%，农药使用量增长8.3%。

(三)有利于提高农产品产量

农产品价格对农业生产的综合影响表现为产品产量的变化。农产品价格变动直接影响播种面积，同时影响农业生产投入，在其他条件不变的情况下，投入增加单产增加。以粮食生产为例，"十五"时期我国粮食生产价格对粮食产量的影响具有明显的正相关性。2004年全国粮食生产价格比上年上涨26.2%，粮食产量增产9%；2005年粮食生产价格比2000年上涨23%，全国粮食产量增产4.7%。

(四)有利于增加农民收入

1.农业收入是农民收入的重要来源。"十五"期间，全国农民人均纯收入增加1002元，其中农业纯收入增加379元，对农民纯收入增收的贡献率为37.9%。2005年我国农民人均纯收入3255元，其中来自农业的人均纯收入为1470元，占45.2%。

2.农产品价格回升是农民农业纯收入增加的主要因素。"十五"时期农产品生产价格总指数变动率和农民人均农业纯收入变动率的相关系数为0.97，存在强相关性。2004年全国农民人均农业纯收入1398元，其中来自粮食的纯收入621元，比上年增加172元，粮食纯收入对农业纯收入增长的贡献率达到97.7%。在粮食纯收入中，粮价大幅回升使农民增收165元，粮价对当年农业纯收入增加的贡献率为93.8%。

3.农产品价格上涨更有利于中低收入农户增收。中低收农户收入来源集中于农业特别是种植业收入。2004年在农产品生产价格上涨13.1%的带动下，低收入户和中低收入户农民人均纯收入分别增长16.3%和14.7%；中等收入户增长13.4%。当年中高收入户和高收入户分别增收12.5%和9.2%。低收入户和中低收入户收入对农产品价格波动的反应更为灵敏。

(五)有利于保持居民消费价格的稳定

"十五"以来，我国大多数工业品产能过剩，上游产品价格向下游产品的传导机制不畅，农产品价格回升对居民消费价格的稳定效应明显增强。2004和2005年居民消费价格分别上涨3.9%和1.8%，其中食品价格分别上涨9.9%和2.9%，如扣除食品价格上涨的影响3.3%和1%，全国居民消费价格仅上涨0.6%和0.8%。农产品价格回升对缓解全国物价总水平"紧缩"压力发挥重要作用。

四、保持农产品价格平稳运行的政策建议

(一)进一步完善农产品市场体系

建立发达完善的市场体系是发挥市场机制形成合理农产品价格的必要条件，也是新农村建设的重要内容。批发市场是农产品市场体系的龙头，应充分发挥其信息集中、反应灵敏的优势，加强市场信息体系和配套的产品加工、冷藏、运输等基础设施建设，严把产品质量检验检疫关。积极发展农产品零售市场，减少流通环节，鼓励农业流通合作组织或龙头企业到城镇建立农产品连锁超市或便利店，鼓励大型超市、连锁店直接从生产基地直接采购。充分发挥期货市场的价格发现功能，加强对农民的信息服务，降低生产与需求信息的不对称性。大力发展电子商务、拍卖和经纪人代理等新型交易方式。

(二)提高农户抵御市场风险能力

积极探索分散的家庭经营和大市场对接的可能途径，引导农民参与各种形式的协会及专业合作组织，壮大农村经纪人队伍，提高农民进入市场的组织化程度。通过专业化合作，在了解市场信息、组织生产和市场谈判中形成合力，改变市场交易中的劣势地位，提高抵御市场风险的能力。应加快建

立政策性农业保险制度，为农民抵御自然灾害和市场风险提供支持。

（三）遏制农资价格的过快上涨

农资价格上涨抬高生产成本，降低生产效益，不利于农产品价格稳定和农民增收。遏制农资价格过快上涨，一是要采取优惠措施扶持农资生产企业，降低农资生产成本，增加农资供给；二是理顺农资流通，减少中间流通环节，降低流通费用；三是加大监督执法力度，规范农资流通秩序，防止随意抬高价格；四是加大对农户购买生产资料的直接补贴力度，提高补贴标准，扩大补贴覆盖面。

（四）加强对粮食价格的宏观调控

保持粮价在合理水平上的基本稳定，重在把好储备调节和进出口两道关。根据市场供求状况和粮价走势，把握好储备粮进出库的时机和规模，平抑粮价的大幅波动。随着我国粮食进口规模逐年扩大，进口粮食对调节国内产需缺口的积极作用持续增强，进口粮食品种、数量及其投放市场的时机都会直接影响到国内市场粮食价格走势。进出口与储备调节是国家对粮食市场实施宏观调控的两个重要手段，在具体操作上必须注意二者的有效配合。

（五）坚持和完善对重点粮食品种的最低收购价政策

国家对短缺的重点粮食品种实行最低收购价政策，是促进粮食增产、农民增收以及稳定市场粮价的重要政策措施。从调查情况来看，主产区农民反映近两年的最低保护价标准偏低，种粮比较收益仍不高。建议适当提高最低保护价标准，进一步提高农民种粮积极性，确保粮食安全和农民稳定增收。

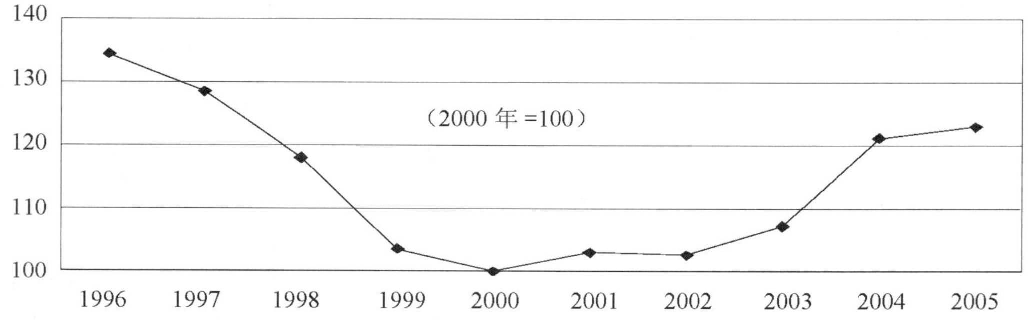

图 1 “九五”和“十五”期间农产品生产价格总指数①走势

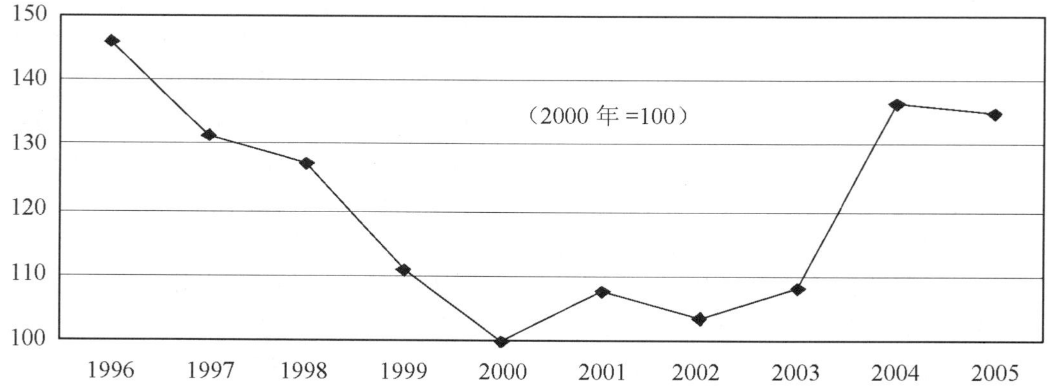

图 2 “九五”和“十五”我国粮食生产价格指数走势

① a. 资料来源：《中国农产品价格调查年鉴 2005》。b. 农产品生产价格同比指数以 2000 年为基期（2000 年＝100），环比指数以上年为 100。c. 1978～2005 年农产品生产价格指数：2000 年以前为农产品收购价格指数，2001 年后为生产价格指数，下同。

Characteristics and Effects of the Rise of Price of Agricultural Products in the 10th Five-Year Plan Period

Taking the opportunity of entry into WTO, China has accelerated the construction of market system in the rural area in the 10th Five-Year Plan period. China has implemented important policies on market-oriented reform for grain and cotton distribution system one after another during last five years. The market environment of agricultural trade has been improved, and the price of agricultural products has played an increasing important role in regulating agricultural production, trading and consumption. Because of the changes of the relationship between supply and demand for grain, the price of agricultural products rose sharply in 10th Five-Year plan period. The national producer price of agricultural products in 2005 rose by 23.1% as compared with 2000. Of the total, that of grain rose by 35.2%. The rise has contributed great much to the growth of grain yield and farmer income.

I Trend of the Price of Agricultural Products in the 10th Five-Year Plan Period

1. The price of agricultural products rose sharply

The price of agricultural products rose mildly at first and then sharply grew as a whole in the 10th Five-Year plan period, contrasting to the situation of that declining continuously in the 9th Five-Year plan period (see graph 1). The chain price index showed that the producer price of the agricultural products rose in all years except that declined by 0.3% in 2002. As compared with preceding year, the producer price rose by 3.1%, 4.4% and 1.4% respectively in 2001, 2003 and 2005. In 2004, the producer price rose by 13.1% and the increase rate was the highest in the 10th Five-Year period. The producer price of agricultural products rose by 23.1% in 2005 as compared with 2000. The annual average price of agricultural products rose by 4.2% in the 10th Five-Year plan period and the increase rate was higher since the reform and opening up to the outside world. The price of agricultural products rose sharply in 10th Five-Year plan period in contrast to that declined continuously in the 9th Five-Year plan period. However, the producer price of agricultural products in 2005 was 4.7% down from that in 1995.

2. The price of grain approached the peak in history

In the 10th Five-Year plan period, the price of grain fluctuated and tended to rise as a whole because of the continuous decline of grain production from 1999 to 2003, the tight supply of grain and the policy of grain purchasing at the lowest price of protection (see graph 2). As compared with previous year, the producer price of grain rose by 7.6%, 4.5% and 26.2% in 2001, 2003 and 2004 respectively, while that declined slightly by 3.8% and 0.9% respectively in 2002 and 2005. The annual average producer price of grain in the 10th Five-Year plan period was all higher than that in 2000. The producer price of grain in 2004 rose by 36.5% as compared with 2000 and was the highest level in the 10th Five-Year plan period. It's only down 6.5% from 1996 in which the producer price of grain was the highest in the history . The annual average producer price of grain rose by 6.2% as compared with the previous year. The producer price of grain in 2005 rose by 23% as compared with 2000. Generally speaking, at present, the price of grain is reasonable and hundreds of millions farmers especially those in major grain producing areas benefited great much from the rise of price of grain. It is a positive effect of exercise of macroeconomic regulation policy.

3. The price of cotton fluctuated sharply

The producer price of cotton rose slightly by 6. 7% and 3. 4% respectively in 2001 and 2002. In 2003, the price of cotton rose sharply and the increase rate reached 35. 3%. However, the price declined sharply by 20. 5% in 2004 and rose by 11. 8% in 2005. The average price of cotton in the 10th Five-Year plan period was higher than that in the 9th Five-Year plan period due to domestic demand for cotton increasing rapidly. As compared with the end year of the 9th Five-Year plan period, the annual price of cotton was all higher in the 10th Five-Year plan period. The price of cotton in 2003 rose by 49. 2% as compared with 2000 and was the highest level since the 9th Five-Year plan period. The annual increase rate of price of cotton was 5. 8% in the 10th Five-Year plan period. As compared with 1995 and 2000, the producer price of cotton rose by 2. 6% and 32. 7% respectively.

4. The price of oil-bearing crops rose at first and then declined

The movement trail of the price of oil-bearing crops looks like "S". The producer price of oil-bearing crops declined by 10% and 8. 7% respectively in 2001 and 2005, and rose by 4. 8%, 19. 4% and 16. 6% respectively in 2002, 2003 and 2004. Except for 2001, the annual average price of oil-bearing crops in 10th Five-Year plan period was higher than that in 2000. The producer price of oil-bearing crops in 2004 rose by 3. 1% and 31. 3% respectively as compared with that in 1995 and 2000 and was the highest since the 9th Five-Year plan. The annual average producer price of oil-bearing crops rose by 3. 7% over the previous year in the 10th Five-Year plan period. The price of oil-bearing crops in 2005 rose by 20% over 2000.

5. The price of livestock products rose steadily

The producer price of livestock products rose steadily in the 10th Five-Year plan period. The increase rate of the producer price of livestock products was less than 5% in the 10th Five-Year plan period except that in 2004 rose by 11. 1% as the price of grain rose rapidly and the cost of livestock rose with a big margin. The annual average producer price of livestock products rose by 3. 4% over previous year. As compared with 2000, the price of livestock products rose by 18. 4% in 2005.

6. The price of fishery products declined at first and then rose

The price of fishery products declined at first and rose then in the 10th Five-Year plan period. As compared with the previous year, the producer price of fishery products declined by 1. 4% and 4. 1% respectively in 2001 and 2002, and rose by 0. 3%, 10. 2% and 4. 7% respectively from 2003 to 2005. As compared with 2000, the producer price of fishery products declined by 1. 4%, 5. 5% and 5. 2% respectively in 2001, 2002 and 2003, and rose by 4. 5% and 9. 4% respectively in 2004 and 2005.

Ⅱ Main Characteristics of the Change of Price of Agricultural Products in the 10th Five-Year Plan Period

1. The price fluctuated with a big margin

The price of agricultural products fluctuated frequently with a big margin in the 10th Five-Year plan period. The price of grain which rose rapidly was one of prominent characteristics. As compared with the previous year, the producer price of grain rose by 26. 2% in 2004. Of the total, that of cereal, paddy, wheat and soybean rose by 28. 1%, 36. 3%, 31. 2% and 20. 2% respectively. The increase rate of grain crops went up beyond the market expectation. Judging by the annual changing rate, the price of cotton fluctuated most frequently. The price of cotton rose sharply and the increase rate reached 35. 3% in 2003. However, that declined sharply by 20. 5% in 2004 and rose again by 11. 8% in 2005. It is noticeable that the price of fresh agricultural products such as fruits and vegetables fluctuated seasonably.

2. The price of agricultural products showed a recovering rise

Since the reform and opening up to the outside world, the price of agricultural products has risen for 4 rounds with a big margin. The rise of price of agricultural products in the 8th Five-Year plan period lasted for a long period and the increase rate was the highest. The price of most of agricultural products reached the history peak in 1996. Because the relationship of supply and demand changed, the rise of price of agricultural products in the 10th Five-Year plan period recovered from the situation that declined continuously in the 9th Five-Year plan period and started to rise from the lower level before. As compared with 1995 and 1996, the national producer price of agricultural products was down by 4.7% and 8.5% respectively in 2005. The prices of grain, cotton, oil-bearing crops and livestock products in 2005 declined by 7.4%, 0.5%, 2.5% and 8.2% respectively as compared with 1996, and the price of fishery products declined by 12.4% over 1996.

3. Market mechanism has become the decisive factor affecting the price trend of agricultural products

The market-oriented reform of circulation of agricultural products has been strengthened and the market mechanism has become decisive factor affecting the price trend of agricultural products in the 10th Five-Year plan period. As far as the reform of cotton distribution system is concerned, the prices of cotton selling and purchasing were deregulated early in 1999 and the government only publishes reference prices. In order to break the trade monopoly and regional blockade, the central government allowed all qualified enterprises to compete at the cotton market. The cotton market has been becoming more qualified than before. The reform of grain distribution system has been deepened in the 10th Five-Year plan period. The government stopped the control over the purchasing price of grain and implemented the policy of purchasing grain at the lowest price of protection in the major producing areas in 2004.

So, the rise of price of agricultural products in 10th Five-Year plan period was mainly due to tight supply, and the market mechanism played a basic role at the market. The reason for this round rise of the price of agricultural products was different from the last 3 round rises before in which the government played a basic role in putting the price upward.

4. The international market became more important factor affecting the domestic price of agricultural products

With the development of economic globalization and opening up to the outside world, the price of agricultural products at domestic and international market linked closely. The foreign trade of agricultural products in China increased rapidly in the 10th Five-Year plan period, up 71% over the 9th Five-Year plan period. Of the total, the export and import of agricultural products rose by 47.5% and 105.8% respectively. The average ratio of foreign trade of agricultural products to GDP was 18.2% in the 10th Five-Year plan period, a rise of 4.2% over the 9th Five-Year plan period. It shows that foreign trade of agricultural products has more important impacts on the supply and demand at domestic market. Consequently, the international market has become an important factor affecting the price of agricultural products at the domestic market.

The import of land-intensive agricultural products such as grain, cotton and oil-bearing crops etc compensated the gap between the domestic production and consumption and played an important role in keeping balance on domestic market The net import of grain reached 24.1 billion kilogram and 21.5 billion kilogram in 2004 and 2005 respectively, accounting for 5.1% and 4.4% of domestic production. The import of soybean continued to surpass the domestic production in the middle and later of 10th Five-Year plan period. The import of soybean reached 20.7 billion kilogram in 2003, 20.2 billion kilogram in 2004 and 26.6 billion kilogram in 2005, which were higher than domestic production at the same year, 5.4 billion kilogram, 2.8 billion kilogram and 10.2 billion kilogram respectively. So, above half of the domestic consumption of soybeans depended on import and the price of soybean at the domestic market closely followed the price at the international market.

Ⅲ Positive Effects of the Rise of the Price of Agricultural Products in the 10th Five-Year Plan Period

1. The rise is favorable to making full use of the potential production capacity and expansion of planting area of crops

The price of agricultural products in China was at the lower level as a whole in the first half of 10th Five-Year plan period and the total sown area of crops decreased 58.25 million mu, from 2.35 billion mu in 2000 to 2.29 billion mu in 2003. The sown area of grain decreased 0.14 billon mu from 2000 to 2003. Of the total, that of paddy decreased 51 million mu, that of wheat decreased by 69 million mu. The main reason for the decrease of sown area was that the price of agricultural products continued to decline, the agricultural benefits declined and even could not cover the costs of agricultural production. The lower benefits affected the production enthusiasm of farmer, and the farmer tended to decrease the multiple cropping area and even abandoned some. So the total sown area decreased. Because of the sharp rise of the price of agricultural products beginning in the third quarter in 2003, the total sown area in 2004 increased 17 million mu over 2003, the grain sown area increased 32.94 million mu, that of paddy increased 28 million mu, that of corn increased 20.67 million mu, that of soybean increased 4.14 million mu.

2. The rise is favorable to the increase of input in agricultural production and adoption of advanced and applicable agricultural technique

The increase rate of input in agricultural production was higher as a whole than that of the price of agricultural products in the 10th Five-Year plan period. In 2001, the price of agricultural products rose by 3.1% and it stimulated the input in agricultural production, up by 7.2%. The input in agricultural production rose by 24.2, caused by a rise of 13.1% of the price of agricultural products. More than 95% sown area has been sown with seed of good quality in the 10th Five-Year plan period. The modern machine and equipment for agricultural production and crop processing have been widely used in China, and the traditional planting mode which mainly depended on labor and animal in. plain area has been given up. Up to 2004, the total power of machine for agriculture has reached 640.3 billion watt, a rise of 21.8% over 2000. As compared with 2000, the effective irrigation area rose by 1.2%, the amount of chemical fertilizer and the plastic pellicle for agriculture rose by 11.8% and 25.8% respectively and the amount of pesticide rose by 8.3%.

3. The rise is favorable to increase of yield of agricultural products

The positive effect of the price of agricultural products on agricultural production is the change in product yield. The change of price affects the sown area and input directly. Assuming other influencing factors stable, the increase of inputs will result in the increase of unit yield. Taking the production of grain as an example, the producer price of grain has obvious positive correlation with the yield in the 10th Five-Year plan period. The producer price of grain rose by 26.2% in 2004 and the grain yield rose by 9% at the same year. In 2005, the producer price rose by 23%, it resulted in 4.7% up of the yield of grain.

4. The rise is favorable to the increase of farmer income

(1) Income from agricultural products is an important part of farmer's income. The national average per capita net income increased 1002 yuan in the 10th Five-Year plan period. Of the total,

the net income from agricultural products increased 379 yuan and the contribution rate from agriculture to the farmer's net income was 37.9%. The national average per capita net income was 3255 yuan in 2005. Of the total, net income from agricultural products was 1470 yuan, accounting for 45.2% of the total net income.

(2) The rise of the price of agricultural products contributed great much to the increase of farmer's agricultural net income. The correlation coefficient between the change rate of the national producer price index of agricultural products and that of farmer's per capita agricultural net income was 0.97 in the 10th Five-Year plan period, which showed that there was a strong correlation between the price of agricultural products and farmer's income. The national average agricultural net income was 1398 yuan in 2004. Of the total, that from grain was 621 yuan, a rise of 172 yuan over previous year. The contribution rate from grain net income to farmer net income of agricultural products reached 97.7%. The sharp rise of price of grain caused an increase of 165 yuan of farmer's net income from grain and the contribution rate from the rise of price of grain to farmer's net income was 93.8%.

(3) The rise of price of agricultural products was more favorable for farmers of low and middle level of incomes.

The main source of income of farmer with low middle income was mainly from agriculture especially crop planting. Accompanied with the rise by 13.1% of the price of agricultural products, the average per capita income of low and middle income farmers rose by 16.3% and 14.7% respectively in 2004, that for those of middle income rose by 13.4%, that for those of upper-middle income and high income rose by 12.5 and 9.2% respectively. The low and middle income farmers were more sensitive to the change of the price of agricultural products.

5. The rise is favorable to keep consumer price stable

Since the beginning of the 10th Five-year plan, Most of industrial products was surplus, the transmission of the price from upstream products to downstream products was not unobstructed in the 10th Five-Year plan period. The rise of price of agricultural products contributed great much to the stability of consumer price, which rose by 3.9% and 1.8% in 2004 and 2005 respectively. Of the total, the price of foodstuff rose by 9.9% and 2.9% respectively. The consumer price only rose by 0.6% and 0.8%, if the rise of price of foodstuff, which was 3.3% and 1% in 2004 and 2005, is excluded. the rise of price of agricultural products has contributed great much to counteract the pressure of the national deflation in the 10th Five-Year plan period.

Ⅳ Suggestions on Keeping the Price of Agricultural Products at a Reasonable Level

1. To improve the market system of agricultural products

The construction of complete market system is necessary for making use of the basic role of market mechanism in keeping reasonable price of agricultural products. It is also an important content of building a new socialist countryside. The wholesale market plays a primary role in the agricultural market system. The wholesale market for its quick response to and intense information on price of agricultural products should be put into full use. The infrastructure of wholesale market such as information system, products processing, cold storage and transportation etc should be strengthened. The inspection and quarantine should be excised strictly at the wholesale market. The retail market of agricultural products should be improved, and the links in circulation of agricultural products should be reduced. The Cooperative Organization of Agricultural Products Circulation should be encouraged to set up. Agricultural products in the supermarket or store in town and city should be encouraged to purchase directly from production bases. To avoid the asymmetric information between production and demand, the function of price of the futures market should be made full use and more information service should be provided to farmer. New trade pattern such as electronic business, auction and broker proxy should be adopted.

2. To enhance the farmer's ability in preventing the market risks

To make farmer to access to the agricultural market, any access for disperse mode of family production and management to the modern market should be explored to guide farmer to participate in any form of cooperative economic organizations and increase the number of the agricultural broker in rural area. Through participating in the professional, cooperative economic organization, farmer can cooperate to get market information, to organize production and to negotiate prices and change the inferior position at the agricultural market so as to enhance farmer's ability in preventing market risks. The establishment of system of agricultural insurance should be accelerated to help farmer to prevent natural disasters and market risks.

3. To keep the price of materials for agricultural production not to rise fast

The rise of the price of materials for agricultural production increases the cost of agricultural production and decreases the profits. It is unfavorable for keeping the price of agricultural products stable and the increase of farmer's income. To keep the price of materials for agricultural production under reasonable level, necessary policies should be excised. First, favorable policy should be adopted to support the production of the materials so as to decrease the production cost and increase the supply of materials for agricultural production at the market. Second, it is necessary to simplify the circulation and reduce the links of circulation and the cost of materials for agricultural production. Third, inspection and supervision on the production and circulation of materials for agricultural production should be strengthened to prevent the price rising sharply. Fourth, direct subsidy to farmer who purchases the materials for agricultural production should be strengthened. The subsidy standard should be increased and the subsidy should cover more items.

4. To strengthen macro-regulation on price of grain

To keep price of grain stable at a reasonable level, more attention should be paid to regulate the reserve and import and export of grain. To prevent the price of grain from fluctuating sharply, the time and quantity for reserved grain flowing in and out of storage should be regulated properly according to the situation of supply of and demand for grain at the market and the trend of grain price. With the annual increase of grain import, the grain from international market plays an important role in regulating the supply of and demand for grain at the domestic market. The variety, quantity and time of grain import have direct impacts on the price of grain at domestic market. Import and export of grain and the regulation on reserved grain are important measure to regulate the price. It should be noted to integrate two measures closely in practice.

5. To insist and improve the policy of purchasing grain at the lowest price of protection.

The government implements the policy of purchasing grain at the lowest price of protection in the major grain producing areas. The policy can stimulate the growth of grain production, the increase of farmer income and stabilize the price of grain. According to survey, farmer in the major grain producing areas thought that the purchasing price (the lowest price of protection) was still low in recent two years and profits from planting grain were not high enough. It is recommended that the level of the price of protection should be increased to ensure the safety of grain and the increase of farmer's income.

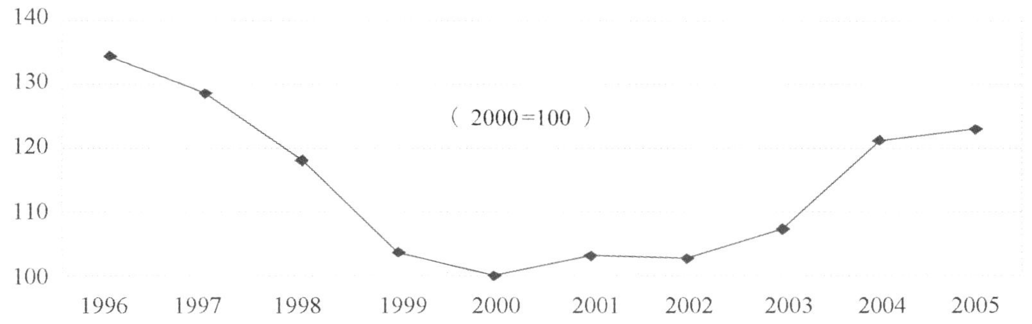

Graph 1 Gross Index of the Producer Price of Agricultural Products in the 9th and 10th Five-Year Plan Period

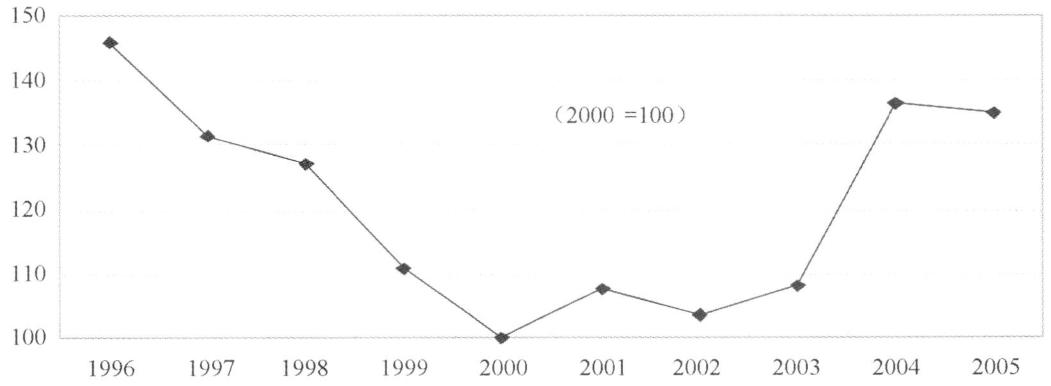

Graph 2 Index of Producer Price of Grain in the 9th and 10th Five-Year Plan Period

2

农产品生产价格指数

Indices of the Producer Prices of Agricultural Products

2—1 全国农产品生产价格总指数
National Gross Indices of Producer Prices of Agricultural Products

（上年＝100） (preceding year＝100)

年份 Year	农产品生产价格总指数 Gross Indices of Producer Prices of Agricultural Products				
	总指数 Gross Index	种植业产品 Crop products	林业产品 Forest products	畜牧业产品 Livestock products	渔业产品 Fishery products
1978	103.90	104.69	101.00	100.50	102.50
1979	122.10	122.39	115.00	122.60	118.20
1980	107.10	107.78	115.80	103.40	101.80
1981	105.90	106.09	127.00	101.10	100.60
1982	102.20	102.48	105.90	100.30	101.00
1983	104.40	105.74	100.20	100.50	103.20
1984	104.00	103.82	103.30	104.10	109.80
1985	108.60	101.66	155.50	124.10	151.30
1986	106.40	106.62	114.90	103.00	110.40
1987	112.00	108.83	120.30	117.90	122.80
1988	123.00	113.46	136.70	140.20	134.30
1989	115.00	118.90	105.20	110.20	99.80
1990	97.40	100.73	84.50	92.30	98.80
1991	98.00	97.31	102.40	97.40	104.70
1992	103.40	101.14	107.30	106.30	108.10
1993	113.40	112.05	111.10	114.20	122.10
1994	139.90	141.91	111.80	144.60	122.00
1995	119.90	123.95	105.10	115.80	112.40
1996	104.20	104.71	104.40	103.30	103.40
1997	95.50	92.81	98.90	101.80	91.70
1998	92.00	93.64	101.10	86.90	93.90
1999	87.80	85.75	101.40	88.50	92.50
2000	96.40	94.66	90.00	99.00	100.50
2001	103.10	105.65	94.15	103.07	98.57
2002	99.70	100.04	98.31	100.15	95.89
2003	104.37	107.42	107.01	101.76	100.34
2004	113.09	115.86	104.62	111.08	110.19
2005	101.39	101.55	104.79	100.52	104.67

注：2000年以前农产品生产价格总指数为农产品收购价格指数。

Note: The gross indices of Producer prices of agricultural products before 2000 were the indices of state purchase prices of agricultural products.

2—2 全国分品种农产品生产价格指数
Nationlal Indices of Producer Prices of Agricultural Products by Category

(上年=100) (preceding year=100)

农产品名称	Categories of agricultural products	2002	2003	2004	2005
总指数	Gross Index	99.70	104.37	113.09	101.39
一、种植业产品	I. Crop products	100.04	107.42	115.86	101.55
粮食	Grain	96.16	104.48	126.21	99.08
谷物(原粮)	Cereal (unprocessed food grains)	95.83	102.34	128.06	99.23
小麦	Wheat	98.14	102.99	131.16	96.41
硬粒小麦	Hard wheat	99.70	103.96	132.28	96.25
软粒小麦	Soft wheat	87.66	103.12	130.97	97.78
混合小麦	Mixed wheat	98.76	101.84	132.88	97.70
稻谷	Paddy	97.17	99.89	136.30	101.57
早籼稻	Early long-grain nonglutinous rice	99.39	101.69	133.57	95.22
晚籼稻	Late long-grain nonglutinous rice	100.79	103.70	134.39	99.13
粳稻	Round-grain rice	94.71	97.85	137.68	105.39
玉米	Maize (corn)	91.50	104.58	116.92	97.97
黄玉米	Yellow maize	91.25	104.59	116.89	97.99
白玉米	White maize	102.89	101.33	117.43	103.19
混合玉米	Mixed maize	109.95	104.66	117.48	93.90
薯类	Potato	93.71	92.87	105.75	106.14
红薯	Sweet potato	142.94	94.54	108.97	103.59
马铃薯	White Potato	75.42	92.21	104.89	107.43
豆类	Beans	98.11	119.33	120.29	95.70
大豆	Soybeans	98.95	120.62	120.17	94.24
绿豆	Mung beans	86.11	100.45	116.73	105.95
红小豆	Small red beans	99.30	103.60	128.26	105.17
油料	Oil-bearing Crops	104.82	119.40	116.58	91.33
花生	Peanut	102.71	124.19	117.07	97.60
油菜籽	Rapeseeds	103.14	119.15	116.33	86.97
芝麻	Sesame	88.64	128.92	122.34	102.98
胡麻籽	Flaxseeds	118.53	116.34	115.44	103.21
棉花	Cotton (unginned cotton)	103.35	135.33	79.54	111.82
细绒棉(籽棉)	Thin-staple cotton	103.83	135.81	79.80	112.04
长绒棉(籽棉)	Long-staple cotton	94.40	121.21	83.50	103.70
麻类	Fiber crops	93.84	111.11	124.99	104.77

2—2 续表 1 continued 1

农产品名称	Categories of agricultural products	2002	2003	2004	2005
黄红麻	Jute and blueish dogbane	96.63	107.67	116.59	108.91
苎麻	Ramie	86.27	113.83	131.10	103.36
糖料	Sugar crops	86.01	90.50	104.86	111.57
甘蔗	Sugarcane	86.57	90.49	104.86	111.22
甜菜	Beet	97.14	106.56	106.10	102.82
烟叶	Tobacco	132.78	97.21	108.42	103.26
烤烟叶	Flue-cured tobacco	153.69	94.94	106.42	103.15
晒烟叶	Sun-cured tobacco	99.09	112.40	113.45	107.64
蔬菜	Vegetable	95.06	110.44	105.17	107.22
叶菜类	Leaf vegetable	98.09	113.21	101.85	108.92
菠菜	Spinach	85.62	113.94	101.57	108.99
芹菜	Celery	81.62	127.10	99.28	107.77
大白菜	Chinese cabbage	81.37	115.76	102.10	108.06
元白菜	Cabbage	90.32	99.55	106.45	112.93
甘蓝	Wild cabbage	146.08	97.81	100.78	110.42
花椰菜	Cauliflower	89.66	112.08	101.29	97.89
莴笋	Asparagus lettuce	119.20	102.77	107.36	109.72
油菜	Rape	155.50	109.50	101.61	110.88
瓜菜类	Gourd vegetable	98.01	110.71	101.10	105.08
黄瓜	Cucumber	96.97	113.37	103.66	104.99
冬瓜	White gourd	93.21	122.81	92.92	105.86
西葫芦	Summer squash	146.05	107.46	99.41	103.53
块根、块茎菜类	Root and tuber vegetable	85.86	111.62	103.59	106.06
萝卜	Radish	86.33	110.46	103.08	108.67
胡萝卜	Carrot	99.17	115.09	102.90	103.33
生姜	Ginger	67.06	95.91	145.13	93.80
茄果菜类	Eggplant, tomato and chili, etc.	86.18	108.55	103.18	104.75
茄子	Eggplant	101.74	117.82	108.01	104.76
西红柿	Tomato	79.20	103.82	104.06	104.39
辣椒	Chili	87.87	111.06	103.62	100.35
青椒	Sweetbell	109.39	109.38	96.48	105.72
葱蒜类	Onion and Garlic	96.39	105.98	115.91	109.76
大葱	Scallion	173.41	110.21	111.81	103.04

2—2 续表 2 continued 2

农产品名称	Categories of agricultural products	2002	2003	2004	2005
蒜苔	Garlic stalk	109.81	115.60	115.10	107.28
蒜头	Garlic head	84.59	94.67	117.72	118.93
菜用豆类	Garden beans	100.38	109.98	104.96	107.98
四季豆	Kidney beans	98.54	104.16	108.45	106.42
豇豆	Cowpeas	103.14	117.49	101.77	110.38
水生菜类	Water vegetable	129.38	112.41	113.37	124.53
莲藕	Lotus root	112.73	114.53	108.84	105.14
茭白	Wild ruice stem	143.37	102.64	106.81	154.49
荸荠	Water chestnut	85.94	99.69	122.09	106.09
水果	Garden fruits	109.91	102.04	97.44	107.41
苹果	Apples	106.53	103.51	102.50	114.55
红富士苹果	Hongfushi apples	120.67	103.84	102.48	112.23
国光苹果	Guoguang apples	94.63	91.60	98.21	105.47
秦冠苹果	Qinguan apples	88.92	107.81	108.62	102.19
香蕉苹果	Banana apples	49.18	110.85	105.10	113.33
梨	Pears	112.35	102.91	95.31	104.53
雪花梨	Snowflake pears	125.20	109.54	93.96	104.66
鸭梨	Ya-pears	103.04	103.56	98.29	104.82
酥梨	Soft-pears	90.75	106.64	95.31	103.32
香梨	Bergamot pears	146.51	142.19	108.04	99.81
柑桔类	Citruses	103.02	100.50	94.73	104.91
柑	Mandarin oranges	109.41	99.24	95.73	103.76
桔	Tangerines	107.11	106.19	91.83	124.51
橙	Oranges	93.44	109.41	102.14	101.58
柚	Shaddocks	79.90	93.89	99.23	113.46
热带亚热带水果	Tropical and subtropics area fruits	104.50	114.98	101.61	103.66
香蕉	Bananas	143.80	111.31	114.25	92.78
荔枝	Litchis	76.89	125.03	64.76	118.69
龙眼	Longans	49.66	115.09	79.61	92.00
果用瓜	Melons	168.06	88.59	109.63	
西瓜	Watermelons	287.81	88.54	110.00	112.96
甜瓜	Muskmelons	90.94	91.83	107.34	110.07
桃	Peachs	113.45	89.42	96.66	109.93

2—2 续表 3 continued 3

农产品名称	Categories of agricultural products	2002	2003	2004	2005
杏	Apricots	91.66	98.72	99.61	89.10
杨梅	Red bayberries	277.56	81.29	106.76	100.04
草莓	Strawberries	95.65	110.38	105.37	99.36
猕猴桃	Yangtaoes	101.85	87.77	113.20	109.35
葡萄	Grapes	136.62	99.14	95.36	112.53
红枣	Chinese dates	101.96	91.62	108.02	95.83
柿子	Persimmons	113.64	97.86	92.29	104.20
红毛茶	Black tea	105.33	83.22	109.41	112.57
绿毛茶	Green tea	180.71	100.56	110.48	110.95
乌龙茶	Oolong tea	106.26	94.56	107.50	95.89
二、林业产品	II. Forest products	98.31	107.01	104.62	104.79
工业用原料	Products of natural and artificial forest	110.48	121.49	104.05	105.76
橡胶	Rubber	110.48	121.49	117.47	114.44
油桐籽	Seeds of tung oil tree	84.93	180.53	114.47	118.64
油茶籽	Seeds of tea-oil tree	75.08	113.54	115.56	101.09
坚果	Nuts	142.89	96.39	108.36	
核桃	Walnut	142.89	96.39	102.66	111.31
花椒	Chinese prickly ash	101.11	98.68	93.49	97.88
八角	Anise	82.52	74.93	77.36	88.03
桂皮	Cassia bark	81.44	92.07	96.73	102.57
三、畜牧业产品	III. Livestock products	100.15	101.76	111.08	100.52
猪	Hog (gross weight)	97.96	102.86	112.84	97.58
肉牛	Live cattle (gross weight)	91.44	101.68	103.93	101.66
家禽(毛重)	Poultry (gross weight)	106.09	101.00	111.25	105.61
鸡	Chicken	105.94	101.02	111.22	105.83
鸭	Duck	100.69	95.81	116.32	105.05
鹅	Goose	115.09	101.83	113.47	105.28
蛋类	Eggs	102.80	101.06	112.58	106.38
鸡蛋	Chicken's eggs	102.58	101.06	112.54	106.52
鸭蛋	Duck 's eggs	110.74	101.61	113.95	107.01
鹅蛋	Goose' s eggs	79.36	100.35	105.95	105.68
奶类	Milk products	99.71	103.68	103.73	99.62
牛奶	Cow milk	99.76	103.67	103.73	99.62

2—2 续表 4 continued 4

农产品名称	Categories of agricultural products	2002	2003	2004	2005
羊奶	Sheep milk	62.67	105.90	105.30	101.41
毛绒类	Hair and down products	80.11	102.23	103.10	106.51
山羊毛	Goat's wool	175.45	85.72	98.98	102.77
山羊绒	Cashmere	67.54	104.92	104.71	107.78
蚕茧	Silkworm cocoon	64.38	106.29	125.01	112.54
蜂蜜	Honey	137.68	106.87	99.07	102.45
四、渔业产品	IV. Fishery products	95.89	100.34	110.19	104.67
海水水产品	Seawater aquatic products	98.09	101.13	109.00	104.10
海水鱼类	Seawater Fish	104.87	103.98	109.16	104.18
大黄鱼	Large yellow croaker	76.64	94.01	108.66	102.11
小黄鱼	Small yellow croaker	91.57	97.68	110.53	102.70
带鱼	Hairtail	94.92	102.75	107.29	103.01
石斑鱼	Grouper	468.10	84.24	116.27	104.81
海水虾蟹类	Seawater shrimp and crab	149.68	110.19	108.80	103.43
海水贝类	Seawater shellfish	106.68	97.80	109.17	103.28
贻贝	Mussel	89.10	99.63	136.84	113.47
扇贝	Scallop	101.40	102.41	134.07	107.85
牡蛎	Oyster	107.78	96.65	102.39	96.34
鲍鱼	Abalone	99.20	111.12	117.06	95.91
蛤	Clam	107.05	98.35	106.35	103.61
蚶	Blood clam	93.05	138.03	94.30	101.99
藻类	Seaweeds	118.13	102.66	120.68	102.53
海带	Kelp	108.75	103.98	114.47	105.97
紫菜	Laver	132.98	103.19	95.60	91.64
内陆水域水产品	Aquatic products in inland water areas	93.07	98.83	112.30	107.90
淡水鱼类	Freshwater fish	93.07	98.65	111.52	106.24
青鱼	Black carp	59.97	99.28	106.65	107.52
草鱼	Grass carp	90.97	97.33	115.47	110.17
鲤鱼	Carp	93.92	101.06	112.06	103.91
鲢鱼	Silver carp	89.03	97.28	113.29	107.37
鲫鱼	Crucian carp	85.06	98.06	109.33	107.91
罗非鱼	Tilapia	104.73	96.57	104.88	103.02
淡水虾蟹类	Freshwater shrimps and crabs	91.72	104.13	122.97	116.18

2—3 全国农产品生产价格指数(第一季度)
National Indices of Producer Prices of Agricultural Products

(上年同期=100) (1st quarter) (the same period of the preceding year=100)

农产品名称	Categories of agricultural products	2002	2003	2004	2005
		第一季度 1st quarter			
总指数	**Gross Index**	**99.30**	**101.15**	**113.75**	**106.40**
一、种植业产品	I. Crop products	95.13	105.01	114.82	104.20
1. 谷物及其他作物	1. Cereal and other crops			119.93	103.90
粮食	Grain	96.06	98.33	120.69	106.62
谷物(原粮)	Cereal (unprocessed food grains)	98.21	95.92	121.00	107.95
小麦	Wheat	103.79	96.00	124.36	109.41
硬粒小麦	Hard wheat	112.72	98.69	130.45	109.15
软粒小麦	Soft wheat	97.43	94.69	117.34	110.81
混合小麦	Mixed wheat	101.00	94.95	123.38	109.93
其他小麦	Other wheat			120.71	105.04
稻谷	Paddy	98.21	94.12	129.55	112.98
早籼稻	Early long-grain nonglutinous rice	102.68	99.11	124.73	110.33
晚籼稻	Late long-grain nonglutinous rice	101.33	99.93	127.20	112.33
粳稻	Round-grain rice	96.67	92.02	130.67	114.44
其他稻谷	Other paddy			119.22	110.68
玉米	Maize (corn)	97.21	97.48	112.86	101.15
黄玉米	Yellow maize	97.20	97.48	112.86	100.97
白玉米	White maize	111.68	96.15	113.63	107.05
混合玉米	Mixed maize	90.97	98.53	112.09	106.99
其他玉米	Other maize		87.83	114.42	103.26
杂粮	Coarse cereals		116.43	0.00	110.45
谷子	Millet		117.82	117.63	106.83
高粱	Chinese sorghum		97.47	116.19	110.38
大麦	Barley		102.79	108.25	105.73
荞麦	Buckwheat		109.02	103.52	112.38
元麦	poulard wheat		129.34	0.00	
青稞	Highland barley		107.74	103.02	123.29
莜麦	Naked oats		103.86	109.55	113.10
燕麦	Oats		130.85		107.14
其他杂粮	Other coarse cereals			109.48	105.06
谷物副产品	By-products of cereals				
小麦秸	Wheat straw		96.57	123.29	113.32
稻草	Rice straw		95.07	117.98	97.48
玉米秆	Corn stover		92.23	111.45	95.29

2—3 续表 1 continued 1

农产品名称	Categories of agricultural products	2002	2003	2004	2005
		第一季度 1st quarter			
谷子秆	Millet stalk		107.56	123.63	100.68
高粱秆	Chinese sorghum stalk		113.10		114.41
薯类	Potato	90.81	89.44	100.65	103.06
红薯	Sweet potato	120.60	92.27	100.86	103.52
马铃薯	White Potato	73.93	87.83	100.53	102.84
其他薯类	Other potatoes			101.79	96.46
薯藤	Potato vines		99.15	94.07	104.17
油料	Oil-bearing crops	108.55	109.02	120.27	99.40
花生	Peanut	80.98	129.34	120.47	100.66
油菜籽	Rapeseeds	110.09	107.74	120.06	98.29
芝麻	Sesame	92.55	103.86	148.68	106.84
向日葵	Sunflower		100.74	109.87	104.72
胡麻籽	Flaxseeds	153.38	123.78	111.23	100.52
苏籽	Perillaseeds		112.32	105.77	92.85
其他油料作物	Other oil-bearing crops			112.77	102.88
花生蔓	Peanut vine		106.67	125.00	100.00
豆类	Beans	82.87	116.43	123.15	99.95
大豆	Soybeans	83.15	117.82	123.92	98.12
绿豆	Mung beans	76.05	97.47	108.89	117.21
红小豆	Small red beans	107.91	102.79	150.78	110.28
蚕豆	Broad beans		91.97	117.80	105.79
豌豆	Peas		112.72	109.02	106.91
芸豆	Kidney beans		126.87	108.85	102.32
其他杂豆	Other beans			113.32	107.47
豆秸	Beanstalk		100.00	85.71	112.70
棉花(籽棉)	Cotton (unginned cotton)	77.20	130.85	136.52	77.98
细绒棉	Thin-staple cotton	77.30	131.16	136.93	77.72
长绒棉	Long-staple cotton	73.76	119.36	121.51	83.59
棉籽	Cottonseeds		94.44	110.89	94.12
麻类	Fiber crops	106.71	95.45	118.04	106.99
黄红麻	Jute and blueish dogbane	115.14	93.92	114.18	109.00
亚麻	Flax		98.03		0.00
苎麻	Ramie	82.74	99.80	129.00	105.26
线麻	Thread hemp		106.06	0.00	105.00

2—3 续表 2 continued 2

农产品名称 Categories of agricultural products		2002	2003	2004	2005
		第一季度 1st quarter			
苘麻	Piemarker		105.08	0.00	
剑麻	Steel hemp		81.57		100.00
其他麻类	Other fiber crops			102.37	100.00
麻秆	Stalks of fiber crops				
糖料	Sugar crops	81.41	88.38	101.75	107.60
甘蔗	Sugarcane	81.39	88.38	101.77	107.60
甜菜	Beet	98.20	99.68	86.90	111.72
烟草	Tobacco	83.23	95.10	101.21	101.04
烤烟叶	Flue-cured tobacco	86.05	91.97	96.75	100.81
晒烟叶	Sun-cured tobacco	67.32	112.72	126.41	109.79
白肋烟	Whiteerib tobacco		95.44	91.01	100.00
香料烟	Perfume tobacco		124.75	0.00	
其他烟叶	Other tobacco			106.94	102.25
青饲料	Greenfeed		130.73	108.73	78.33
牧草	Herbage		130.73	98.57	121.11
绿肥	Green manure		97.03		115.47
桑叶	Mulberry leaves		109.04		
席草	Stems or leaves of cattail		95.65	62.39	0.00
蓖麻籽	Castor beans		110.30	99.48	105.42
除虫菊	Pyrethrum		102.29	0.00	
薄荷油	Peppermint oil		102.87	0.00	116.04
野生植物的采集	Gathering of wild plants			102.41	104.68
未列明的其他农作物	Other agricultural crops			110.31	113.38
2.蔬菜、园艺作物	2. Vegetable and Horticulture crops		126.87	98.73	105.52
蔬菜	Vegetable	77.48	126.87	98.73	105.52
叶菜类	Leaf vegetable	77.05	131.15	96.09	110.62
菠菜	Spinach	95.47	142.97	101.47	115.43
芹菜	Celery	68.07	152.13	94.25	106.48
大白菜	Chinese cabbage	53.29	124.52	108.26	101.28
元白菜	Cabbage	63.48	100.74	100.36	118.56
甘蓝	Wild cabbage	21.03	123.78	97.17	115.97
花椰菜	Cauliflower	87.03	112.32	88.86	112.63
莴笋	Asparagus lettuce	120.53	106.48	102.77	108.07
油菜	Rape	87.83	119.23	91.36	113.12

2—3 续表 3 continued 3

农产品名称	Categories of agricultural products	2002	2003	2004	2005
		第一季度 1st quarter			
其他叶菜	Other leaf vegetable			96.29	113.52
瓜菜类	Gourd vegetable	85.70	128.78	94.11	108.97
黄瓜	Cucumber	86.82	147.41	94.37	111.08
冬瓜	White gourd	55.66	158.76	92.77	109.52
西葫芦	Summer squash	67.51	107.56	91.97	126.18
苦瓜	Balsam pear		126.68	127.24	77.33
丝瓜	Towed gourd		98.03	96.34	95.37
南瓜	Pumpkin		74.03	103.46	99.00
打瓜	Seeded watermelon		108.65		92.64
瓠子	Bottle gourd		108.65	83.33	
其他瓜菜	Other gourd vegetable			71.49	115.01
块根、块茎菜类	Root and tuber vegetable	75.21	105.33	107.69	102.44
萝卜	Radish	75.63	106.06	105.48	102.29
胡萝卜	Carrot	134.46	105.08	109.96	102.38
生姜	Ginger	52.12	81.57	150.92	112.66
芋头	Taro		119.88	112.94	111.67
苔干	Dried bryophyte		71.74	89.44	102.06
百合(根)	Lily (root)		97.63	97.64	102.74
芋艿	Taro		63.45	124.81	126.36
山药	Chinese yam		97.23	116.56	99.39
其他块根、块茎菜	Other root and tuber vegetable			91.51	109.24
茄果菜类	Eggplant, tomato and chili, etc.	58.98	128.74	97.98	96.74
茄子	Eggplant	79.65	152.02	104.87	99.93
西红柿	Tomato	56.46	116.87	103.41	99.18
辣椒	Chili	59.23	116.70	100.37	87.13
青椒	Sweetbell	88.31	139.46	75.16	96.20
其他茄果菜类	Others			111.71	97.72
葱蒜类	Onion and Garlic	135.35	111.64	110.24	108.18
大葱	Scallion	171.63	107.40	125.90	92.91
蒜苔	Garlic stalk	177.80	122.06	111.24	109.11
蒜头	Garlic head	116.54	95.44	101.06	114.80
洋葱	Onion		98.24	98.40	95.10
蒜苗	Garlic bolt		98.21	106.30	122.74
小葱	Shallot		99.33	99.92	115.66

2—3 续表 4 continued 4

农产品名称	Categories of agricultural products	2002	2003	2004	2005
		第一季度 1st quarter			
韭菜	Fragrant-flowered garlic		89.15	107.79	112.20
其他葱蒜类	Others			102.34	128.58
菜用豆类	Garden beans	46.54	124.75	95.90	97.58
四季豆	Kidney beans	47.51	106.21	102.73	105.62
豇豆	Cowpeas	35.24	150.18	86.53	91.79
其他菜用豆	Other garden beans			102.18	115.90
水生菜类	Water vegetable	99.47	130.73	110.67	109.30
莲藕	Lotus root	100.24	130.73	111.28	112.14
茭白	Wild ruice stem	100.00	96.32	100.00	107.02
荸荠	Water chestnut	85.94	99.83	120.52	112.45
其他水生菜	Other water vegetable			109.98	105.88
食用菌(干鲜混合)	Mushroom		97.03	103.91	101.42
香菇(干品)	Mushroom (dried)		109.04	98.64	97.75
蘑菇(鲜品)	Mushroom (fresh)		95.65	104.12	101.45
黑木耳(干品)	Black edible fungus (dried)		110.30	106.26	105.41
白木耳(干品)	Tremella (dried)		79.50		0.00
金针菇(鲜品)	Golden mushroom		90.49	110.54	99.92
猴头菌(干品)	Bearded tooth(dried)		100.00	0.00	0.00
平菇(鲜品)	Oyster mushroom		100.00	112.67	106.48
花菇(干品)	Black forest mushroom		97.34	100.15	
其他食用菌	Other edible mushrooms			98.58	91.54
椿芽	Chinese cedrela sprouts		95.15	126.49	0.00
未列明的其他蔬菜	Other vegetable			104.45	109.99
花卉	Flowers		96.63	0.00	0.00
鲜切花	Fresh flowers		97.29	0.00	0.00
百合花	Lily		99.46	54.49	76.82
康乃馨	Carnation		100.00	98.33	107.29
满天星	June snow (serissa)		95.65	117.10	113.88
勿忘我	Forgetmenot		78.22	70.08	95.41
非洲菊	Flameray Gerbera		100.00	98.00	88.74
玫瑰	Rugosa rose		78.70	130.25	74.58
郁金香	Tulip			83.33	101.05
情人草	Evans begonia		100.00	96.20	90.31
其他鲜切花	Other fresh flowers			121.36	105.29

2—3 续表 5 continued 5

农产品名称 Categories of agricultural products		2002	2003	2004	2005
		第一季度 1st quarter			
盆栽植物	Potted plants		102.08	0.00	0.00
观赏苗木	Ornamental plants		91.71	0.00	0.00
草坪草皮	Sod for lawn		98.46	87.40	110.29
其他园艺作物	Other horticulture crops			104.58	108.60
3.水果、坚果、饮料和香料	3. Fruit, beverage and perfume		102.29	104.97	103.65
水果、坚果	Fruits and nuts		102.87	104.80	102.48
园林水果	Garden fruits	125.09		104.78	103.48
苹果	Apples	141.53	111.26	96.42	95.65
红富士苹果	Hongfushi apples	143.08	111.05	95.76	97.02
国光苹果	Guoguang apples	111.80	84.29	99.07	92.58
秦冠苹果	Qinguan apples	115.87	124.80	101.70	94.79
香蕉苹果	Banana apples	100.00	96.68	113.79	104.08
元帅苹果	Yuanshuai (Marshal) apples		95.24	112.78	97.33
新红星苹果	New Hongxing apples		111.11	98.62	101.18
其他苹果	Other apples			112.04	97.92
梨	Pears	104.56	98.26	107.33	112.75
雪花梨	Snowflake pears	149.65	118.98	113.26	112.76
鸭梨	Ya-pears	104.33	98.21	107.48	113.64
酥梨	Soft-pears	110.92	95.40	86.39	103.18
香梨	Bergamot pears	100.00	100.00		0.00
苹果梨	Apple pears		103.45	91.66	105.42
其他梨	Other pears			79.37	116.32
柑桔	Citrus	89.67	101.97	102.38	106.71
柑	Mandarin oranges	90.04	98.62	104.68	108.71
桔	Tangerines	89.29	117.80	89.82	97.70
橙	Oranges	81.64	119.23	98.79	95.04
柚	Shaddocks	85.49	95.58	95.50	108.45
其他柑桔	Others			96.32	103.02
其他水果	Other fruits			125.77	90.80
香蕉	Bananas	267.44	103.51	125.77	94.18
菠萝	Pineapples		60.58	71.79	124.75
芒果	Mangoes		202.51		111.07
木瓜	Papayas		60.83	89.44	101.72
桃	Peachs	100.00	100.00	98.57	87.71

2—3 续表 6 continued 6

农产品名称	Categories of agricultural products	2002	2003	2004	2005
		第一季度 1st quarter			
猕猴桃	Yangtaoes	100.00	100.00	101.67	114.74
葡萄	Grapes	191.12	75.65	89.99	109.14
红枣	Chinese dates	115.16	97.87	108.36	103.74
柿子	Persimmons	139.41	89.51	105.66	105.56
其他园林水果	Other garden fruits			114.08	89.22
瓜果类	Melons	420.22	52.79	119.18	91.68
西瓜	Watermelons	900.54	53.28	121.15	91.57
甜瓜	Muskmelons	100.00	52.46	117.87	91.36
草莓	Strawberries	93.48	109.25	106.24	95.60
其他瓜果	Others			100.22	92.63
坚果类	Nuts				99.93
椰子	Coconut			128.96	99.93
槟榔	Areca			78.30	146.04
其他坚果	Other nuts			106.27	108.70
茶及其他饮料(干品)	Tea and other beverages			112.02	111.23
茶	Tea	114.40		112.02	111.01
红毛茶	Black tea	100.00	74.03	102.37	0.00
绿毛茶	Green tea	114.40	103.20	112.02	111.95
乌龙茶	Oolong tea	100.00	103.48	94.33	101.62
其他茶	Others			81.16	117.67
咖啡豆	Coffee bean		102.79	92.46	117.44
茴香	Fennel			101.89	0.00
其他	Others			179.31	0.00
4. 中药材	4. Traditional Chinese medicinal materials				
茯苓	Fuling (poris cocos)		100.00	108.01	90.49
党参	Tangshen (pilose asiabell)		208.82	92.20	92.19
当归	Chinese angelica		119.06	142.01	105.42
黄芪	Root of membranous milk vetch		125.00	106.26	101.08
金银花	Honeysuckle		100.00	111.55	93.66
黄连	Rhizome of Chinese goldthread		100.00	118.42	
甘草	Licorice root		112.34	100.00	105.10
贝母	Bulb of fritillary		212.45	143.94	17.10
元胡	Amur corydalis		119.65		0.00
枸杞	Fruit of Chinese wolfberry		119.09	156.00	81.74

2—3 续表 7 continued 7

农产品名称	Categories of agricultural products	2002	2003	2004	2005
		第一季度 1st quarter			
菊花	Chrysanthemum		92.09	145.97	59.07
白术	Largehead atractyldes		88.34	116.45	112.69
半夏	Tuber of pinelia		94.63	100.00	104.24
麦冬	Tuber of dwarf lilyturf			105.26	0.00
生地	Dried rhizome of rehmannia		101.14	83.33	103.55
杜仲	Bark of eucommia		100.00	100.54	0.00
板蓝根	Root of common baphicacanthus		100.00	71.39	79.54
苦丁茶	Kudin crotoxylum (bitter tea tree)		41.65	173.84	
天麻	Tuber of elevated gastrodia		102.82	78.25	81.55
灵芝	Glossy ganoderma			96.00	0.00
穿心莲	Creat		100.00	147.73	49.06
桔梗	Rampion		169.97	107.33	48.36
丹参	Root of red-rooted salvia		82.97	193.01	103.71
大青叶	Common conehead		125.00		75.00
二、林业产品	II. Forest products	86.42	108.65	107.04	102.58
1.竹木采运	1. Felling and transport of bamboo and wood			108.79	102.97
木材采运	Felling and transport of wood	96.40		106.97	102.92
原木	Log	94.80		106.97	102.92
红松	Korean pine		93.04	107.55	100.83
落叶松	Larch		82.72	111.93	103.48
马尾松	Masson pine		99.75	109.10	104.62
杉木	China fir		99.67	105.29	102.37
云南松	Yunnan pine		100.12	94.30	101.72
薪材	Firewood	211.21	99.27	104.53	120.48
竹材采运	Felling and transport of bamboo	71.42		112.90	105.97
水竹	Water bamboo		90.98	109.39	116.39
斑竹	Mottled bamboo		89.93	108.11	101.67
毛竹(楠竹)	Mao bamboo		102.39	117.53	105.97
蒿竹	Hao bamboo		83.12	105.25	108.29
淡竹	Henon bamboo		140.00	99.34	107.34
其他竹材	Other bamboo		102.56	103.87	97.52
2.林产品的采集	2. Gathering of forest products	79.97	108.65	105.34	102.40
天然和人工林的果实	Products of natural and artificial forest			105.34	102.40
橡胶	Rubber	76.05	127.31	127.89	106.16

2—3 续表 8 continued 8

农产品名称	Categories of agricultural products	2002	2003	2004	2005
		第一季度 1st quarter			
生漆	Raw lacquer			96.43	0.00
油桐籽	Seeds of tung oil tree	84.93	164.07	113.44	122.43
乌桕籽	Seeds of Chinese tallow tree		100.39	110.87	116.07
油茶籽	Seeds of tea-oil tree	75.08	101.65	120.39	100.91
棕片	Palm fibre		96.99	102.95	100.00
松脂	Rosin		97.28	94.18	102.82
核桃	Walnut	124.96	119.88	95.31	106.83
板栗	Chinese chestnut		100.04	103.35	100.49
白果	Ginkgo		104.50	95.98	106.02
花椒	Chinese prickly ash	197.96	97.63	86.04	97.69
八角	Anise	52.20	63.45	71.17	101.84
胡椒	Pepper		81.18	107.39	82.06
其他果实	Other products			90.67	120.94
柳条	Willow twigs		96.00	117.63	110.00
藤条	Rattan		99.39	107.72	108.32
竹笋干	Dried bamboo shoots		101.76	101.07	118.50
未列明的其他林产品采集	Gathering of other wild plants			107.28	110.30
三、牧业(畜产品)	III. Livestock products	103.42	97.23	114.47	109.95
1. 牲畜的饲养	1. Livestock raising			102.06	103.93
牛的饲养	Cattle raising	92.22		101.88	102.92
活牛(毛重)	Live cattle (gross weight)	92.22	100.39	101.88	102.89
牛肉	Beef		101.56	111.49	104.14
羊的饲养	Sheep raising			101.21	105.08
活羊(毛重)	Live sheep		92.96	101.21	105.08
羊肉	Mutton		96.51	97.16	102.29
马	Horse		100.43	100.31	106.92
驴	Donkey		104.74	62.23	103.62
骡	Mule		99.10	102.64	44.89
其他未列牲畜的饲养	Other livestock raising			111.34	112.64
奶产品	Milk products	97.09	98.99	107.64	101.15
牛奶	Cow milk	97.12	98.99	107.63	101.15
羊奶	Sheep milk	77.49	100.85	111.52	100.14
其他奶类	Other milk			100.64	110.01
毛绒产品	Hair and down products	120.24	103.99	92.44	107.56

2—3 续表 9 continued 9

农产品名称 Categories of agricultural products		2002	2003	2004	2005
		第一季度 1st quarter			
山羊毛	Goat's wool	419.69	67.95	100.00	111.45
绵羊毛	Sheep's wool		96.00	108.21	101.38
山羊绒	Cashmere	82.81	108.49	91.50	106.62
牦牛毛	Yak hair		63.63	160.00	100.00
骆驼绒	Camel hair cloth		103.33		113.51
其他毛绒产品	Other Hair and down products			107.75	136.97
其他牲畜产品	Other animal products			111.76	103.22
2. 猪的饲养	2. Hog raising	97.67		119.96	111.91
活猪(毛重)	Hog (gross weight)	97.67	96.51	119.96	111.91
猪肉	Pork		99.99	120.07	112.07
猪鬃	Bristles			96.51	107.95
3. 家禽	3. Poultry	127.93	99.20	106.02	111.14
肉禽(毛重)	Poultry (gross weight)	127.93		105.53	110.51
鸡	Chicken	127.96	99.20	105.53	110.50
鸭	Duck	105.74	97.57	106.41	110.43
鹅	Goose	100.00	106.01	104.54	111.15
鹌鹑	Furs			100.00	109.09
其他家禽	Other poultry			103.95	109.30
禽蛋	Eggs	108.18	98.24	106.72	111.98
鸡蛋	Chicken's eggs	108.09	98.21	106.68	112.19
鸭蛋	Duck 's eggs	111.78	99.33	108.15	109.37
鹅蛋	Goose' s eggs	60.59	89.15	102.87	107.00
其他蛋	Other eggs			98.92	127.44
羽绒	Eider down		94.03	0.00	0.00
鸭绒	Duck 's down			113.33	104.29
其他羽绒	Other down			99.78	109.34
4. 狩猎和捕捉动物	4. Hunting and catching animals				
兽皮	Furs		96.72	107.21	103.26
未列明的动物皮张	Furs not identified			115.25	108.51
5. 其他畜牧业	5. Other livestock prolucts				
鸽子	Pigeon		109.23	105.40	103.91
兔	Rabbit		110.72	99.89	110.73
狗	Dog		100.69	94.61	102.81
猫	Cat			96.72	115.42

2—3 续表 10 continued 10

农产品名称 Categories of agricultural products		2002	2003	2004	2005
		第一季度 1st quarter			
兔毛	Rabbit hair		96.05	119.07	133.05
其他家养动物	Other domestic animals			97.81	105.73
蛇	Snake		97.28		90.74
蚯蚓	Earthworm			110.00	0.00
蚕茧	Silkworm cocoon	75.41	86.82	114.14	100.85
蜂蜜	Honey	115.91	128.72	89.25	101.27
动物皮张	Animals' furs		99.99	120.94	105.20
四、渔业	IV. Fishery products	106.00	96.88	106.95	105.80
1.海水水产品	1. Seawater aquatic products	114.64	96.32	106.72	100.88
鱼类	Seawater Fish	148.51	99.83	105.47	100.17
大黄鱼	Large yellow croaker	110.68	72.42	120.01	97.05
小黄鱼	Small yellow croaker	98.03	111.81	102.88	97.89
带鱼	Hairtail	122.27	90.11	107.93	104.91
鲈鱼	Perch			101.81	103.86
沙丁鱼	Sardine		100.00	101.31	105.42
鳕鱼	Cod	164.65		93.92	100.00
石斑鱼	Grouper	100.00	91.98	108.99	105.29
鳀鱼	Anchovy		100.24	105.81	129.28
梭鱼	Mullet		100.00	105.40	112.22
鲳鱼	Silvery pomfret		106.16	121.69	96.83
海鳗	Conger pike		94.77	99.63	101.26
鲅鱼	Spanish mackerel		103.93	103.62	115.05
鲐鱼	Chub mackerel		100.37	103.34	100.90
马面鱼	Black scraper		94.88	108.56	100.33
鳓鱼	Chinese herring			103.45	95.24
马鲛	Japanese Spanish mackerel		87.94	125.25	108.35
梅童鱼	Baby croaker		95.59	99.79	106.37
梭参	Barrachuda		101.46	0.00	
鲷鱼	Porgy			101.70	96.96
蓝圆	Blue scad		101.38	103.39	
远东拟沙丁鱼	Far East imitation sardine			109.09	
鲆鲽	Left-eyed flounder		100.00	111.11	
其他海水鱼类	Other seawater fish			103.29	101.23
海水虾蟹类	Seawater shrimp and crab	276.24	100.00	113.85	95.64

2—3 续表 11 continued 11

农产品名称	Categories of agricultural products	2002	2003	2004	2005
		第一季度 1st quarter			
对虾	Prawn		99.88	116.78	88.10
毛虾	Shrimp		93.42	105.04	106.36
爬虾	Mantis shrimp		96.01		100.11
鹰爪虾	Trachypemaeus curvirostris		124.49	103.45	
梭子蟹	Swimming crab		106.54	118.74	107.22
其他海水虾蟹类	Other seawater shrimps and crabs			104.53	98.91
海水贝类	Seawater shellfish	59.02	90.40	106.52	105.05
贻贝	Mussel	100.00	100.00	104.00	0.00
扇贝	Scallop	100.00	100.00	103.45	94.83
牡蛎	Oyster	156.00	79.50	102.71	84.20
鲍鱼	Abalone	35.29	113.31	110.37	104.20
蛤	Clam	58.96	90.49	106.55	107.81
蚶	Blood clam	93.05	160.05	94.58	0.00
海螺	Conch		85.95	106.67	103.99
蛏	Razor clam		90.77	102.54	100.95
其他海水贝类	Other seawater shellfish			84.53	97.31
藻类	Seaweeds	114.41	100.00	100.24	83.79
海带	Kelp	76.87	100.00	81.63	0.00
紫菜	Laver	121.44	100.00	103.73	83.79
其他藻类	Other seaweeds			101.91	162.37
其他海水产品	Other seawater products				
墨鱼	Inkfish		114.97	115.92	98.54
鱿鱼	Squid		100.00	108.01	107.73
章鱼	Octopus		114.51	64.49	90.76
海蜇	Jellyfish		131.67		102.22
未列明的其他海水产品	Other seawater products			105.51	101.31
2. 内陆水域水产品	2. Aquatic products in inland water areas	93.62	97.34	107.15	110.36
淡水鱼类	Freshwater fish	93.62	97.34	105.41	110.00
青鱼	Black carp	69.60	98.66	108.12	108.61
草鱼	Grass carp	94.33	95.15	108.40	112.24
鲤鱼	Carp	101.84	99.63	103.85	107.61
鲢鱼	Silver carp	101.03	96.63	105.28	110.92
鲫鱼	Crucian carp	79.73	97.29	104.71	112.40
罗非鱼	Tilapia	68.20	99.46	100.27	104.92

2—3 续表 12 continued 12

农产品名称	Categories of agricultural products	2002	2003	2004	2005
		第一季度 1st quarter			
虹鳟鱼	Rainbow trout	83.89		100.00	102.57
白鱼	Whitefish		86.36	96.19	116.51
鳜鱼	Mandarin fish		110.41	82.93	104.80
白昌鱼	Round spadefish		80.76	95.47	109.75
黑鱼	Snakeheaded fish		105.48	110.00	100.46
鲶鱼	Oriental sheatfish		97.94	103.73	102.82
武昌鱼	Blunt-snout bream		96.36	89.37	113.35
鳙鱼	Variegated carp		100.36	109.34	110.21
鲮鱼	Dace		93.45	109.96	100.34
鳊	Bream		92.56	102.20	100.43
黄颡鱼	Yellowcat fish			106.67	82.92
银鱼	Whitebait		90.91	66.67	
淡水鲈	Freshwater perch		85.36	104.17	103.57
其他淡水鱼类	Other freshwater fish			93.11	101.48
淡水虾蟹类	Freshwater shrimps and crabs	89.48	100.00	120.96	116.78
龙虾	Lobster		111.80	107.24	117.33
罗氏沼虾	M. rosenbergii		100.00	106.38	117.62
青虾	Freshwater shrimp		97.90	131.96	116.51
基围虾	Greasybaek shrimp			103.45	98.16
红螯螯虾	Red clow		100.00	128.24	100.00
大闸蟹	Dazha crab		88.50	99.67	99.66
其他淡水虾蟹类	Other freshwater shrimps and crabs			106.05	108.42
淡水贝类	Freshwater shellfish				
淡水珍珠	Freshwater pearl			5.67	86.19
螺蛳	Spiral shell		97.33	98.23	118.93
其他淡水贝类	Other freshwater shellfish			116.03	104.45
其他淡水养殖产品	Other freshwater breeding products				
河鳗	River eel		92.69		0.00
牛蛙	Bullfrog		104.11		116.77
甲鱼	Soft-shelled turtle		98.56	102.54	89.62
黄鳝	Ricefield eel		104.51	112.17	115.90
泥鳅	Loach		103.87	103.88	111.81
蛙	Frog		93.75		0.00
未列明的其他淡水养殖产品	Other freshwater breeding products			90.54	0.00

2—4 全国农产品生产价格指数(第二季度)
National Indices of Producer Prices of Agricultural Products

(上年同期=100)　　(2nd quarter)　　(the same period of the preceding year=100)

农产品名称	Categories of agricultural products	2002	2003	2004	2005
		第二季度 2nd quarter			
总指数	**Gross Index**	**98.90**	**102.65**	**110.89**	**101.75**
一、种植业产品	I. Crop products	99.70	106.73	117.37	100.59
1.谷物及其他作物	1. Cereal and other crops			126.63	98.07
粮食	Grain	94.60	103.89	128.55	99.46
谷物(原粮)	Cereal (unprocessed food grains)	95.60	101.51	129.98	99.74
小麦	Wheat	93.20	103.2	138.13	99.07
硬粒小麦	Hard wheat	90.20	104.22	137.97	98.62
软粒小麦	Soft wheat	81.30	103.40	142.73	99.73
混合小麦	Mixed wheat	100.60	100.76	138.39	100.42
其他小麦	Other wheat			139.14	98.88
稻谷	Paddy	101.20	97.29	141.42	101.41
早籼稻	Early long-grain nonglutinous rice	101.60	98.04	135.86	99.13
晚籼稻	Late long-grain nonglutinous rice	103.50	101.26	140.71	99.94
粳 稻	Round-grain rice	98.20	93.23	144.72	102.94
其他稻谷	Other paddy			132.91	102.21
玉米	Maize (corn)	93.30	103.44	118.97	97.64
黄玉米	Yellow maize	93.10	103.45	118.96	97.55
白玉米	White maize	115.50	99.63	120.55	103.79
混合玉米	Mixed maize	165.00	102.26	120.81	100.08
其他玉米	Other maize		94.15	112.21	100.21
杂粮	Coarse cereals		120.92	0.00	108.20
谷子	Millet		121.54	122.12	114.39
高粱	Chinese sorghum		95.74	133.14	100.52
大麦	Barley		98.48	116.95	105.85
荞麦	Buckwheat		125.83	121.55	126.74
元麦	poulard wheat		124.75	0.00	
青稞	Highland barley		126.29	119.55	0.00
莜麦	Naked oats		113.88	102.10	107.99
燕麦	Oats		131.67	66.67	0.00
其他杂粮	Other coarse cereals			107.86	105.63
谷物副产品	By-products of cereals			0.00	0.00
小麦秸	Wheat straw		99.26	127.46	110.47
稻草	Rice straw		93.12	125.17	121.71

2—4 续表 1 continued 1

农产品名称 Categories of agricultural products		2002	2003	2004	2005
		第二季度 2nd quarter			
玉米秆	Corn stover		132.80	108.47	98.38
大麦秸	Barley straw			101.10	99.02
谷子秆	Millet stalk		162.54	107.74	114.89
高粱秆	Chinese sorghum stalk		100.00	122.79	107.19
薯类	Potato	88.30	94.88	101.94	106.47
红薯	Sweet potato	139.00	97.87	112.87	102.78
马铃薯	White Potato	76.00	94.15	99.27	108.27
其他薯类	Other potatoes			110.59	102.83
薯藤	Potato vines		103.20	122.17	124.78
油料	Oil-bearing crops	103.20	125.83	121.61	88.70
花生	Peanut	104.70	124.75	120.45	97.19
油菜籽	Rapeseeds	102.80	126.29	121.80	83.37
芝麻	Sesame	88.20	113.88	129.58	101.59
向日葵	Sunflower		93.83	114.70	106.85
胡麻籽	Flaxseeds	112.50	112.70	106.54	110.47
苏籽	Perillaseeds		114.76	99.01	96.00
其他油料作物	Other oil-bearing crops			101.14	105.76
花生蔓	Peanut vine		103.08	125.00	98.13
豆类	Beans	90.20	120.92	127.09	95.41
大豆	Soybeans	90.40	121.54	127.48	94.02
绿豆	Mung beans	77.10	95.74	110.61	104.98
红小豆	Small red beans	117.20	98.48	117.48	108.40
蚕豆	Broad beans		112.03	140.84	98.10
豌豆	Peas		108.47	112.75	106.88
芸豆	Kidney beans		108.47	123.52	102.73
其他杂豆	Other beans			114.62	100.34
豆秸	Beanstalk		101.03	79.06	109.51
棉花(籽棉)	Cotton (unginned cotton)	88.00	131.67	122.61	87.05
细绒棉	Thin-staple cotton	88.00	131.67	122.61	86.74
长绒棉	Long-staple cotton	100.00	125.04	141.71	93.75
棉籽	Cottonseeds		97.56	121.00	97.29
棉花秆	Cotton stalk			87.50	0.00
麻类	Fiber crops	85.20	90.68	135.33	104.84
黄红麻	Jute and blueish dogbane	95.70	78.56	115.39	113.96

2—4 续表 2　　continued 2

农产品名称	Categories of agricultural products	2002	2003	2004	2005
		第二季度 2nd quarter			
亚麻	Flax		108.75	98.71	73.03
苎麻	Ramie	77.90	99.14	149.25	107.62
线麻	Thread hemp		108.16	0.00	0.00
苘麻	Piemarker		100.94	0.00	
剑麻	Steel hemp		74.47		0.00
麻秆	Stalks of fiber crops			104.43	
糖料	Sugar crops	105.20	87.14	104.59	104.16
甘蔗	Sugarcane	105.20	87.09	104.59	104.16
甜菜	Beet	96.10	120.00		100.00
其他糖料	Other sugar crops			104.94	111.11
烟草	Tobacco	183.30	105.99	107.00	106.58
烤烟叶	Flue-cured tobacco	263.90	100.29	103.41	106.63
晒烟叶	Sun-cured tobacco	97.80	112.03	110.80	104.67
白肋烟	Whiteerib tobacco		99.20		100.00
香料烟	Perfume tobacco		107.15	0.00	
其他烟叶	Other tobacco			104.64	103.43
其他农作物	Other agricultural crops				
青饲料	Greenfeed		110.68	102.60	103.20
牧草	Herbage		113.13	105.00	96.24
绿肥	Green manure		106.16	81.65	133.33
桑叶	Mulberry leaves		97.70	111.80	
席草	Stems or leaves of cattail		102.34	113.89	0.00
蓖麻籽	Castor beans		96.45	119.69	121.57
除虫菊	Pyrethrum		103.74	0.00	
薄荷油	Peppermint oil		98.01	0.00	114.29
野生植物的采集	Gathering of wild plants			175.51	111.20
未列明的其他农作物	Other agricultural crops			115.94	106.20
2.蔬菜、园艺作物	2. Vegetable and Horticulture crops		108.47	102.56	105.65
蔬菜	Vegetable	95.90	108.47	102.56	105.65
叶菜类	Leaf vegetable	86.80	110.54	100.34	107.59
菠菜	Spinach	94.10	109.35	103.13	104.78
芹菜	Celery	78.60	114.03	101.01	103.36
大白菜	Chinese cabbage	50.70	120.44	101.08	105.94
元白菜	Cabbage	73.90	102.59	102.30	114.55

2—4 续表 3 continued 3

农产品名称	Categories of agricultural products	2002	2003	2004	2005
		第二季度 2nd quarter			
甘蓝	Wild cabbage	38.70	93.83	99.41	108.75
花椰菜	Cauliflower	72.10	112.70	94.97	94.47
莴笋	Asparagus lettuce	105.80	114.76	97.94	110.33
油菜	Rape	107.30	111.19	98.64	109.62
其他叶菜	Other leaf vegetable			101.89	107.04
瓜菜类	Gourd vegetable	86.80	107.80	100.47	103.25
黄瓜	Cucumber	86.90	100.16	108.94	103.45
冬瓜	White gourd	63.60	125.04	73.55	100.95
西葫芦	Summer squash	99.90	96.55	102.06	98.49
苦瓜	Balsam pear		120.04	110.64	109.52
丝瓜	Towed gourd		108.75	111.39	108.31
南瓜	Pumpkin		93.35	109.93	106.25
打瓜	Seeded watermelon		96.87	100.00	122.69
瓠子	Bottle gourd		96.87	109.17	114.35
其他瓜菜	Other gourd vegetable			109.00	103.52
块根、块茎菜类	Root and tuber vegetable	82.30	104.98	103.68	102.92
萝卜	Radish	81.40	108.16	99.07	105.43
胡萝卜	Carrot	144.50	100.94	110.33	98.53
生姜	Ginger	92.90	74.47	133.12	88.58
芋头	Taro		117.29	95.05	106.40
苔干	Dried bryophyte		117.29	113.01	106.67
百合(根)	Lily (root)		78.37	89.57	99.90
芋艿	Taro		78.37	114.34	109.54
山药	Chinese yam		76.76	104.03	117.20
其他块根、块茎菜	Other root and tuber vegetable			102.92	107.87
茄果菜类	Eggplant, tomato and chili, etc.	108.80	107.64	102.80	100.80
茄子	Eggplant	123.70	112.51	112.44	102.62
西红柿	Tomato	105.50	108.75	98.41	99.69
辣椒	Chili	87.50	115.41	113.30	92.17
青椒	Sweetbell	106.60	98.31	100.20	106.96
其他茄果菜类	Others			109.15	106.02
葱蒜类	Onion and Garlic	60.90	114.85	110.87	109.93
大葱	Scallion	250.10	109.17	109.05	96.09
蒜苔	Garlic stalk	81.40	118.58	110.14	107.09

2—4 续表 4 continued 4

农产品名称 Categories of agricultural products		2002	2003	2004	2005
		第二季度 2nd quarter			
蒜头	Garlic head	50.30	99.20	114.08	117.00
洋葱	Onion		94.17	90.55	97.18
蒜苗	Garlic bolt		94.19	103.70	104.82
小葱	Shallot		83.86	99.11	104.04
韭菜	Fragrant-flowered garlic		98.74	106.87	98.18
其他葱蒜类	Others			97.59	109.77
菜用豆类	Garden beans	111.40	107.15	110.19	110.90
四季豆	Kidney beans	97.60	101.55	110.87	107.66
豇豆	Cowpeas	136.90	112.51	109.55	113.23
其他菜用豆	Other garden beans			102.57	106.26
水生菜类	Water vegetable	105.10	110.68	105.07	152.99
莲藕	Lotus root	98.60	113.13	114.07	105.81
茭白	Wild ruice stem	115.30	106.16	88.51	190.74
荸荠	Water chestnut	100.00	94.62	121.04	101.71
其他水生菜	Other water vegetable			110.22	106.45
食用菌(干鲜混合)	Mushroom		97.70	101.73	95.58
香菇(干品)	Mushroom (dried)		102.34	99.70	90.91
蘑菇(鲜品)	Mushroom (fresh)		96.45	100.05	96.94
黑木耳(干品)	Black edible fungus (dried)		103.74	124.89	82.80
白木耳(干品)	Tremella (dried)		112.20	87.43	111.12
金针菇(鲜品)	Golden mushroom		89.64	108.47	99.58
猴头菌(干品)	Bearded tooth(dried)		100.67	0.00	91.15
平菇(鲜品)	Oyster mushroom		105.42	104.08	102.72
花菇(干品)	Black forest mushroom		89.59	81.47	
其他食用菌	Other edible mushrooms			112.29	95.74
椿芽	Chinese cedrela sprouts		98.23	107.42	104.75
未列明的其他蔬菜	Other vegetable			103.20	109.15
花卉	Flowers		96.18	0.00	0.00
鲜切花	Fresh flowers		97.55	0.00	0.00
百合花	Lily		98.55	100.29	106.35
康乃馨	Carnation		94.56	125.36	130.22
满天星	June snow (serissa)		99.75	89.37	114.13
勿忘我	Forgetmenot		87.43	92.64	109.39
非洲菊	Flameray Gerbera		100.00	86.58	68.60

2—4 续表 5 continued 5

农产品名称	Categories of agricultural products	2002	2003	2004	2005
		第二季度 2nd quarter			
玫瑰	Rugosa rose		113.18	74.49	114.97
郁金香	Tulip			83.33	101.00
情人草	Evans begonia		59.54	71.21	100.00
其他鲜切花	Other fresh flowers			106.84	111.81
其他园艺作物	Other holticulture crops				
盆栽植物	Potted plants		101.21	0.00	0.00
观赏苗木	Ornamental plants		85.66	0.00	0.00
草坪草皮	Sod for lawn		90.72	97.49	100.48
其他园艺作物	Other horticulture crops			96.27	115.88
3.水果、坚果、饮料和香料	3. Fruit, beverage and perfume		98.01	106.93	107.34
水果、坚果	Fruits and nuts			101.09	107.27
园林水果	Garden fruits	117.90	98.69	98.16	106.99
苹果	Apples	100.50	100.74	111.25	95.46
红富士苹果	Hongfushi apples	93.10	103.47	108.83	96.88
国光苹果	Guoguang apples	117.30	78.56	109.29	104.26
秦冠苹果	Qinguan apples	107.30	99.50	115.42	78.25
香蕉苹果	Banana apples	100.00	103.36		113.64
金冠苹果	Jinguan apples				93.33
元帅苹果	Yuanshuai (Marshal) apples		100.00	175.28	94.57
新红星苹果	New Hongxing apples		93.94		115.16
梨	Pears	95.60	107.84	93.38	116.18
雪花梨	Snowflake pears	99.90	114.22	82.53	125.25
鸭梨	Ya-pears	102.00	100.00	99.99	84.64
酥梨	Soft-pears	69.60	104.34	102.08	99.77
香梨	Bergamot pears	100.00	100.00		0.00
其他梨	Other pears			101.00	99.68
柑桔	Citrus	96.20	96.96	81.05	103.72
柑	Mandarin oranges	94.30	95.72	83.81	102.51
桔	Tangerines	101.00	100.05	78.63	111.22
橙	Oranges	100.00	103.74	93.99	103.49
柚	Shaddocks	100.00	75.00	107.78	56.11
其他水果	Other fruits			96.20	101.89
香蕉	Bananas	186.10	104.79	122.34	91.27
菠萝	Pineapples		74.48	105.72	107.67

2—4 续表 6 continued 6

农产品名称	Categories of agricultural products	2002	2003	2004	2005
		第二季度 2nd quarter			
荔枝	Litchis	26.10	138.03	74.52	113.50
芒果	Mangoes		71.56	118.37	96.30
木瓜	Papayas		98.04	107.17	100.00
橄榄	Chinese olives		80.00		91.29
桃	Peachs	161.80	93.35	95.31	100.92
杏	Apricots	90.60	99.15	103.29	88.26
杨梅	Red bayberries	133.40	91.01	120.27	84.55
猕猴桃	Yangtaoes	100.00	87.50		104.50
葡萄	Grapes	196.70	113.52	97.47	109.26
红枣	Chinese dates	100.90	78.72	108.81	102.17
柿子	Persimmons	100.00	100.00	73.68	0.00
其他园林水果	Other garden fruitss			93.35	91.12
瓜果类	Melon	44.00	93.61	104.04	110.33
西瓜	Watermelons	38.40	93.62	102.73	110.68
甜瓜	Muskmelons	140.60	93.36	111.73	110.37
哈蜜瓜	Hami melons	100.00		100.00	
香瓜	Musk melons		116.82	111.05	108.67
伊利沙白瓜	Elizabeth melons		98.52	120.00	
草莓	Strawberries	77.70	104.81	107.14	99.77
其他瓜果	Others			109.23	101.40
坚果类	Nuts				101.06
椰子	Coconut			106.25	102.12
杏仁	Apricot kerne				100.00
槟榔	Areca			113.24	121.88
沙棘果	Seabuck thorn			0.00	
其他坚果	Other nuts			125.00	77.08
茶及其他饮料(干品)	Tea and other beverages			116.86	107.79
茶	Tea	144.40		116.86	107.50
红毛茶	Black tea	135.30	91.14	106.34	113.13
绿毛茶	Green tea	145.30	97.19	117.38	109.04
乌龙茶	Oolong tea	109.00	90.31	110.16	90.39
其他茶	Others			104.41	99.87
可可和咖啡	Cocoa and Coffee				116.04
咖啡豆	Coffee bean	88.00	99.68	86.57	116.04
香料作物	Perfume crops				

2—4 续表 7 continued 7

农产品名称 Categories of agricultural products		2002	2003	2004	2005
		第二季度 2nd quarter			
茴香	Fennel			100.95	0.00
4. 中药材	4. Traditional Chinese medicinal materials				
茯苓	Fuling (poris cocos)		104.39	121.82	83.51
党参	Tangshen (pilose asiabell)		311.35	88.04	96.69
当归	Chinese angelica		164.20	81.55	71.43
黄芪	Root of membranous milk vetch		113.21	105.64	96.75
金银花	Honeysuckle		120.02	85.56	103.83
人参	Ginseng			85.00	
黄连	Rhizome of Chinese goldthread		100.00	100.78	
甘草	Licorice root		98.55	85.00	87.15
贝母	Bulb of fritillary		186.21	90.91	89.22
红花	Safflower		95.35	109.54	0.00
元胡	Amur corydalis		100.00	83.08	88.46
枸杞	Fruit of Chinese wolfberry		100.00	83.77	100.91
砂仁	Villous amomum			90.00	0.00
菊花	Chrysanthemum		104.20	139.48	104.00
白术	Largehead atractyldes		92.31	89.82	98.91
半夏	Tuber of pinelia		117.08	106.90	107.28
麦冬	Tuber of dwarf lilyturf			90.91	101.08
三七	Pseudo-ginseng			111.11	107.83
麻黄草	Chinese ephedra			90.91	
玄参	Root of Zhejiang figwort			87.50	99.80
肉桂	Cinnamon			102.25	
生地	Dried rhizome of rehmannia		100.00	86.07	100.78
厚朴	Bark of official magnolia			130.00	100.00
杜仲	Bark of eucommia		99.41	100.36	89.79
薄荷	Peppermint			80.00	0.00
田七	Notoginseng			80.00	
板蓝根	Root of common baphicacanthus		137.92	72.13	90.96
苦丁茶	Kudin crotoxylum (bitter tea tree)		54.70	103.84	
霍香	Wrinkled giant hyssop			90.00	118.12
天麻	Tuber of elevated gastrodia		107.92	99.69	100.39
穿心莲	Creat		98.33	127.44	0.00
桔梗	Rampion		137.07	102.58	101.23
干姜	Dried ginger			111.11	112.59

2—4 续表 8 continued 8

农产品名称	Categories of agricultural products	2002	2003	2004	2005
		第二季度 2nd quarter			
丹参	Root of red-rooted salvia		99.75	84.81	84.02
大青叶	Common conehead		100.00	50.00	116.67
白芷	Root of Dahurian angelica			90.91	0.00
川芎	Ligusticum wallichii			97.56	
虫草	Chinese caterpillar fungus			112.19	103.61
其他药材	Other medicinal materials			109.96	99.12
二、林业产品	II. Forest products	88.40	101.24	108.91	102.45
1.竹木采运	1. Felling and transport of bamboo and wood				104.47
木材采运	Felling and transport of wood	104.50			104.54
原木	Log	104.40			104.54
红松	Korean pine		105.93	103.28	112.32
落叶松	Larch		89.69	97.94	101.77
马尾松	Masson pine		102.32	100.70	103.77
杉木	China fir		101.82	102.22	100.71
云南松	Yunnan pine		101.43	104.98	102.82
薪材	Firewood	165.20	98.41	105.57	101.69
竹材采运	Felling and transport of bamboo	149.90			100.57
水竹	Water bamboo		64.03	118.89	104.08
斑竹	Mottled bamboo		100.00	99.02	100.00
毛竹(楠竹)	Mao bamboo		99.02	101.50	100.57
蒿竹	Hao bamboo		89.63	97.93	104.88
淡竹	Henon bamboo		113.14	183.40	108.67
其他竹材	Other bamboo		91.00	112.16	101.94
2.林产品的采集	2. Gathering of forest products	83.30	101.24	108.91	101.50
天然和人工林的果实	Products of natural and artificial forest			108.91	101.50
橡胶	Rubber	92.00	117.29	123.43	104.54
油桐籽	Seeds of tung oil tree	100.00	214.46	98.17	136.28
油茶籽	Seeds of tea-oil tree	100.00	118.48	129.73	112.30
棕片	Palm fibre		104.99	93.45	99.36
松脂	Rosin		105.39	110.32	97.85
核桃	Walnut	184.60	78.37	103.19	101.98
板栗	Chinese chestnut		81.23		88.89
花椒	Chinese prickly ash	72.60	93.73	98.30	100.20
八角	Anise	57.70	77.76	73.64	94.92
桂皮	Cassia bark	90.60	67.35	111.73	103.34

2—4 续表 9 continued 9

农产品名称 Categories of agricultural products		2002	2003	2004	2005
		第二季度 2nd quarter			
胡椒	Pepper		112.23	110.13	103.40
茴油	Fennel oil			0.00	
桂油	Cassia oil			0.00	
其他果实	Other products			99.78	108.01
其他林产品采集	Gathering of other wild plants				
柳条	Willow twigs		100.27	133.33	0.00
藤条	Rattan		100.00	83.33	0.00
竹笋干	Dried bamboo shoots		94.36	109.70	105.48
桉树叶	Eucalyptus leaves			81.89	101.21
黄 柏	Chinese weeping cypress			104.65	98.66
未列明的其他林产品采集	Gathering of other wild plants			100.91	93.15
三、牧业(畜产品)	III. Livestock products	99.80	99.08	103.87	102.52
1.牲畜的饲养	1. Livestock raising			105.80	102.10
牛的饲养	Cattle raising			103.77	101.38
活牛(毛重)	Live cattle (gross weight)	78.70	103.49	103.77	101.37
牛肉	Beef		113.47	91.91	101.71
羊的饲养	Sheep raising			104.30	102.21
活羊(毛重)	Live sheep		100.29	104.30	102.21
羊肉	Mutton		127.38	110.11	108.18
其他牲畜饲养	Other livestock raising				
马	Horse		101.20	104.99	103.10
驴	Donkey		96.75	103.12	93.11
骡	Mule		106.70	100.00	102.46
奶产品	Milk products	98.50	99.97	102.13	99.32
牛奶	Cow milk	98.50	99.97	102.12	99.32
羊奶	Sheep milk	60.50	102.21	104.41	102.19
其他奶类	Other milk			100.08	95.09
毛绒产品	Hair and down products	80.70	92.92	112.29	106.47
山羊毛	Goat's wool	139.90	77.49	104.29	100.50
绵羊毛	Sheep's wool		94.71	108.46	104.15
山羊绒	Cashmere	74.20	94.62	113.17	107.93
绵羊绒	Sheep's down		100.00	106.93	101.86
牦牛毛	Yak hair		100.00	76.55	100.00
骆驼绒	Camel hair cloth		103.67	160.00	89.78
2.猪的饲养	2. Hog raising			100.76	100.62

2—4 续表 10 continued 10

农产品名称	Categories of agricultural products	2002	2003	2004	2005
		第二季度 2nd quarter			
活猪(毛重)	Hog (gross weight)	97.50	99.88	100.76	100.60
猪肉	Pork		100.62	122.46	103.07
猪鬃	Bristles			109.54	99.24
3. 家禽	3. Poultry	107.90	94.17	110.62	107.34
肉禽(毛重)	Poultry (gross weight)			109.76	107.23
鸡	Chicken	107.90	94.19	109.74	107.02
鸭	Duck	103.50	83.86	116.63	109.04
鹅	Goose	100.00	90.70	114.43	106.99
其他家禽	Other poultry			111.77	100.84
禽蛋	Eggs	104.80	98.74	111.77	107.48
鸡蛋	Chicken's eggs	104.50		111.73	107.53
鸭蛋	Duck 's eggs	119.90		113.48	107.58
鹅蛋	Goose' s eggs	98.10		109.12	105.63
鹌鹑蛋	Quail 's eggs			98.89	
其他蛋	Other eggs			93.99	101.69
羽绒	Eider down		76.83	0.00	0.00
鸭绒	Duck 's down			107.08	105.84
其他羽绒	Other down			105.69	94.47
4. 狩猎和捕捉动物	4. Hunting and catching animals				
兽皮	Furs		100.00	108.57	100.18
未列明的动物皮张	Furs not identified			112.47	105.86
5. 其他畜牧业	5. Other livestock products				
各种鸟类	Birds				
鸽子	Pigeon		112.75	101.62	102.39
其他鸟类	Other birds			118.18	103.30
家养动物	Domestic animals				
兔	Rabbit		112.22	111.30	105.72
狗	Dog		90.86	105.62	99.88
猫	Cat			104.05	98.58
兔毛	Rabbit hair		99.06	139.95	116.37
珍贵动物	Rare animals				
狐狸	Fox		100.00	125.00	100.00
蛇	Snake		101.25	109.21	99.38
虫类	Worms				
蚯蚓	Earthworm			112.14	0.00

2—4 续表 11 continued 11

农产品名称	Categories of agricultural products	2002	2003	2004	2005
		第二季度 2nd quarter			
蝎子	Scorpion			94.28	0.00
其他虫类	Other Worms			109.16	99.20
活的家畜产品	Domestic livestock products				
蚕茧	Silkworm cocoon	65.90	98.39	149.73	110.54
蜂蜜	Honey	223.80	104.29	107.54	103.09
蜂蜡	Beeswax			100.90	0.00
鹿茸	Pilose antler			70.18	141.30
其他活的家畜产品	Other livestock products			118.71	101.24
毛皮的生产	Production of furs				
动物皮张	Animals' furs		99.35	117.36	79.34
四、渔业	IV. Fishery products	93.40	98.99	111.91	103.95
1. 海水水产品	1. Seawater aquatic products	98.60	99.29	111.44	103.63
鱼类	Seawater Fish	94.50	108.65	113.27	104.51
大黄鱼	Large yellow croaker	61.10	105.63	103.88	102.39
小黄鱼	Small yellow croaker	63.00	88.16	119.53	100.01
带鱼	Hairtail	59.30	112.20	112.24	101.36
鲈鱼	Perch			106.14	104.78
沙丁鱼	Sardine		100.00	105.72	102.01
石斑鱼	Grouper	100.00	66.28	98.36	105.24
鳀鱼	Anchovy		105.86	109.72	102.34
梭鱼	Mullet		99.98	105.94	113.54
鲳鱼	Silvery pomfret		93.51	114.91	103.86
海鳗	Conger pike		103.71	96.77	107.02
鲅鱼	Spanish mackerel		114.38	106.98	123.29
鲐鱼	Chub mackerel		149.69	113.07	129.88
马面鱼	Black scraper		75.81	126.75	91.78
黄姑鱼	Spotted maigre			0.00	99.57
鳓鱼	Chinese herring			114.59	
马鲛	Japanese Spanish mackerel		92.91	115.95	105.32
梅童鱼	Baby croaker		151.72		99.63
梭参	Barrachuda		100.01	0.00	
鲷鱼	Porgy			115.22	103.08
蓝圆	Blue scad		113.09	98.85	
鲆鲽	Left-eyed flounder		109.59	116.95	99.14
舌鳎	Tonguefish			123.08	126.84

2—4 续表 12 continued 12

农产品名称 Categories of agricultural products		2002	2003	2004	2005
		第二季度 2nd quarter			
其他海水鱼类	Other seawater fish			105.75	102.44
海水虾蟹类	Seawater shrimp and crab	164.50	100.00		106.82
对虾	Prawn		103.22	97.50	108.31
毛虾	Shrimp		125.25	108.71	118.37
爬虾	Mantis shrimp		87.82	121.11	109.82
脊尾白虾	Exopataemom carimicauda		100.00	104.17	109.96
鹰爪虾	Trachypemaeus curvirostris		151.32	113.13	98.57
梭子蟹	Swimming crab		91.65	108.93	99.77
其他海水虾蟹类	Other seawater shrimps and crabs			115.63	100.38
海水贝类	Seawater shellfish	111.30	89.64	108.49	100.94
贻贝	Mussel	87.50	100.67	104.66	0.00
扇贝	Scallop	101.40	100.00	111.11	0.00
牡蛎	Oyster	97.10	105.42	104.92	98.95
鲍鱼	Abalone	51.80	102.76	124.95	95.46
蛤	Clam	111.60	89.59	108.50	102.80
蚶	Blood clam	100.00	116.82	101.03	100.00
海螺	Conch		107.56	114.13	114.23
蛏	Razor clam		86.00	106.45	92.76
其他海水贝类	Other seawater shellfish			107.29	101.96
藻类	Seaweeds	144.80	101.04	129.88	90.34
海带	Kelp	144.80	100.00	129.88	90.17
紫菜	Laver	144.50	100.00		90.91
其他藻类	Other seaweeds			96.38	100.97
其他海水产品	Other seawater products				
墨鱼	Inkfish		70.64	132.21	109.31
鱿鱼	Squid		100.00	125.24	102.73
章鱼	Octopus		115.52	104.42	104.27
海参	Sea cucumber			112.50	100.00
未列明的其他海水产品	Other seawater products			178.05	109.64
2. 内陆水域水产品	2. Aquatic products in inland water areas	85.90	98.23	113.10	104.25
淡水鱼类	Freshwater fish	85.90	97.71	112.57	103.96
青鱼	Black carp	61.60	96.18	99.37	106.70
草鱼	Grass carp	88.40	97.55	117.92	105.09
鲤鱼	Carp	82.60	98.55	114.44	100.76
鲢鱼	Silver carp	75.70	94.56	110.30	105.06

2—4 续表 13 continued 13

农产品名称	Categories of agricultural products	2002	2003	2004	2005
		第二季度 2nd quarter			
鲫鱼	Crucian carp	91.50	99.75	109.55	105.10
罗非鱼	Tilapia	66.90	87.43	105.30	106.70
虹鳟鱼	Rainbow trout	115.40		100.00	100.01
白鱼	Whitefish		97.59	115.94	111.15
鳜鱼	Mandarin fish		100.00	106.77	99.02
黑鱼	Snakeheaded fish		100.08	98.14	102.84
鲶鱼	Oriental sheatfish		101.82	110.51	102.57
武昌鱼	Blunt-snout bream		95.39	126.75	109.86
鳙鱼	Variegated carp		102.04	116.55	102.18
鲮鱼	Dace		83.91	128.02	99.79
鳊	Bream		88.92	97.12	102.12
黄颡鱼	Yellowcat fish			101.83	100.00
银鱼	Whitebait		80.00		
淡水鲈	Freshwater perch		79.55	87.87	110.98
其他淡水鱼类	Other freshwater fish			106.84	110.01
淡水虾蟹类	Freshwater shrimps and crabs	99.90	113.18	128.35	109.31
龙虾	Lobster		113.18	128.35	118.11
罗氏沼虾	M. rosenbergii		99.24	99.72	102.06
青虾	Freshwater shrimp		103.28	104.79	98.54
基围虾	Greasyback shrimp			120.00	0.00
红螯螯虾	Red clow		179.64	123.87	108.43
大闸蟹	Steamed crab		81.44	113.71	96.81
其他淡水虾蟹类	Other freshwater shrimps and crabs			107.67	116.13
淡水贝类	Freshwater shellfish				
螺蛳	Spiral shell		105.51	108.08	110.70
河蚌	Freshwater mussel		68.04	104.17	
其他淡水贝类	Other freshwater shellfish			84.58	103.44
其他淡水养殖产品	Other freshwater breeding products				
河鳗	River eel			111.11	91.89
牛蛙	Bullfrog		215.38	104.46	113.60
甲鱼	Soft-shelled turtle		111.57	93.63	104.62
黄鳝	Ricefield eel		102.88	107.94	106.44
泥鳅	Loach		102.41	123.87	105.91
蛙	Frog		92.78	107.16	61.56
未列明的其他淡水养殖产品	Other freshwater breeding products			94.35	100.00

2—5 全国农产品生产价格指数(第三季度)

National Indices of the Producer Prices of Agricultural Products

(上年同期=100) (3rd quarter) (the same period of the preceding year=100)

农产品名称	Categories of agricultural products	2002	2003	2004	2005
		第三季度 3rd quarter			
总指数	Gross Index	98.10	102.05	114.71	99.72
一、种植业产品	I. Crop products	98.10	102.91	122.26	100.60
1. 谷物及其他作物	1. Cereal and other crops			129.07	96.75
粮食	Grain	95.30	101.47	135.09	96.78
谷物(原粮)	Cereal (unprocessed food grains)	93.00	100.15	137.26	97.11
小麦	Wheat	98.00	100.69	137.74	95.81
硬粒小麦	Hard wheat	97.90	100.81	136.48	96.00
软粒小麦	Soft wheat	82.30	103.99	134.38	93.59
混合小麦	Mixed wheat	100.20	99.86	143.52	95.72
其他小麦	Other wheat			136.36	95.71
稻谷	Paddy	93.10	97.81	143.12	98.35
早籼稻	Early long-grain nonglutinous rice	95.10	102.73	140.82	94.85
晚籼稻	Late long-grain nonglutinous rice	97.80	102.99	139.68	94.62
粳 稻	Round-grain rice	90.60	93.10	145.47	101.17
其他稻谷	Other paddy			134.27	99.72
玉米	Maize (corn)	79.40	103.27	124.49	95.67
黄玉米	Yellow maize	78.20	103.06	124.57	95.87
白玉米	White maize	91.10	104.10	117.90	99.48
混合玉米	Mixed maize	92.40	105.60	124.25	87.30
其他玉米	Other maize		103.99	112.63	96.46
杂粮	Coarse cereals				108.52
谷子	Millet		105.98	119.90	114.04
高粱	Chinese sorghum		106.17	131.30	115.13
大麦	Barley		101.33	132.26	90.19
荞麦	Buckwheat		95.31	110.87	123.15
青稞	Highland barley		102.55	108.20	100.29
莜麦	Naked oats		101.36	110.08	98.80
燕麦	Oats		92.61	151.05	0.00
其他杂粮	Other coarse cereals			111.32	103.12
谷物副产品	By-products of cereals				

2—5 续表 1 continued 1

农产品名称 Categories of agricultural products		2002	2003	2004	2005
		第三季度 3rd quarter			
小麦秸	Wheat straw			115.87	98.63
稻草	Rice straw			114.65	113.20
玉米秆	Corn stover			107.68	83.69
大麦秸	Barley straw			117.14	100.00
高粱秆	Chinese sorghum stalk			111.11	120.00
薯类	Potato	118.70	84.92	111.10	102.92
红薯	Sweet potato	223.20	91.29	110.71	99.00
马铃薯	White Potato	79.30	82.52	111.24	104.84
其他薯类	Other potatoes			120.18	93.27
薯藤	Potato vines			139.27	110.07
油料	Oil-bearing crops	102.10	120.55	115.20	89.02
花生	Peanut	110.90	115.13	116.91	95.62
油菜籽	Rapeseeds	97.90	123.27	114.50	84.74
芝麻	Sesame	89.20	110.12	111.07	101.41
向日葵	Sunflower		99.65	110.30	104.41
胡麻籽	Flaxseeds	112.10	110.16	125.67	105.03
其他油料作物	Other oil-bearing crops			102.05	97.46
油菜籽秆	Rapeseed stalk			115.39	149.48
豆类	Beans	109.50	114.80	121.86	92.74
大豆	Soybeans	110.60	116.77	122.66	90.89
绿豆	Mung beans	99.10	95.18	113.72	107.75
红小豆	Small red beans	62.40	86.94	120.20	109.77
蚕豆	Broad beans		105.58	126.59	91.49
豌豆	Peas		99.99	115.68	102.51
芸豆	Kidney beans		100.42	94.57	102.11
其他杂豆	Other beans			108.47	97.91
豆秸	Beanstalk			109.71	105.53
棉花(籽棉)	Cotton (unginned cotton)	110.10	127.91	95.55	106.00
细绒棉	Thin-staple cotton	110.80	128.83	95.14	104.91
长绒棉	Long-staple cotton	89.00	100.00	107.95	129.73
麻类	Fiber crops	92.50	120.28	136.75	108.09
黄红麻	Jute and blueish dogbane	90.50	140.33	123.38	115.33
亚麻	Flax		92.93	137.53	101.17

2—5 续表 2 continued 2

农产品名称	Categories of agricultural products	2002	2003	2004	2005
		第三季度 3rd quarter			
苎麻	Ramie	92.70	115.89	139.68	104.18
其他麻类	Other fiber crops			101.01	0.00
糖料	Sugar crops	70.90	87.56	103.20	94.93
甘蔗	Sugarcane	73.20	87.56	103.20	94.93
甜菜	Beet	100.00	104.00		99.67
其他糖料	Other sugar crops				
烟草	Tobacco	111.40	92.26	112.91	100.80
烤烟叶	Flue-cured tobacco	111.60	92.08	112.96	100.71
晒烟叶	Sun-cured tobacco	80.30	117.43	105.13	104.37
其他烟叶	Other tobacco			104.10	104.00
其他农作物	Other agricultural crops				
青饲料	Greenfeed		104.45	102.31	91.29
牧草	Herbage		94.65	129.82	94.76
绿肥	Green manure		100.00	105.41	0.00
桑叶	Mulberry leaves		123.38	100.00	
席草	Stems or leaves of cattail		75.69	111.07	95.50
薄荷油	Peppermint oil		108.11	0.00	109.09
野生植物的采集	Gathering of wild plants			141.54	110.78
未列明的其他农作物	Other agricultural crops			104.24	101.65
2.蔬菜、园艺作物	2. Vegetable and Horticulture crops		99.22	116.33	109.41
蔬菜	Vegetable	84.70	99.22	116.33	109.41
叶菜类	Leaf vegetable	77.20	100.19	115.60	108.94
菠菜	Spinach	87.20	94.08	107.15	101.62
芹菜	Celery	89.50	130.12	112.07	106.25
大白菜	Chinese cabbage	42.20	101.80	112.23	111.33
元白菜	Cabbage	84.20	91.36	120.19	108.46
甘蓝	Wild cabbage	52.50	60.80	106.21	107.66
花椰菜	Cauliflower	61.60	110.32	114.44	97.20
莴笋	Asparagus lettuce	118.50	75.84	125.35	115.76
油菜	Rape	105.30	101.61	116.55	113.33
其他叶菜	Other leaf vegetable			109.55	108.56
瓜菜类	Gourd vegetable	102.90	102.03	111.30	106.11
黄瓜	Cucumber	99.60	102.72	111.84	105.96

2—5 续表 3 continued 2

农产品名称	Categories of agricultural products	2002	2003	2004	2005
		第三季度 3rd quarter			
冬瓜	White gourd	122.20	97.34	112.86	105.58
西葫芦	Summer squash	283.30	105.09	104.42	101.82
苦瓜	Balsam pear		106.57	103.26	110.83
丝瓜	Towed gourd		94.98	103.70	110.06
南瓜	Pumpkin		99.52	106.26	105.62
打瓜	Seeded watermelon		104.90	96.25	101.24
瓠子	Bottle gourd		86.78	119.39	113.10
其他瓜菜	Other gourd vegetable			109.40	101.07
块根、块茎菜类	Root and tuber vegetable	60.40	122.40	106.54	108.74
萝卜	Radish	60.70	116.21	109.76	110.01
胡萝卜	Carrot	54.90	136.40	98.25	106.83
生姜	Ginger	49.90	104.68	160.91	92.37
芋头	Taro		107.43	115.49	101.67
苔干	Dried bryophyte		100.00	133.34	138.71
百合(根)	Lily (root)		115.31	116.83	89.08
芋艿	Taro		146.66	124.67	137.14
山药	Chinese yam		113.87	112.13	105.46
其他块根、块茎菜	Other root and tuber vegetable			107.79	105.09
茄果菜类	Eggplant, tomato and chili, etc.	82.10	99.11	110.15	107.44
茄子	Eggplant	97.00	106.79	113.52	105.82
西红柿	Tomato	67.40	89.70	112.06	107.15
辣椒	Chili	74.80	106.93	100.82	109.77
青椒	Sweetbell	133.10	104.31	108.65	107.63
其他茄果菜类	Others			108.91	105.40
葱蒜类	Onion and Garlic	84.70	89.35	127.40	118.41
大葱	Scallion	182.70	106.61	106.79	115.41
蒜苔	Garlic stalk	54.30	106.00	136.38	112.84
蒜头	Garlic head	55.60	83.32	133.18	121.37
洋葱	Onion		106.02	117.30	94.71
蒜苗	Garlic bolt		145.57	102.88	107.06
小葱	Shallot		90.94	96.44	110.26
韭菜	Fragrant-flowered garlic		107.00	109.39	108.29
菜用豆类	Garden beans	105.90	98.49	112.12	108.39

2—5 续表 4 continued 3

农产品名称	Categories of agricultural products	2002	2003	2004	2005
		第三季度 3rd quarter			
四季豆	Kidney beans	124.90	95.82	114.58	105.93
豇豆	Cowpeas	95.20	99.40	111.28	110.16
水生菜类	Water vegetable	129.70	109.45	131.62	103.49
莲藕	Lotus root	153.90	106.13	108.84	105.74
茭白	Wild ruice stem	128.80	109.57	132.45	101.69
荸荠	Water chestnut	100.00	99.73		93.33
其他水生菜	Other water vegetable			99.52	86.59
食用菌(干鲜混合)	Mushroom		98.00	105.24	100.91
香菇(干品)	Mushroom (dried)		87.17	111.82	100.48
蘑菇(鲜品)	Mushroom (fresh)		97.76	104.33	101.27
黑木耳(干品)	Black edible fungus (dried)		114.20	125.29	96.53
白木耳(干品)	Tremella (dried)		89.09	103.33	110.40
金针菇(鲜品)	Golden mushroom		113.04	134.62	108.02
猴头菌(干品)	Bearded tooth(dried)		100.00	0.00	97.34
平菇(鲜品)	Oyster mushroom		105.69	109.61	103.11
花菇(干品)	Black forest mushroom		99.98	94.86	
其他食用菌	Other edible mushrooms			110.09	108.14
椿芽	Chinese cedrela sprouts		106.07	115.47	101.71
花卉	Flowers				
鲜切花	Fresh flowers				0.00
百合花	Lily		62.43	94.28	96.26
康乃馨	Carnation		296.79	59.77	103.13
满天星	June snow (serissa)		128.51	87.05	106.06
勿忘我	Forgetmenot		100.00	78.36	100.00
非洲菊	Flameray Gerbera		109.99	121.12	73.41
玫瑰	Rugosa rose		92.81	84.74	100.01
郁金香	Tulip			42.82	90.00
情人草	Evans begonia		57.15	40.00	125.00
其他鲜切花	Other fresh flowers			91.49	105.26
其他园艺作物	Other horticulture crops				
盆栽植物	Potted plants		134.83	0.00	0.00
观赏苗木	Ornamental plants		100.09	0.00	0.00
草坪草皮	Sod for lawn		91.84	93.38	91.19

2—5 续表 5 continued 4

农产品名称	Categories of agricultural products	2002	2003	2004	2005
		第三季度 3rd quarter			
其他园艺作物	Other horticulture crops			133.63	101.21
3.水果、坚果、饮料和香料	3. Fruit, beverage and perfume			98.16	108.87
水果、坚果	Fruits and nuts			97.18	108.87
园林水果	Garden fruits	103.00	104.91	96.47	108.11
苹果	Apples	124.40	107.19	104.18	112.89
红富士苹果	Hongfushi apples	181.40	107.25	104.40	108.84
国光苹果	Guoguang apples	60.00	107.15	97.47	107.31
秦冠苹果	Qinguan apples	73.70	106.83	110.10	125.19
香蕉苹果	Banana apples	60.80	124.57	102.31	114.55
金冠苹果	Jinguan apples			108.46	121.99
元帅苹果	Yuanshuai (Marshal) apples		104.73	103.34	94.33
新红星苹果	New Hongxing apples		116.12	98.11	105.31
其他苹果	Other apples			88.06	112.06
梨	Pears	123.40	95.79	95.42	104.67
雪花梨	Snowflake pears	125.50	95.29	94.90	104.04
鸭梨	Ya-pears	103.50	118.26	96.81	107.13
酥梨	Soft-pears	43.30	108.75	111.38	104.06
香梨	Bergamot pears	181.90	142.19	108.04	85.16
苹果梨	Apple pears		99.79	103.01	83.33
其他梨	Other pears			105.68	99.59
柑桔	Citruses	91.70	99.37	96.48	106.19
柑	Mandarin oranges	90.40	98.62	95.16	105.81
桔	Tangerines	120.10	109.85	97.07	110.29
橙	Oranges	100.00	100.00	119.19	100.00
柚	Shaddocks	83.50	108.00	100.77	102.33
其他柑桔	Others			108.79	98.96
其他水果	Other fruits			89.46	110.32
香蕉	Bananas	47.10	113.74	105.71	109.27
菠萝	Pineapples		116.67	109.12	126.22
荔枝	Litchis	104.60	170.40	42.08	120.30
龙眼	Longans	33.90	138.64	75.69	91.80
芒果	Mangoes		115.81	106.38	102.11
橄榄	Chinese olives		96.17	90.50	100.00

2—5 续表 6 continued 5

农产品名称 Categories of agricultural products		2002	2003	2004	2005
		第三季度 3rd quarter			
桃	Peaches	88.30	94.75	94.39	110.76
杏	Apricots	103.70	97.02	93.34	89.68
杨梅	Red bayberries	100.00	69.53	93.26	106.15
猕猴桃	Yangtaoes	101.50	91.37	125.00	101.28
葡萄	Grapes	96.20	93.52	98.57	113.12
红枣	Chinese dates	101.20	84.02	115.21	88.15
柿子	Persimmons	70.60	103.91	91.54	105.44
其他园林水果	Other garden fruits			101.97	107.88
瓜果类	Melons	135.40	105.01	106.38	117.15
西瓜	Watermelons	138.00	104.47	106.84	118.88
甜瓜	Muskmelons	88.20	115.16	97.92	102.75
哈蜜瓜	Hami melons	135.20			
香瓜	Musk melons		100.06	110.67	105.34
草莓	Strawberries			97.77	97.91
其他瓜果	Others			107.49	98.71
坚果类	Nuts				99.14
椰子	Coconut			107.00	96.59
杏仁	Apricot kerne			117.47	90.18
沙棘果	Seabuck thorn			0.00	
其他坚果	Other nuts			136.84	106.43
茶及其他饮料(干品)	Tea and other beverages			108.14	108.87
茶	Tea	255.20		108.14	108.87
红毛茶	Black tea	119.80	83.83	112.52	106.34
绿毛茶	Green tea	320.00	103.61	105.70	110.93
乌龙茶	Oolong tea	70.70	75.66	115.12	89.16
紧压茶原料	Raw material for pressed tea	81.00		0.00	92.63
其他茶	Others			102.60	99.67
可可和咖啡	Cocoa and Coffee				0.00
咖啡豆	Coffee bean		215.48	102.86	0.00
香料作物	Perfume crops				
茴香	Fennel			150.36	93.57
香茅草	Lemon grass			0.00	
留兰香	Spearmint			76.87	98.67

2—5 续表 7 continued 6

农产品名称	Categories of agricultural products	2002	2003	2004	2005
		第三季度 3rd quarter			
百里香	Chinese thyme			112.35	
其他	Others			108.58	101.80
4.中药材	4. Traditional Chinese medicinal materials				
茯苓	Fuling (poris cocos)		107.99	126.49	98.23
当归	Chinese angelica		200.00	93.66	0.00
黄芪	Root of membranous milk vetch		104.66	105.98	104.80
金银花	Honeysuckle		148.85	99.41	107.48
人参	Ginseng			83.69	
黄连	Rhizome of Chinese goldthread		100.90	124.24	
甘草	Licorice root		103.79	100.00	0.00
贝母	Bulb of fritillary		141.28	50.71	48.78
红花	Safflower		164.10	98.01	144.75
元胡	Amur corydalis		100.30	104.03	82.70
枸杞	Fruit of Chinese wolfberry		133.59	106.91	98.87
砂仁	Villous amomum			101.38	90.83
菊花	Chrysanthemum		100.00		97.23
白术	Largehead atractyldes		100.00	107.21	100.00
半夏	Tuber of pinelia		116.46	122.77	106.62
三七	Pseudo-ginseng			108.29	0.00
玄参	Root of Zhejiang figwort			113.44	0.00
生地	Dried rhizome of rehmannia		103.07		100.00
杜仲	Bark of eucommia		105.39	72.94	104.82
枳壳	Trifoliate-orange			100.07	103.04
板蓝根	Root of common baphicacanthus		111.11	87.71	91.83
苦丁茶	Kudin crotoxylum (bitter tea tree)		39.80	113.36	
天麻	Tuber of elevated gastrodia		157.89	120.59	109.54
灵芝	Glossy ganoderma			121.97	135.44
白芍	Root of herbaceous peony			108.83	102.71
虫草	Chinese caterpillar fungus			121.96	104.39
其他药材	Other medicinal materials			104.56	94.11
二、林业产品	II. Forest products	106.90	112.79	103.84	104.42
1.竹木采运	1. Felling and transport of bamboo and wood			102.91	105.06
木材采运	Felling and transport of wood	95.60		102.90	105.06

2—5 续表 8 continued 7

农产品名称	Categories of agricultural products	2002	2003	2004	2005
		第三季度 3rd quarter			
原木	Log	95.50		102.90	105.06
红松	Korean pine		98.35		114.28
落叶松	Larch		100.17	100.00	106.17
马尾松	Masson pine		96.96	105.49	96.91
杉木	China fir		101.21	102.91	102.31
云南松	Yunnan pine		101.72	104.71	0.00
薪材	Firewood		100.69	107.43	102.71
竹材采运	Felling and transport of bamboo			106.06	105.14
水竹	Water bamboo		175.28	91.01	100.84
斑竹	Mottled bamboo		100.00	113.76	
毛竹(楠竹)	Mao bamboo		93.24	106.06	105.14
蒿竹	Hao bamboo		82.33	112.34	98.44
淡竹	Henon bamboo		93.75	116.71	100.00
其他竹材	Other bamboo		98.74	96.61	107.73
2.林产品的采集	2.Gathering of forest products		112.79	104.02	104.11
天然和人工林的果实	Products of natural and artificial forest			104.02	104.11
橡胶	Rubber	116.30	124.41	113.92	113.47
生漆	Raw lacquer			105.00	0.00
山苍籽	Seeds of mountain spicy tree			117.63	109.11
五倍籽	Chinese gall (gall nut)		137.32	108.01	102.35
油茶籽	Seeds of tea-oil tree	100.00	124.61	103.46	99.38
棕片	Palm fibre		77.20	113.54	102.96
松脂	Rosin		101.80	112.25	123.53
核桃	Walnut	179.00	78.37	98.60	104.62
板栗	Chinese chestnut		81.23	87.03	107.24
白果	Ginkgo		100.00	81.29	89.22
花椒	Chinese prickly ash	84.30	93.73	93.82	97.81
八角	Anise	139.90	91.37	80.17	68.58
桂皮	Cassia bark	66.40	88.00	102.15	101.68
胡椒	Pepper		109.88	94.71	101.25
其他果实	Other products			96.02	82.89
其他林产品采集	Gathering of other wild plants				
柳条	Willow twigs		110.06		100.64

2—5 续表 9 continued 8

农产品名称	Categories of agricultural products	2002	2003	2004	2005
		第三季度 3rd quarter			
竹笋干	Dried bamboo shoots		96.50	104.32	108.94
黄柏	Chinese weeping cypress			109.49	100.00
未列明的其他林产品采集	Gathering of other wild plants			86.90	100.49
三、牧业(畜产品)	III. Livestock products	98.80	101.49	107.05	96.78
1.牲畜的饲养	1. Livestock raising	99.50		105.21	101.64
牛的饲养	Cattle raising			106.10	101.47
活牛(毛重)	Live cattle (gross weight)	96.80	98.92	106.10	101.60
牛肉	Beef		103.05	106.61	95.89
羊的饲养	Sheep raising			105.74	100.08
活羊(毛重)	Live sheep		94.01	105.74	100.08
羊肉	Mutton		89.76	99.22	96.93
其他牲畜饲养	Other livestock raising				0.00
马	Horse		103.19	123.88	108.21
驴	Donkey		90.07	102.89	99.58
骡	Mule		100.00	101.19	73.83
奶产品	Milk products	99.20	104.69	103.87	99.06
牛奶	Cow milk	99.30	104.69	103.88	99.05
羊奶	Sheep milk	58.20	107.27	101.01	103.09
其他奶类	Other milk			100.19	100.41
毛绒产品	Hair and down products	62.30	98.13	103.99	106.72
山羊毛	Goat's wool	86.80	97.45	87.99	102.19
绵羊毛	Sheep's wool		114.62	107.49	103.30
山羊绒	Cashmere	55.40	98.33	108.50	107.83
绵羊绒	Sheep's down		101.02	102.17	118.17
牦牛毛	Yak hair		100.00	125.17	100.00
牦牛绒	Yak down			0.00	100.61
骆驼绒	Camel hair cloth		100.00	107.95	90.02
其他毛绒产品	Other Hair and down products			88.37	95.52
其他牲畜产品	Other livestock products			117.33	102.70
2.猪的饲养	2. Hog raising			104.28	90.96
活猪(毛重)	Hog (gross weight)	97.20	102.09	104.28	90.88
猪肉	Pork		103.51	128.08	98.37
猪鬃	Bristles			114.25	100.99

2—5 续表 10 continued 9

农产品名称	Categories of agricultural products	2002	2003	2004	2005
		第三季度 3rd quarter			
3. 家禽	3. Poultry			116.81	105.68
肉禽(毛重)	Poultry (gross weight)	93.90	104.59	115.97	105.61
鸡	Chicken	93.30	104.67	115.88	105.75
鸭	Duck	97.10	98.41	123.86	104.63
鹅	Goose	115.10	101.42	119.10	104.51
鹌鹑	Furs			139.40	0.00
其他家禽	Other poultry			116.26	106.38
禽蛋	Eggs	98.60	102.27	118.07	105.77
鸡蛋	Chicken's eggs	98.50	102.34	118.04	105.79
鸭蛋	Duck 's eggs	102.70	99.94	118.93	105.89
鹅蛋	Goose' s eggs	100.00	96.79	107.99	105.01
其他蛋	Other eggs			103.09	106.07
羽绒	Eider down		96.75	0.00	0.00
鸭绒	Duck 's down			109.40	104.26
其他羽绒	Other down			109.35	106.68
4. 狩猎和捕捉动物	4. Hunting and catching animals				
兽皮	Furs			92.77	72.03
未列明的动物皮张	Furs not identified			102.93	92.96
5. 其他畜牧业	5. Other livestock products				
各种鸟类	Birds				
鸽子	Pigeon		112.53	98.66	106.96
山鸡	Pheasant			103.28	125.00
家养动物	Domestic animals				
兔	Rabbit		94.06	114.59	103.03
狗	Dog		91.44	104.70	94.80
猫	Cat			98.25	102.70
兔毛	Rabbit hair			167.40	102.43
珍贵动物	Rare animals				
鹿	Deer			79.29	0.00
狐狸	Fox		102.65		0.00
水 貂	Marten			128.42	100.11
蛇	Snake		72.07	117.62	91.13
虫类	Worms				

2—5 续表 11 continued 10

农产品名称	Categories of agricultural products	2002	2003	2004	2005
		第三季度 3rd quarter			
蚯蚓	Earthworm			122.75	100.00
蝎子	Scorpion			88.95	88.92
其他虫类	Other Worms			134.16	104.95
活的家畜产品	Domestic animal products				
蚕茧	Silkworm cocoon	69.30	94.87	135.42	107.63
蜂蜜	Honey	152.70	93.59	98.45	100.31
鹿茸	Pilose antler			76.66	116.45
其他活的家畜产品	Other domestic animal products			134.46	85.45
毛皮的生产	Production of furs				
动物皮张	Animals' furs		100.61	98.95	71.80
其他毛皮的生产	Production of other furs			110.00	0.00
四、渔业	IV. Fishery products	93.30	99.37	112.08	103.76
1. 海水水产品	1. Seawater aquatic products	92.30	99.37	109.57	104.58
鱼类	Seawater Fish	93.10	97.28	109.91	105.88
大黄鱼	Large yellow croaker	80.60	85.18	109.19	93.97
小黄鱼	Small yellow croaker	120.40	88.09	115.20	103.37
带鱼	Hairtail	93.50	98.53	100.48	116.58
沙丁鱼	Sardine		100.98	121.61	93.45
鳕鱼	Cod	224.60			
石斑鱼	Grouper	110.60	94.46	138.19	104.01
鳀鱼	Anchovy		117.59	110.85	104.62
梭鱼	Mullet		100.00	116.18	94.41
鲳鱼	Silvery pomfret		86.56	106.60	122.10
海鳗	Conger pike		89.33	101.36	106.47
鲅鱼	Spanish mackerel		118.89	112.84	0.00
鲐鱼	Chub mackerel		102.13	100.00	
马面鱼	Black scraper		102.12	113.26	97.52
马鲛	Japanese Spanish mackerel		88.18	108.38	106.67
梭参	Barrachuda		100.82	0.00	
鲷鱼	Porgy			106.67	106.25
蓝圆	Blue scad		102.74		
鲆鲽	Left-eyed flounder		112.27	94.71	0.00
舌鳎	Tonguefish			123.06	105.26

2—5 续表 12 continued 11

农产品名称	Categories of agricultural products	2002	2003	2004	2005
		第三季度 3rd quarter			
其他海水鱼类	Other seawater fish			105.25	106.22
海水虾蟹类	Seawater shrimp and crab	276.24	110.19	95.83	102.73
对虾	Prawn		110.15	95.44	103.52
毛虾	Shrimp		111.81	105.10	109.78
爬虾	Mantis shrimp		108.67	106.01	102.85
脊尾白虾	Exopataemom carimicauda		100.29	102.72	91.56
鹰爪虾	Trachypemaeus curvirostris		69.93	162.87	0.00
梭子蟹	Swimming crab		135.34	92.55	102.23
其他海水虾蟹类	Other seawater shrimps and crabs			98.55	104.96
海水贝类	Seawater shellfish		108.99	122.73	101.35
贻贝	Mussel		84.43	201.86	104.62
扇贝	Scallop		103.66	176.49	100.00
牡蛎	Oyster		102.90	94.13	94.05
鲍鱼	Abalone		101.55	120.12	97.12
蛤	Clam		112.81	111.61	103.05
蚶	Blood clam		100.00	90.00	126.36
海螺	Conch		112.90	112.00	102.74
蛏	Razor clam		106.94	98.35	105.91
其他海水贝类	Other seawater shellfish			117.36	109.43
藻类	Seaweeds		100.00	131.91	105.46
海带	Kelp		100.00	131.91	105.46
其他藻类	Other seaweeds			125.65	98.05
其他海水产品	Other seawater products				
墨鱼	Inkfish		106.16	92.16	98.60
鱿鱼	Squid		108.60	137.64	99.82
章鱼	Octopus		107.60	110.28	104.41
海蜇	Jellyfish		105.25	100.39	98.88
2. 内陆水域水产品	2. Aquatic products in inland water areas	95.10	99.60	116.46	103.00
淡水鱼类	Freshwater fish	95.10	99.37	115.82	102.33
青鱼	Black carp	60.90	99.25	107.66	103.51
草鱼	Grass carp	89.80	95.42	120.06	102.42
鲤鱼	Carp	94.70	105.45	117.91	100.07
鲢鱼	Silver carp	88.00	96.62	120.99	104.94

2—5 续表 13　　continued 12

农产品名称	Categories of agricultural products	2002	2003	2004	2005
		第三季度 3rd quarter			
鲫鱼	Crucian carp	90.80	96.95	109.59	101.98
罗非鱼	Tilapia	122.00	99.19	113.27	107.00
虹鳟鱼	Rainbow trout	125.10		100.00	105.20
白鱼	Whitefish		101.26	117.74	113.53
鳜鱼	Mandarin fish		100.00	108.94	106.25
白昌鱼	Round spadefish		97.51	131.64	77.17
黑鱼	Snakeheaded fish		104.49	108.56	101.30
鲶鱼	Oriental sheatfish		91.30	112.43	96.39
武昌鱼	Blunt-snout bream		99.23	114.91	112.31
鳙鱼	Variegated carp		106.26	114.99	100.25
鲮鱼	Dace		100.85	128.19	83.64
鳊	Bream		108.80	115.47	101.91
银鱼	Whitebait		93.25	111.11	
淡水鲈	Freshwater perch		94.59	106.73	95.25
其他淡水鱼类	Other freshwater fish			104.08	107.64
淡水虾蟹类	Freshwater shrimps and crabs	91.30	103.47	126.76	114.88
龙虾	Lobster		103.47	130.33	120.66
罗氏沼虾	M. rosenbergii		94.27	96.93	94.95
青虾	Freshwater shrimp		98.80	113.60	108.42
红螯螯虾	Red clow		110.76	127.99	117.09
大闸蟹	Steamed crab		86.43	98.15	107.96
其他淡水虾蟹类	Other freshwater shrimp and crab			90.74	101.76
淡水贝类	Freshwater shellfish				
淡水珍珠	Freshwater pearl			97.48	140.42
螺蛳	Spiral shell		97.62	109.57	103.74
其他淡水养殖产品	Other freshwater breeding products				
河鳗	River eel		102.79		0.00
甲鱼	Soft-shelled turtle		100.37	104.62	99.04
黄鳝	Ricefield eel		105.77	112.74	101.05
泥鳅	Loach		102.46	112.26	102.77
龟	Tortoise			86.44	72.46
蛙	Frog		129.23	134.27	103.63
未列明的其他淡水养殖产品	Other freshwater breeding products			88.68	100.63

2—6 全国农产品生产价格指数(第四季度)
National Indices of the Producer Prices of Agricultural Products

(上年同期=100) (4th quarter) (the same period of the preceding year=100)

农产品名称	Categories of agricultural products	2002	2003	2004	2005
		第四季度 4th quarter			
总指数	**Gross Index**	**102.29**	**111.64**	**113.02**	**98.81**
一、种植业产品	I. Crop products	107.25	115.03	108.98	101.99
1. 谷物及其他作物	1. Cereal and other crops			112.77	99.11
粮食	Grain	98.60	114.21	120.50	97.75
谷物(原粮)	Cereal (unprocessed food grains)	96.43	111.79	124.01	97.81
小麦	Wheat	97.56	114.21	124.43	95.18
硬粒小麦	Hard wheat	98.03	111.79	124.22	95.06
软粒小麦	Soft wheat	89.67	114.21	129.42	95.13
混合小麦	Mixed wheat	93.20	111.79	126.21	95.58
其他小麦	Other wheat			131.80	95.62
稻谷	Paddy	96.17	110.35	131.09	100.13
早籼稻	Early long-grain nonglutinous rice	98.15	106.87	132.88	94.46
晚籼稻	Late long-grain nonglutinous rice	100.54	110.64	129.98	96.25
粳 稻	Round-grain rice	93.40	113.04	129.87	104.02
其他稻谷	Other paddy			125.04	97.68
玉米	Maize (corn)	96.11	114.12	111.35	96.30
黄玉米	Yellow maize	96.53	114.36	111.17	96.37
白玉米	White maize	93.31	105.43	117.66	101.50
混合玉米	Mixed maize	91.35	112.24	112.76	92.98
其他玉米	Other maize		111.58	108.87	98.84
杂粮	Coarse cereals		100.00	0.00	106.84
谷子	Millet		105.41	126.30	104.73
高粱	Chinese sorghum		106.22	128.62	102.38
大麦	Barley		106.72	117.54	101.76
荞麦	Buckwheat		109.39	108.30	147.75
元麦	poulard wheat		100.00	0.00	
青稞	Highland barley		105.35	102.47	103.11
莜麦	Naked oats		101.88	104.03	104.83
燕麦	Oats		100.00	100.00	113.44
其他杂粮	Other coarse cereals			117.78	101.90
谷物副产品	By-products of cereals				
小麦秸	Wheat straw			122.69	107.40
稻草	Rice straw			103.04	97.13

2—6 续表 1 continued 1

农产品名称	Categories of agricultural products	2002	2003	2004	2005
		第四季度 4th quarter			
玉米秆	Corn stover			107.63	105.02
谷子秆	Millet stalk			177.80	98.28
高粱杆	Chinese sorghum stalk			100.00	102.37
薯类	Potato	76.97	102.25	109.31	109.13
红薯	Sweet potato	88.97	96.73	111.44	105.17
马铃薯	White Potato	72.45	104.33	108.51	111.07
其他薯类	Other potatoes			108.02	101.32
薯藤	Potato vines			100.00	102.41
油料	Oil-bearing crops	105.47	122.22	109.25	91.07
花生	Peanut	114.21	127.54	110.46	96.95
油菜籽	Rapeseeds	101.75	119.31	108.96	87.55
芝麻	Sesame	84.58	187.81	100.04	101.73
向日葵	Sunflower		105.66	119.35	99.12
胡麻籽	Flaxseeds	96.12	118.73	118.33	102.64
苏籽	Perillaseeds		123.26	108.81	99.3
其他油料作物	Other oil-bearing crops			107.41	105.26
花生蔓	Peanut vine			79.95	76.59
豆类	Beans	109.90	125.17	109.07	93.49
大豆	Soybeans	111.65	126.33	106.63	92.14
绿豆	Mung beans	92.22	113.41	133.69	103.41
红小豆	Small red beans	109.68	126.18	124.58	99.55
蚕豆	Broad beans		115.13	125.23	101.37
豌豆	Peas		99.90	120.00	102.41
芸豆	Kidney beans		105.58	103.48	103.60
其他杂豆	Other beans			117.08	101.04
豆秸	Beanstalk			99.55	156.88
棉花(籽棉)	Cotton (unginned cotton)	138.13	150.90	76.09	113.73
细绒棉	Thin-staple cotton	139.27	151.57	75.61	113.96
长绒棉	Long-staple cotton	120.46	140.45	83.47	108.71
棉籽	Cottonseeds			85.15	112.05
麻类	Fiber crops	90.95	138.03	109.85	101.97
黄红麻	Jute and blueish dogbane	85.27	117.89	113.40	107.56
亚麻	Flax		100.00	121.77	101.59
苎麻	Ramie	91.64	140.50	106.50	97.31
剑麻	Steel hemp		112.42	110.49	150.00

2—6 续表 2 continued 2

农产品名称	Categories of agricultural products	2002	2003	2004	2005
		第四季度 4th quarter			
麻秆	Stalks of fiber crops			208.16	96.75
糖料	Sugar crops	86.51	98.93	109.89	117.66
甘蔗	Sugarcane	86.51	98.93	109.89	117.67
甜菜	Beet	100.00	102.55	125.30	102.61
其他糖料	Other sugar crops				0.00
烟草	Tobacco	86.51	95.51	112.56	104.46
烤烟叶	Flue-cured tobacco	86.51	95.42	112.57	104.36
晒烟叶	Sun-cured tobacco	100.00	107.44	111.44	108.32
白肋烟	Whiteerib tobacco		109.62	98.95	101.63
其他烟叶	Other tobacco			105.60	103.59
其他农作物	Other agricultural crops				
青饲料	Greenfeed		101.33	113.31	90.54
牧草	Herbage		102.96	112.59	98.36
桑叶	Mulberry leaves		100.00	154.20	
席草	Stems or leaves of cattail		69.46	86.52	0.00
蓖麻籽	Castor beans		111.11	106.58	80.13
野生植物的采集	Gathering of wild plants			107.93	121.72
未列明的其他农作物	Other agricultural crops			77.33	101.73
2.蔬菜、园艺作物	2. Vegetable and Horticulture crops		107.20	103.05	108.23
蔬菜	Vegetable	122.21	107.20	103.05	108.23
叶菜类	Leaf vegetable	151.35	110.95	95.36	110.32
菠菜	Spinach	65.66	109.35	94.52	110.22
芹菜	Celery	90.29	112.12	89.79	118.25
大白菜	Chinese cabbage	179.29	116.29	86.84	110.05
元白菜	Cabbage	139.64	103.49	102.94	107.83
甘蓝	Wild cabbage	472.05	112.81	100.34	101.64
花椰菜	Cauliflower	137.90	113.00	106.90	106.73
莴笋	Asparagus lettuce	132.01	114.01	103.38	107.29
油菜	Rape	321.62	105.99	99.89	106.79
其他叶菜	Other leaf vegetable			102.25	108.77
瓜菜类	Gourd vegetable	116.64	104.23	98.53	104.48
黄瓜	Cucumber	114.62	103.20	99.50	104.07
冬瓜	White gourd	131.46	110.09	92.49	108.47
西葫芦	Summer squash	133.52	120.64	99.19	105.75
苦瓜	Balsam pear		89.64	111.64	96.47

2—6 续表 3 continued 3

农产品名称 Categories of agricultural products		2002	2003	2004	2005
		第四季度 4th quarter			
丝瓜	Towed gourd		103. 95	103. 75	102. 64
南瓜	Pumpkin		107. 08	108. 91	108. 15
打瓜	Seeded watermelon		104. 28	113. 51	100. 41
瓠子	Bottle gourd		105. 80	100. 33	115. 04
其他瓜菜	Other gourd vegetable			97. 39	110. 36
块根、块茎菜类	Root and tuber vegetable	125. 50	113. 77	96. 45	109. 23
萝卜	Radish	127. 59	111. 42	98. 02	111. 49
胡萝卜	Carrot	62. 79	117. 95	93. 07	105. 49
生姜	Ginger	73. 31	122. 94	135. 59	89. 72
芋头	Taro		101. 54	106. 04	108. 56
苔干	Dried bryophyte		119. 29	77. 36	0. 00
百合(根)	Lily (root)		113. 49	94. 45	110. 06
芋艿	Taro		122. 03	112. 76	118. 31
山药	Chinese yam		112. 17	119. 19	106. 19
其他块根、块茎菜	Other root and tuber vegetable			104. 43	106. 77
茄果菜类	Eggplant, tomato and chili, etc.	94. 88	98. 71	101. 79	105. 40
茄子	Eggplant	106. 62	99. 94	101. 19	105. 22
西红柿	Tomato	87. 35	99. 94	102. 35	106. 03
辣椒	Chili	129. 96	105. 20	100. 00	103. 86
青椒	Sweetbell	109. 55	95. 43	101. 90	105. 36
其他茄果菜类	Others			110. 96	107. 98
葱蒜类	Onion and Garlic	104. 59	108. 08	115. 11	111. 48
大葱	Scallion	89. 26	117. 67	105. 50	107. 03
蒜苔	Garlic stalk	125. 74	115. 76	102. 64	100. 10
蒜头	Garlic head	115. 92	100. 70	122. 57	116. 79
洋葱	Onion		98. 11	98. 36	89. 95
蒜苗	Garlic bolt		114. 95	106. 37	112. 29
小葱	Shallot		108. 83	97. 25	111. 10
韭菜	Fragrant-flowered garlic		101. 46	107. 01	108. 12
其他葱蒜类	Others			99. 61	105. 47
菜用豆类	Garden beans	137. 59	109. 55	101. 62	106. 24
四季豆	Kidney beans	124. 18	113. 07	105. 61	106. 35
豇豆	Cowpeas	145. 18	107. 88	99. 72	106. 16
其他菜用豆	Other garden beans			104. 52	108. 64
水生菜类	Water vegetable	183. 24	98. 80	106. 14	105. 51

2—6 续表 4 continued 4

农产品名称	Categories of agricultural products	2002	2003	2004	2005
		第四季度 4th quarter			
莲藕	Lotus root	98.13	108.12	101.16	104.20
茭白	Wild ruice stem	185.99	98.50	106.30	106.56
荸荠	Water chestnut	100.00	104.58	124.73	98.14
其他水生菜	Other water vegetable			111.92	99.78
食用菌(干鲜混合)	Mushroom		104.15	94.76	104.34
香菇(干品)	Mushroom (dried)		89.19	91.17	99.88
蘑菇(鲜品)	Mushroom (fresh)		102.54	93.51	104.99
黑木耳(干品)	Black edible fungus (dried)		123.33	105.46	100.85
白木耳(干品)	Tremella (dried)		102.50	91.34	107.25
金针菇(鲜品)	Golden mushroom		99.07	100.00	104.83
猴头菌(干品)	Bearded tooth(dried)		100.00	0.00	104.09
平菇(鲜品)	Oyster mushroom		110.90	94.83	99.99
花菇(干品)	Black forest mushroom		100.00	92.68	
其他食用菌	Other edible mushrooms			106.33	106.65
未列明的其他蔬菜	Other vegetable			104.41	108.73
花卉	Flowers				
鲜切花	Fresh flowers				0.00
百合花	Lily		87.89	115.95	88.65
康乃馨	Carnation		210.94	166.42	64.78
满天星	June snow (serissa)		388.07	81.76	102.71
勿忘我	Forgetmenot		135.23	143.98	96.82
非洲菊	Flameray Gerbera		100.00	78.81	97.00
玫瑰	Rugosa rose		108.57	94.11	74.55
情人草	Evans begonia		100.00	90.33	111.11
其他鲜切花	Other fresh flowers			101.08	97.69
其他园艺作物	Other horticulture crops				
盆栽植物	Potted plants		107.76	0.00	0.00
观赏苗木	Ornamental plants		108.62	0.00	0.00
草坪草皮	Sod for lawn		85.94	91.72	92.11
3.水果、坚果、饮料和香料	3. Fruit, beverage and perfume			92.14	108.84
水果、坚果	Fruits and nuts			91.44	108.10
园林水果	Garden fruits	93.65	101.70	90.37	108.01
苹果	Apples	59.71	94.83	98.15	118.51
红富士苹果	Hongfushi apples	65.11	93.60	100.94	115.35
国光苹果	Guoguang apples	89.38	96.39	87.00	106.29

2—6 续表 5 continued 5

农产品名称 Categories of agricultural products		2002	2003	2004	2005
		第四季度 4th quarter			
秦冠苹果	Qinguan apples	58.90	100.10	107.24	139.05
香蕉苹果	Banana apples	37.52	118.78	99.18	112.68
元帅苹果	Yuanshuai (Marshal) apples		95.58	104.11	106.04
新红星苹果	New Hongxing apples		107.36	110.03	109.13
其他苹果	Other apples			96.94	110.66
梨	Pears	125.84	109.76	85.10	102.55
雪花梨	Snowflake pears	125.71	109.67	85.15	101.43
鸭梨	Ya-pears	102.32	97.75	88.89	106.55
酥梨	Soft-pears	139.24	118.05	81.40	104.08
香梨	Bergamot pears	111.11	100.00		100.02
苹果梨	Apple pears		108.09	105.08	80.84
冬果梨	Dongguo pears			100.00	100.00
其他梨	Other pears			100.21	105.81
柑桔	Citrus	134.56	103.71	99.01	104.77
柑	Mandarin oranges	162.88	103.99	99.26	101.35
桔	Tangerines	118.07	97.07	101.79	126.34
橙	Oranges	98.68	105.25	96.60	103.02
柚	Shaddocks	70.70	96.98	92.88	119.63
其他柑桔	Others			108.50	101.83
其他水果	Other fruits			95.00	107.41
香蕉	Bananas	74.57	123.20	103.18	102.49
菠萝	Pineapples		100.00	114.82	98.00
荔枝	Litchis	100.00	66.67	77.69	0.00
龙眼	Longans	15.04	91.55	83.53	95.83
芒果	Mangoes		98.06		0.00
木瓜	Papayas		92.02	119.35	100.00
橄榄	Chinese olives		101.56	126.07	77.97
桃	Peachs	103.72	80.14	98.38	109.02
杏	Apricots	80.65	100.00	102.20	101.98
杨梅	Red bayberries	100.00	83.33		0.00
猕猴桃	Yangtaoes	105.88	72.23	112.93	116.56
葡萄	Grapes	62.50	113.87	95.43	108.56
红枣	Chinese dates	90.54	105.85	99.71	97.43
柿子	Persimmons	130.97	100.17	98.27	104.19
其他园林水果	Other garden fruits			98.82	82.18

2—6 续表 6 continued 6

农产品名称 Categories of agricultural products		2002	2003	2004	2005
		第四季度 4th quarter			
瓜果类	Melons	72.64	102.96	108.91	109.10
西瓜	Watermelons	74.30	102.79	109.28	109.22
甜瓜	Muskmelons	34.96	106.33	101.83	111.34
香瓜	Musk melons		108.89		0.00
草莓	Strawberries			110.34	101.31
其他瓜果	Others			103.13	110.45
坚果类	Nuts			108.36	105.61
椰子	Coconut			108.36	105.61
杏仁	Apricot kerne			446.43	95.00
槟榔	Areca			120.04	123.19
其他坚果	Other nuts			117.93	105.56
茶及其他饮料(干品)	Tea and other beverages			107.85	113.60
茶	Tea	140.89		107.85	113.86
红毛茶	Black tea	60.84	83.86	116.41	112.67
绿毛茶	Green tea	143.11	98.23	106.84	114.91
乌龙茶	Oolong tea	139.09	108.80	110.38	103.78
其他茶	Others			99.01	111.25
可可和咖啡	Cocoa and Coffee				106.33
咖啡豆	Coffee bean		106.46	110.38	106.33
香料作物	Perfume crops				
茴香	Fennel			138.82	0.00
留兰香	Spearmint			97.78	0.00
其他	Others			90.82	74.41
4.中药材	4. Traditional Chinese medicinal materials				
茯苓	Fuling (poris cocos)		112.28	123.37	119.78
党参	Tangshen (pilose asiabell)		107.97	94.62	91.27
当归	Chinese angelica		100.00	103.52	
黄芪	Root of membranous milk vetch		113.03	88.08	116.73
金银花	Honeysuckle		103.04	79.73	109.73
黄连	Rhizome of Chinese goldthread		91.64		93.93
甘草	Licorice root		100.00	207.12	100.00
贝母	Bulb of fritillary		153.54	104.76	109.53
红花	Safflower		100.17	104.00	100.00
元胡	Amur corydalis		111.87		110.92
枸杞	Fruit of Chinese wolfberry		107.19	89.00	100.33

2—6 续表 7 continued 7

农产品名称	Categories of agricultural products	2002	2003	2004	2005
		第四季度 4th quarter			
菊花	Chrysanthemum		201.98	31.07	103.06
白术	Largehead atractyldes		137.56	84.86	101.28
半夏	Tuber of pinelia		100.00	99.82	102.60
西洋参	American ginseng			100.47	
生地	Dried rhizome of rehmannia		105.80	121.55	98.32
杜仲	Bark of eucommia		101.35	96.00	100.00
板蓝根	Root of common baphicacanthus		101.85	90.38	97.89
苦丁茶	Kudin crotoxylum (bitter tea tree)		68.66	130.98	
天麻	Tuber of elevated gastrodia		94.21	93.46	89.70
穿心莲	Creat		181.29	101.78	168.15
桔梗	Rampion		118.27	100.26	101.65
其他药材	Other medicinal materials			93.00	99.45
二、林业产品	II. Forest products	111.49	105.36	98.69	107.20
1. 竹木采运	1. Felling and transport of bamboo and wood			102.74	101.64
木材采运	Felling and transport of wood	105.26		102.71	101.64
原木	Log	105.54		102.71	101.64
红松	Korean pine		100.90		98.04
落叶松	Larch		101.69	93.95	105.08
马尾松	Masson pine		103.32	103.74	99.46
杉木	China fir		101.73	108.40	103.55
云南松	Yunnan pine		93.63	111.11	95.74
薪材	Firewood		99.49	99.72	99.24
竹材采运	Felling and transport of bamboo			107.69	102.09
水竹	Water bamboo		101.63	106.27	86.73
斑竹	Mottled bamboo		101.29		100.00
毛竹(楠竹)	Mao bamboo		104.05	107.69	102.09
蒿竹	Hao bamboo		97.44	117.66	104.28
淡竹	Henon bamboo		104.48	107.28	172.72
其他竹材	Other bamboo		113.63	106.32	107.70
2. 林产品的采集	2. Gathering of forest products		105.36	97.93	109.83
天然和人工林的果实	Products of natural and artificial forest			97.93	109.83
橡胶	Rubber	157.52	116.94	104.62	120.41
生漆	Raw lacquer			99.80	106.62
油桐籽	Seeds of tung oil tree	100.00	163.07	131.79	104.58
乌桕籽	Seeds of Chinese tallow tree		183.15	101.39	0.00

2—6 续表 8 continued 8

农产品名称	Categories of agricultural products	2002	2003	2004	2005
		第四季度 4th quarter			
五倍籽	Chinese gall (gall nut)		177.86	105.27	100.49
油茶籽	Seeds of tea-oil tree	100.00	109.41	108.66	98.34
棕片	Palm fibre		97.24	99.26	97.59
松脂	Rosin		106.94	114.19	130.73
核桃	Walnut	83.02	98.46	113.53	113.70
板栗	Chinese chestnut		97.77	98.72	97.57
白果	Ginkgo		76.75	83.73	102.04
松子	Pine nut		113.27	127.72	100.00
花椒	Chinese prickly ash	49.58	100.47	95.82	101.34
八角	Anise	80.28	67.15	84.46	88.77
桂皮	Cassia bark	87.27	120.86	73.04	101.31
胡椒	Pepper		106.70	79.61	111.18
其他果实	Other products			106.20	100.07
其他林产品采集	Gathering of other wild plants				
藤条	Rattan		100.00	113.71	100.00
竹笋干	Dried bamboo shoots		97.71	112.70	115.48
桉树叶	Eucalyptus leaves			96.00	140.00
黄柏	Chinese weeping cypress			104.17	0.00
未列明的其他林产品采集	Gathering of other wild plants			103.20	100.74
三、牧业(畜产品)	III. Livestock products	98.59	109.25	118.92	92.10
1. 牲畜的饲养	1. Livestock raising	102.03		103.57	100.63
牛的饲养	Cattle raising			103.96	100.49
活牛(毛重)	Live cattle (gross weight)	98.04	103.92	103.96	100.48
牛肉	Beef		102.73	99.11	100.82
羊的饲养	Sheep raising			103.61	99.32
活羊(毛重)	Live sheep		98.11	103.61	99.32
羊肉	Mutton		106.06	106.02	101.24
其他牲畜饲养	Other livestock raising				
马	Horse		105.27	105.31	104.67
驴	Donkey		108.50	94.22	104.67
骆驼	Camel		130.01	0.00	96.91
其他未列牲畜的饲养	Other livestock raising			100.08	97.27
奶产品	Milk products	104.09	111.06	101.29	99.25
牛奶	Cow milk	104.16	111.06	101.28	99.25
羊奶	Sheep milk	54.49	113.28	104.25	97.63

2—6 续表 9 continued 9

农产品名称	Categories of agricultural products	2002	2003	2004	2005
		第四季度 4th quarter			
毛绒产品	Hair and down products	57.25	113.89	103.67	104.43
山羊毛	Goat's wool	55.39	100.00	103.67	109.36
绵羊毛	Sheep's wool		98.16	97.72	101.85
山羊绒	Cashmere	57.83	118.24	105.66	103.24
绵羊绒	Sheep's down		146.25		100.20
骆驼绒	Camel hair cloth		106.38		0.00
其他毛绒产品	Other Hair and down products			113.03	99.38
2.猪的饲养	2. Hog raising			126.36	85.56
活猪(毛重)	Hog (gross weight)	99.46	112.97	126.36	85.47
猪肉	Pork		109.54	117.34	94.66
猪鬃	Bristles			121.27	67.87
3.家禽	3. Poultry			113.74	99.13
肉禽(毛重)	Poultry (gross weight)	94.59	106.03	113.73	97.38
鸡	Chicken	94.58	106.03	113.72	97.24
鸭	Duck	96.36	103.40	118.39	98.14
鹅	Goose	100.00	109.18	115.80	99.19
其他家禽	Other poultry			115.38	99.76
禽蛋	Eggs	99.57	104.99	113.75	101.48
鸡蛋	Chicken's eggs	99.27	105.09	113.70	101.51
鸭蛋	Duck 's eggs	108.56	101.65	115.24	102.97
鹅蛋	Goose' s eggs	100.00	102.79	103.83	98.51
其他蛋	Other eggs			90.61	86.18
羽绒	Eider down		111.60	0.00	0.00
鸭绒	Duck 's down			117.84	111.13
其他羽绒	Other down			115.54	107.12
4.狩猎和捕捉动物	4. Hunting and catching animals				
兽皮	Furs			96.89	104.66
未列明的动物皮张	Furs not identified			108.06	96.54
5.其他畜牧业	5. Other livestock products			0.00	
各种鸟类	Birds			0.00	0.00
鸽子	Pigeon		104.36	122.04	101.11
家养动物	Domestic animals				0.00
兔	Rabbit		95.10	112.25	102.88
狗	Dog		100.91	103.93	98.14
猫	Cat			102.61	90.98

2—6 续表 10 continued 10

农产品名称 Categories of agricultural products		2002	2003	2004	2005
		第四季度 4th quarter			
兔毛	Rabbit hair			163.91	102.65
其他家养动物	Other domestic animals			120.00	100.32
珍贵动物	Rare animals				
水貂	Marten			76.65	100.00
蛇	Snake		100.33	95.64	101.82
活的家畜产品	Domestic animal products				
蚕茧	Silkworm cocoon	46.95	145.09	100.76	118.38
蜂蜜	Honey	58.30	100.90	101.03	103.34
鹿茸	Pilose antler			15.50	97.64
其他活的家畜产品	Other domestic animal products			128.38	62.77
毛皮的生产	Production of furs				
动物皮张	Animals' furs		105.93	97.02	75.92
四、渔业	IV. Fishery products	90.87	106.12	109.82	103.73
1. 海水水产品	1. Seawater aquatic products	86.81	109.53	108.30	105.27
鱼类	Seawater Fish	83.38	110.15	107.99	104.92
大黄鱼	Large yellow croaker	54.21	112.79	101.55	106.91
小黄鱼	Small yellow croaker	84.82	102.64	104.51	105.75
带鱼	Hairtail	104.61	110.15	108.49	102.40
鲈鱼	Perch			92.01	135.96
沙丁鱼	Sardine		107.49	111.88	100.89
鳕鱼	Cod	83.15			
石斑鱼	Grouper	100.00	100.00	119.55	103.84
醍鱼	Anchovy		106.62	111.74	116.00
梭鱼	Mullet		89.29	117.01	106.29
鲳鱼	Silvery pomfret		101.56	111.31	106.13
海鳗	Conger pike		95.49	107.65	108.74
鲅鱼	Spanish mackerel		91.51	115.60	102.58
鲐鱼	Chub mackerel		102.12	113.99	100.00
马面鱼	Black scraper		87.50	100.77	70.82
马鲛	Japanese Spanish mackerel		108.72	105.19	106.61
梅童鱼	Baby croaker		104.85		100.85
梭参	Barrachuda		103.55	0.00	
鲷鱼	Porgy			105.62	102.04
蓝圆	Blue scad		111.29	166.67	
鲆鲽	Left-eyed flounder		116.14		104.16

2—6 续表 11 continued 11

农产品名称	Categories of agricultural products	2002	2003	2004	2005
		第四季度 4th quarter			
舌鳎	Tonguefish			145.20	116.58
其他海水鱼类	Other seawater fish			112.23	101.67
海水虾蟹类	Seawater shrimp and crab	88.76	100.00	116.72	105.00
对虾	Prawn		94.47	103.56	104.69
毛虾	Shrimp		109.89	103.77	110.62
爬虾	Mantis shrimp		98.87	133.30	108.47
脊尾白虾	Exopataemom carimicauda		100.00	104.88	94.07
鹰爪虾	Trachypemaeus curvirostris		129.70		107.13
梭子蟹	Swimming crab		105.16	114.24	106.30
其他海水虾蟹类	Other seawater shrimps and crabs			97.22	106.11
海水贝类	Seawater shellfish		102.17	98.93	106.17
贻贝	Mussel		113.79		132.55
扇贝	Scallop		101.17	145.22	108.16
牡蛎	Oyster		98.81	107.79	106.38
鲍鱼	Abalone		126.87	112.81	89.03
蛤	Clam		100.52	98.73	110.74
蚶	Blood clam		137.23	91.60	107.93
海螺	Conch		117.14	115.57	104.23
蛏	Razor clam		109.44	106.13	107.57
其他海水贝类	Other seawater shellfish			80.12	58.05
藻类	Seaweeds		106.93		108.53
海带	Kelp		106.93		108.01
紫菜	Laver		106.38	87.46	110.24
其他藻类	Other seaweeds			133.06	
其他海水产品	Other seawater products				
墨鱼	Inkfish		107.22	94.39	123.16
鱿鱼	Squid		133.65	136.84	103.69
章鱼	Octopus		103.01	84.22	109.18
海蜇	Jellyfish		110.68	43.78	107.97
未列明的其他海水产品	Other seawater products			98.53	105.70
2. 内陆水域水产品	2. Aquatic products in inland water areas	97.64	100.16	112.49	102.31
淡水鱼类	Freshwater fish	97.64	100.18	112.29	101.81
青鱼	Black carp	47.77	103.04	111.47	102.10
草鱼	Grass carp	91.35	101.20	115.51	104.66
鲤鱼	Carp	96.56	100.63	112.04	101.99

2—6 续表 12 continued 12

农产品名称 Categories of agricultural products		2002	2003	2004	2005
		第四季度 4th quarter			
鲢鱼	Silver carp	91.39	101.30	116.61	101.41
鲫鱼	Crucian carp	78.25	98.25	113.50	100.80
罗非鱼	Tilapia	161.80	100.20	100.67	91.46
虹鳟鱼	Rainbow trout	111.09		103.34	117.17
白鱼	Whitefish		90.72	104.34	110.68
鳜鱼	Mandarin fish		107.73	102.29	101.29
白昌鱼	Round spadefish		104.36	118.51	0.00
黑鱼	Snakeheaded fish		99.69	99.97	98.91
鲶鱼	Oriental sheatfish		101.01	107.82	87.41
武昌鱼	Blunt-snout bream		106.77	107.24	99.28
鳙鱼	Variegated carp		103.43	110.21	97.29
鲮鱼	Dace		96.50	112.92	99.98
鳊	Bream		93.15	107.41	102.02
黄颡鱼	Yellowcat fish			110.00	114.91
淡水鲈	Freshwater perch		110.64	123.53	89.21
其他淡水鱼类	Other freshwater fish			103.91	101.29
淡水虾蟹类	Freshwater shrimps and crabs	86.23	99.87	115.82	111.08
龙虾	Lobster		99.87	128.76	117.15
罗氏沼虾	M. rosenbergii		93.82	100.72	104.63
青虾	Freshwater shrimp		98.74	103.43	103.82
基围虾	Greasyback shrimp			102.33	102.60
红螯螯虾	Red clow		113.96	145.61	106.67
大闸蟹	Steamed crab		91.20	101.69	101.98
其他淡水虾蟹类	Other freshwater shrimps and crabs			103.84	104.84
淡水贝类	Freshwater shellfish				
螺蛳	Spiral shell		114.07		100.61
其他淡水贝类	Other freshwater shellfish			104.76	103.57
其他淡水养殖产品	Other freshwater breeding products				
河鳗	River eel		94.57	114.29	111.11
牛蛙	Bullfrog		120.00	107.77	0.00
甲鱼	Soft-shelled turtle		101.95	85.76	97.26
黄鳝	Ricefield eel		104.10	105.30	102.60
泥鳅	Loach		109.18	117.56	93.88
龟	Tortoise			86.52	80.86
蛙	Frog		104.17		100.77

2—7 各地区农产品生产价格总指数
Gross Indices of the Producer Prices of Agricultural Products by Region

(上年=100) (the preceding year=100)

地 区 Region	2002	2003	2004	2005
全 国 National	**99.65**	**104.37**	**113.09**	**101.39**
北 京 Beijing	104.10	102.46	105.76	103.53
天 津 Tianjin	104.17	104.44	108.06	103.38
河 北 Hebei	97.70	107.48	110.09	102.45
山 西 Shanxi	94.74	103.94	110.61	103.50
内蒙古 Inner Mongolia	99.34	106.45	112.00	103.17
辽 宁 Liaoning	99.41	103.33	120.41	101.50
吉 林 Jilin	98.60	136.86	118.11	100.29
黑龙江 Heilongjiang	102.39	110.23	117.27	101.01
上 海 Shanghai	100.00	102.15	110.84	105.71
江 苏 Jiangsu	97.28	107.21	122.68	100.32
浙 江 Zhejiang	101.22	101.88	116.77	105.88
安 徽 Anhui	99.85	106.42	117.78	98.71
福 建 Fujian	99.10	101.72	106.80	103.90
江 西 Jiangxi	100.00	105.09	119.48	100.45
山 东 Shandong	102.15	108.55	112.31	102.93
河 南 Henan	99.70	111.84	121.95	100.74
湖 北 Hubei	100.90	106.94	121.66	100.30
湖 南 Hunan	99.91	111.69	127.31	99.54
广 东 Guangdong	98.45	101.30	110.70	103.47
广 西 Guangxi	100.00	104.51	118.93	100.02
海 南 Hainan	100.00	104.26	106.36	102.20
重 庆 Chongqing	101.10	103.80	125.53	100.03
四 川 Sichuan	101.82	103.54	120.38	103.18
贵 州 Guizhou	103.89	101.93	111.14	101.82
云 南 Yunnan	108.12	100.33	112.91	103.99
陕 西 Shaanxi	101.12	105.48	111.66	104.85
甘 肃 Gansu	97.81	103.36	113.06	103.06
青 海 Qinghai	101.16	105.75	108.75	103.28
宁 夏 Ningxia	93.40	104.40	114.23	103.26
新 疆 Xinjiang	100.91	126.16	100.80	108.29

2—8 各地区农林牧渔业产品生产价格指数

Indices of Producer Prices of Agricultural Products by Region

(上年=100) (the preceding year=100)

地区	Region	总指数 Gross Index		种植业产品 Crop products		林业产品 Forest products	
		2004	2005	2004	2005	2004	2005
全国	**National**	**113.09**	**101.39**	**115.86**	**101.55**	**104.62**	**104.79**
北京	Beijing	105.76	103.53	103.21	107.15	111.40	108.26
天津	Tianjin	108.06	103.38	103.11	103.49	98.80	101.95
河北	Hebei	110.09	102.45	107.10	103.85	112.34	100.58
山西	Shanxi	110.61	103.50	109.14	104.24	106.33	102.18
内蒙古	Inner Mongolia	112.00	103.17	112.26	103.11	98.97	103.18
辽宁	Liaoning	120.41	101.50	117.73	100.30	95.05	101.67
吉林	Jilin	118.11	100.29	119.78	100.75	250.55	106.06
黑龙江	Heilongjiang	117.27	101.01	117.14	100.46	83.75	99.64
上海	Shanghai	110.84	105.71	108.12	108.17	0.00	0.00
江苏	Jiangsu	122.68	100.32	124.96	100.33	99.36	104.82
浙江	Zhejiang	116.77	105.88	116.98	109.64	98.75	101.28
安徽	Anhui	117.78	98.71	117.73	97.30	102.78	107.39
福建	Fujian	106.80	103.90	104.70	105.10	102.30	104.00
江西	Jiangxi	119.48	100.45	122.60	98.87	109.06	108.14
山东	Shandong	112.31	102.93	111.40	103.40	110.24	101.01
河南	Henan	121.95	100.74	118.43	99.81	103.81	104.94
湖北	Hubei	121.66	100.30	119.58	97.92	100.09	104.77
湖南	Hunan	127.31	99.54	118.13	103.44	111.10	99.84
广东	Guangdong	110.70	103.47	108.88	104.46	108.26	103.93
广西	Guangxi	118.93	100.02	104.11	107.36	105.29	98.41
海南	Hainan	106.36	102.20	105.70	101.03	106.26	106.79
重庆	Chongqing	125.53	100.03	120.26	102.16	0.00	100.60
四川	Sichuan	120.38	103.18	121.03	103.89	104.37	102.04
贵州	Guizhou	111.14	101.82	110.72	102.49	106.00	102.79
云南	Yunnan	112.91	103.99	110.68	103.93	115.79	115.34
陕西	Shaanxi	111.66	104.85	110.28	108.49	95.09	96.93
甘肃	Gansu	113.06	103.06	112.98	103.31	100.01	99.68
青海	Qinghai	108.75	103.28	111.51	102.24	0.00	
宁夏	Ningxia	114.23	103.26	120.21	103.00	0.00	0.00
新疆	Xinjiang	100.80	108.29	96.76	118.40	98.77	87.29

2—8 续表 continued

地区 Region	畜牧业产品 Livestock products		渔业产品 Fishery products	
	2004	2005	2004	2005
全国 National	**111.08**	**100.52**	**110.19**	**104.67**
北京 Beijing	107.42	101.22	106.46	98.44
天津 Tianjin	113.65	103.22	104.41	103.21
河北 Hebei	112.06	100.40	126.99	107.08
山西 Shanxi	113.86	102.59	102.79	102.34
内蒙古 Inner Mongolia	112.48	103.47	112.35	100.23
辽宁 Liaoning	124.93	103.31	117.77	107.33
吉林 Jilin	111.81	98.89	87.34	100.15
黑龙江 Heilongjiang	119.57	102.01	104.84	100.99
上海 Shanghai	107.81	102.07	114.74	104.94
江苏 Jiangsu	127.44	98.47	111.85	102.58
浙江 Zhejiang	131.17	103.24	110.30	104.89
安徽 Anhui	120.18	99.71	110.10	105.56
福建 Fujian	113.90	100.90	107.00	103.75
江西 Jiangxi	125.45	98.44	110.61	104.98
山东 Shandong	115.13	102.77	110.05	103.29
河南 Henan	129.27	101.98	109.30	103.01
湖北 Hubei	128.15	100.48	113.67	109.12
湖南 Hunan	134.80	96.54	111.76	105.40
广东 Guangdong	118.08	100.81	106.09	104.57
广西 Guangxi	132.33	94.49	109.86	97.90
海南 Hainan	115.20	98.83	101.46	104.96
重庆 Chongqing	128.83	98.76	107.83	105.72
四川 Sichuan	121.50	102.26	109.37	106.53
贵州 Guizhou	111.69	100.97	106.20	102.69
云南 Yunnan	116.84	100.87	111.63	111.34
陕西 Shaanxi	115.89	96.48	110.25	95.38
甘肃 Gansu	113.66	102.70	100.00	101.35
青海 Qinghai	106.67	104.07	0.00	
宁夏 Ningxia	109.22	103.47	132.87	106.33
新疆 Xinjiang	102.95	92.70	122.90	96.06

2—9 各地区种植业产品生产价格指数
Indices of Producer Prices of Crop Products by Region

(上年=100) (the preceding year=100)

地 区 Region	种植业产品 Crop products		种植业产品 Crop products 谷物(原粮) Cereal (unprocessed food grains)	
	2004	2005	2004	2005
全 国 National	**115.86**	**101.55**	**128.06**	**99.23**
北 京 Beijing	103.21	107.15	118.18	90.43
天 津 Tianjin	103.11	103.49	123.60	99.44
河 北 Hebei	107.10	103.85	123.91	98.03
山 西 Shanxi	109.14	104.24	116.71	102.17
内蒙古 Inner Mongolia	112.26	103.11	114.92	101.30
辽 宁 Liaoning	117.73	100.30	122.18	99.64
吉 林 Jilin	119.78	100.75	120.41	101.79
黑龙江 Heilongjiang	117.14	100.46	122.62	101.76
上 海 Shanghai	108.12	108.17	184.25	108.79
江 苏 Jiangsu	124.96	100.33	130.11	98.76
浙 江 Zhejiang	116.98	109.64	136.95	105.64
安 徽 Anhui	117.73	97.30	132.18	95.41
福 建 Fujian	104.70	105.10	138.09	97.66
江 西 Jiangxi	122.60	98.87	129.64	95.18
山 东 Shandong	111.40	103.40	126.51	97.32
河 南 Henan	118.43	99.81	131.12	96.51
湖 北 Hubei	119.58	97.92	141.53	92.64
湖 南 Hunan	118.13	103.44	140.58	97.38
广 东 Guangdong	108.88	104.46	134.62	99.67
广 西 Guangxi	104.11	107.36	125.70	97.61
海 南 Hainan	105.70	101.03	125.63	101.24
重 庆 Chongqing	120.26	102.16	139.59	101.29
四 川 Sichuan	121.03	103.89	132.87	101.97
贵 州 Guizhou	110.72	102.49	117.47	101.57
云 南 Yunnan	110.68	103.93	123.54	102.91
陕 西 Shaanxi	110.28	108.49	126.98	95.35
甘 肃 Gansu	112.98	103.31	118.05	105.05
青 海 Qinghai	111.51	102.24	115.63	105.57
宁 夏 Ningxia	120.21	103.00	125.85	106.62
新 疆 Xinjiang	96.76	118.40	119.81	102.19

2—9 续表 1 continued 1

地 区 Region	种植业产品 Crop products			
	蔬菜与园艺作物 Vegetable and Horticulture crops		水果、饮料和香料作物 Fruit, beverage and perfume	
	2004	2005	2004	2005
全 国 National	**105.17**	**107.17**	**100.55**	**107.78**
北 京 Beijing	101.92	108.20	101.33	113.69
天 津 Tianjin	97.44	106.75	107.23	111.65
河 北 Hebei	105.64	106.03	92.88	113.25
山 西 Shanxi	107.43	108.48	100.90	104.46
内蒙古 Inner Mongolia	97.44	106.04	99.03	102.99
辽 宁 Liaoning	107.45	101.50	116.23	100.61
吉 林 Jilin	117.03	102.63	128.22	95.21
黑龙江 Heilongjiang	97.46	110.63	0.00	0.00
上 海 Shanghai	97.90	108.91	111.17	105.84
江 苏 Jiangsu	104.30	106.73	124.65	87.99
浙 江 Zhejiang	115.33	110.21	103.81	120.22
安 徽 Anhui	101.73	102.78	100.93	112.30
福 建 Fujian	100.64	107.57	103.49	108.49
江 西 Jiangxi	105.58	110.32	124.29	81.17
山 东 Shandong	105.63	106.79	113.50	113.89
河 南 Henan	109.90	111.30	112.15	117.98
湖 北 Hubei	106.20	105.45	116.28	102.71
湖 南 Hunan	101.36	111.79	86.53	115.80
广 东 Guangdong	105.55	107.98	85.13	103.27
广 西 Guangxi	137.60	107.20	94.68	95.97
海 南 Hainan	91.31	96.60	113.32	102.85
重 庆 Chongqing	106.01	103.82	103.40	103.36
四 川 Sichuan	109.77	107.15	102.93	106.97
贵 州 Guizhou	102.80	104.59	102.35	103.21
云 南 Yunnan	109.06	101.60	95.11	107.52
陕 西 Shaanxi	125.91	100.71	98.99	115.48
甘 肃 Gansu	115.44	101.41	106.07	106.95
青 海 Qinghai	100.30	103.92	0.00	
宁 夏 Ningxia	112.08	93.41	119.24	105.69
新 疆 Xinjiang	112.40	73.70	119.19	106.40

2—9 续表 2 continued 2

地区 Region	种植业产品 Crop products					
	薯类 Potato		豆类 Beans		油料 Oil-bearing crops	
	2004	2005	2004	2005	2004	2005
全国 National	**105.75**	**106.14**	**120.29**	**95.70**	**116.58**	**91.33**
北京 Beijing	101.61	105.64	113.43	102.97	109.17	0.00
天津 Tianjin	0.00	0.00	111.83	93.99	104.28	93.37
河北 Hebei	117.51	111.47	127.48	92.69	117.76	98.75
山西 Shanxi	108.44	108.36	111.00	102.22	110.55	106.87
内蒙古 Inner Mongolia	107.33	116.13	119.30	101.12	117.43	102.33
辽宁 Liaoning	105.68	134.16	114.52	95.51	108.24	97.42
吉林 Jilin	123.49	101.59	120.09	97.68	110.57	95.15
黑龙江 Heilongjiang	113.90	100.07	112.20	98.75	113.30	99.74
上海 Shanghai	100.28	106.07	121.56	100.00	111.10	0.00
江苏 Jiangsu	107.74	106.02	118.93	97.15	113.84	92.78
浙江 Zhejiang	107.47	118.52	112.30	102.31	107.43	97.86
安徽 Anhui	103.54	102.95	112.55	88.64	111.34	89.23
福建 Fujian	110.72	106.97	109.07	97.06	106.58	106.33
江西 Jiangxi	115.89	99.91	117.62	102.12	118.01	102.20
山东 Shandong	109.05	98.03	119.76	96.30	113.20	95.83
河南 Henan	108.10	111.49	119.89	88.76	118.88	96.95
湖北 Hubei	109.69	112.08	119.37	87.02	117.99	93.14
湖南 Hunan	110.19	106.32	125.70	89.72	117.09	95.17
广东 Guangdong	113.99	103.18	106.42	107.09	113.57	102.93
广西 Guangxi	100.67	110.04	121.87	93.90	119.33	96.22
海南 Hainan	101.26	103.24	102.62	99.87	118.78	95.22
重庆 Chongqing	102.21	101.58	118.63	99.30	123.22	93.07
四川 Sichuan	104.51	105.47	124.03	104.98	122.65	99.49
贵州 Guizhou	100.30	102.59	108.15	97.90	112.05	96.36
云南 Yunnan	102.84	103.39	119.86	101.74	108.65	94.27
陕西 Shaanxi	105.22	122.87	118.18	105.82	121.89	97.58
甘肃 Gansu	101.23	105.42	110.63	101.07	118.63	101.11
青海 Qinghai	91.07	105.41	115.82	104.37	111.28	97.07
宁夏 Ningxia	97.65	109.32	110.01	93.03	116.54	99.89
新疆 Xinjiang	90.80	75.11	106.90	95.63	110.92	109.68

2—9 续表 3 continued 3

地 区 Region	种植业产品 Crop products			
	棉花(籽棉) Cotton (unginned cotton)		麻类 Fiber crops	
	2004	2005	2004	2005
全 国 National	**79.54**	**111.82**	**124.99**	**104.77**
北 京 Beijing	100.00	0.00	0.00	0.00
天 津 Tianjin	106.42	94.25	0.00	0.00
河 北 Hebei	85.73	104.86	0.00	0.00
山 西 Shanxi	94.28	99.66	0.00	0.00
内蒙古 Inner Mongolia	0.00	0.00	0.00	0.00
辽 宁 Liaoning	107.84	0.00	0.00	0.00
吉 林 Jilin	0.00	0.00	0.00	0.00
黑龙江 Heilongjiang	0.00	0.00	100.00	0.00
上 海 Shanghai	0.00	0.00	0.00	0.00
江 苏 Jiangsu	73.07	117.71	100.00	100.00
浙 江 Zhejiang	85.81	108.56	0.00	0.00
安 徽 Anhui	78.11	109.54	0.00	0.00
福 建 Fujian	0.00	0.00	102.49	0.00
江 西 Jiangxi	96.80	112.12	110.18	0.00
山 东 Shandong	88.60	92.76	0.00	0.00
河 南 Henan	97.38	100.39	0.00	0.00
湖 北 Hubei	84.23	107.65	128.71	107.84
湖 南 Hunan	101.31	105.72	127.51	98.47
广 东 Guangdong	0.00	0.00	0.00	102.35
广 西 Guangxi	0.00	0.00	110.84	143.25
海 南 Hainan	0.00	0.00	0.00	0.00
重 庆 Chongqing	0.00	0.00	122.11	108.53
四 川 Sichuan	104.80	101.93	126.07	112.44
贵 州 Guizhou	0.00	0.00	0.00	0.00
云 南 Yunnan	0.00	0.00	98.71	73.30
陕 西 Shaanxi	99.45	121.91	0.00	0.00
甘 肃 Gansu	86.80	98.17	0.00	0.00
青 海 Qinghai	0.00		0.00	
宁 夏 Ningxia	0.00	0.00	0.00	0.00
新 疆 Xinjiang	87.78	122.63	0.00	0.00

2—9 续表 4 continued 4

地区 Region	种植业产品 Crop products			
	糖料 Sugar crops		烟叶 Tobacco	
	2004	2005	2004	2005
全国 National	**104.86**	**111.57**	**108.42**	**103.26**
北京 Beijing	0.00	0.00	0.00	0.00
天津 Tianjin	0.00	0.00	0.00	0.00
河北 Hebei	0.00	0.00	0.00	0.00
山西 Shanxi	0.00	0.00	0.00	0.00
内蒙古 Inner Mongolia	108.55	105.66	105.37	87.66
辽宁 Liaoning	0.00	0.00	117.20	112.45
吉林 Jilin	0.00	0.00	108.52	119.14
黑龙江 Heilongjiang	157.89	103.16	140.15	104.53
上海 Shanghai	0.00	0.00	0.00	0.00
江苏 Jiangsu	100.00	100.00	100.00	100.00
浙江 Zhejiang	128.67	106.84	0.00	0.00
安徽 Anhui	99.14	129.34	0.00	0.00
福建 Fujian	105.82	106.07	111.32	101.79
江西 Jiangxi	120.91	104.50	123.47	108.67
山东 Shandong	0.00	0.00	82.66	125.68
河南 Henan	0.00	0.00	95.06	104.29
湖北 Hubei	144.90	112.73	128.46	104.41
湖南 Hunan	102.48	107.01	130.68	95.26
广东 Guangdong	95.74	107.32	120.90	86.74
广西 Guangxi	103.27	112.38	129.97	102.39
海南 Hainan	99.41	118.25	0.00	0.00
重庆 Chongqing	101.85	0.00	116.98	105.26
四川 Sichuan	108.91	96.85	106.41	105.08
贵州 Guizhou	98.98	100.67	109.51	104.78
云南 Yunnan	102.02	106.61	113.19	105.10
陕西 Shaanxi	0.00	0.00	118.10	100.26
甘肃 Gansu	0.00	0.00	111.11	92.38
青海 Qinghai	0.00		0.00	
宁夏 Ningxia	0.00	0.00	0.00	0.00
新疆 Xinjiang	113.83	103.84	0.00	0.00

2—9 续表 5 continued 5

地　区 Region	种植业产品 Crop products			
	小麦 Wheat		稻谷 Paddy	
	2004	2005	2004	2005
全　国 National	**131.16**	**96.41**	**136.30**	**101.57**
北　京 Beijing	123.54	86.36	141.67	83.33
天　津 Tianjin	142.11	95.68	0.00	106.74
河　北 Hebei	135.25	100.25	119.90	107.02
山　西 Shanxi	129.49	105.76	0.00	0.00
内蒙古 Inner Mongolia	122.05	109.34	112.29	110.30
辽　宁 Liaoning	0.00	0.00	138.76	106.20
吉　林 Jilin	0.00	0.00	134.69	107.03
黑龙江 Heilongjiang	131.61	98.36	134.18	105.33
上　海 Shanghai	127.68	96.71	189.86	110.08
江　苏 Jiangsu	147.39	93.99	119.38	102.42
浙　江 Zhejiang	0.00	99.64	137.10	104.67
安　徽 Anhui	137.56	91.51	136.42	98.98
福　建 Fujian	0.00	0.00	139.57	95.93
江　西 Jiangxi	0.00	0.00	129.64	95.18
山　东 Shandong	136.58	96.88	123.86	103.94
河　南 Henan	138.21	97.38	135.23	97.51
湖　北 Hubei	150.07	84.51	138.85	96.79
湖　南 Hunan	96.81	0.00	141.10	97.42
广　东 Guangdong	0.00	0.00	135.24	99.81
广　西 Guangxi	0.00	0.00	136.15	99.77
海　南 Hainan	0.00	0.00	126.28	101.22
重　庆 Chongqing	131.58	102.71	141.46	101.18
四　川 Sichuan	136.92	99.83	133.70	103.77
贵　州 Guizhou	113.15	105.70	119.90	101.31
云　南 Yunnan	126.46	102.42	126.79	102.41
陕　西 Shaanxi	140.11	94.76	119.60	93.08
甘　肃 Gansu	117.42	106.43	0.00	0.00
青　海 Qinghai	118.27	104.05	0.00	
宁　夏 Ningxia	129.63	108.51	129.29	108.92
新　疆 Xinjiang	126.22	98.39	107.43	99.54

2—9 续表 6 continued 6

地 区 Region	种植业产品 Crop products			
	玉米 Maize (corn)		杂粮 Coarse cereals	
	2004	2005	2004	2005
全 国 National	**116.92**	**97.97**	**0.00**	**107.98**
北 京 Beijing	114.03	94.11	0.00	0.00
天 津 Tianjin	119.53	100.38	0.00	0.00
河 北 Hebei	115.97	95.90	0.00	0.00
山 西 Shanxi	113.40	100.99	108.44	104.97
内蒙古 Inner Mongolia	114.59	99.45	119.26	114.76
辽 宁 Liaoning	115.25	97.40	127.75	104.32
吉 林 Jilin	114.89	99.84	137.82	103.02
黑龙江 Heilongjiang	114.78	99.53	0.00	0.00
上 海 Shanghai	145.99	0.00	0.00	100.00
江 苏 Jiangsu	115.85	97.60	0.00	
浙 江 Zhejiang	122.84	104.12	0.00	110.55
安 徽 Anhui	110.24	96.96	116.49	108.05
福 建 Fujian	106.00	122.75	116.61	104.08
江 西 Jiangxi	0.00	0.00	0.00	0.00
山 东 Shandong	118.29	96.27	0.00	0.00
河 南 Henan	115.57	94.44	0.00	0.00
湖 北 Hubei	123.63	97.86	0.00	0.00
湖 南 Hunan	125.07	96.06	0.00	0.00
广 东 Guangdong	115.93	94.63	0.00	108.42
广 西 Guangxi	122.90	97.03	0.00	0.00
海 南 Hainan	112.63	101.55	0.00	0.00
重 庆 Chongqing	130.43	101.71	0.00	0.00
四 川 Sichuan	126.92	98.71	129.82	106.40
贵 州 Guizhou	113.42	101.02	0.00	0.00
云 南 Yunnan	116.01	104.08	0.00	0.00
陕 西 Shaanxi	115.39	96.15	104.71	98.24
甘 肃 Gansu	116.93	101.35	123.30	107.91
青 海 Qinghai	0.00		113.27	106.93
宁 夏 Ningxia	119.32	99.36	110.47	0.00
新 疆 Xinjiang	118.74	106.30	117.29	102.60

2—9 续表 7 continued 7

地　区 Region	种植业产品 Crop products			
	红薯 Sweet potato		马铃薯 White potato	
	2004	2005	2004	2005
全　国 National	**108.97**	**103.59**	**104.89**	**107.43**
北　京 Beijing	101.01	105.64	110.22	0.00
天　津 Tianjin	0.00	0.00	0.00	0.00
河　北 Hebei	131.83	103.56	110.72	115.23
山　西 Shanxi	98.89	98.63	110.53	110.49
内蒙古 Inner Mongolia	0.00	0.00	107.33	116.13
辽　宁 Liaoning	102.42	105.89	111.74	145.56
吉　林 Jilin	143.49	95.47	113.38	104.67
黑龙江 Heilongjiang	125.00	0.00	112.60	100.07
上　海 Shanghai	0.00	0.00	100.28	106.07
江　苏 Jiangsu	0.00		0.00	
浙　江 Zhejiang	114.22	121.45	100.30	103.29
安　徽 Anhui	98.98	101.59	110.14	109.16
福　建 Fujian	111.05	109.79	108.73	107.49
江　西 Jiangxi	115.89	99.91	145.06	116.84
山　东 Shandong	107.37	96.10	121.53	112.44
河　南 Henan	108.10	111.49	76.15	93.72
湖　北 Hubei	106.77	107.16	111.18	114.59
湖　南 Hunan	108.79	105.99	113.93	107.21
广　东 Guangdong	120.80	102.76	92.69	99.52
广　西 Guangxi	109.99	115.26	77.37	102.02
海　南 Hainan	101.34	103.68	0.00	0.00
重　庆 Chongqing	103.60	101.19	101.66	101.74
四　川 Sichuan	104.41	103.34	104.78	111.41
贵　州 Guizhou	100.15	105.43	100.31	102.42
云　南 Yunnan	105.80	87.86	102.61	104.62
陕　西 Shaanxi	115.66	111.25	102.16	126.28
甘　肃 Gansu	0.00	129.03	101.23	105.42
青　海 Qinghai	0.00		91.07	105.41
宁　夏 Ningxia	0.00	0.00	97.65	109.32
新　疆 Xinjiang	0.00	90.00	90.80	75.11

2—9 续表 8 continued 8

地　区 Region	种植业产品 Crop products			
	大豆 Soybeans		绿豆 Mung beans	
	2004	2005	2004	2005
全　国 National	**120.17**	**94.24**	**116.73**	**105.95**
北　京 Beijing	114.89	102.97	100.00	0.00
天　津 Tianjin	111.83	93.99	0.00	0.00
河　北 Hebei	128.05	92.60	102.05	99.30
山　西 Shanxi	112.77	102.92	108.32	99.62
内蒙古 Inner Mongolia	116.07	98.27	127.33	107.47
辽　宁 Liaoning	112.35	95.21	99.28	100.83
吉　林 Jilin	109.57	97.22	147.23	96.98
黑龙江 Heilongjiang	112.20	98.75	100.00	0.00
上　海 Shanghai	120.99	100.00	0.00	0.00
江　苏 Jiangsu	108.09	95.99	100.00	100.00
浙　江 Zhejiang	104.93	98.46	0.00	108.56
安　徽 Anhui	112.91	88.72	110.04	88.17
福　建 Fujian	109.43	93.44	100.00	102.43
江　西 Jiangxi	121.45	101.38	110.66	103.45
山　东 Shandong	119.76	96.30	116.76	115.66
河　南 Henan	119.89	88.76	102.39	104.72
湖　北 Hubei	120.35	85.49	104.17	98.12
湖　南 Hunan	125.78	89.54	122.39	96.99
广　东 Guangdong	119.41	105.84	103.45	0.00
广　西 Guangxi	121.93	93.89	107.11	100.00
海　南 Hainan	103.51	98.20	105.26	100.23
重　庆 Chongqing	122.07	97.40	107.34	104.98
四　川 Sichuan	122.40	100.75	105.84	105.64
贵　州 Guizhou	108.15	97.90	104.44	0.00
云　南 Yunnan	116.75	103.09	100.00	0.00
陕　西 Shaanxi	122.81	90.52	107.65	144.39
甘　肃 Gansu	109.68	99.98	0.00	111.11
青　海 Qinghai	116.63		0.00	
宁　夏 Ningxia	100.00	85.34	0.00	0.00
新　疆 Xinjiang	99.00	95.01	0.00	116.19

2—9 续表 9 continued 9

地　区 Region	种植业产品 Crop products			
	红小豆 Small red beans		蚕豆 Broad beans	
	2004	2005	2004	2005
全　国 National	**128.26**	**105.17**	**127.61**	**100.41**
北　京 Beijing	100.00	0.00	0.00	0.00
天　津 Tianjin	0.00	0.00	0.00	0.00
河　北 Hebei	110.70	0.00	0.00	0.00
山　西 Shanxi	100.68	102.57	120.59	98.25
内蒙古 Inner Mongolia	107.43	104.83	118.84	94.78
辽　宁 Liaoning	127.32	104.60	0.00	0.00
吉　林 Jilin	183.54	117.92	0.00	0.00
黑龙江 Heilongjiang	102.99	101.78	0.00	0.00
上　海 Shanghai	0.00	0.00	0.00	0.00
江　苏 Jiangsu	0.00	102.27	0.00	
浙　江 Zhejiang	0.00	101.23	0.00	100.11
安　徽 Anhui	103.58	104.48	120.41	82.35
福　建 Fujian	0.00	92.24	127.60	90.01
江　西 Jiangxi	0.00	100.00	109.95	100.63
山　东 Shandong	99.56	109.22	0.00	0.00
河　南 Henan	0.00	100.00	0.00	0.00
湖　北 Hubei	125.00	0.00	114.84	99.69
湖　南 Hunan	126.44	88.40	104.45	0.00
广　东 Guangdong	114.29	0.00	0.00	120.00
广　西 Guangxi	200.00	0.00	0.00	0.00
海　南 Hainan	75.64	0.00	0.00	0.00
重　庆 Chongqing	0.00	0.00	116.14	100.70
四　川 Sichuan	102.98	0.00	144.50	120.71
贵　州 Guizhou	112.87	0.00	107.96	101.12
云　南 Yunnan	104.91	103.12	135.60	94.88
陕　西 Shaanxi	100.00	100.00	126.48	0.00
甘　肃 Gansu	105.03	107.92	125.96	110.49
青　海 Qinghai	0.00		124.16	98.49
宁　夏 Ningxia	0.00	0.00	0.00	0.00
新　疆 Xinjiang	0.00	0.00	0.00	87.50

2—9 续表 10 continued 10

地 区 Region	种植业产品 Crop products			
	豌豆 Peas		芸豆 Kidney beans	
	2004	2005	2004	2005
全 国 National	**114.36**	**105.03**	**107.60**	**102.80**
北 京 Beijing	0.00	0.00	0.00	0.00
天 津 Tianjin	0.00	0.00	0.00	0.00
河 北 Hebei	0.00	0.00	0.00	0.00
山 西 Shanxi	100.00	103.26	110.34	0.00
内蒙古 Inner Mongolia	115.06	104.28	105.15	105.72
辽 宁 Liaoning	0.00	0.00	0.00	0.00
吉 林 Jilin	0.00	100.00	104.65	103.22
黑龙江 Heilongjiang	0.00	0.00	108.11	100.19
上 海 Shanghai	0.00	0.00	0.00	0.00
江 苏 Jiangsu	0.00		0.00	
浙 江 Zhejiang	0.00	100.12	0.00	0.00
安 徽 Anhui	116.61	99.29	120.00	0.00
福 建 Fujian	107.77	0.00	0.00	0.00
江 西 Jiangxi	101.56	110.29	0.00	0.00
山 东 Shandong	129.89	104.01	0.00	107.71
河 南 Henan	131.18	99.51	0.00	0.00
湖 北 Hubei	114.97	110.28	0.00	0.00
湖 南 Hunan	106.84	117.55	100.00	0.00
广 东 Guangdong	126.12	116.59	0.00	0.00
广 西 Guangxi	104.72	120.51	0.00	0.00
海 南 Hainan	0.00	0.00	0.00	0.00
重 庆 Chongqing	0.00	99.80	0.00	0.00
四 川 Sichuan	116.76	102.09	0.00	0.00
贵 州 Guizhou	99.73	100.00	123.57	102.19
云 南 Yunnan	121.35	103.45	100.01	99.89
陕 西 Shaanxi	123.02	98.53	0.00	100.00
甘 肃 Gansu	105.59	108.42	96.43	99.49
青 海 Qinghai	108.88	109.27	0.00	
宁 夏 Ningxia	110.90	102.71	0.00	0.00
新 疆 Xinjiang	0.00	0.00	0.00	0.00

2—9 续表 11 continued 11

地 区 Region	种植业产品 Crop products					
	花生 Peanut		油菜籽 Rapeseeds		芝麻 Sesame	
	2004	2005	2004	2005	2004	2005
全 国 National	**117.07**	**97.60**	**116.33**	**86.97**	**122.34**	**102.98**
北 京 Beijing	109.17	0.00	0.00	0.00	0.00	0.00
天 津 Tianjin	100.39	0.00	0.00	0.00	0.00	0.00
河 北 Hebei	117.76	96.78	120.76	106.39	116.59	103.28
山 西 Shanxi	112.83	100.81	105.28	111.11	109.17	103.81
内蒙古 Inner Mongolia	83.61	100.46	112.73	101.87	111.15	98.89
辽 宁 Liaoning	108.24	97.42	0.00	0.00	0.00	103.28
吉 林 Jilin	121.17	95.56	0.00	0.00	89.03	92.93
黑龙江 Heilongjiang	87.26	0.00	0.00	0.00	0.00	0.00
上 海 Shanghai	0.00	0.00	111.10	0.00	0.00	0.00
江 苏 Jiangsu	97.91	95.13	114.22	88.84	0.00	
浙 江 Zhejiang	107.43	106.46	118.21	99.86	117.70	91.74
安 徽 Anhui	111.23	89.78	112.52	85.87	103.83	100.70
福 建 Fujian	106.61	106.37	0.00	0.00	104.08	100.00
江 西 Jiangxi	118.01	102.20	117.34	94.33	109.83	103.07
山 东 Shandong	113.21	95.84	104.50	91.17	100.63	100.00
河 南 Henan	120.93	97.09	114.45	87.29	112.25	105.04
湖 北 Hubei	116.23	95.49	119.57	92.16	96.95	102.64
湖 南 Hunan	121.26	92.63	118.16	83.51	116.76	98.77
广 东 Guangdong	113.57	102.89	0.00	120.00	0.00	102.50
广 西 Guangxi	119.30	96.28	136.94	77.72	100.00	99.06
海 南 Hainan	119.23	94.99	0.00	0.00	106.23	105.85
重 庆 Chongqing	127.84	103.13	117.90	86.63	133.36	101.75
四 川 Sichuan	125.13	100.39	121.27	98.99	92.68	87.68
贵 州 Guizhou	107.41	103.11	112.70	95.42	0.00	0.00
云 南 Yunnan	114.32	107.97	107.74	92.08	0.00	0.00
陕 西 Shaanxi	112.74	106.52	123.38	96.13	97.06	112.13
甘 肃 Gansu	100.00		117.12	97.31	100.00	
青 海 Qinghai	0.00		111.28	97.07	0.00	
宁 夏 Ningxia	0.00	0.00	0.00	0.00	0.00	0.00
新 疆 Xinjiang	94.16	136.01	104.55	99.36	0.00	0.00

2—9 续表 12 continued 12

地区 Region	种植业产品 Crop products					
	黄红麻 Jute and blueish dogbane		亚麻 Flax		苎麻 Ramie	
	2004	2005	2004	2005	2004	2005
全 国 National	**116.59**	**108.91**	**119.34**	**87.91**	**131.10**	**103.36**
北 京 Beijing						
天 津 Tianjin						
河 北 Hebei						
山 西 Shanxi						
内蒙古 Inner Mongolia						
辽 宁 Liaoning						
吉 林 Jilin						
黑龙江 Heilongjiang						
上 海 Shanghai						
江 苏 Jiangsu	100.00	100.00	0.00	0.00	107.14	100.00
浙 江 Zhejiang						
安 徽 Anhui	113.12	114.63	0.00	0.00	128.12	100.81
福 建 Fujian	102.49	0.00	0.00	0.00	0.00	0.00
江 西 Jiangxi	0.00	0.00	105.88	0.00	110.18	0.00
山 东 Shandong	145.84	0.00	0.00	0.00	0.00	0.00
河 南 Henan	117.30	102.15			0.00	0.00
湖 北 Hubei	100.00	0.00			137.05	107.84
湖 南 Hunan	0.00	0.00			127.51	98.47
广 东 Guangdong	0.00	102.35			0.00	0.00
广 西 Guangxi	117.78	112.13			0.00	0.00
海 南 Hainan	0.00	111.11			0.00	0.00
重 庆 Chongqing	0.00	104.48	0.00	0.00	122.11	108.53
四 川 Sichuan	0.00	109.16	0.00	0.00	126.07	112.88
贵 州 Guizhou						
云 南 Yunnan	0.00	0.00	98.71	73.30	0.00	0.00
陕 西 Shaanxi	0.00	0.00	0.00	0.00		
甘 肃 Gansu	0.00		100.00			
青 海 Qinghai	0.00		0.00			
宁 夏 Ningxia	0.00	0.00	0.00	0.00		
新 疆 Xinjiang	0.00	0.00	170.19	101.38		

2—9 续表 13 continued 13

地 区 Region	种植业产品 Crop products			
	甘蔗 Sugarcane		甜菜 Beet	
	2004	2005	2004	2005
全 国 National	**104.86**	**111.22**	**106.10**	**102.82**
北 京 Beijing	0.00	0.00	0.00	0.00
天 津 Tianjin	0.00	0.00	0.00	0.00
河 北 Hebei	0.00	0.00	0.00	0.00
山 西 Shanxi	0.00	0.00	0.00	0.00
内蒙古 Inner Mongolia	0.00	0.00	108.55	105.66
辽 宁 Liaoning	0.00	0.00	0.00	0.00
吉 林 Jilin	0.00	0.00	0.00	103.26
黑龙江 Heilongjiang	0.00	0.00	157.89	103.16
上 海 Shanghai	0.00	0.00	0.00	0.00
江 苏 Jiangsu	100.00	100.00	100.00	100.00
浙 江 Zhejiang	128.67	114.12	101.48	107.49
安 徽 Anhui	99.14	129.34	0.00	0.00
福 建 Fujian	105.82	106.07	0.00	0.00
江 西 Jiangxi	120.91	104.50	0.00	99.71
山 东 Shandong	0.00	0.00	0.00	0.00
河 南 Henan	0.00	0.00	0.00	0.00
湖 北 Hubei	144.90	112.73	0.00	0.00
湖 南 Hunan	102.48	107.01	0.00	0.00
广 东 Guangdong	95.74	107.30	0.00	105.00
广 西 Guangxi	103.27	112.38	0.00	0.00
海 南 Hainan	99.41	118.25	0.00	0.00
重 庆 Chongqing	101.85	0.00	0.00	0.00
四 川 Sichuan	108.91	96.85	0.00	0.00
贵 州 Guizhou	98.98	100.67	98.40	0.00
云 南 Yunnan	102.02	106.61	0.00	0.00
陕 西 Shaanxi	0.00	0.00	0.00	0.00
甘 肃 Gansu	0.00		0.00	
青 海 Qinghai	0.00		0.00	
宁 夏 Ningxia	0.00	0.00	0.00	0.00
新 疆 Xinjiang	0.00	0.00	113.83	103.84

2—9 续表 14 continued 14

地 区 Region	种植业产品 Crop products			
	烤烟叶 Flue-cured tobacco		晒烟叶 Sun-cured tobacco	
	2004	2005	2004	2005
全 国 National	**106.42**	**103.15**	**113.45**	**107.64**
北 京 Beijing	0.00	0.00	0.00	0.00
天 津 Tianjin	0.00	0.00	0.00	0.00
河 北 Hebei	0.00	0.00	0.00	0.00
山 西 Shanxi	0.00	103.68	0.00	0.00
内蒙古 Inner Mongolia	105.37	82.00	0.00	100.85
辽 宁 Liaoning	117.20	112.45	101.09	106.48
吉 林 Jilin	120.25	0.00	100.00	119.14
黑龙江 Heilongjiang	140.15	104.53	99.36	116.12
上 海 Shanghai	0.00	0.00	0.00	0.00
江 苏 Jiangsu	0.00	0.00	100.00	100.00
浙 江 Zhejiang	0.00	0.00	102.29	0.00
安 徽 Anhui	0.00	0.00	0.00	0.00
福 建 Fujian	111.32	101.79	0.00	0.00
江 西 Jiangxi	123.47	108.67	0.00	0.00
山 东 Shandong	82.66	125.68	103.85	0.00
河 南 Henan	95.06	104.29	0.00	0.00
湖 北 Hubei	125.26	101.58	143.17	117.40
湖 南 Hunan	130.68	95.26	104.17	95.24
广 东 Guangdong	120.90	86.32	0.00	100.41
广 西 Guangxi	139.30	102.39	100.63	0.00
海 南 Hainan	0.00	0.00	0.00	0.00
重 庆 Chongqing	123.37	104.28	108.68	106.53
四 川 Sichuan	111.23	104.61	104.12	105.31
贵 州 Guizhou	109.55	104.67	108.43	108.60
云 南 Yunnan	113.23	105.05	108.47	111.40
陕 西 Shaanxi	118.10	100.26	0.00	0.00
甘 肃 Gansu	0.00	92.38	111.11	
青 海 Qinghai	0.00		0.00	
宁 夏 Ningxia	0.00	0.00	0.00	0.00
新 疆 Xinjiang	0.00	0.00	123.03	0.00

2—9 续表 15 continued 15

地 区 Region	蔬菜 Vegetable		蔬菜 Vegetable 叶菜类 Leaf vegetable		瓜菜类 Gourd vegetable	
	2004	2005	2004	2005	2004	2005
全 国 National	**105.17**	**107.22**	**101.85**	**108.92**	**101.10**	**105.08**
北 京 Beijing	102.84	109.34	92.10	111.36	113.29	105.71
天 津 Tianjin	97.62	108.04	85.04	115.96	105.66	111.68
河 北 Hebei	105.64	106.03	95.41	105.59	106.00	107.36
山 西 Shanxi	107.43	108.48	93.98	109.27	101.87	107.44
内蒙古 Inner Mongolia	97.44	106.04	86.21	106.62	112.91	97.12
辽 宁 Liaoning	107.45	101.50	98.48	111.91	126.06	107.68
吉 林 Jilin	117.03	102.63	100.12	104.39	112.16	108.24
黑龙江 Heilongjiang	97.46	110.63	87.07	113.85	120.61	96.27
上 海 Shanghai	98.81	112.85	88.63	115.88	108.70	111.48
江 苏 Jiangsu	104.31	106.89	105.77	110.87	104.22	99.33
浙 江 Zhejiang	115.33	110.25	108.22	111.26	127.34	114.28
安 徽 Anhui	101.99	102.89	95.57	109.74	0.00	0.00
福 建 Fujian	102.98	107.60	102.72	110.77	108.35	115.96
江 西 Jiangxi	105.58	110.32	104.74	123.56	110.57	99.42
山 东 Shandong	106.13	106.82	90.36	111.23	98.07	115.89
河 南 Henan	109.90	111.30	94.92	105.29	107.32	106.55
湖 北 Hubei	106.20	105.45	105.36	104.29	102.81	106.44
湖 南 Hunan	102.07	113.08	101.99	115.59	96.22	107.69
广 东 Guangdong	105.48	108.04	99.26	108.04	112.15	109.43
广 西 Guangxi	137.60	107.20	107.67	106.04	99.72	112.32
海 南 Hainan	91.14	96.24	103.08	104.64	85.40	98.66
重 庆 Chongqing	106.01	103.82	105.89	102.93	110.12	103.09
四 川 Sichuan	109.92	107.15	106.19	108.23	111.93	103.19
贵 州 Guizhou	102.88	104.66	98.42	106.74	96.90	106.04
云 南 Yunnan	111.56	102.70	105.07	103.65	105.81	105.57
陕 西 Shaanxi	125.91	100.71	108.26	118.65	112.99	111.02
甘 肃 Gansu	115.64	101.56	111.59	104.81	112.73	94.54
青 海 Qinghai	100.30	103.92	97.58	99.88	100.95	98.55
宁 夏 Ningxia	112.08	93.41	106.76	95.23	101.08	79.28
新 疆 Xinjiang	112.40	73.70	108.73		131.40	99.64

2—9 续表 16 continued 16

地区 Region	蔬菜 Vegetable 块根、块茎菜类 Root and tuber vegetable 2004	2005	茄果菜类 Eggplant，tomato and chili，etc 2004	2005
全国 National	**103.59**	**106.06**	**103.18**	**104.75**
北京 Beijing	108.15	121.16	110.21	108.08
天津 Tianjin	90.99	100.00	98.69	102.22
河北 Hebei	81.16	102.39	110.89	105.33
山西 Shanxi	93.06	107.58	119.33	109.05
内蒙古 Inner Mongolia	89.59	117.07	107.86	100.30
辽宁 Liaoning	97.44	83.63	109.64	99.10
吉林 Jilin	110.82	89.89	127.60	103.74
黑龙江 Heilongjiang	107.97	106.60	125.97	105.15
上海 Shanghai	105.87	119.95	109.41	103.18
江苏 Jiangsu	96.61	106.73	103.33	103.47
浙江 Zhejiang	109.05	117.89	123.57	103.29
安徽 Anhui	103.47	93.86	82.90	109.37
福建 Fujian	107.24	105.25	102.65	114.24
江西 Jiangxi	106.67	105.09	108.60	98.63
山东 Shandong	135.97	87.02	96.99	111.44
河南 Henan	87.52	119.83	109.64	105.55
湖北 Hubei	98.49	103.49	113.02	106.57
湖南 Hunan	110.04	105.37	87.43	115.00
广东 Guangdong	116.50	109.27	99.04	105.51
广西 Guangxi	215.54	90.19	102.30	115.99
海南 Hainan	102.27	103.96	90.09	84.07
重庆 Chongqing	105.61	104.53	101.92	104.32
四川 Sichuan	109.31	108.90	117.97	105.92
贵州 Guizhou	99.33	104.29	107.03	101.81
云南 Yunnan	117.29	102.25	108.61	103.94
陕西 Shaanxi	135.58	116.34	133.46	87.20
甘肃 Gansu	99.60	100.56	126.55	105.05
青海 Qinghai	100.00	114.47	97.82	101.38
宁夏 Ningxia	123.40	107.99	104.35	85.11
新疆 Xinjiang	113.62	80.34	112.41	79.67

2—9 续表 17 continued 17

地　区 Region	蔬菜 Vegetable			
	葱蒜类 Onion and Garlic		菜用豆类 Garden beans	
	2004	2005	2004	2005
全　国 National	**115.91**	**109.76**	**104.96**	**107.98**
北　京 Beijing	112.77	103.18	115.14	102.73
天　津 Tianjin	108.93	107.52	136.74	113.41
河　北 Hebei	112.12	105.92	127.72	115.34
山　西 Shanxi	117.97	102.56	123.68	115.02
内蒙古 Inner Mongolia	112.18	100.67	0.00	0.00
辽　宁 Liaoning	100.09	103.35	123.61	108.15
吉　林 Jilin	119.54	95.10	133.76	107.13
黑龙江 Heilongjiang	128.76	97.00	0.00	0.00
上　海 Shanghai	118.28	117.02	100.83	112.86
江　苏 Jiangsu	98.19	107.62	116.51	101.27
浙　江 Zhejiang	149.42	115.82	117.13	106.42
安　徽 Anhui	106.23	97.85	0.00	0.00
福　建 Fujian	105.42	113.10	107.72	112.21
江　西 Jiangxi	94.72	121.06	105.07	115.18
山　东 Shandong	117.55	116.60	110.43	110.20
河　南 Henan	143.38	121.82	0.00	0.00
湖　北 Hubei	113.63	105.90	105.34	117.43
湖　南 Hunan	99.20	119.27	103.54	119.55
广　东 Guangdong	96.62	107.21	101.97	115.66
广　西 Guangxi	111.66	97.33	108.91	110.19
海　南 Hainan	110.97	118.26	94.64	99.64
重　庆 Chongqing	105.93	102.30	114.48	102.30
四　川 Sichuan	109.88	112.80	119.46	106.62
贵　州 Guizhou	109.24	107.50	105.03	112.40
云　南 Yunnan	120.32	103.42	122.27	99.42
陕　西 Shaanxi	116.56	106.10	109.73	142.09
甘　肃 Gansu	116.53	101.06	116.10	108.41
青　海 Qinghai	114.69	106.40	0.00	
宁　夏 Ningxia	108.38	103.13	148.00	104.71
新　疆 Xinjiang	103.22	88.08	0.00	0.00

2—9 续表 18 continued 18

地区 Region	蔬菜 Vegetable			
	水生菜类 Water vegetable		食用菌(干鲜混合) Mushroom	
	2004	2005	2004	2005
全国 National	**113.37**	**124.53**	**101.41**	**101.54**
北京 Beijing	103.03	0.00	101.65	98.87
天津 Tianjin	0.00	0.00	91.77	125.83
河北 Hebei	0.00	0.00	93.17	94.14
山西 Shanxi	0.00	0.00	110.12	100.33
内蒙古 Inner Mongolia	0.00	0.00	0.00	0.00
辽宁 Liaoning	0.00	0.00	0.00	85.79
吉林 Jilin	0.00	0.00	141.78	97.65
黑龙江 Heilongjiang	0.00	0.00	119.73	101.93
上海 Shanghai	147.29	112.01	0.00	0.00
江苏 Jiangsu	108.61	106.95	102.86	101.65
浙江 Zhejiang	0.00	119.35	0.00	100.02
安徽 Anhui	131.13	102.43	0.00	0.00
福建 Fujian	102.37	102.34	99.43	103.01
江西 Jiangxi	108.58	114.45	104.45	117.58
山东 Shandong	111.06	116.15	106.09	107.27
河南 Henan	113.86	0.00	116.57	97.22
湖北 Hubei	114.06	111.60	109.41	92.87
湖南 Hunan	109.17	117.06	107.69	102.44
广东 Guangdong	91.91	109.66	103.55	0.00
广西 Guangxi	132.20	92.63	91.81	104.68
海南 Hainan	0.00	0.00	0.00	0.00
重庆 Chongqing	106.90	104.76	0.00	0.00
四川 Sichuan	101.89	101.85	98.40	104.52
贵州 Guizhou	102.65	106.20	95.89	105.88
云南 Yunnan	91.24	95.88	101.77	99.18
陕西 Shaanxi	172.71	88.13	115.29	110.29
甘肃 Gansu	0.00	0.00	92.65	93.11
青海 Qinghai	0.00		0.00	
宁夏 Ningxia	0.00	0.00	0.00	0.00
新疆 Xinjiang	0.00	0.00	0.00	0.00

2—9 续表 19 continued 19

地　区 Region	蔬菜 Vegetable			
	菠菜 Spinach		芹菜 Celery	
	2004	2005	2004	2005
全　国 National	**101.57**	**108.99**	**99.28**	**107.77**
北　京 Beijing	96.87	113.19	105.56	96.47
天　津 Tianjin	0.00	0.00	82.92	126.42
河　北 Hebei	81.96	98.69	125.73	99.03
山　西 Shanxi	111.77	115.36	104.27	107.52
内蒙古 Inner Mongolia	103.15	106.90	100.35	95.46
辽　宁 Liaoning	111.45	103.59	91.16	104.45
吉　林 Jilin	147.24	102.75	101.32	104.62
黑龙江 Heilongjiang	131.32	103.84	108.98	97.90
上　海 Shanghai	95.69	122.03	106.11	118.68
江　苏 Jiangsu	120.10	115.35	110.25	118.78
浙　江 Zhejiang	74.72	108.96	70.94	111.42
安　徽 Anhui	105.14	106.01	90.61	112.30
福　建 Fujian	101.74	113.17	99.12	111.84
江　西 Jiangxi	115.89	111.40	104.11	124.42
山　东 Shandong	86.90	122.38	93.10	105.23
河　南 Henan	98.65	118.90	70.27	87.48
湖　北 Hubei	110.38	108.52	96.33	120.01
湖　南 Hunan	94.99	127.43	94.84	144.52
广　东 Guangdong	99.90	116.71	77.45	104.64
广　西 Guangxi	86.98	122.47	112.20	108.45
海　南 Hainan	105.62	102.12	109.69	108.13
重　庆 Chongqing	108.65	103.14	125.72	104.97
四　川 Sichuan	104.45	115.33	96.33	104.73
贵　州 Guizhou	108.45	109.61	98.33	106.49
云　南 Yunnan	102.69	114.24	100.00	113.79
陕　西 Shaanxi	113.20	115.18	118.04	132.49
甘　肃 Gansu	134.27	90.05	91.79	113.47
青　海 Qinghai	0.00	100.69	0.00	104.30
宁　夏 Ningxia	0.00	0.00	118.58	58.74
新　疆 Xinjiang	76.47	100.88	96.84	194.10

2—9 续表 20 continued 20

地　区 Region	蔬菜 Vegetable			
	大白菜 Chinese cabbage		元白菜 Cabbage	
	2004	2005	2004	2005
全　国 National	**102.10**	**108.06**	**106.45**	**112.93**
北　京 Beijing	69.15	111.20	110.41	133.90
天　津 Tianjin	74.10	108.59	92.30	106.55
河　北 Hebei	77.45	100.76	108.43	116.76
山　西 Shanxi	78.16	108.36	74.73	116.61
内蒙古 Inner Mongolia	83.04	110.44	75.60	101.38
辽　宁 Liaoning	103.33	117.49	110.12	104.36
吉　林 Jilin	90.22	105.29	211.19	92.56
黑龙江 Heilongjiang	86.15	115.12	63.90	96.23
上　海 Shanghai	94.85	119.46	101.09	110.69
江　苏 Jiangsu	97.58	102.91	99.77	114.93
浙　江 Zhejiang	148.85	119.89	100.87	111.22
安　徽 Anhui	98.01	111.19	85.59	107.98
福　建 Fujian	104.49	110.42	101.00	113.33
江　西 Jiangxi	106.13	126.68	98.54	114.08
山　东 Shandong	84.10	109.56	101.17	103.89
河　南 Henan	92.88	110.12	114.38	109.98
湖　北 Hubei	116.85	98.95	107.70	91.60
湖　南 Hunan	103.39	112.74	97.62	118.79
广　东 Guangdong	112.43	105.16	96.17	113.28
广　西 Guangxi	112.96	116.29	156.81	0.00
海　南 Hainan	102.53	105.74	101.45	115.08
重　庆 Chongqing	110.85	102.03	107.01	102.35
四　川 Sichuan	112.50	102.88	111.65	114.55
贵　州 Guizhou	97.07	107.82	96.58	101.59
云　南 Yunnan	104.63	105.72	100.91	86.71
陕　西 Shaanxi	108.76	122.32	105.83	117.07
甘　肃 Gansu	97.32	83.98	103.96	118.92
青　海 Qinghai	99.47	102.20	0.00	0.00
宁　夏 Ningxia	85.24	115.68	95.79	89.94
新　疆 Xinjiang	105.41		165.68	

2—9 续表 21 continued 21

地　区 Region	蔬菜 Vegetable			
	甘蓝 Wild cabbage		花椰菜 Cauliflower	
	2004	2005	2004	2005
全　国 National	**100.78**	**110.42**	**101.29**	**97.89**
北　京 Beijing	107.97	99.17	114.53	104.76
天　津 Tianjin	0.00	0.00	80.43	111.96
河　北 Hebei	0.00	0.00	64.06	107.70
山　西 Shanxi	112.46	102.86	0.00	100.00
内蒙古 Inner Mongolia	117.49	108.97	0.00	0.00
辽　宁 Liaoning	95.08	97.42	80.00	0.00
吉　林 Jilin	0.00	102.27	0.00	0.00
黑龙江 Heilongjiang	116.50	93.32	129.04	0.00
上　海 Shanghai	0.00	0.00	98.27	121.25
江　苏 Jiangsu	100.00	102.91	100.22	110.81
浙　江 Zhejiang	116.36	106.23	0.00	106.24
安　徽 Anhui	98.20	0.00	91.91	0.00
福　建 Fujian	96.74	112.26	101.60	106.20
江　西 Jiangxi	94.58	97.98	95.86	109.28
山　东 Shandong	92.05	120.86	97.13	105.46
河　南 Henan	0.00	93.55	110.30	109.95
湖　北 Hubei	0.00	106.67	85.78	106.55
湖　南 Hunan	105.76	104.98	100.84	104.12
广　东 Guangdong	89.61	105.76	84.53	106.37
广　西 Guangxi	0.00	0.00	0.00	107.69
海　南 Hainan	0.00	0.00	87.48	0.00
重　庆 Chongqing	98.63	106.30	94.98	104.61
四　川 Sichuan	105.83	111.80	85.67	109.74
贵　州 Guizhou	100.00	0.00	96.71	100.42
云　南 Yunnan	104.85	0.00	112.21	89.21
陕　西 Shaanxi	103.72	103.37	51.85	0.00
甘　肃 Gansu	103.80	97.70	126.00	114.07
青　海 Qinghai	100.01	96.53	0.00	
宁　夏 Ningxia	0.00	0.00	0.00	0.00
新　疆 Xinjiang	0.00	0.00	170.68	0.00

2—9 续表 22 continued 22

地　区 Region	蔬菜 Vegetable			
	莴笋 Asparagus lettuce		油菜 Rape	
	2004	2005	2004	2005
全　国 National	**107.36**	**109.72**	**101.61**	**110.88**
北　京 Beijing	98.46	103.18	111.07	120.64
天　津 Tianjin	0.00	0.00	13.00	122.41
河　北 Hebei	105.71	101.08	103.33	99.58
山　西 Shanxi	104.00	0.00	102.03	106.45
内蒙古 Inner Mongolia	0.00	0.00	100.00	105.19
辽　宁 Liaoning	0.00	0.00	92.41	88.89
吉　林 Jilin	0.00	109.66	83.88	110.16
黑龙江 Heilongjiang	0.00	0.00	0.00	128.77
上　海 Shanghai	76.47	109.80	81.44	123.07
江　苏 Jiangsu	102.58	106.25	100.00	104.80
浙　江 Zhejiang	135.57	109.74	98.19	111.55
安　徽 Anhui	98.53	113.03	90.01	115.29
福　建 Fujian	105.28	101.43	115.60	115.74
江　西 Jiangxi	90.01	101.15	95.13	112.97
山　东 Shandong	113.95	102.07	89.87	115.82
河　南 Henan	66.18	100.00	0.00	100.07
湖　北 Hubei	104.13	97.88	0.00	101.79
湖　南 Hunan	100.18	122.88	90.93	139.35
广　东 Guangdong	0.00	97.36	98.95	107.31
广　西 Guangxi	82.81	89.89	0.00	105.10
海　南 Hainan	101.95	0.00	105.17	99.33
重　庆 Chongqing	99.59	103.88	0.00	0.00
四　川 Sichuan	106.69	108.43	116.47	109.39
贵　州 Guizhou	98.72	101.25	117.48	0.00
云　南 Yunnan	109.38	100.33	126.77	0.00
陕　西 Shaanxi	87.16	114.05	99.52	82.46
甘　肃 Gansu	176.17	97.31	115.26	127.61
青　海 Qinghai	105.27	94.12	90.35	95.65
宁　夏 Ningxia	0.00	0.00	108.07	96.11
新　疆 Xinjiang	0.00	0.00	121.21	0.00

2—9 续表 23 continued 23

地区 Region	蔬菜 Vegetable			
	黄瓜 Cucumber		冬瓜 White gourd	
	2004	2005	2004	2005
全国 National	**103.66**	**104.99**	**92.92**	**105.86**
北京 Beijing	110.41	107.24	118.38	95.37
天津 Tianjin	105.66	111.68	0.00	0.00
河北 Hebei	106.01	107.44	139.28	89.32
山西 Shanxi	119.29	104.62	0.00	0.00
内蒙古 Inner Mongolia	112.91	97.12	0.00	0.00
辽宁 Liaoning	126.06	107.68	0.00	0.00
吉林 Jilin	112.16	108.24	0.00	0.00
黑龙江 Heilongjiang	122.40	93.42	0.00	0.00
上海 Shanghai	106.95	112.92	127.89	107.37
江苏 Jiangsu	103.95	100.25	101.25	92.31
浙江 Zhejiang	126.85	109.69	123.12	111.11
安徽 Anhui	112.79	94.81	97.07	98.88
福建 Fujian	100.88	121.02	119.07	114.15
江西 Jiangxi	105.98	101.36	93.03	101.08
山东 Shandong	98.70	116.71	101.09	105.71
河南 Henan	107.32	106.55	117.08	88.59
湖北 Hubei	113.30	109.93	105.02	97.06
湖南 Hunan	102.63	100.30	96.00	107.64
广东 Guangdong	101.66	115.45	120.92	106.74
广西 Guangxi	114.73	113.02	95.29	115.85
海南 Hainan	81.93	107.58	64.94	87.42
重庆 Chongqing	113.32	103.84	111.73	102.43
四川 Sichuan	111.79	103.69	109.02	105.54
贵州 Guizhou	95.73	106.22	95.98	102.75
云南 Yunnan	102.67	116.76	100.66	74.55
陕西 Shaanxi	112.84	111.03	100.00	96.25
甘肃 Gansu	114.45	93.80	0.00	114.29
青海 Qinghai	102.62	100.07	0.00	
宁夏 Ningxia	101.08	79.28	0.00	0.00
新疆 Xinjiang	101.91	111.31	120.93	0.00

2—9 续表 24 continued 24

地　区 Region	蔬菜 Vegetable			
	西葫芦 Summer squash		苦瓜 Balsam pear	
	2004	2005	2004	2005
全　国 National	**99.41**	**103.53**	**113.19**	**109.63**
北　京 Beijing	120.87	134.50	104.59	103.93
天　津 Tianjin	0.00	0.00	0.00	0.00
河　北 Hebei	92.20	92.41	0.00	0.00
山　西 Shanxi	71.69	111.50	0.00	0.00
内蒙古 Inner Mongolia	0.00	100.00	0.00	100.00
辽　宁 Liaoning	0.00	0.00	0.00	111.11
吉　林 Jilin	0.00	92.02	0.00	107.14
黑龙江 Heilongjiang	112.65	109.02	0.00	97.33
上　海 Shanghai	0.00	0.00	0.00	0.00
江　苏 Jiangsu	98.34	99.10	100.00	70.92
浙　江 Zhejiang	0.00	89.24	110.98	102.53
安　徽 Anhui	0.00	105.23	0.00	107.56
福　建 Fujian	100.32	107.18	99.04	116.04
江　西 Jiangxi	107.66	97.44	88.66	107.47
山　东 Shandong	95.68	120.17	100.40	110.65
河　南 Henan	0.00	108.85	0.00	129.09
湖　北 Hubei	119.02	111.04	81.32	108.25
湖　南 Hunan	83.72	113.24	87.52	123.21
广　东 Guangdong	121.27	120.54	121.52	102.32
广　西 Guangxi	115.33	101.72	98.05	106.16
海　南 Hainan	92.45	105.17	118.62	103.56
重　庆 Chongqing	0.00	105.88	105.71	105.76
四　川 Sichuan	95.57	0.00	116.86	98.59
贵　州 Guizhou	107.23	0.00	111.84	135.26
云　南 Yunnan	127.69	0.00	117.53	100.00
陕　西 Shaanxi	143.23	109.09	111.91	31.25
甘　肃 Gansu	109.44	95.67	0.00	
青　海 Qinghai	0.00		0.00	
宁　夏 Ningxia	0.00	0.00	0.00	0.00
新　疆 Xinjiang	0.00	93.75	0.00	0.00

2—9 续表 25 continued 25

地　区 Region	蔬菜 Vegetable			
	萝卜 Radish		胡萝卜 Carrot	
	2004	2005	2004	2005
全　国 National	**103.08**	**108.67**	**102.90**	**103.33**
北　京 Beijing	107.94	121.16	108.78	0.00
天　津 Tianjin	90.99	100.00	0.00	0.00
河　北 Hebei	97.80	106.61	77.95	101.57
山　西 Shanxi	107.60	108.08	79.87	107.12
内蒙古 Inner Mongolia	122.38	98.63	83.08	120.73
辽　宁 Liaoning	97.44	96.91	0.00	88.89
吉　林 Jilin	125.11	86.68	115.13	96.47
黑龙江 Heilongjiang	107.97	97.81	0.00	115.38
上　海 Shanghai	99.86	127.28	0.00	0.00
江　苏 Jiangsu	92.41	100.00	103.07	100.30
浙　江 Zhejiang	115.91	121.66	106.67	112.85
安　徽 Anhui	95.60	118.15	110.57	72.00
福　建 Fujian	95.65	113.85	105.33	115.71
江　西 Jiangxi	104.84	104.65	120.00	108.23
山　东 Shandong	91.76	103.15	100.31	96.24
河　南 Henan	87.52	119.83	114.67	106.77
湖　北 Hubei	93.41	108.56	113.24	102.38
湖　南 Hunan	95.51	104.91	111.09	101.86
广　东 Guangdong	99.98	113.32	103.63	107.63
广　西 Guangxi	114.35	102.63	146.46	115.42
海　南 Hainan	97.37	92.22	0.00	0.00
重　庆 Chongqing	103.49	105.71	110.35	107.24
四　川 Sichuan	103.18	112.08	106.93	109.03
贵　州 Guizhou	96.29	106.02	97.38	102.64
云　南 Yunnan	97.22	134.79	90.50	123.10
陕　西 Shaanxi	128.32	121.10	147.92	114.19
甘　肃 Gansu	114.25	85.73	109.23	106.81
青　海 Qinghai	100.00	114.47	119.47	
宁　夏 Ningxia	120.88	137.53	129.27	88.19
新　疆 Xinjiang	100.00	69.62	83.45	43.24

2—9 续表 26 continued 26

地　区 Region	蔬菜 Vegetable			
	生姜 Ginger		芋头 Taro	
	2004	2005	2004	2005
全　国 National	**145.13**	**93.80**	**107.38**	**107.16**
北　京 Beijing	0.00	0.00	0.00	0.00
天　津 Tianjin	0.00	0.00	0.00	0.00
河　北 Hebei	0.00	0.00	0.00	0.00
山　西 Shanxi	0.00	0.00	0.00	105.08
内蒙古 Inner Mongolia	0.00	0.00	0.00	0.00
辽　宁 Liaoning	0.00	65.86	0.00	0.00
吉　林 Jilin	0.00	0.00	0.00	0.00
黑龙江 Heilongjiang	0.00	0.00	0.00	0.00
上　海 Shanghai	0.00	222.22	0.00	0.00
江　苏 Jiangsu	100.00	98.76	0.00	
浙　江 Zhejiang	0.00	105.64	122.31	114.29
安　徽 Anhui	106.84	83.33	102.04	106.61
福　建 Fujian	116.74	96.13	116.52	92.50
江　西 Jiangxi	102.90	113.58	120.56	101.17
山　东 Shandong	158.82	79.03	101.80	118.02
河　南 Henan	0.00	89.64	0.00	123.65
湖　北 Hubei	114.77	104.53	98.04	102.91
湖　南 Hunan	147.89	107.55	106.40	115.29
广　东 Guangdong	194.40	102.02	101.11	109.79
广　西 Guangxi	237.63	83.10	103.85	114.73
海　南 Hainan	101.18	104.28	0.00	99.12
重　庆 Chongqing	114.67	100.61	92.13	102.62
四　川 Sichuan	132.20	98.59	110.03	107.99
贵　州 Guizhou	108.00	92.11	102.32	90.35
云　南 Yunnan	132.43	79.53	106.62	92.19
陕　西 Shaanxi	0.00	82.77	97.22	114.16
甘　肃 Gansu	0.00		0.00	
青　海 Qinghai	0.00		0.00	
宁　夏 Ningxia	0.00	0.00	0.00	0.00
新　疆 Xinjiang	0.00	100.00	120.00	0.00

2—9 续表 27 continued 27

地区 Region	蔬菜 Vegetable			
	茄子 Eggplant		西红柿 Tomato	
	2004	2005	2004	2005
全国 National	**108.01**	**104.76**	**104.06**	**104.39**
北京 Beijing	114.10	107.20	108.89	108.85
天津 Tianjin	94.02	112.36	104.20	97.24
河北 Hebei	125.11	105.35	110.21	105.34
山西 Shanxi	133.06	106.61	123.94	109.56
内蒙古 Inner Mongolia	137.66	105.52	108.03	98.14
辽宁 Liaoning	110.53	99.56	111.08	105.96
吉林 Jilin	115.61	107.72	119.96	100.08
黑龙江 Heilongjiang	157.02	98.27	78.21	121.07
上海 Shanghai	106.94	97.63	116.05	104.58
江苏 Jiangsu	107.61	101.65	104.09	96.46
浙江 Zhejiang	114.11	96.86	103.80	103.99
安徽 Anhui	103.15	105.00	108.14	109.53
福建 Fujian	105.58	118.44	104.12	118.32
江西 Jiangxi	109.46	103.84	107.18	33.73
山东 Shandong	101.41	113.06	92.04	110.47
河南 Henan	170.70	113.70	96.74	101.15
湖北 Hubei	117.16	108.70	110.87	103.09
湖南 Hunan	97.00	108.01	98.46	102.55
广东 Guangdong	110.31	100.20	102.02	111.82
广西 Guangxi	118.32	103.98	103.67	119.21
海南 Hainan	120.05	104.97	86.22	100.74
重庆 Chongqing	99.93	105.33	99.75	103.72
四川 Sichuan	122.59	111.43	105.37	102.12
贵州 Guizhou	105.01	108.06	106.35	116.61
云南 Yunnan	116.13	94.79	100.19	101.78
陕西 Shaanxi	124.22	98.71	112.80	100.57
甘肃 Gansu	136.54	102.52	117.49	106.23
青海 Qinghai	0.00	0.00	96.23	99.77
宁夏 Ningxia	82.29	63.70	112.33	86.42
新疆 Xinjiang	84.34	77.19	125.04	96.90

2—9 续表 28 continued 28

地　区 Region	蔬菜 Vegetable			
	辣椒 Chili		青椒 Sweetbell	
	2004	2005	2004	2005
全　国 National	**103.62**	**100.35**	**96.48**	**105.72**
北　京 Beijing	109.90	113.98	109.03	102.62
天　津 Tianjin	110.24	77.34	0.00	99.10
河　北 Hebei	68.56	106.25	109.29	104.73
山　西 Shanxi	97.41	99.29	96.60	115.88
内蒙古 Inner Mongolia	88.86	95.15	98.78	103.14
辽　宁 Liaoning	103.57	97.32	105.20	97.59
吉　林 Jilin	130.49	104.23	118.82	96.56
黑龙江 Heilongjiang	115.74	105.30	107.44	101.76
上　海 Shanghai	100.00	139.25	86.18	107.24
江　苏 Jiangsu	97.59	107.09	103.11	104.65
浙　江 Zhejiang	139.55	106.24	146.28	104.78
安　徽 Anhui	82.90	109.37	102.40	110.17
福　建 Fujian	112.61	117.85	94.86	98.77
江　西 Jiangxi	108.37	102.12	98.01	101.82
山　东 Shandong	100.61	111.11	99.29	112.20
河　南 Henan	99.61	110.26	122.74	106.70
湖　北 Hubei	111.46	107.98	112.57	97.23
湖　南 Hunan	81.66	119.70	95.97	116.37
广　东 Guangdong	88.61	108.47	95.42	114.44
广　西 Guangxi	103.22	104.31	85.63	107.32
海　南 Hainan	92.46	73.45	73.73	101.53
重　庆 Chongqing	106.77	102.06	109.35	104.79
四　川 Sichuan	125.99	102.85	110.63	108.20
贵　州 Guizhou	107.38	98.87	105.28	104.36
云　南 Yunnan	108.04	100.54	107.90	125.03
陕　西 Shaanxi	138.51	83.64	107.49	107.89
甘　肃 Gansu	127.22	106.58	115.31	100.00
青　海 Qinghai	100.00	103.59	140.16	96.61
宁　夏 Ningxia	107.68	103.88	0.00	0.00
新　疆 Xinjiang	108.41	81.27	0.00	0.00

2—9 续表 29　　continued 29

地　区 Region	蔬菜 Vegetable			
	大葱 Scallion		蒜苔 Garlic stalk	
	2004	2005	2004	2005
全　国 National	**111.81**	**103.04**	**115.10**	**107.28**
北　京 Beijing	106.28	110.81	157.14	109.09
天　津 Tianjin	141.16	102.56	0.00	0.00
河　北 Hebei	108.82	106.56	138.94	0.00
山　西 Shanxi	123.25	101.53	0.00	0.00
内蒙古 Inner Mongolia	117.02	97.26	0.00	106.90
辽　宁 Liaoning	105.10	103.19	0.00	0.00
吉　林 Jilin	101.62	94.33	89.50	100.00
黑龙江 Heilongjiang	128.76	97.00	134.93	153.61
上　海 Shanghai	0.00	0.00	0.00	0.00
江　苏 Jiangsu	121.04	110.80	103.08	104.17
浙　江 Zhejiang	98.15	109.86	0.00	108.67
安　徽 Anhui	108.27	99.30	89.93	86.23
福　建 Fujian	105.40	103.93	0.00	104.02
江　西 Jiangxi	113.54	101.74	100.82	116.85
山　东 Shandong	113.75	101.29	110.10	112.97
河　南 Henan	120.34	104.37	128.31	119.38
湖　北 Hubei	110.51	114.46	115.39	101.11
湖　南 Hunan	105.90	112.59	113.17	112.94
广　东 Guangdong	109.04	109.43	58.40	106.30
广　西 Guangxi	94.43	0.00	0.00	105.39
海　南 Hainan	98.20	100.96	93.99	0.00
重　庆 Chongqing	108.79	106.93	109.36	95.62
四　川 Sichuan	103.03	113.90	95.94	107.10
贵　州 Guizhou	110.71	107.60	108.52	106.30
云　南 Yunnan	119.33	105.13	113.70	105.98
陕　西 Shaanxi	119.88	108.22	90.72	0.00
甘　肃 Gansu	91.26	100.95	102.82	111.28
青　海 Qinghai	99.97	95.23	168.02	100.00
宁　夏 Ningxia	87.42	90.88	0.00	0.00
新　疆 Xinjiang	130.86	108.83	0.00	108.99

2—9 续表 30　　continued 30

地　区 Region	蔬菜 Vegetable			
	蒜头 Garlic head		洋葱 Onion	
	2004	2005	2004	2005
全　国 National	**117.72**	**118.93**	**101.15**	**91.05**
北　京 Beijing	146.67	0.00	123.75	85.71
天　津 Tianjin	81.28	100.60	0.00	0.00
河　北 Hebei	109.38	107.10	101.01	0.00
山　西 Shanxi	111.06	102.35	0.00	98.09
内蒙古 Inner Mongolia	83.33	105.96	83.30	122.39
辽　宁 Liaoning	102.46	105.50	0.00	0.00
吉　林 Jilin	139.28	97.04	0.00	101.32
黑龙江 Heilongjiang	110.17	109.45	0.00	0.00
上　海 Shanghai	116.15	117.27	121.75	85.75
江　苏 Jiangsu	91.55	121.87	0.00	
浙　江 Zhejiang	119.38	105.22	0.00	0.00
安　徽 Anhui	116.40	99.52	103.68	101.51
福　建 Fujian	100.52	116.82	114.37	100.49
江　西 Jiangxi	105.47	92.20	107.77	100.00
山　东 Shandong	127.41	131.49	115.01	79.64
河　南 Henan	188.27	156.19	0.00	101.37
湖　北 Hubei	123.03	97.69	113.36	112.19
湖　南 Hunan	99.76	115.22	104.82	83.16
广　东 Guangdong	95.94	104.65	0.00	0.00
广　西 Guangxi	102.06	94.36	0.00	0.00
海　南 Hainan	125.00	0.00	0.00	0.00
重　庆 Chongqing	104.33	101.32	0.00	0.00
四　川 Sichuan	113.60	124.37	105.68	116.50
贵　州 Guizhou	105.12	108.50	111.11	0.00
云　南 Yunnan	121.23	102.81	54.09	132.83
陕　西 Shaanxi	105.41	98.97	0.00	100.00
甘　肃 Gansu	116.12	100.21	137.36	71.24
青　海 Qinghai	114.90	118.11	111.11	
宁　夏 Ningxia	117.17	0.00	0.00	0.00
新　疆 Xinjiang	0.00	110.69	0.00	76.94

2—9 续表 31　　continued 31

地　区 Region	食用菌 Mushroom		食用菌 Mushroom 香菇(干品) Mushroom (dried)	
	2004	2005	2004	2005
全　国 National	**101.41**	**101.54**	**100.33**	**98.87**
北　京 Beijing	101.65	98.87	100.00	81.50
天　津 Tianjin	91.77	125.83	0.00	0.00
河　北 Hebei	93.17	94.14	89.45	101.23
山　西 Shanxi	110.12	100.33	101.28	0.00
内蒙古 Inner Mongolia	0.00	0.00	0.00	0.00
辽　宁 Liaoning	0.00	85.79	0.00	0.00
吉　林 Jilin	141.78	97.65	0.00	0.00
黑龙江 Heilongjiang	119.73	101.93	100.00	115.21
上　海 Shanghai	0.00	0.00	0.00	0.00
江　苏 Jiangsu	102.86	101.65	100.00	100.00
浙　江 Zhejiang	0.00	100.02	0.00	92.58
安　徽 Anhui	0.00	0.00	86.81	121.27
福　建 Fujian	99.43	103.01	94.96	105.01
江　西 Jiangxi	104.45	117.58	106.37	123.11
山　东 Shandong	106.09	107.27	101.59	119.32
河　南 Henan	116.57	97.22	116.57	97.22
湖　北 Hubei	109.41	92.87	105.50	91.08
湖　南 Hunan	107.69	102.44	0.00	121.46
广　东 Guangdong	103.55	0.00	0.00	0.00
广　西 Guangxi	91.81	104.68	0.00	113.58
海　南 Hainan	0.00	0.00	0.00	0.00
重　庆 Chongqing	0.00	0.00	0.00	0.00
四　川 Sichuan	98.40	104.52	77.78	0.00
贵　州 Guizhou	95.89	105.88	100.00	0.00
云　南 Yunnan	101.77	99.18	0.00	0.00
陕　西 Shaanxi	115.29	110.29	94.70	110.29
甘　肃 Gansu	92.65	93.11	0.00	129.73
青　海 Qinghai	0.00		0.00	
宁　夏 Ningxia	0.00	0.00	0.00	0.00
新　疆 Xinjiang	0.00	0.00	0.00	0.00

2—9 续表 32 continued 32

地　　区 Region	食用菌 Mushroom			
	蘑菇(鲜品) Mushroom (fresh)		黑木耳(干品) Black edible fungus (dried)	
	2004	2005	2004	2005
全　　国 National	**100.50**	**101.58**	**115.47**	**99.71**
北　　京 Beijing	102.58	107.58	0.00	0.00
天　　津 Tianjin	91.77	125.83	0.00	0.00
河　　北 Hebei	93.17	92.61	0.00	0.00
山　　西 Shanxi	113.84	100.33	0.00	0.00
内 蒙 古 Inner Mongolia	106.38	97.84	0.00	0.00
辽　　宁 Liaoning	100.00	85.79	0.00	0.00
吉　　林 Jilin	141.78	97.65	0.00	96.93
黑 龙 江 Heilongjiang	0.00	118.62	119.73	101.93
上　　海 Shanghai	0.00	0.00	0.00	0.00
江　　苏 Jiangsu	100.00	102.45	100.00	100.00
浙　　江 Zhejiang	0.00	110.89	0.00	99.46
安　　徽 Anhui	97.71	0.00	108.45	0.00
福　　建 Fujian	100.20	98.15	111.80	100.19
江　　西 Jiangxi	104.37	117.58	0.00	0.00
山　　东 Shandong	107.15	104.41	0.00	0.00
河　　南 Henan	141.19	99.30	0.00	0.00
湖　　北 Hubei	106.13	98.93	127.97	95.26
湖　　南 Hunan	106.33	105.94	162.86	125.00
广　　东 Guangdong	0.00	0.00	0.00	0.00
广　　西 Guangxi	97.85	90.48	0.00	89.44
海　　南 Hainan	0.00	0.00	0.00	0.00
重　　庆 Chongqing	111.11	0.00	0.00	0.00
四　　川 Sichuan	97.46	102.83	111.43	103.28
贵　　州 Guizhou	95.89	0.00	0.00	0.00
云　　南 Yunnan	101.77	99.18	108.01	0.00
陕　　西 Shaanxi	0.00	102.00	118.98	0.00
甘　　肃 Gansu	86.12	95.55	0.00	
青　　海 Qinghai	18.54		0.00	
宁　　夏 Ningxia	90.11	0.00	0.00	0.00
新　　疆 Xinjiang	0.00	97.78	0.00	0.00

2—9 续表 33 continued 33

地　区 Region	花卉 Flower		花卉 Flower 康乃馨 Carnation	
	2004	2005	2004	2005
全　国 National	**94.65**	**97.02**	**112.47**	**106.36**
北　京 Beijing	98.68	97.00	0.00	0.00
天　津 Tianjin	99.30	87.13	0.00	0.00
河　北 Hebei	0.00	0	0.00	0.00
山　西 Shanxi	0.00	0	0.00	0.00
内蒙古 Inner Mongolia	0.00	0	0.00	0.00
辽　宁 Liaoning	0.00	0	0.00	0.00
吉　林 Jilin	0.00	0	0.00	0.00
黑龙江 Heilongjiang	0.00	0	0.00	0.00
上　海 Shanghai	96.56	92.22	0.00	0.00
江　苏 Jiangsu	100.00	105.61	99.99	99.99
浙　江 Zhejiang	0.00	100	0.00	0.00
安　徽 Anhui	0.00	0	0.00	0.00
福　建 Fujian	68.76	103.39	0.00	0.00
江　西 Jiangxi	0.00	0	0.00	0.00
山　东 Shandong	79.22	105.13	98.00	96.30
河　南 Henan	0.00	0	0.00	0.00
湖　北 Hubei	0.00	0	0.00	0.00
湖　南 Hunan	0.00	0	0.00	0.00
广　东 Guangdong	119.31	95.96	0.00	0.00
广　西 Guangxi	0.00	0	0.00	0.00
海　南 Hainan	93.70	101.53	0.00	0.00
重　庆 Chongqing	0.00	0	0.00	0.00
四　川 Sichuan	0.00	0	0.00	0.00
贵　州 Guizhou	0.00	0	0.00	0.00
云　南 Yunnan	105.92	100.22	110.62	106.66
陕　西 Shaanxi	0.00	0	0.00	0.00
甘　肃 Gansu	85.03	79.06	0.00	92.03
青　海 Qinghai	0.00		0.00	
宁　夏 Ningxia	0.00	0	0.00	0.00
新　疆 Xinjiang	0.00	0	0.00	0.00

2—9 续表 34 continued 34

地区 Region	水果 Fruit		水果 Fruit 苹果 Apples	
	2004	2005	2004	2005
全国 National	**98.63**	**107.41**	**102.50**	**114.55**
北京 Beijing	101.33	113.69	89.14	108.87
天津 Tianjin	107.23	111.65	104.76	117.63
河北 Hebei	92.88	113.25	92.77	111.72
山西 Shanxi	100.90	104.46	100.38	105.82
内蒙古 Inner Mongolia	99.03	102.99	97.24	106.38
辽宁 Liaoning	116.23	100.61	106.28	101.30
吉林 Jilin	128.22	95.21	0.00	0.00
黑龙江 Heilongjiang	0.00	0.00	0.00	0.00
上海 Shanghai	111.17	105.84	0.00	0.00
江苏 Jiangsu	113.83	100.34	0.00	100.00
浙江 Zhejiang	101.23	119.63	0.00	0.00
安徽 Anhui	100.81	112.18	0.00	0.00
福建 Fujian	102.15	110.59	0.00	0.00
江西 Jiangxi	0.00	0.00	0.00	0.00
山东 Shandong	113.50	113.89	104.46	111.57
河南 Henan	112.15	117.98	101.93	117.52
湖北 Hubei	111.04	108.37	0.00	0.00
湖南 Hunan	85.50	115.83	0.00	0.00
广东 Guangdong	83.19	103.13	0.00	106.63
广西 Guangxi	90.96	92.36	0.00	0.00
海南 Hainan	113.32	102.85	0.00	0.00
重庆 Chongqing	103.04	103.36	0.00	0.00
四川 Sichuan	100.96	106.05	92.59	0.00
贵州 Guizhou	103.75	102.65	0.00	0.00
云南 Yunnan	87.75	103.75	88.35	0.00
陕西 Shaanxi	99.00	115.48	98.82	116.09
甘肃 Gansu	106.07	106.95	97.07	103.89
青海 Qinghai	0.00		0.00	
宁夏 Ningxia	119.24	105.69	81.81	82.27
新疆 Xinjiang	119.09	106.45	123.64	101.07

2—9 续表 35 continued 35

地　区 Region	水果 Fruit			
	梨 Pears		柑桔 Citruses	
	2004	2005	2004	2005
全　国 National	**95.31**	**104.53**	**94.73**	**104.91**
北　京 Beijing	104.37	106.22	0.00	0.00
天　津 Tianjin	82.80	97.66	0.00	0.00
河　北 Hebei	87.70	110.80	0.00	0.00
山　西 Shanxi	89.44	98.79	0.00	0.00
内蒙古 Inner Mongolia	91.66	100.12	0.00	0.00
辽　宁 Liaoning	103.29	102.78	0.00	0.00
吉　林 Jilin	113.74	78.84	0.00	0.00
黑龙江 Heilongjiang	0.00	0.00	0.00	0.00
上　海 Shanghai	0.00	100.00	127.40	115.99
江　苏 Jiangsu	110.78	100.00	100.00	100.00
浙　江 Zhejiang	0.00	103.65	100.59	112.32
安　徽 Anhui	104.60	0.00	102.04	111.11
福　建 Fujian	0.00	0.00	103.77	103.03
江　西 Jiangxi	0.00	0.00	113.59	101.64
山　东 Shandong	112.03	100.28	0.00	0.00
河　南 Henan	84.00	95.24	0.00	0.00
湖　北 Hubei	0.00	0.00	106.32	107.69
湖　南 Hunan	0.00	0.00	84.39	112.40
广　东 Guangdong	94.64	113.10	106.94	101.28
广　西 Guangxi	95.92	155.54	102.93	104.19
海　南 Hainan	0.00	0.00	0.00	0.00
重　庆 Chongqing	107.58	109.22	100.02	102.38
四　川 Sichuan	102.23	110.87	97.40	103.25
贵　州 Guizhou	96.36	112.00	103.51	104.97
云　南 Yunnan	60.00	100.12	84.20	101.68
陕　西 Shaanxi	95.71	107.50	0.00	0.00
甘　肃 Gansu	116.00	113.30	0.00	0.00
青　海 Qinghai	0.00		0.00	
宁　夏 Ningxia	132.94	0.00	0.00	0.00
新　疆 Xinjiang	100.01	99.19	0.00	0.00

2—9 续表 36 continued 36

地　区 Region	水果 Fruit			
	红富士苹果 Hongfushi apples		国光苹果 Guoguang apples	
	2004	2005	2004	2005
全　国 National	**102.48**	**112.23**	**98.21**	**105.47**
北　京 Beijing	85.77	102.01	100.31	153.13
天　津 Tianjin	113.33	112.02	0.00	0.00
河　北 Hebei	97.60	112.08	81.55	110.89
山　西 Shanxi	101.52	103.03	94.51	109.53
内蒙古 Inner Mongolia	0.00	106.38	93.75	0.00
辽　宁 Liaoning	120.26	105.78	92.31	95.98
吉　林 Jilin	0.00	0.00	0.00	0.00
黑龙江 Heilongjiang	0.00	0.00	0.00	0.00
上　海 Shanghai	0.00	0.00	0.00	0.00
江　苏 Jiangsu	100.00	100.00	100.00	100.00
浙　江 Zhejiang	0.00	99.01	0.00	0.00
安　徽 Anhui	0.00	0.00	0.00	0.00
福　建 Fujian	0.00	0.00	0.00	0.00
江　西 Jiangxi	0.00	0.00	0.00	0.00
山　东 Shandong	104.32	111.66	106.04	110.64
河　南 Henan	101.93	117.52	0.00	0.00
湖　北 Hubei	0.00	0.00	0.00	0.00
湖　南 Hunan	0.00	0.00	0.00	0.00
广　东 Guangdong	0.00	0.00	0.00	0.00
广　西 Guangxi	0.00	0.00	0.00	0.00
海　南 Hainan	0.00	0.00	0.00	0.00
重　庆 Chongqing	0.00	101.11	0.00	0.00
四　川 Sichuan	0.00	0.00	92.59	0.00
贵　州 Guizhou	0.00	0.00	0.00	0.00
云　南 Yunnan	87.07	0.00	0.00	0.00
陕　西 Shaanxi	98.15	114.99	0.00	100.00
甘　肃 Gansu	93.65	106.86	100.02	91.29
青　海 Qinghai	97.61		42.44	
宁　夏 Ningxia	81.81	71.27	0.00	81.00
新　疆 Xinjiang	123.64	101.07	0.00	0.00

2—9 续表 37 continued 37

地　区 Region	水果 Fruit			
	秦冠苹果 Qinguan apples		香蕉苹果 Banana apples	
	2004	2005	2004	2005
全　国 National	**108.62**	**102.19**	**105.10**	**113.33**
北　京 Beijing	0.00	0.00	160.00	100.00
天　津 Tianjin	0.00	0.00	87.06	120.88
河　北 Hebei	0.00	0.00	0.00	0.00
山　西 Shanxi	102.32	114.22	0.00	102.12
内蒙古 Inner Mongolia	112.50	0.00	0.00	0.00
辽　宁 Liaoning	0.00	0.00	0.00	0.00
吉　林 Jilin	0.00	0.00	0.00	0.00
黑龙江 Heilongjiang	0.00	0.00	0.00	0.00
上　海 Shanghai	0.00	0.00	0.00	0.00
江　苏 Jiangsu	0.00		0.00	
浙　江 Zhejiang	0.00	0.00	0.00	0.00
安　徽 Anhui	0.00	0.00	0.00	0.00
福　建 Fujian	0.00	0.00	0.00	0.00
江　西 Jiangxi	0.00	0.00	0.00	0.00
山　东 Shandong	97.41	100.00	94.04	120.26
河　南 Henan	109.40	89.42	110.56	129.40
湖　北 Hubei	0.00	0.00	0.00	0.00
湖　南 Hunan	0.00	0.00	0.00	0.00
广　东 Guangdong	0.00	0.00	0.00	0.00
广　西 Guangxi	0.00	0.00	0.00	0.00
海　南 Hainan	0.00	0.00	0.00	0.00
重　庆 Chongqing	0.00	0.00	0.00	0.00
四　川 Sichuan	0.00	0.00	0.00	0.00
贵　州 Guizhou	0.00	0.00	0.00	0.00
云　南 Yunnan	91.86	0.00	0.00	0.00
陕　西 Shaanxi	109.48	134.00	0.00	0.00
甘　肃 Gansu	79.06	108.31	114.75	100.00
青　海 Qinghai	0.00		0.00	
宁　夏 Ningxia	0.00	0.00	0.00	0.00
新　疆 Xinjiang	0.00	0.00	0.00	0.00

2—9 续表 38　　　　continued 38

地　区 Region	水果 Fruit					
	雪花梨 Snowflake pears		鸭梨 Ya-pears		酥梨 Soft-pears	
	2004	2005	2004	2005	2004	2005
全　国 National	**93.96**	**104.66**	**98.29**	**104.82**	**95.31**	**103.32**
北　京 Beijing	0.00	115.63	104.37	101.60	0.00	103.21
天　津 Tianjin	86.18	87.48	80.33	103.50	0.00	0.00
河　北 Hebei	88.64	114.93	86.60	105.96	0.00	0.00
山　西 Shanxi	0.00	0.00	0.00	125.00	89.44	98.79
内蒙古 Inner Mongolia	0.00	0.00	0.00	104.58	0.00	0.00
辽　宁 Liaoning	0.00	0.00	0.00	0.00	119.77	88.50
吉　林 Jilin	0.00	0.00	0.00	0.00	0.00	0.00
黑龙江 Heilongjiang	0.00	0.00	0.00	0.00	0.00	0.00
上　海 Shanghai	0.00	0.00	0.00	0.00	0.00	0.00
江　苏 Jiangsu	100.00	100.00	0.00	100.00	0.00	100.00
浙　江 Zhejiang	81.02	105.26	105.41	0.00	0.00	0.00
安　徽 Anhui	0.00	0.00	0.00	0.00	104.60	0.00
福　建 Fujian	0.00	110.74	0.00	0.00	0.00	129.20
江　西 Jiangxi	111.11	0.00	0.00	0.00	0.00	0.00
山　东 Shandong	100.00	100.38	112.03	100.28	105.41	116.67
河　南 Henan	0.00	92.93	85.71	100.00	84.00	95.24
湖　北 Hubei	103.92	93.94	109.39	100.00	0.00	0.00
湖　南 Hunan	94.23	97.54	85.94	100.00	0.00	0.00
广　东 Guangdong	0.00	0.00	0.00	0.00	0.00	0.00
广　西 Guangxi	69.44	0.00	0.00	0.00	0.00	0.00
海　南 Hainan	0.00	0.00	0.00	0.00	0.00	0.00
重　庆 Chongqing	107.58	110.84	0.00	104.36	0.00	0.00
四　川 Sichuan	99.58	106.77	95.74	162.38	106.25	0.00
贵　州 Guizhou	104.73	0.00	96.23	0.00	100.00	112.00
云　南 Yunnan	60.00	100.00	0.00	0.00	0.00	100.92
陕　西 Shaanxi	97.40	101.61	0.00	100.00	95.66	111.68
甘　肃 Gansu	108.08		0.00		121.65	118.27
青　海 Qinghai	0.00		0.00		0.00	
宁　夏 Ningxia	0.00	100.00	0.00	0.00	132.94	142.86
新　疆 Xinjiang	100.01	0.00	0.00	0.00	0.00	0.00

2—9 续表 39 continued 39

地　区 Region	水果 Fruit			
	西瓜 Watermelons		甜瓜 Muskmelons	
	2004	2005	2004	2005
全　国 National	**110.00**	**112.96**	**107.34**	**110.07**
北　京 Beijing	106.41	116.27	103.14	104.04
天　津 Tianjin	95.39	108.12	0.00	0.00
河　北 Hebei	131.40	112.52	115.96	117.61
山　西 Shanxi	123.57	106.32	94.69	104.56
内蒙古 Inner Mongolia	101.17	103.17	90.19	98.09
辽　宁 Liaoning	204.65	92.32	122.24	104.69
吉　林 Jilin	131.10	96.51	0.00	86.22
黑龙江 Heilongjiang	104.41	95.26	0.00	108.96
上　海 Shanghai	124.54	96.45	116.05	103.28
江　苏 Jiangsu	0.00	100.00	0.00	100.00
浙　江 Zhejiang	94.29	116.29	110.51	108.46
安　徽 Anhui	109.91	119.16	112.85	0.00
福　建 Fujian	99.73	135.11	99.61	105.30
江　西 Jiangxi	95.07	115.74	102.44	123.09
山　东 Shandong	119.75	119.85	118.78	116.86
河　南 Henan	136.44	121.11	150.45	106.86
湖　北 Hubei	128.02	110.82	97.78	112.10
湖　南 Hunan	87.43	134.01	93.38	107.45
广　东 Guangdong	82.63	104.76	78.83	139.86
广　西 Guangxi	88.23	120.64	119.92	0.00
海　南 Hainan	116.12	99.70	110.31	108.70
重　庆 Chongqing	120.51	105.26	0.00	0.00
四　川 Sichuan	91.69	102.35	0.00	0.00
贵　州 Guizhou	104.88	99.06	100.00	0.00
云　南 Yunnan	94.14	137.71	0.00	124.68
陕　西 Shaanxi	114.81	180.45	79.50	0.00
甘　肃 Gansu	140.45	106.91	101.46	106.79
青　海 Qinghai	0.00		0.00	
宁　夏 Ningxia	126.04	114.41	0.00	0.00
新　疆 Xinjiang	95.98	202.02	86.37	102.90

2—9 续表 40 continued 40

地 区 Region	水果 Fruit			
	香瓜 Musk melons		草莓 Strawberries	
	2004	2005	2004	2005
全 国 National	**110.86**	**105.67**	**105.37**	**99.36**
北 京 Beijing	0.00	0.00	0.00	100.00
天 津 Tianjin	0.00	0.00	0.00	0.00
河 北 Hebei	0.00	0.00	101.81	110.85
山 西 Shanxi	178.10	105.00	105.26	105.20
内蒙古 Inner Mongolia	149.99	0.00	0.00	0.00
辽 宁 Liaoning	0.00	0.00	84.92	92.40
吉 林 Jilin	98.60	102.50	82.08	102.81
黑龙江 Heilongjiang	108.18	114.56	0.00	0.00
上 海 Shanghai	0.00	0.00	0.00	0.00
江 苏 Jiangsu	0.00		0.00	
浙 江 Zhejiang	0.00	100.04	117.81	125.89
安 徽 Anhui	0.00	118.75	0.00	104.00
福 建 Fujian	0.00	108.72	0.00	105.91
江 西 Jiangxi	109.05	112.50	0.00	0.00
山 东 Shandong	102.06	0.00	120.65	95.91
河 南 Henan	0.00	0.00	0.00	98.24
湖 北 Hubei	0.00	87.99	0.00	0.00
湖 南 Hunan	94.79	106.05	102.23	92.05
广 东 Guangdong	106.30	106.00	0.00	0.00
广 西 Guangxi	126.20	106.63	0.00	0.00
海 南 Hainan	100.00	99.42	0.00	0.00
重 庆 Chongqing	0.00	0.00	0.00	0.00
四 川 Sichuan	0.00	0.00	138.74	99.17
贵 州 Guizhou	0.00	0.00	97.30	92.55
云 南 Yunnan	0.00	0.00	0.00	0.00
陕 西 Shaanxi	0.00	0.00	158.67	0.00
甘 肃 Gansu	0.00		0.00	79.37
青 海 Qinghai	0.00		0.00	
宁 夏 Ningxia	0.00	0.00	0.00	0.00
新 疆 Xinjiang	0.00	0.00	0.00	0.00

2—9 续表 41　　continued 41

地　区 Region	水果 Fruit 桃 Peachs 2004	2005	杏 Apricots 2004	2005
全　国 National	**96.66**	**109.93**	**99.61**	**89.10**
北　京 Beijing	96.64	134.24	95.83	94.63
天　津 Tianjin	92.21	113.11	0.00	0.00
河　北 Hebei	75.61	115.64	142.85	98.97
山　西 Shanxi	96.39	103.60	95.14	91.43
内蒙古 Inner Mongolia	0.00	0.00	0.00	121.72
辽　宁 Liaoning	93.93	101.04	117.85	0.00
吉　林 Jilin	0.00	100.00	0.00	103.70
黑龙江 Heilongjiang	0.00	0.00	0.00	0.00
上　海 Shanghai	100.25	103.24	0.00	0.00
江　苏 Jiangsu	93.56	100.00	0.00	
浙　江 Zhejiang	105.06	108.26	0.00	90.23
安　徽 Anhui	85.72	102.07	100.00	104.56
福　建 Fujian	85.06	105.71	0.00	0.00
江　西 Jiangxi	104.66	99.00	0.00	0.00
山　东 Shandong	106.90	109.88	101.44	95.45
河　南 Henan	108.32	119.91	0.00	83.24
湖　北 Hubei	95.34	97.56	0.00	0.00
湖　南 Hunan	86.55	110.35	109.25	73.58
广　东 Guangdong	83.04	130.02	0.00	0.00
广　西 Guangxi	59.13	99.82	0.00	0.00
海　南 Hainan	0.00	0.00	0.00	0.00
重　庆 Chongqing	105.81	100.00	111.11	0.00
四　川 Sichuan	109.34	107.37	111.11	114.29
贵　州 Guizhou	93.47	101.29	120.00	0.00
云　南 Yunnan	102.74	114.47	114.58	100.00
陕　西 Shaanxi	90.43	112.25	88.87	0.00
甘　肃 Gansu	95.81	115.97	94.20	98.65
青　海 Qinghai	83.58		91.29	
宁　夏 Ningxia	143.59	81.90	0.00	0.00
新　疆 Xinjiang	100.00	96.67	85.78	96.50

2—9 续表 42 continued 42

地区 Region	水果 Fruit					
	葡萄 Grapes		红枣 Chinese dates		柿子 Persimmons	
	2004	2005	2004	2005	2004	2005
全国 National	**95.36**	**112.53**	**108.02**	**95.83**	**92.29**	**104.20**
北京 Beijing	91.39	116.68	124.85	115.74	96.63	104.28
天津 Tianjin	122.58	132.70	0.00	104.25	0.00	0.00
河北 Hebei	85.65	125.49	114.67	103.75	105.06	103.01
山西 Shanxi	100.19	95.18	89.87	99.18	97.79	105.14
内蒙古 Inner Mongolia	0.00	0.00	0.00	0.00	0.00	0.00
辽宁 Liaoning	111.02	100.00	54.48	0.00	0.00	0.00
吉林 Jilin	113.19	101.04	0.00	0.00	0.00	0.00
黑龙江 Heilongjiang	0.00	0.00	0.00	0.00	0.00	0.00
上海 Shanghai	0.00	123.77	0.00	0.00	0.00	0.00
江苏 Jiangsu	97.87	100.00	100.00	100.00	0.00	
浙江 Zhejiang	84.91	120.48	162.96	100.89	96.32	105.26
安徽 Anhui	0.00	125.00	100.00	0.00	84.50	101.70
福建 Fujian	96.26	102.26	0.00	0.00	87.25	110.62
江西 Jiangxi	0.00	0.00	113.64	100.55	0.00	88.33
山东 Shandong	116.58	113.90	105.04	93.54	87.41	90.55
河南 Henan	0.00	112.09	0.00	0.00	269.22	115.95
湖北 Hubei	0.00	101.25	0.00	0.00	99.51	108.14
湖南 Hunan	81.59	104.12	90.88	99.40	100.28	133.08
广东 Guangdong	0.00	0.00	0.00	0.00	103.85	108.49
广西 Guangxi	92.00	104.87	0.00	0.00	115.01	98.67
海南 Hainan	0.00	0.00	0.00	0.00	0.00	0.00
重庆 Chongqing	124.37	0.00	0.00	0.00	106.67	0.00
四川 Sichuan	104.85	103.74	127.85	0.00	105.46	107.89
贵州 Guizhou	119.64	108.61	0.00	0.00	0.00	80.09
云南 Yunnan	86.78	97.22	0.00	0.00	103.96	100.89
陕西 Shaanxi	114.17	100.87	90.88	84.19	97.13	107.55
甘肃 Gansu	65.21		101.01		86.18	93.84
青海 Qinghai	0.00		0.00		0.00	
宁夏 Ningxia	118.13	89.52	75.00	109.95	0.00	0.00
新疆 Xinjiang	106.14	108.82	133.77	85.77	0.00	0.00

2—9 续表 43　　continued 43

地　区 Region	其他水果 Other fruits		其他水果 Other fruits 香蕉 Bananas		其他水果 Other fruits 菠萝 Pineapples	
	2004	2005	2004	2005	2004	2005
全　国 National	**101.61**	**103.66**	**114.25**	**92.78**	**100.36**	**108.26**
北　京 Beijing	97.44	115.04				
天　津 Tianjin	123.33	116.96				
河　北 Hebei	93.08	114.41				
山　西 Shanxi	94.87	101.60				
内蒙古 Inner Mongolia	0.00	121.72				
辽　宁 Liaoning	101.66	100.28				
吉　林 Jilin	113.19	101.04	0.00	142.86	0.00	0.00
黑龙江 Heilongjiang	0.00	0.00	0.00	0.00	0.00	0.00
上　海 Shanghai	100.25	112.08	0.00	0.00	0.00	0.00
江　苏 Jiangsu	0.00		0.00		0.00	
浙　江 Zhejiang	0.00	111.17	0.00	0.00	0.00	0.00
安　徽 Anhui	85.72	103.32	0.00	0.00	0.00	0.00
福　建 Fujian	92.25	108.43	115.87	107.75	125.63	0.00
江　西 Jiangxi	108.18	97.24				
山　东 Shandong	109.64	106.68				
河　南 Henan	108.32	116.78	0.00	0.00	0.00	0.00
湖　北 Hubei	95.34	97.56	0.00	0.00	0.00	0.00
湖　南 Hunan	85.87	106.51	0.00	0.00	0.00	0.00
广　东 Guangdong	73.01	103.37	102.22	105.27	108.65	111.14
广　西 Guangxi	82.94	81.93	107.00	82.21	116.67	0.00
海　南 Hainan	115.98	99.80	120.15	97.23	91.66	113.14
重　庆 Chongqing	115.09	100.00	101.02	106.67	0.00	0.00
四　川 Sichuan	106.64	109.72	110.06	104.52	0.00	0.00
贵　州 Guizhou	104.10	104.26	0.00	0.00	0.00	0.00
云　南 Yunnan	98.18	106.56	113.96	88.85	100.30	0.00
陕　西 Shaanxi	103.80	112.41				
甘　肃 Gansu	87.47	107.37				
青　海 Qinghai	0.00					
宁　夏 Ningxia	116.07	92.44				
新　疆 Xinjiang	105.39	105.14				

2—9 续表 44 continued 44

地区 Region	茶叶 Tea					
	红毛茶 Black tea		绿毛茶 Green tea		乌龙茶 Oolong tea	
	2004	2005	2004	2005	2004	2005
全国 National	**109.41**	**112.57**	**110.48**	**110.95**	**107.50**	**95.89**
北京 Beijing	0.00	0.00	0.00	0.00	0.00	0.00
天津 Tianjin	0.00	0.00	0.00	0.00	0.00	0.00
河北 Hebei	0.00	0.00	0.00	0.00	0.00	0.00
山西 Shanxi	0.00	0.00	0.00	0.00	0.00	0.00
内蒙古 Inner Mongolia	0.00	0.00	0.00	0.00	0.00	0.00
辽宁 Liaoning	0.00	0.00	0.00	0.00	0.00	0.00
吉林 Jilin	0.00	0.00	0.00	0.00	0.00	0.00
黑龙江 Heilongjiang	0.00	0.00	0.00	0.00	0.00	0.00
上海 Shanghai	0.00	0.00	0.00	0.00	0.00	0.00
江苏 Jiangsu	100.00	117.92	102.05	84.26	0.00	
浙江 Zhejiang	0.00	0.00	112.51	122.47	0.00	0.00
安徽 Anhui	97.70	112.11	102.11	112.41	0.00	0.00
福建 Fujian	108.64	0.00	99.34	106.02	113.48	98.35
江西 Jiangxi	0.00	92.86	124.29	81.17	0.00	0.00
山东 Shandong	0.00	0.00	104.85	0.00	0.00	0.00
河南 Henan	0.00	0.00	141.26	105.39	0.00	0.00
湖北 Hubei	0.00	0.00	119.75	98.95	0.00	0.00
湖南 Hunan	39.53	141.42	138.85	105.32	0.00	0.00
广东 Guangdong	0.00	0.00	103.58	103.97	105.75	105.04
广西 Guangxi	0.00	0.00	105.50	106.42	0.00	0.00
海南 Hainan	0.00	0.00	0.00	0.00	0.00	0.00
重庆 Chongqing	0.00	0.00	107.69	0.00	0.00	0.00
四川 Sichuan	0.00	0.00	121.46	115.57	0.00	0.00
贵州 Guizhou	0.00	0.00	97.08	105.33	0.00	0.00
云南 Yunnan	117.51	110.08	108.17	123.06	0.00	0.00
陕西 Shaanxi	0.00	0.00	93.23	0.00	0.00	0.00
甘肃 Gansu	0.00		0.00		0.00	
青海 Qinghai	0.00		0.00		0.00	
宁夏 Ningxia	0.00	0.00	0.00	0.00	0.00	0.00
新疆 Xinjiang	0.00	0.00	0.00	0.00	0.00	0.00

2—10 各地区林业产品生产价格指数
Indices of the Producer Prices of Forest Products by Region

(上年=100) (the preceding year=100)

地 区 Region	林业产品 Forest products		林业产品 Forest products: 竹木采运 Felling and transport of bamboo and wood		林业产品 Forest products: 林产品的采集 Gathering of forest products	
	2004	2005	2004	2005	2004	2005
全 国 National	**104.62**	**104.79**	**104.81**	**103.17**	**104.05**	**106.15**
北 京 Beijing	111.40	108.26	0.00	0.00	111.40	108.26
天 津 Tianjin	98.80	101.95	0.00	0.00	98.80	101.95
河 北 Hebei	112.34	100.58	0.00	0.00	112.34	100.58
山 西 Shanxi	106.33	102.18	105.56	99.81	107.49	104.05
内蒙古 Inner Mongolia	98.97	103.18	103.69	103.18	0.00	0.00
辽 宁 Liaoning	95.05	101.67	90.10	106.13	95.35	93.33
吉 林 Jilin	250.55	106.06	0.00	106.06	250.55	0.00
黑龙江 Heilongjiang	83.75	99.64	83.75	99.64	0.00	0.00
上 海 Shanghai	0.00	0.00	0.00	0.00	0.00	0.00
江 苏 Jiangsu	99.36	104.82	101.95	104.28	94.38	102.11
浙 江 Zhejiang	98.75	101.28	98.75	99.79	0.00	100.28
安 徽 Anhui	102.78	107.39	106.26	107.65	75.52	105.33
福 建 Fujian	102.30	104.00	102.88	105.45	102.78	103.85
江 西 Jiangxi	109.06	108.14	109.14	108.38	107.82	103.84
山 东 Shandong	110.24	101.01	106.35	103.78	111.70	99.97
河 南 Henan	103.81	104.94	103.81	104.94	0.00	0.00
湖 北 Hubei	100.09	104.77	100.09	104.77	0.00	0.00
湖 南 Hunan	111.10	99.84	111.23	98.86	110.86	101.76
广 东 Guangdong	108.26	103.93	107.59	103.16	111.23	105.53
广 西 Guangxi	105.29	98.41	105.28	98.42	107.63	94.59
海 南 Hainan	106.26	106.79	103.33	99.41	106.72	107.94
重 庆 Chongqing	0.00	100.60	0.00	104.08	0.00	97.89
四 川 Sichuan	104.37	102.04	102.52	103.33	97.60	104.43
贵 州 Guizhou	106.00	102.79	103.41	102.62	109.84	103.04
云 南 Yunnan	115.79	115.34	104.33	101.59	119.70	120.04
陕 西 Shaanxi	95.09	96.93	105.53	0.00	94.90	96.93
甘 肃 Gansu	100.01	99.68	0.00	0.00	100.01	99.68
青 海 Qinghai	0.00		0.00		0.00	
宁 夏 Ningxia	0.00	0.00	0.00	0.00	0.00	0.00
新 疆 Xinjiang	98.77	87.29	95.40	90.10	104.71	102.10

2—10 续表 1 continued 1

地　区 Region	木材采运 Felling and transport of wood				竹材采运 Felling and transport of bamboo	
	原木 Log		薪材 Firewood			
	2004	2005	2004	2005	2004	2005
全　国 National	**104. 19**	**103. 17**	**104. 31**	**106. 85**	**108. 89**	**103. 67**
北　京 Beijing	0. 00	0. 00	0. 00	0. 00	0. 00	0. 00
天　津 Tianjin	0. 00	0. 00	0. 00	0. 00	0. 00	0. 00
河　北 Hebei	0. 00	0. 00	0. 00	100. 97	0. 00	0. 00
山　西 Shanxi	105. 56	99. 81	0. 00	0. 00	0. 00	0. 00
内蒙古 Inner Mongolia	104. 79	103. 90	100. 13	100. 88	0. 00	0. 00
辽　宁 Liaoning	96. 28	106. 13	83. 91	0. 00	0. 00	0. 00
吉　林 Jilin	0. 00	106. 06	0. 00	0. 00	0. 00	0. 00
黑龙江 Heilongjiang	83. 75	99. 64	0. 00	100. 00	0. 00	0. 00
上　海 Shanghai	0. 00	0. 00	0. 00	0. 00	0. 00	0. 00
江　苏 Jiangsu	102. 09	103. 53	0. 00		99. 93	101. 33
浙　江 Zhejiang	96. 91	101. 23	0. 00	100. 12	113. 77	99. 89
安　徽 Anhui	103. 92	106. 74	106. 17	107. 92	114. 24	110. 39
福　建 Fujian	98. 28	104. 78	107. 18	108. 40	106. 81	104. 13
江　西 Jiangxi	109. 47	108. 47	110. 07	101. 74	102. 70	106. 79
山　东 Shandong	106. 35	103. 78	103. 17	0. 00	0. 00	0. 00
河　南 Henan	103. 81	104. 94	101. 74	0. 00	0. 00	0. 00
湖　北 Hubei	105. 34	104. 28	96. 18	100. 96	85. 16	106. 18
湖　南 Hunan	104. 91	97. 54	90. 45	94. 20	124. 40	101. 60
广　东 Guangdong	106. 52	104. 30	93. 66	102. 17	110. 94	101. 24
广　西 Guangxi	105. 28	98. 43	101. 13	98. 79	110. 42	96. 31
海　南 Hainan	100. 51	100. 00	107. 69	97. 96	101. 79	101. 17
重　庆 Chongqing	0. 00	104. 08	0. 00	98. 96	0. 00	0. 00
四　川 Sichuan	103. 67	97. 58	0. 00	0. 00	100. 68	112. 52
贵　州 Guizhou	103. 15	102. 05	108. 68	0. 00	104. 75	105. 56
云　南 Yunnan	99. 87	99. 76	103. 30	104. 88	134. 98	114. 11
陕　西 Shaanxi	0. 00	0. 00	111. 06	0. 00	100. 40	0. 00
甘　肃 Gansu	0. 00	0. 00	0. 00		0. 00	0. 00
青　海 Qinghai	0. 00		94. 95		0. 00	
宁　夏 Ningxia	0. 00	0. 00	0. 00	0. 00	0. 00	0. 00
新　疆 Xinjiang	95. 94	90. 10	88. 76	0. 00	0. 00	0. 00

2—10 续表 2 continued 2

地　区 Region	林产品采集 Gathering of forest products					
	橡胶 Rubber		油桐籽 Seeds of tung oil tree		油茶籽 Seeds of tea-oil tree	
	2004	2005	2004	2005	2004	2005
全　国 National	**117.47**	**114.44**	**114.47**	**118.64**	**115.56**	**101.09**
北　京 Beijing	0.00	0.00	0.00	0.00	0.00	0.00
天　津 Tianjin	0.00	0.00	0.00	0.00	0.00	0.00
河　北 Hebei	0.00	0.00	0.00	0.00	0.00	0.00
山　西 Shanxi	0.00	0.00	0.00	0.00	0.00	0.00
内蒙古 Inner Mongolia	0.00	0.00	0.00	0.00	0.00	0.00
辽　宁 Liaoning	0.00	0.00	0.00	0.00	0.00	0.00
吉　林 Jilin	0.00	0.00	0.00	0.00	0.00	0.00
黑龙江 Heilongjiang	0.00	0.00	0.00	0.00	0.00	0.00
上　海 Shanghai	0.00	0.00	0.00	0.00	0.00	0.00
江　苏 Jiangsu	0.00		0.00	0.00	0.00	0.00
浙　江 Zhejiang	0.00	0.00	0.00	0.00	0.00	100.00
安　徽 Anhui	0.00	0.00	0.00	0.00	0.00	0.00
福　建 Fujian	0.00	0.00	102.22	93.91	100.00	0.00
江　西 Jiangxi	0.00	0.00	102.15	96.61	111.73	103.84
山　东 Shandong	0.00	0.00	0.00	0.00	0.00	0.00
河　南 Henan	0.00	0.00	0.00	0.00	0.00	107.14
湖　北 Hubei	0.00	0.00	114.10	116.30	0.00	0.00
湖　南 Hunan	0.00	0.00	129.02	130.69	111.92	99.13
广　东 Guangdong	0.00	0.00	0.00	0.00	116.67	109.22
广　西 Guangxi	0.00	0.00	167.18	99.98	133.98	112.03
海　南 Hainan	112.28	109.68	0.00	0.00	0.00	0.00
重　庆 Chongqing	0.00	0.00	0.00	102.25	106.67	95.24
四　川 Sichuan	0.00	0.00	103.91	124.63	100.00	0.00
贵　州 Guizhou	0.00	0.00	109.52	105.79	0.00	0.00
云　南 Yunnan	126.65	122.72	124.22	117.31	0.00	0.00
陕　西 Shaanxi	0.00	0.00	93.40	0.00	0.00	0.00
甘　肃 Gansu	0.00		0.00		0.00	103.00
青　海 Qinghai	0.00		0.00		0.00	
宁　夏 Ningxia	0.00	0.00	0.00	0.00	0.00	0.00
新　疆 Xinjiang	0.00	0.00	0.00	0.00	0.00	0.00

2—10 续表 3　　　　continued 3

地　区 Region	林产品采集 Gathering of forest products			
	棕片 Palm fibre		松脂 Rosin	
	2004	2005	2004	2005
全　国 National	**102.30**	**100.85**	**107.74**	**125.63**
北　京 Beijing	0.00	0.00	0.00	0.00
天　津 Tianjin	0.00	0.00	0.00	0.00
河　北 Hebei	0.00	0.00	0.00	0.00
山　西 Shanxi	0.00	0.00	0.00	0.00
内蒙古 Inner Mongolia	0.00	0.00	0.00	0.00
辽　宁 Liaoning	0.00	0.00	0.00	0.00
吉　林 Jilin	0.00	0.00	0.00	0.00
黑龙江 Heilongjiang	0.00	0.00	0.00	0.00
上　海 Shanghai	0.00	0.00	0.00	0.00
江　苏 Jiangsu	0.00		0.00	
浙　江 Zhejiang	0.00	0.00	0.00	0.00
安　徽 Anhui	0.00	0.00	0.00	128.44
福　建 Fujian	0.00	0.00	0.00	0.00
江　西 Jiangxi	96.00	100.49	106.77	0.00
山　东 Shandong	0.00	0.00	0.00	0.00
河　南 Henan	0.00	0.00	0.00	0.00
湖　北 Hubei	0.00	100.00	0.00	0.00
湖　南 Hunan	112.00	104.27	0.00	100.80
广　东 Guangdong	113.33	0.00	116.85	108.33
广　西 Guangxi	0.00	0.00	112.78	115.02
海　南 Hainan	0.00	0.00	94.40	0.00
重　庆 Chongqing	0.00	100.74	0.00	0.00
四　川 Sichuan	101.23	101.62	0.00	0.00
贵　州 Guizhou	112.50	0.00	0.00	0.00
云　南 Yunnan	80.00	80.00	121.94	135.80
陕　西 Shaanxi	0.00	0.00	0.00	0.00
甘　肃 Gansu	0.00		0.00	
青　海 Qinghai	0.00		0.00	
宁　夏 Ningxia	0.00	0.00	0.00	0.00
新　疆 Xinjiang	0.00	0.00	0.00	0.00

2—10 续表 4 continued 4

地 区 Region	林产品采集 Gathering of forest products			
	核桃 Walnut		板栗 Chinese chestnut	
	2004	2005	2004	2005
全 国 National	**102.66**	**111.31**	**96.37**	**98.80**
北 京 Beijing	106.82	136.74	115.25	91.28
天 津 Tianjin	98.80	103.23	0.00	100.00
河 北 Hebei	104.05	120.05	134.85	75.52
山 西 Shanxi	116.71	104.36	0.00	0.00
内 蒙 古 Inner Mongolia	0.00	0.00	0.00	0.00
辽 宁 Liaoning	90.28	0.00	96.44	93.33
吉 林 Jilin	61.47	116.43	0.00	0.00
黑 龙 江 Heilongjiang	0.00	0.00	0.00	0.00
上 海 Shanghai	0.00	0.00	0.00	0.00
江 苏 Jiangsu	0.00	100.00	0.00	100.44
浙 江 Zhejiang	0.00	88.36	89.65	99.99
安 徽 Anhui	129.65	94.02	64.70	110.99
福 建 Fujian	0.00	0.00	75.47	121.94
江 西 Jiangxi	0.00	0.00	91.51	94.83
山 东 Shandong	104.38	102.24	114.14	98.77
河 南 Henan	122.70	104.01	110.95	100.47
湖 北 Hubei	100.00	0.00	86.65	103.27
湖 南 Hunan	0.00	92.40	85.16	106.06
广 东 Guangdong	0.00	0.00	85.71	99.78
广 西 Guangxi	0.00	0.00	99.03	101.86
海 南 Hainan	0.00	0.00	0.00	0.00
重 庆 Chongqing	0.00	109.54	0.00	100.00
四 川 Sichuan	98.08	108.71	111.83	97.42
贵 州 Guizhou	102.69	103.36	108.08	95.71
云 南 Yunnan	113.83	114.68	124.98	90.80
陕 西 Shaanxi	111.20	129.41	105.98	77.26
甘 肃 Gansu	126.55	101.40	0.00	
青 海 Qinghai	114.29		0.00	
宁 夏 Ningxia	0.00	0.00	0.00	0.00
新 疆 Xinjiang	104.71	102.41	0.00	0.00

2－11 各地区畜牧业产品生产价格指数
Indices of the Producer Prices of Livestock Products by Region

（上年＝100） (the preceding year＝100)

地区 Region	畜牧业产品 Livestock products		畜产品 Livestock products 大牲畜 Livestock		猪 Hogs	
	2004	2005	2004	2005	2004	2005
全国 National	**111.08**	**100.52**	**104.16**	**102.09**	**112.84**	**97.65**
北京 Beijing	107.42	101.22	102.20	102.14	117.57	93.62
天津 Tianjin	113.65	103.22	100.16	102.67	125.29	104.57
河北 Hebei	112.06	100.40	102.25	100.17	125.25	98.50
山西 Shanxi	113.86	102.59	102.35	103.34	126.72	102.33
内蒙古 Inner Mongolia	112.48	103.47	107.76	103.26	119.96	103.97
辽宁 Liaoning	124.93	103.31	105.87	103.90	133.99	101.80
吉林 Jilin	111.81	98.89	104.60	99.11	116.11	97.40
黑龙江 Heilongjiang	119.57	102.01	96.85	95.88	124.47	97.71
上海 Shanghai	107.81	102.07	102.75	102.51	127.27	96.85
江苏 Jiangsu	127.44	98.47	91.00	108.77	138.92	96.89
浙江 Zhejiang	131.17	103.24	0.00	106.45	137.46	101.11
安徽 Anhui	120.18	99.71	105.25	108.01	132.86	91.37
福建 Fujian	113.90	100.90	105.40	100.08	121.77	97.40
江西 Jiangxi	125.45	98.44	108.00	108.99	126.84	97.52
山东 Shandong	115.13	102.77	103.29	104.12	128.07	97.18
河南 Henan	129.27	101.98	103.84	113.59	147.50	96.40
湖北 Hubei	128.15	100.48	103.70	102.42	132.95	98.25
湖南 Hunan	134.80	96.54	106.62	103.60	137.66	94.85
广东 Guangdong	118.08	100.81	99.36	100.50	124.86	98.14
广西 Guangxi	132.33	94.49	125.63	101.20	133.76	93.78
海南 Hainan	115.20	98.83	109.71	102.48	123.64	93.96
重庆 Chongqing	128.83	98.76	103.62	103.64	130.79	97.71
四川 Sichuan	121.50	102.26	101.99	97.95	129.71	100.32
贵州 Guizhou	111.69	100.97	104.60	104.00	112.95	100.02
云南 Yunnan	116.84	100.87	104.26	102.13	119.65	100.28
陕西 Shaanxi	115.89	96.48	109.07	97.91	132.84	98.89
甘肃 Gansu	113.66	102.70	110.50	101.58	115.89	103.04
青海 Qinghai	106.67	104.07	105.10	104.27	122.32	102.04
宁夏 Ningxia	109.22	103.47	105.48	99.80	122.59	104.92
新疆 Xinjiang	102.95	92.70	100.07	83.39	118.51	113.65

2—11 续表 1 continued 1

地 区 Region	畜牧业产品 Livestock products			
	家禽(毛重) Poultry		禽蛋 Eggs	
	2004	2005	2004	2005
全 国 National	**111.25**	**105.61**	**112.58**	**106.38**
北 京 Beijing	103.68	99.35	109.66	103.78
天 津 Tianjin	104.08	98.17	118.54	104.99
河 北 Hebei	111.27	103.92	113.91	103.08
山 西 Shanxi	103.33	100.50	111.97	102.30
内蒙古 Inner Mongolia	112.76	102.21	119.98	103.06
辽 宁 Liaoning	111.64	104.28	115.94	103.82
吉 林 Jilin	119.65	100.74	116.24	106.89
黑龙江 Heilongjiang	119.76	106.72	125.63	105.60
上 海 Shanghai	95.12	103.82	116.19	114.82
江 苏 Jiangsu	112.00	99.15	114.05	100.39
浙 江 Zhejiang	114.72	114.87	115.02	109.47
安 徽 Anhui	112.78	103.51	112.01	110.74
福 建 Fujian	113.23	104.00	116.71	106.10
江 西 Jiangxi	106.27	111.71	113.57	106.07
山 东 Shandong	104.28	106.74	114.61	106.61
河 南 Henan	114.35	98.84	117.20	104.89
湖 北 Hubei	111.52	103.88	114.08	108.67
湖 南 Hunan	116.55	111.98	116.62	112.78
广 东 Guangdong	106.23	105.26	114.83	115.16
广 西 Guangxi	111.10	103.98	103.19	108.46
海 南 Hainan	105.94	104.41	103.12	101.95
重 庆 Chongqing	117.21	104.34	111.95	103.85
四 川 Sichuan	114.40	106.53	109.33	105.32
贵 州 Guizhou	108.46	104.10	107.61	101.77
云 南 Yunnan	109.51	104.62	105.29	103.04
陕 西 Shaanxi	113.83	97.85	111.23	94.58
甘 肃 Gansu	110.84	103.60	113.16	103.57
青 海 Qinghai	101.88	103.15	108.21	108.54
宁 夏 Ningxia	109.39	123.93	111.02	109.14
新 疆 Xinjiang	106.29	104.58	94.67	102.99

2—11 续表 2 continued 2

地 区 Region	畜产品 Livestock products					
	牛 Live cattle		羊 Sheep raising		马 Horse	
	2004	2005	2004	2005	2004	2005
全 国 National	**103.93**	**101.66**	**103.72**	**101.70**	**108.63**	**105.35**
北 京 Beijing	103.63	106.96	102.44	101.48	0.00	0.00
天 津 Tianjin	99.47	103.37	97.38	104.50	0.00	0.00
河 北 Hebei	103.07	100.24	100.72	100.14	0.00	0.00
山 西 Shanxi	107.44	99.32	101.18	108.56	0.00	0.00
内蒙古 Inner Mongolia	103.34	101.93	106.99	101.75	112.37	108.86
辽 宁 Liaoning	105.33	105.56	109.27	94.72	0.00	0.00
吉 林 Jilin	100.40	99.28	98.36	97.05	0.00	108.33
黑龙江 Heilongjiang	96.58	97.94	97.48	90.96	0.00	0.00
上 海 Shanghai	0.00	0.00	0.00	0.00	0.00	0.00
江 苏 Jiangsu	100.00	108.43	0.00	0.00	0.00	
浙 江 Zhejiang	0.00	0.00	139.31	112.49	0.00	0.00
安 徽 Anhui	102.45	108.76	108.34	112.56	0.00	0.00
福 建 Fujian	102.04	99.45	114.77	101.55	0.00	0.00
江 西 Jiangxi	108.00	108.99	100.88	104.75	0.00	0.00
山 东 Shandong	103.96	103.79	102.05	105.03	0.00	0.00
河 南 Henan	104.17	112.56	102.82	116.72	0.00	0.00
湖 北 Hubei	105.99	101.80	97.70	104.50	0.00	0.00
湖 南 Hunan	108.44	103.89	105.62	103.57	125.00	0.00
广 东 Guangdong	102.73	100.97	113.42	83.33	0.00	0.00
广 西 Guangxi	129.37	107.07	105.30	97.81	0.00	99.69
海 南 Hainan	109.22	103.05	110.69	101.32	0.00	0.00
重 庆 Chongqing	101.75	103.85	111.09	102.80	0.00	0.00
四 川 Sichuan	100.04	102.32	102.75	103.42	0.00	85.00
贵 州 Guizhou	104.41	104.27	106.12	104.65	108.74	106.20
云 南 Yunnan	107.18	101.45	103.77	103.30	103.21	105.67
陕 西 Shaanxi	101.14	98.58	105.33	109.46	0.00	0.00
甘 肃 Gansu	104.58	99.54	114.58	101.53	0.00	
青 海 Qinghai	101.80	106.48	103.27	103.04	100.40	
宁 夏 Ningxia	102.61	102.16	101.76	100.43	0.00	0.00
新 疆 Xinjiang	101.05	85.55	102.00	80.65	100.00	82.36

2—11 续表 3

continued 3

地　区 Region	畜产品 Livestock products					
	牛肉 Beef		羊肉 Mutton		猪肉 Pork	
	2004	2005	2004	2005	2004	2005
全　国 National	**102.28**	**100.17**	**103.13**	**103.52**	**121.99**	**104.83**
北　京 Beijing	102.93	101.97	100.00	0.00	109.77	99.25
天　津 Tianjin		0.00	0.00	0.00	0.00	0.00
河　北 Hebei	0.00	100.00	100.00	102.08	124.78	107.24
山　西 Shanxi	100.55	120.86	107.03	103.20	110.56	106.49
内蒙古 Inner Mongolia	110.39	103.00	113.56	106.80	119.18	107.20
辽　宁 Liaoning	0.00	95.60	118.68	107.50	127.71	116.87
吉　林 Jilin	0.00	87.63	130.43	97.24	112.39	102.52
黑龙江 Heilongjiang	88.23	0.00	114.29	0.00	113.92	107.73
上　海 Shanghai	0.00	0.00	0.00	0.00	102.27	116.89
江　苏 Jiangsu	100.00	100.00	0.00	0.00	0.00	0.00
浙　江 Zhejiang	0.00	101.28	0.00	109.25	123.18	103.26
安　徽 Anhui	115.74	105.04	0.00	0.00	129.00	94.12
福　建 Fujian	111.80	111.66	0.00	98.99	121.77	101.19
江　西 Jiangxi	112.88	111.98	0.00	0.00	127.61	111.85
山　东 Shandong	105.73	106.99	95.97	105.82	122.22	102.04
河　南 Henan	0.00	0.00	0.00	0.00	117.97	107.38
湖　北 Hubei	100.00	0.00	107.58	0.00	119.25	107.53
湖　南 Hunan	0.00	104.10	100.00	110.92	128.68	107.41
广　东 Guangdong	109.09	125.00	0.00	0.00	130.65	105.30
广　西 Guangxi	0.00	101.52	0.00	0.00	115.18	97.09
海　南 Hainan	109.16	66.43	112.51	0.00	113.85	99.49
重　庆 Chongqing	0.00	0.00	106.30	0.00	115.89	104.76
四　川 Sichuan	103.35	107.01	98.17	105.47	108.36	110.13
贵　州 Guizhou	93.75	106.62	0.00	0.00	114.65	105.13
云　南 Yunnan	100.00	99.99	0.00	100.11	110.98	105.94
陕　西 Shaanxi	112.22	0.00	104.01	0.00	117.71	92.68
甘　肃 Gansu	105.49	105.23	114.45	104.69	116.69	108.32
青　海 Qinghai	0.00		102.94		107.21	
宁　夏 Ningxia	107.39	0.00	95.44	98.23	114.16	102.24
新　疆 Xinjiang	90.05	91.77	85.72	93.16	105.63	115.73

2—11 续表 4 continued 4

地　区 Region	畜产品 Livestock products					
	鸡 Chicken		鸭 Duck		鹅 Goose	
	2004	2005	2004	2005	2004	2005
全　国 National	**111.22**	**105.83**	**116.32**	**105.05**	**113.47**	**105.28**
北　京 Beijing	105.08	100.18	100.74	97.62	0.00	0.00
天　津 Tianjin	102.46	97.70	113.65	101.07	0.00	0.00
河　北 Hebei	111.28	104.01	114.12	110.09	110.55	97.95
山　西 Shanxi	103.33	100.50	0.00	0.00	0.00	0.00
内蒙古 Inner Mongolia	112.27	102.37	113.22	95.53	116.86	100.99
辽　宁 Liaoning	111.62	102.48	117.40	115.88	110.28	109.19
吉　林 Jilin	117.88	100.59	125.78	95.35	122.44	101.54
黑龙江 Heilongjiang	118.69	108.24	132.75	96.45	112.10	101.18
上　海 Shanghai	95.12	103.82	0.00	0.00	0.00	0.00
江　苏 Jiangsu	112.24	98.19	111.34	97.12	112.42	108.30
浙　江 Zhejiang	116.80	108.49	112.58	117.82	134.80	115.96
安　徽 Anhui	113.77	103.76	107.94	102.41	122.12	105.48
福　建 Fujian	113.23	102.00	114.10	106.00	100.29	117.47
江　西 Jiangxi	101.08	106.58	109.06	108.95	115.60	135.65
山　东 Shandong	103.94	106.92	108.92	105.15	102.07	104.46
河　南 Henan	114.35	98.84	116.87	98.81	109.99	103.57
湖　北 Hubei	112.52	105.55	105.83	94.32	0.00	0.00
湖　南 Hunan	111.31	112.20	121.51	109.50	123.59	119.22
广　东 Guangdong	104.96	105.23	106.60	104.68	106.58	115.78
广　西 Guangxi	109.76	104.49	114.89	102.37	122.95	101.83
海　南 Hainan	106.06	104.18	105.65	105.63	103.10	108.97
重　庆 Chongqing	114.54	106.04	119.46	103.34	116.41	102.26
四　川 Sichuan	111.89	107.50	121.35	105.55	112.16	104.43
贵　州 Guizhou	108.91	104.07	107.32	105.47	105.65	101.08
云　南 Yunnan	109.50	104.63	110.66	103.19	107.96	107.85
陕　西 Shaanxi	113.86	97.85	95.24	100.00	0.00	0.00
甘　肃 Gansu	110.84	103.60	0.00		0.00	
青　海 Qinghai	101.88	103.15	0.00		0.00	
宁　夏 Ningxia	109.39	123.93	0.00	0.00	0.00	0.00
新　疆 Xinjiang	106.29	104.58	150.94	113.46	0.00	97.31

2—11 续表 5　　　　continued 5

地　区 Region	畜产品 Livestock products					
	鸡蛋 Chicken's eggs		鸭蛋 Duck's eggs		鹅蛋 Goose's eggs	
	2004	2005	2004	2005	2004	2005
全　国 National	**112.54**	**106.52**	**113.95**	**107.01**	**105.95**	**105.68**
北　京 Beijing	109.66	103.78	0.00	0.00	0.00	0.00
天　津 Tianjin	118.54	104.99	0.00	0.00	0.00	0.00
河　北 Hebei	113.98	103.09	100.00	101.38	112.24	102.49
山　西 Shanxi	111.97	102.30	0.00	0.00	0.00	0.00
内蒙古 Inner Mongolia	119.99	103.04	110.24	105.87	118.50	107.68
辽　宁 Liaoning	115.45	103.83	125.42	103.26	115.44	108.59
吉　林 Jilin	116.90	107.81	116.58	102.52	106.87	103.30
黑龙江 Heilongjiang	125.78	105.60	118.16	102.08	115.88	108.77
上　海 Shanghai	116.19	104.24	0.00	129.62	0.00	0.00
江　苏 Jiangsu	113.99	100.37	124.75	103.33	100.14	100.00
浙　江 Zhejiang	100.39	108.67	128.61	106.53	0.00	0.00
安　徽 Anhui	112.43	110.67	109.90	111.07	0.00	0.00
福　建 Fujian	111.36	105.89	120.00	107.80	0.00	102.82
江　西 Jiangxi	111.32	102.80	114.39	107.27	0.00	0.00
山　东 Shandong	115.10	106.90	113.06	105.33	104.50	101.56
河　南 Henan	117.20	104.89	106.03	107.17	0.00	104.30
湖　北 Hubei	112.26	108.21	120.69	110.33	0.00	0.00
湖　南 Hunan	113.93	114.36	118.29	111.81	0.00	0.00
广　东 Guangdong	106.76	103.27	118.07	119.92	0.00	0.00
广　西 Guangxi	108.31	102.07	103.12	108.55	0.00	0.00
海　南 Hainan	99.23	101.20	108.58	103.01	0.00	0.00
重　庆 Chongqing	112.27	103.75	115.20	105.02	99.25	101.19
四　川 Sichuan	110.44	105.89	108.09	104.92	104.80	102.33
贵　州 Guizhou	108.15	102.32	105.35	99.90	108.33	100.27
云　南 Yunnan	104.74	102.56	110.00	106.99	101.51	103.58
陕　西 Shaanxi	111.23	94.58	0.00	0.00	0.00	0.00
甘　肃 Gansu	113.16	103.57	0.00	100.00	0.00	
青　海 Qinghai	108.21	108.54	0.00		0.00	
宁　夏 Ningxia	111.02	109.14	0.00	0.00	0.00	0.00
新　疆 Xinjiang	94.67	102.99	103.64	93.42	96.70	105.94

2—11 续表 6 continued 6

地区 Region	畜产品 Livestock products			
	牛奶 Cow milk		羊奶 Sheep milk	
	2004	2005	2004	2005
全国 National	**103.73**	**99.62**	**105.30**	**101.41**
北京 Beijing	100.75	98.23	0.00	0.00
天津 Tianjin	103.31	101.29	0.00	0.00
河北 Hebei	102.66	100.10	95.37	0.00
山西 Shanxi	95.23	98.25	0.00	0.00
内蒙古 Inner Mongolia	100.19	99.92	100.00	0.00
辽宁 Liaoning	0.00	93.13	0.00	112.38
吉林 Jilin	102.85	98.73	0.00	0.00
黑龙江 Heilongjiang	102.62	99.02	0.00	0.00
上海 Shanghai	102.75	101.87	0.00	0.00
江苏 Jiangsu	100.00	99.47	100.00	100.00
浙江 Zhejiang	124.41	96.58	0.00	0.00
安徽 Anhui	105.35	98.86	0.00	0.00
福建 Fujian	101.81	99.07	100.00	111.53
江西 Jiangxi	0.00	0.00	0.00	0.00
山东 Shandong	100.48	105.02	77.79	106.47
河南 Henan	0.00	99.63	0.00	100.00
湖北 Hubei	0.00	0.00	0.00	0.00
湖南 Hunan	87.84	100.00	0.00	0.00
广东 Guangdong	88.43	100.00	0.00	100.00
广西 Guangxi	0.00	0.00	0.00	0.00
海南 Hainan	0.00	0.00	0.00	0.00
重庆 Chongqing	0.00	0.00	0.00	0.00
四川 Sichuan	105.68	74.30	101.40	93.75
贵州 Guizhou	99.84	86.54	0.00	0.00
云南 Yunnan	104.84	99.90	87.08	0.00
陕西 Shaanxi	111.04	95.75	104.62	96.85
甘肃 Gansu	108.06	102.17	103.40	
青海 Qinghai	100.48	102.48	0.00	
宁夏 Ningxia	111.85	97.68	0.00	0.00
新疆 Xinjiang	101.21	98.38	0.00	100.00

2－11 续表 7 continued 7

地　区 Region	畜产品 Livestock products			
	山羊毛 Goat's wool		绵羊毛 Sheep's wool	
	2004	2005	2004	2005
全　国 National	**98.98**	**102.77**	**105.47**	**103.31**
北　京 Beijing	0.00	0.00	100.00	0.00
天　津 Tianjin	0.00	0.00	0.00	0.00
河　北 Hebei	95.88	92.92	122.57	96.86
山　西 Shanxi	99.47	108.48	109.30	102.37
内蒙古 Inner Mongolia	87.56	109.42	100.35	98.91
辽　宁 Liaoning	123.44	100.00	0.00	125.43
吉　林 Jilin	0.00	102.08	86.50	107.26
黑龙江 Heilongjiang	0.00	0.00	95.94	90.07
上　海 Shanghai	0.00	0.00	0.00	0.00
江　苏 Jiangsu	0.00	0.00	100.00	100.00
浙　江 Zhejiang	0.00	0.00	0.00	113.56
安　徽 Anhui	0.00	0.00	0.00	0.00
福　建 Fujian	0.00	0.00	0.00	0.00
江　西 Jiangxi	0.00	0.00	0.00	0.00
山　东 Shandong	104.81	0.00	116.13	92.91
河　南 Henan	100.00	104.17	0.00	100.94
湖　北 Hubei	0.00	0.00	0.00	0.00
湖　南 Hunan	0.00	124.28	0.00	0.00
广　东 Guangdong	0.00	0.00	0.00	0.00
广　西 Guangxi	0.00	0.00	0.00	0.00
海　南 Hainan	0.00	0.00	0.00	0.00
重　庆 Chongqing	0.00	0.00	0.00	0.00
四　川 Sichuan	0.00	96.88	101.62	100.45
贵　州 Guizhou	0.00	0.00	0.00	0.00
云　南 Yunnan	0.00	0.00	0.00	0.00
陕　西 Shaanxi	0.00	100.00	0.00	0.00
甘　肃 Gansu	100.00	105.74	108.41	101.42
青　海 Qinghai	85.71		114.43	105.08
宁　夏 Ningxia	107.35	103.60	112.38	116.19
新　疆 Xinjiang	0.00	73.17	97.79	100.80

2—11 续表 8　　continued 8

地　　区 Region	畜产品 Livestock products			
	山羊绒 Cashmere		绵羊绒 Sheep's down	
	2004	2005	2004	2005
全　　国 National	**104.71**	**107.78**	**104.55**	**101.88**
北　　京 Beijing	101.15	103.45	0.00	0.00
天　　津 Tianjin	0.00	0.00	0.00	0.00
河　　北 Hebei	0.00	98.56	0.00	0.00
山　　西 Shanxi	107.53	100.37	0.00	100.00
内 蒙 古 Inner Mongolia	110.56	104.48	0.00	0.00
辽　　宁 Liaoning	95.73	123.19	0.00	0.00
吉　　林 Jilin	527.71	118.18	0.00	0.00
黑 龙 江 Heilongjiang	120.00	95.52	0.00	0.00
上　　海 Shanghai	0.00	0.00	0.00	0.00
江　　苏 Jiangsu	0.00	0.00	0.00	
浙　　江 Zhejiang	0.00	0.00	0.00	0.00
安　　徽 Anhui	0.00	0.00	0.00	0.00
福　　建 Fujian	0.00	0.00	0.00	0.00
江　　西 Jiangxi	0.00	0.00	0.00	0.00
山　　东 Shandong	114.56	100.00	0.00	0.00
河　　南 Henan	0.00	0.00	0.00	0.00
湖　　北 Hubei	0.00	0.00	0.00	0.00
湖　　南 Hunan	0.00	0.00	0.00	0.00
广　　东 Guangdong	0.00	0.00	0.00	0.00
广　　西 Guangxi	0.00	0.00	0.00	0.00
海　　南 Hainan	0.00	0.00	0.00	0.00
重　　庆 Chongqing	0.00	0.00	0.00	0.00
四　　川 Sichuan	104.81	96.61	102.17	103.23
贵　　州 Guizhou	0.00	0.00	0.00	0.00
云　　南 Yunnan	0.00	0.00	0.00	0.00
陕　　西 Shaanxi	84.63	0.00	0.00	0.00
甘　　肃 Gansu	99.06	109.96	106.93	98.07
青　　海 Qinghai	108.50	105.64	0.00	
宁　　夏 Ningxia	111.11	107.98	0.00	0.00
新　　疆 Xinjiang	126.68	110.63	0.00	103.80

2—12 各地区渔业产品生产价格指数
Indices of the Producers Prices of Fishery Products by Region

(上年=100) (the preceding year=100)

地区 Region	渔业产品 Fishery products		渔业产品 Fishery products: 海水产品 Seawater aquatic products		渔业产品 Fishery products: 内陆水域水产品 Aquatic products in inland water areas	
	2004	2005	2004	2005	2004	2005
全国 National	**110.19**	**104.67**	**109.00**	**104.10**	**112.30**	**107.90**
北京 Beijing	106.46	98.44	0.00	0.00	106.46	98.44
天津 Tianjin	104.41	103.21	104.10	99.22	105.99	103.68
河北 Hebei	126.99	107.08	136.98	110.55	107.47	100.28
山西 Shanxi	102.79	102.34	0.00	0.00	102.79	102.34
内蒙古 Inner Mongolia	112.35	100.23	0.00	0.00	112.35	100.23
辽宁 Liaoning	117.77	107.33	119.03	110.97	103.97	100.24
吉林 Jilin	87.34	100.15	0.00	0.00	87.34	100.15
黑龙江 Heilongjiang	104.84	100.99	0.00	0.00	104.84	100.99
上海 Shanghai	114.74	104.94	105.91	103.43	124.46	105.50
江苏 Jiangsu	111.85	102.58	105.11	107.50	112.02	102.71
浙江 Zhejiang	110.30	104.89	0.00	101.25	110.30	109.79
安徽 Anhui	110.10	105.56	0.00	0.00	110.10	105.56
福建 Fujian	107.00	103.75	106.10	102.41	107.40	107.93
江西 Jiangxi	110.61	104.98	0.00	0.00	110.61	104.98
山东 Shandong	110.05	103.29	109.10	104.39	114.26	98.12
河南 Henan	109.30	103.01	0.00	0.00	109.30	103.01
湖北 Hubei	113.67	109.12	0.00	0.00	113.67	109.12
湖南 Hunan	111.76	105.40	0.00	0.00	111.76	105.40
广东 Guangdong	106.09	104.57	108.68	103.41	105.67	104.76
广西 Guangxi	109.86	97.90	90.39	96.47	115.75	98.33
海南 Hainan	101.46	104.96	100.55	105.12	108.67	103.67
重庆 Chongqing	107.83	105.72	0.00	0.00	107.83	105.72
四川 Sichuan	109.37	106.53	0.00	0.00	109.37	106.53
贵州 Guizhou	106.20	102.69	0.00	0.00	106.20	102.69
云南 Yunnan	111.63	111.34	0.00	0.00	111.63	111.34
陕西 Shaanxi	110.25	95.38	0.00	0.00	110.25	95.38
甘肃 Gansu	100.00	101.35	0.00	0.00	100.00	101.35
青海 Qinghai	0.00		0.00		0.00	
宁夏 Ningxia	132.87	106.33	0.00	0.00	132.87	106.33
新疆 Xinjiang	122.90	96.06	0.00	0.00	122.90	96.06

2—12 续表 1 continued 1

地　区 Region	海水产品 Seawater aquatic products		海水产品 Seawater aquatic products 鱼类 Seawater Fish	
	2004	2005	2004	2005
全　国 National	**109.00**	**104.10**	**109.16**	**104.18**
天　津 Tianjin	104.10	99.22	103.64	0.00
河　北 Hebei	136.98	110.55	0.00	0.00
辽　宁 Liaoning	119.03	110.97	127.51	113.34
上　海 Shanghai	105.91	103.43	93.92	103.34
江　苏 Jiangsu	105.11	107.50	105.50	107.19
浙　江 Zhejiang	0.00	101.25	0.00	98.78
福　建 Fujian	106.10	102.41	109.27	99.65
山　东 Shandong	109.10	104.39	115.46	103.76
广　东 Guangdong	108.68	103.41	97.65	99.70
广　西 Guangxi	90.39	96.47	88.79	92.92
海　南 Hainan	100.55	105.12	100.13	105.01

2—12 续表 2 continued 2

地　区 Region	海水产品 Seawater aquatic products			
	贝类 Seawater shellfish		藻类 Seaweeds	
	2004	2005	2004	2005
全　国 National	**109.17**	**103.28**	**120.68**	**102.53**
天　津 Tianjin	0.00	0.00	0.00	0.00
河　北 Hebei	163.16	108.90	0.00	0.00
辽　宁 Liaoning	101.91	103.40	87.84	0.00
上　海 Shanghai	0.00	0.00	0.00	0.00
江　苏 Jiangsu	100.00	110.62	100.00	101.12
浙　江 Zhejiang	0.00	99.99	0.00	96.84
福　建 Fujian	105.18	100.75	107.59	98.45
山　东 Shandong	103.97	102.66	135.00	0.00
广　东 Guangdong	113.86	104.76	0.00	0.00
广　西 Guangxi	92.36	95.45	0.00	0.00
海　南 Hainan	111.11	0.00	131.62	106.53

2—12 续表 3 continued 3

地　区 Region	海水产品 Seawater aquatic products					
	大黄鱼 Large yellow croaker		小黄鱼 Small yellow croaker		带鱼 Hairtail	
	2004	2005	2004	2005	2004	2005
全　国 National	**108.66**	**102.11**	**110.53**	**102.70**	**107.29**	**103.01**
天　津 Tianjin	0.00	0.00	0.00	0.00	0.00	0.00
河　北 Hebei	0.00	0.00	0.00	0.00	0.00	0.00
辽　宁 Liaoning	115.44	0.00	130.60	0.00	138.13	0.00
上　海 Shanghai	0.00	0.00	0.00	0.00	0.00	0.00
江　苏 Jiangsu	100.00	102.40	100.36	102.35	118.38	101.66
浙　江 Zhejiang	0.00	0.00	0.00	0.00	0.00	0.00
福　建 Fujian	105.54	94.46	95.85	97.16	112.01	101.99
山　东 Shandong	120.00	108.33	108.05	98.07	134.27	99.63
广　东 Guangdong	0.00	0.00	0.00	0.00	100.34	119.09
广　西 Guangxi	0.00	0.00	97.33	101.84	0.00	0.00
海　南 Hainan	0.00	109.55	104.28	101.10	96.05	102.81

2—12 续表 4 continued 4

地 区 Region	海水产品 Seawater aquatic products					
	鳕鱼 Cod		鲳鱼 Silvery pomfret		鲅鱼 Spanish mackerel	
	2004	2005	2004	2005	2004	2005
全 国 National	**93.92**	**100.77**	**113.63**	**104.65**	**109.76**	**111.18**
天 津 Tianjin	0.00	0.00	103.64	0.00	0.00	0.00
河 北 Hebei	0.00	0.00	0.00	0.00	0.00	0.00
辽 宁 Liaoning	0.00	0.00	0.00	0.00	125.33	102.65
上 海 Shanghai	93.92	0.00	0.00	0.00	0.00	0.00
江 苏 Jiangsu	0.00		117.93	101.31	100.00	100.00
浙 江 Zhejiang	0.00	0.00	0.00	0.00	0.00	0.00
福 建 Fujian	0.00	0.00	109.65	104.51	0.00	0.00
山 东 Shandong	0.00	100.77	94.91	101.44	113.11	109.13
广 东 Guangdong	0.00	0.00	0.00	98.44	0.00	0.00
广 西 Guangxi	0.00	0.00	0.00	0.00	0.00	0.00
海 南 Hainan	0.00	0.00	111.92	99.11	0.00	0.00

2—12 续表 5 continued 5

地 区 Region	海水产品 Seawater aquatic products					
	对虾 Prawn		毛虾 Shrimp		梭子蟹 Swimming crab	
	2004	2005	2004	2005	2004	2005
全 国 National	**103.32**	**102.34**	**105.65**	**107.88**	**108.61**	**103.48**
天 津 Tianjin	0.00	99.50	0.00	0.00	135.53	98.79
河 北 Hebei	90.14	113.46	82.14	0.00	99.45	0.00
辽 宁 Liaoning	103.35	102.87	0.00	0.00	81.19	100.83
上 海 Shanghai	109.88	104.90	0.00	0.00	101.23	102.31
江 苏 Jiangsu	100.00	105.33	100.00	108.44	100.00	101.55
浙 江 Zhejiang	0.00	100.00	0.00	0.00	0.00	0.00
福 建 Fujian	100.13	107.52	105.47	108.82	133.33	111.21
山 东 Shandong	100.12	101.34	0.00	100.87	106.94	101.27
广 东 Guangdong	122.91	104.32	95.86	109.66	0.00	0.00
广 西 Guangxi	92.71	103.49	0.00	0.00	98.58	0.00
海 南 Hainan	102.00	105.19	109.27	0.00	119.75	94.54

2—12 续表 6 continued 6

地　区 Region	内陆水域水产品 Aquatic products in inland water areas		淡水产品 Aquatic products in inland water areas 淡水鱼类 Freshwater fish		淡水虾蟹类 Freshwater shrimps and crabs	
	2004	2005	2004	2005	2004	2005
全　国 National	**112.30**	**107.90**	**111.52**	**106.24**	**122.97**	**116.18**
北　京 Beijing	106.46	98.44	111.09	94.37	0.00	0.00
天　津 Tianjin	105.99	103.68	107.56	101.97	101.24	108.65
河　北 Hebei	107.47	100.28	107.47	100.28	0.00	0.00
山　西 Shanxi	102.79	102.34	102.79	102.34	0.00	0.00
内蒙古 Inner Mongolia	112.35	100.23	112.35	100.23	0.00	0.00
辽　宁 Liaoning	103.97	100.24	103.97	100.24	0.00	0.00
吉　林 Jilin	87.34	100.15	87.34	100.15	0.00	0.00
黑龙江 Heilongjiang	104.84	100.99	104.84	100.99	0.00	0.00
上　海 Shanghai	124.46	105.50	130.59	108.42	100.17	103.06
江　苏 Jiangsu	112.02	102.71	119.36	103.67	102.74	102.10
浙　江 Zhejiang	110.30	109.79	120.42	112.85	92.37	114.25
安　徽 Anhui	110.10	105.56	109.33	104.93	113.35	108.08
福　建 Fujian	107.40	107.93	114.97	109.42	118.05	94.88
江　西 Jiangxi	110.61	104.98	110.61	104.98	0.00	0.00
山　东 Shandong	114.26	98.12	113.64	98.12	120.00	0.00
河　南 Henan	109.30	103.01	109.30	103.01	0.00	0.00
湖　北 Hubei	113.67	109.12	113.41	108.10	120.36	135.97
湖　南 Hunan	111.76	105.40	112.15	107.96	162.90	108.70
广　东 Guangdong	105.67	104.76	106.82	104.27	90.38	111.44
广　西 Guangxi	115.75	98.33	115.75	98.33	0.00	0.00
海　南 Hainan	108.67	103.67	110.12	103.44	101.46	105.76
重　庆 Chongqing	107.83	105.72	107.83	105.72	0.00	0.00
四　川 Sichuan	109.37	106.53	109.37	106.35	0.00	0.00
贵　州 Guizhou	106.20	102.69	106.20	102.69	0.00	0.00
云　南 Yunnan	111.63	111.34	111.63	111.34	0.00	0.00
陕　西 Shaanxi	110.25	95.38	110.25	95.38	0.00	0.00
甘　肃 Gansu	100.00	101.35	100.00	101.35	0.00	0.00
青　海 Qinghai	0.00		0.00		0.00	
宁　夏 Ningxia	132.87	106.33	132.87	106.33	0.00	0.00
新　疆 Xinjiang	122.90	96.06	122.90	96.06	0.00	0.00

2—12 续表 7 continued 7

地　区 Region	内陆水域水产品 Aquatic products in inland water areas			
	青鱼 Black carp		草鱼 Grass carp	
	2004	2005	2004	2005
全　国 National	**106.65**	**107.52**	**115.47**	**110.17**
北　京 Beijing	0.00	96.77	114.35	98.48
天　津 Tianjin	0.00	0.00	101.74	111.25
河　北 Hebei	0.00	0.00	109.00	103.30
山　西 Shanxi	0.00	0.00	0.00	0.00
内蒙古 Inner Mongolia	0.00	0.00	111.19	108.37
辽　宁 Liaoning	0.00	0.00	0.00	102.33
吉　林 Jilin	0.00	0.00	0.00	132.53
黑龙江 Heilongjiang	0.00	0.00	0.00	109.09
上　海 Shanghai	0.00	108.33	128.04	105.13
江　苏 Jiangsu	101.53	101.23	120.08	103.31
浙　江 Zhejiang	0.00	107.92	123.78	113.99
安　徽 Anhui	111.99	101.52	111.42	113.41
福　建 Fujian	133.98	101.89	112.86	105.65
江　西 Jiangxi	105.26	0.00	115.26	104.55
山　东 Shandong	134.12	104.45	111.25	91.53
河　南 Henan	103.06	104.53	123.60	100.91
湖　北 Hubei	102.91	102.81	113.55	105.69
湖　南 Hunan	98.99	106.24	117.07	110.30
广　东 Guangdong	114.89	97.96	110.68	106.69
广　西 Guangxi	0.00	0.00	108.61	102.33
海　南 Hainan	0.00	103.36	114.61	103.44
重　庆 Chongqing	107.69	0.00	108.50	105.22
四　川 Sichuan	104.12	0.00	110.78	106.44
贵　州 Guizhou	0.00	0.00	98.28	0.00
云　南 Yunnan	0.00	0.00	112.62	111.64
陕　西 Shaanxi	0.00	0.00	115.42	97.34
甘　肃 Gansu	0.00		0.00	95.20
青　海 Qinghai	0.00		0.00	
宁　夏 Ningxia	0.00	0.00	157.58	109.86
新　疆 Xinjiang	0.00	0.00	114.36	101.21

2—12 续表 8 continued 8

地　区 Region	内陆水域水产品 Aquatic products in inland water areas			
	鲤鱼 Carp		鲢鱼 Silver carp	
	2004	2005	2004	2005
全　国 National	**112.06**	**103.91**	**113.29**	**107.37**
北　京 Beijing	116.79	89.80	106.17	88.89
天　津 Tianjin	107.78	99.00	115.87	106.72
河　北 Hebei	118.22	98.74	101.91	99.00
山　西 Shanxi	113.79	100.00	107.21	105.41
内蒙古 Inner Mongolia	110.25	96.74	118.31	100.00
辽　宁 Liaoning	0.00	109.80	0.00	94.77
吉　林 Jilin	0.00	102.10	0.00	99.46
黑龙江 Heilongjiang	103.27	101.79	110.75	97.74
上　海 Shanghai	0.00	0.00	128.89	117.58
江　苏 Jiangsu	109.41	103.56	122.89	105.52
浙　江 Zhejiang	100.00	108.14	0.00	112.25
安　徽 Anhui	111.91	104.31	104.69	107.59
福　建 Fujian	107.76	108.27	103.02	110.48
江　西 Jiangxi	108.08	111.17	110.14	99.40
山　东 Shandong	118.64	98.48	111.86	95.88
河　南 Henan	117.90	105.16	99.82	100.64
湖　北 Hubei	110.97	112.73	118.80	110.29
湖　南 Hunan	101.90	106.95	114.48	108.15
广　东 Guangdong	103.85	103.59	103.79	105.71
广　西 Guangxi	107.59	102.62	122.53	97.86
海　南 Hainan	108.92	101.47	105.17	101.06
重　庆 Chongqing	123.29	106.56	104.71	103.05
四　川 Sichuan	108.79	107.76	106.55	107.15
贵　州 Guizhou	110.20	102.94	104.86	98.41
云　南 Yunnan	102.59	102.13	101.55	110.82
陕　西 Shaanxi	112.61	96.06	101.41	92.20
甘　肃 Gansu	100.00	102.21	0.00	
青　海 Qinghai	0.00		0.00	
宁　夏 Ningxia	129.77	107.36	95.38	106.15
新　疆 Xinjiang	126.66	94.87	108.97	101.21

2—12 续表 9 continued 9

地 区 Region	内陆水域水产品 Aquatic products in inland water areas					
	鲫鱼 Crucian carp		罗非鱼 Tilapia		鲶鱼 Oriental sheatfish	
	2004	2005	2004	2005	2004	2005
全 国 National	**109.33**	**107.91**	**104.88**	**103.02**	**108.62**	**100.54**
北 京 Beijing	0.00	0.00	109.30	98.22	0.00	0.00
天 津 Tianjin	110.68	98.25	0.00	0.00	0.00	0.00
河 北 Hebei	104.43	98.62	0.00	0.00	0.00	0.00
山 西 Shanxi	0.00	100.00	101.59	102.59	0.00	0.00
内蒙古 Inner Mongolia	110.37	103.77	100.00	116.11	0.00	0.00
辽 宁 Liaoning	103.97	0.00	0.00	0.00	0.00	0.00
吉 林 Jilin	87.34	124.48	0.00	0.00	0.00	79.53
黑龙江 Heilongjiang	107.73	0.00	0.00	0.00	0.00	0.00
上 海 Shanghai	136.40	110.12	0.00	0.00	0.00	0.00
江 苏 Jiangsu	115.38	102.57	100.00	100.00	100.00	100.00
浙 江 Zhejiang	127.53	116.43	0.00	107.50	0.00	0.00
安 徽 Anhui	109.44	95.24	0.00	0.00	106.16	0.00
福 建 Fujian	106.99	105.24	106.80	104.37	0.00	0.00
江 西 Jiangxi	102.56	101.14	0.00	0.00	90.97	98.82
山 东 Shandong	110.06	106.02	102.86	0.00	104.59	95.37
河 南 Henan	118.22	0.00	0.00	0.00	0.00	0.00
湖 北 Hubei	111.13	113.18	0.00	0.00	111.80	83.33
湖 南 Hunan	99.65	105.39	0.00	0.00	108.68	106.56
广 东 Guangdong	99.76	106.46	101.94	99.11	111.23	99.91
广 西 Guangxi	0.00	100.64	80.44	85.62	93.82	95.27
海 南 Hainan	105.90	110.27	112.94	103.89	0.00	0.00
重 庆 Chongqing	102.54	108.47	0.00	92.30	0.00	111.11
四 川 Sichuan	113.55	101.95	0.00	0.00	102.89	107.17
贵 州 Guizhou	103.77	100.00	0.00	0.00	0.00	0.00
云 南 Yunnan	107.41	108.49	99.97	114.77	0.00	0.00
陕 西 Shaanxi	100.00	0.00	0.00	0.00	0.00	0.00
甘 肃 Gansu	0.00		0.00		0.00	
青 海 Qinghai	0.00		0.00		0.00	
宁 夏 Ningxia	127.95	96.87	0.00	0.00	0.00	0.00
新 疆 Xinjiang	121.04	101.48	107.14	96.91	0.00	0.00

3

农产品集贸市场价格

Prices of the Agricultural Products at the Rural Market Fairs

3—1 全国农产品集贸市场年度价格走势
Annual RMF Prices of the Agricultural Products

品 种	Categories	2000	2001	2002	2003	2004	2005
一、价格	Price						
（元/公斤）	（yuan/ kg）						
籼 稻	Long-grain nonglutinous rice	1.01	1.05	1.04	1.08	1.51	1.50
优质籼稻	High quality long-grain nonglutinous rice	1.18	1.24	1.16	1.25	1.72	1.72
粳 稻	Round-grain rice	1.27	1.31	1.15	1.20	1.72	1.78
小 麦	Wheat	1.02	1.09	1.06	1.14	1.52	1.51
玉 米	Corn	0.88	1.08	1.03	1.14	1.40	1.30
大 豆	Soybeans	2.53	2.43	2.38	2.96	3.88	3.59
籼 米	Milled long-grain nonglutinous rice			1.62	1.79	2.48	2.51
优质籼米	High quality milled long-grain nonglutinous rice			1.90	2.10	2.87	2.95
粳 米	Milled round-grain rice			1.92	2.02	2.84	2.94
面 粉	Wheat flour			1.71	1.82	2.35	2.36
二、价格变动	Index						
（上年＝100）	（preceding year＝100）						
籼 稻	Long-grain nonglutinous rice	82.44	104.70	98.63	103.63	140.41	99.48
优质籼稻	High quality long-grain nonglutinous rice		105.10	93.62	107.46	137.92	99.61
粳 稻	Round-grain rice	91.39	102.89	87.99	104.06	143.26	103.80
小 麦	Wheat	82.02	107.09	96.46	107.64	133.30	99.55
玉 米	Corn	81.99	122.78	95.18	111.31	122.57	93.30
大 豆	Soybeans	93.23	96.36	97.75	124.51	130.98	92.61
籼 米	Milled long-grain nonglutinous rice				110.56	138.91	101.00
优质籼米	High quality milled long-grain nonglutinous rice				110.41	136.75	102.66
粳 米	Milled round-grain rice				105.03	140.48	103.46
面 粉	Wheat flour				106.20	129.65	100.20

NOTE：RMF refer to the selected Rural Market Faires

3—1 续表 1　　continued 1

品　种　Categories		2000	2001	2002	2003	2004	2005
一、价格	Price						
(元/公斤)	(yuan/ kg)						
棉花(籽棉)	Cotton (unginned cotton)	3.33	3.55	3.35	4.80	5.60	5.09
花生仁	Peanut kernel			4.32	5.60	6.75	6.59
油菜籽	Rapeseeds			1.92	2.40	2.85	2.67
花生油	Peanut oil	8.49	8.04	7.88	9.43	11.15	10.80
菜籽油	Rape oil	6.73	5.98	5.79	6.85	7.99	7.43
豆 油	Soybean oil	6.37	5.50	5.50	6.74	7.71	6.93
烤 烟	Flue-cured tobacco			7.70	8.54	10.08	12.19
大白菜	Chinese cabbage			0.75	1.01	1.00	1.19
黄 瓜	Cucumber			1.81	2.07	2.03	2.31
西红柿	Tomato			1.88	2.21	2.18	2.39
菜 椒	Green bell			2.21	2.62	2.60	2.88
四季豆	Kidney beans			2.48	2.69	2.80	3.10
红富士苹果	Hongfushi apples			2.93	3.35	3.47	3.49
香 蕉	Bananas			2.91	3.11	3.49	3.29
橙 子	Oranges			2.88	3.41	3.55	3.27
二、价格变动	Index						
(上年=100)	(preceding year=100)						
棉花(籽棉)	Cotton (unginned cotton)		106.65	94.41	143.16	116.59	91.02
花生仁	Peanut kernel				129.60	120.66	97.66
油菜籽	Rapeseeds				125.07	118.98	93.57
花生油	Peanut oil		94.69	97.99	119.78	118.18	96.86
菜籽油	Rape oil		88.95	96.73	118.43	116.64	92.90
豆 油	Soybean oil		86.43	99.92	122.53	114.47	89.78
烤 烟	Flue-cured tobacco				110.97	117.98	121.01
大白菜	Chinese cabbage				134.02	98.68	119.40
黄 瓜	Cucumber				114.14	98.06	113.82
西红柿	Tomato				117.08	98.93	109.75
菜 椒	Green bell				118.89	99.21	110.84
四季豆	Kidney beans				108.47	104.08	110.78
红富士苹果	Hongfushi apples				114.22	103.81	100.52
香 蕉	Bananas				107.03	112.22	94.16
橙 子	Oranges				118.58	104.07	92.02

3—1续表2 continued 2

品　　种	Categories	2000	2001	2002	2003	2004	2005
一、价格	Price						
(元/公斤)	(yuan/ kg)						
草鱼	Grass carp	7.25	7.24	7.10	7.24	9.10	9.43
鲤鱼	Carp	7.73	7.52	6.84	7.01	8.90	8.67
鲢鱼	Silver carp			5.71	5.70	7.03	7.36
带鱼	Hairtail			8.95	9.33	10.13	10.50
活猪	Hogs	5.51	5.80	5.56	6.12	8.44	8.05
仔猪	Piglet	7.16	7.64	7.37	7.91	12.14	12.35
猪肉	Pork	9.68	10.18	9.85	10.70	13.97	13.39
牛肉	Beef	12.53	12.86	13.66	14.99	16.21	17.35
羊肉	Mutton	14.55	14.58	15.16	16.16	16.98	18.17
活鸡	Live chicken			8.39	8.80	10.09	10.46
鸡蛋	Eggs	4.98	5.20	5.43	5.37	6.40	6.61
二、价格变动	Index						
(上年=100)	(preceding year=100)						
草鱼	Grass carp		99.83	98.04	102.06	125.70	103.60
鲤鱼	Carp		97.31	90.94	102.48	126.98	97.44
鲢鱼	Silver carp				99.85	123.28	104.71
带鱼	Hairtail				104.26	108.49	103.67
活猪	Hogs		105.31	95.92	109.90	137.97	95.36
仔猪	Piglet		106.81	96.46	107.23	153.60	101.68
猪肉	Pork		105.27	96.74	108.54	130.60	95.85
牛肉	Beef		102.62	106.25	109.74	108.10	107.06
羊肉	Mutton		100.14	103.99	106.61	105.05	107.04
活鸡	Live chicken				104.90	114.68	103.65
鸡蛋	Eggs		104.27	104.51	98.89	119.14	103.26

3－2 全国农产品集贸市场季度价格走势
Quarterly RMF Prices of the Agricultural Products

（第一季度） (1st quarter)

品　　种	Categories	2000	2001	2002	2003	2004	2005
一、价格	Price						
（元/公斤）	(yuan/ kg)						
籼稻	Long-grain nonglutinous rice	1.06	1.01	1.02	1.05	1.36	1.56
优质籼稻	High quality long-grain nonglutinous rice	1.22	1.21	1.15	1.22	1.56	1.77
粳稻	Round-grain rice	1.31	1.28	1.17	1.14	1.53	1.76
小麦	Wheat	1.09	1.06	1.08	1.12	1.39	1.57
玉米	Corn	0.85	1.01	1.01	1.06	1.31	1.31
大豆	Soybeans	2.43	2.47	2.31	2.74	3.61	3.72
籼米	Milled long-grain nonglutinous rice			1.60	1.73	2.23	2.55
优质籼米	High quality milled long-grain nonglutinous rice			1.88	2.04	2.59	2.99
粳米	Milled round-grain rice			1.92	1.96	2.50	2.93
面粉	Wheat flour			1.72	1.78	2.22	2.40
棉花	Cotton (unginned cotton)	2.96	3.72	2.97	4.22	6.00	4.77
花生仁	Peanut kernel			4.08	5.11	6.56	6.68
油菜籽	Rapeseeds			1.93	2.22	2.79	2.85
花生油	Peanut oil	8.70	8.19	7.78	8.85	11.00	11.07
菜籽油	Rape oil	7.31	6.17	5.62	6.41	8.01	7.75
豆油	Soybean oil	6.80	5.61	5.25	6.31	7.84	7.19
烤烟	Flue-cured tobacco			7.58	8.19	9.30	11.70
活猪	Hogs	5.48	5.90	5.71	5.77	7.54	8.77
仔猪	Piglet	6.60	7.79	7.56	7.54	9.65	13.53
猪肉	Pork	9.48	10.37	10.01	10.05	12.64	14.23
牛肉	Beef	12.32	13.02	13.45	14.82	16.00	17.36
羊肉	Mutton	14.72	14.80	15.22	16.32	16.98	18.65
活鸡	Live chicken			8.53	8.79	9.44	10.83
鸡蛋	Eggs	4.96	5.01	5.53	5.28	5.93	6.71
草鱼	Grass carp	6.93	7.22	7.18	7.14	8.01	9.56
鲤鱼	Carp	7.31	7.69	6.76	6.86	7.92	8.99
鲢鱼	Silver carp			5.53	5.51	6.38	7.35
带鱼	Hairtail			8.95	9.47	9.60	10.44
大白菜	Chinese cabbage			0.54	0.95	0.90	0.89
黄瓜	Cucumber			2.54	3.06	3.01	3.21
西红柿	Tomato			2.47	2.89	3.03	2.73
菜椒	Green bell			3.14	3.61	3.55	3.53
四季豆	Kidney beans			3.40	3.81	3.80	3.90
红富士苹果	Hongfushi apples			2.72	3.13	3.14	3.29
香蕉	Bananas			3.24	3.13	3.51	3.31
橙子	Oranges			2.87	3.17	3.49	3.22

3—2 续表 continued

品 种 Categories		2000	2001	2002	2003	2004	2005
二、价格变动	Index						
(上季度=100)	(preceding quarter=100)						
籼稻	Long-grain nonglutinous rice	98.32	101.77	95.63	102.49	117.09	100.88
优质籼稻	High quality long-grain nonglutinous rice		102.38	92.03	106.84	115.64	100.88
粳稻	Round-grain rice	103.06	100.03	90.26	102.35	116.27	100.70
小麦	Wheat	96.34	103.48	96.53	107.17	111.94	100.20
玉米	Corn	89.59	108.82	95.21	106.54	106.61	95.28
大豆	Soybeans	95.28	100.43	97.49	111.24	109.94	97.29
籼米	Milled long-grain nonglutinous rice				106.45	115.60	100.84
优质籼米	High quality milled long-grain nonglutinous rice				106.38	114.21	101.75
粳米	MIlled round-grain rice				102.58	114.71	100.30
面粉	Wheat flour				105.18	112.36	99.54
棉花	Cotton (unginned cotton)		104.47	99.08	104.14	99.75	100.08
花生仁	Peanut kernel				113.29	107.05	98.55
油菜籽	Rapeseeds				110.84	101.19	98.94
花生油	Peanut oil		99.18	99.51	109.78	103.76	99.51
菜籽油	Rape oil		96.98	96.66	103.80	103.96	99.40
豆油	Soybean oil		94.37	97.95	106.76	103.11	97.57
烤烟	Flue-cured tobacco				114.16	106.95	105.86
活猪	Hogs		102.12	96.50	101.21	106.07	97.50
仔猪	Piglet		103.68	101.92	103.01	108.28	97.62
猪肉	Pork		101.28	97.03	100.48	102.64	96.83
牛肉	Beef		102.50	103.13	103.60	102.53	104.78
羊肉	Mutton		101.85	103.07	105.65	102.84	108.01
活鸡	Live chicken				105.49	100.90	102.08
鸡蛋	Eggs		98.33	102.61	97.51	99.35	99.21
草鱼	Grass carp		99.16	99.86	102.94	108.80	104.30
鲤鱼	Carp		101.56	93.71	101.78	110.49	103.68
鲢鱼	Silver carp				97.35	108.51	104.35
带鱼	Hairtail				106.00	102.66	101.42
大白菜	Chinese cabbage				136.19	95.21	117.38
黄瓜	Cucumber				146.48	126.55	157.18
西红柿	Tomato				146.34	123.01	130.75
菜椒	Green bell				167.37	137.48	146.64
四季豆	Kidney beans				156.22	141.90	150.05
红富士苹果	Hongfushi apples				112.00	101.77	101.95
香蕉	Bananas				115.06	107.15	103.70
橙子	Oranges				114.18	98.90	94.23

3—3 全国农产品集贸市场季度价格走势
Quarterly RMF Prices of the Agricultural Products

（第二季度） (2nd quarter)

品　种	Categories	2000	2001	2002	2003	2004	2005
一、价格	Price						
（元/公斤）	(yuan/ kg)						
籼 稻	long-grain nonglutinous rice	1.01	1.06	1.06	1.05	1.58	1.53
优质籼稻	High quality long-grain nonglutinous rice	1.19	1.26	1.19	1.21	1.79	1.75
粳 稻	Round-grain rice	1.23	1.32	1.17	1.16	1.79	1.80
小 麦	Wheat	1.01	1.10	1.06	1.10	1.55	1.54
玉 米	Corn	0.84	1.10	1.04	1.13	1.45	1.32
大 豆	Soybeans	2.61	2.47	2.35	2.89	4.02	3.64
籼 米	Milled long-grain nonglutinous rice			1.61	1.74	2.59	2.54
优质籼米	High quality milled long-grain nonglutinous rice			1.89	2.05	2.98	2.97
粳 米	Milled round-grain rice			1.92	1.97	2.97	2.93
面 粉	Wheat flour			1.72	1.76	2.40	2.37
棉 花	Cotton (unginned cotton)	3.37	3.80	3.14	4.39	6.04	4.89
花生仁	Peanut kernel			4.22	5.52	6.79	6.59
油菜籽	Rapeseeds			1.82	2.22	2.85	2.73
花生油	Peanut oil	8.53	8.15	7.68	9.10	11.22	10.78
菜籽油	Rape oil	6.80	6.05	5.55	6.59	8.13	7.56
豆 油	Soybean oil	6.55	5.62	5.22	6.52	7.94	6.98
烤 烟	Flue-cured tobacco			8.07	8.62	9.65	11.88
活 猪	Hogs	5.27	5.65	5.34	5.57	8.23	8.28
仔 猪	Piglet	7.08	7.82	7.36	7.35	11.44	13.53
猪 肉	Pork	9.22	9.92	9.57	9.84	13.63	13.60
牛 肉	Beef	12.51	12.69	13.29	14.65	15.90	17.18
羊 肉	Mutton	14.45	14.45	14.97	15.86	16.85	17.92
活 鸡	Live chicken			8.32	8.36	9.78	10.74
鸡 蛋	Eggs	4.82	5.02	5.31	5.00	6.08	6.53
草 鱼	Grass carp	7.35	7.26	7.11	7.19	9.60	9.57
鲤 鱼	Carp	8.06	7.68	6.82	6.90	9.63	8.75
鲢 鱼	Silver carp			5.78	5.64	7.25	7.44
带 鱼	Hairtail			8.82	9.29	10.14	10.44
大白菜	Chinese cabbage			0.77	1.05	1.05	1.27
黄 瓜	Cucumber			1.46	1.56	1.61	1.95
西红柿	Tomato			1.76	2.05	1.95	2.30
菜 椒	Green bell			2.14	2.69	2.71	2.98
四季豆	Kidney beans			2.32	2.51	2.70	3.02
红富士苹果	Hongfushi apples			3.15	3.42	3.67	3.31
香 蕉	Bananas			3.08	3.05	3.84	3.14
橙 子	Oranges			2.91	3.30	3.59	3.24

3－3 续表 continued

品　种 Categories		2000	2001	2002	2003	2004	2005
二、价格变动 Index							
（上季度＝100）（preceding quarter＝100）							
籼稻	long-grain nonglutinous rice	95.27	104.51	104.12	99.46	116.49	98.51
优质籼稻	High quality long-grain nonglutinous rice	97.28	104.54	103.40	98.99	114.82	99.30
粳稻	Round-grain rice	93.88	103.05	100.54	102.27	116.88	102.15
小麦	Wheat	93.25	103.78	98.27	98.41	111.36	97.96
玉米	Corn	99.61	108.73	102.77	105.97	110.61	100.48
大豆	Soybeans	107.69	99.84	101.95	105.53	111.37	97.82
籼米	Milled long-grain nonglutinous rice			100.70	100.49	116.51	99.52
优质籼米	High quality milled long-grain nonglutinous rice			100.30	100.64	115.33	99.10
粳米	Milled round-grain rice			100.29	100.25	119.04	100.13
面粉	Wheat flour			99.78	98.63	108.04	98.93
棉花	Cotton (unginned cotton)	113.84	102.16	105.53	103.98	100.60	102.46
花生仁	Peanut kernel			103.37	108.05	103.61	98.71
油菜籽	Rapeseeds			94.27	99.79	102.14	95.72
花生油	Peanut oil	98.05	99.51	98.81	102.82	101.94	97.35
菜籽油	Rape oil	92.98	98.00	98.71	102.70	101.57	97.53
豆油	Soybean oil	96.42	100.18	99.56	103.39	101.24	97.08
烤烟	Flue-cured tobacco			106.41	105.25	103.77	101.54
活猪	Hogs	96.17	95.81	93.48	96.56	109.21	94.39
仔猪	Piglet	107.33	100.30	97.35	97.40	118.52	100.05
猪肉	Pork	97.33	95.67	95.58	97.98	107.82	95.56
牛肉	Beef	101.54	97.43	98.79	98.84	99.42	98.94
羊肉	Mutton	98.14	97.63	98.40	97.21	99.23	96.08
活鸡	Live chicken			97.52	95.10	103.57	99.23
鸡蛋	Eggs	97.11	100.20	96.13	94.69	102.63	97.37
草鱼	Grass carp	106.06	100.60	99.00	100.72	119.97	100.16
鲤鱼	Carp	110.21	99.93	100.89	100.63	121.61	97.42
鲢鱼	Silver carp			104.60	102.47	113.70	101.32
带鱼	Hairtail			98.52	98.07	105.57	100.00
大白菜	Chinese cabbage			143.86	109.85	116.46	143.56
黄瓜	Cucumber			57.31	51.05	53.53	60.78
西红柿	Tomato			71.40	71.16	64.12	84.34
菜椒	Green bell			68.00	74.46	76.36	84.61
四季豆	Kidney beans			68.12	65.95	71.17	77.37
红富士苹果	Hongfushi apples			115.72	109.17	116.85	100.64
香蕉	Bananas			95.10	97.51	109.54	94.76
橙子	Oranges			101.30	103.97	102.97	100.89

3—4 全国农产品集贸市场季度价格走势
Quarterly RMF Prices of the Agricultural Products

（第三季度） (3rd quarter)

品 种	Categories	2000	2001	2002	2003	2004	2005
一、价格	Price						
（元/公斤）	(yuan/ kg)						
籼 稻	long-grain nonglutinous rice	0.96	1.07	1.05	1.05	1.56	1.47
优质籼稻	High quality long-grain nonglutinous rice	1.13	1.24	1.16	1.22	1.79	1.67
粳 稻	Round-grain rice	1.28	1.35	1.16	1.17	1.79	1.79
小 麦	Wheat	0.96	1.10	1.05	1.09	1.55	1.47
玉 米	Corn	0.89	1.14	1.06	1.15	1.46	1.31
大 豆	Soybeans	2.60	2.43	2.39	2.93	4.07	3.54
籼 米	Milled long-grain nonglutinous rice			1.63	1.76	2.58	2.47
优质籼米	High quality milled long-grain nonglutinous rice			1.92	2.04	2.97	2.90
粳 米	Milled round-grain rice			1.94	1.97	2.96	2.93
面 粉	Wheat flour			1.71	1.75	2.39	2.34
棉 花	Cotton (unginned cotton)	3.43	3.69	3.25	4.58	5.58	5.17
花生仁	Peanut kernel			4.46	5.63	6.87	6.57
油菜籽	Rapeseeds			1.92	2.40	2.90	2.52
花生油	Peanut oil	8.46	7.98	7.98	9.17	11.25	10.71
菜籽油	Rape oil	6.43	5.91	5.81	6.72	8.04	7.24
豆 油	Soybean oil	6.18	5.43	5.62	6.52	7.71	6.85
烤 烟	Flue-cured tobacco			7.96	8.66	10.31	12.50
活 猪	Hogs	5.51	5.74	5.51	6.01	8.99	7.92
仔 猪	Piglet	7.43	7.54	7.24	7.82	13.62	12.48
猪 肉	Pork	9.76	10.12	9.83	10.58	14.91	13.28
牛 肉	Beef	12.59	12.69	13.62	14.91	16.37	17.27
羊 肉	Mutton	14.52	14.29	15.00	15.95	16.81	17.83
活 鸡	Live chicken			8.38	8.70	10.54	10.61
鸡 蛋	Eggs	5.06	5.37	5.46	5.23	6.82	6.78
草 鱼	Grass carp	7.43	7.28	7.16	7.28	9.64	9.40
鲤 鱼	Carp	7.97	7.49	7.04	7.11	9.38	8.60
鲢 鱼	Silver carp			5.88	5.78	7.44	7.40
带 鱼	Hairtail			9.10	9.22	10.47	10.62
大白菜	Chinese cabbage			1.00	1.09	1.29	1.47
黄 瓜	Cucumber			1.16	1.27	1.44	1.61
西红柿	Tomato			1.33	1.42	1.66	1.92
菜 椒	Green bell			1.39	1.62	1.75	2.08
四季豆	Kidney beans			1.78	1.77	2.11	2.41
红富士苹果	Hongfushi apples			3.05	3.75	3.86	3.78
香 蕉	Bananas			2.59	3.00	3.44	3.26
橙 子	Oranges			2.95	3.66	3.72	3.30

3—4 续表 continued

品 种 Categories		2000	2001	2002	2003	2004	2005
二、价格变动	Index						
(上季度=100)	(preceding quarter=100)						
籼 稻	long-grain nonglutinous rice	95.36	100.81	98.67	100.12	98.90	95.67
优质籼稻	High quality long-grain nonglutinous rice	94.96	98.23	97.50	100.81	99.64	95.51
粳 稻	Round-grain rice	104.08	102.60	98.66	100.33	99.56	99.07
小 麦	Wheat	95.07	99.88	98.72	98.92	99.88	95.57
玉 米	Corn	105.53	103.55	102.02	101.88	100.42	99.65
大 豆	Soybeans	99.49	98.40	101.61	101.27	101.30	97.34
籼 米	Milled long-grain nonglutinous rice			101.06	101.23	99.31	97.41
优质籼米	High quality milled long-grain nonglutinous rice			101.41	99.78	99.42	97.90
粳 米	Milled round-grain rice			100.60	100.12	99.77	99.91
面 粉	Wheat flour			99.84	99.94	99.86	98.52
棉 花	Cotton (unginned cotton)	101.69	97.14	103.55	104.28	92.30	105.76
花生仁	Peanut kernel			105.60	101.94	101.18	99.64
油菜籽	Rapeseeds			105.61	107.88	102.00	92.44
花生油	Peanut oil	99.26	97.93	103.80	100.79	100.32	99.42
菜籽油	Rape oil	94.61	97.66	104.73	101.99	98.79	95.71
豆 油	Soybean oil	94.25	96.59	107.52	100.05	97.08	98.06
烤 烟	Flue-cured tobacco			98.59	100.42	106.89	105.21
活 猪	Hogs	104.55	101.70	103.25	107.82	109.26	95.68
仔 猪	Piglet	104.94	96.47	98.31	106.38	119.05	92.23
猪 肉	Pork	105.82	102.00	102.73	107.45	109.44	97.65
牛 肉	Beef	100.61	100.02	102.51	101.77	102.91	100.55
羊 肉	Mutton	100.53	98.92	100.13	100.57	99.79	99.49
活 鸡	Live chicken			100.77	104.07	107.76	98.77
鸡 蛋	Eggs	104.91	107.13	102.82	104.47	112.14	103.82
草 鱼	Grass carp	101.04	100.20	100.80	101.35	100.32	98.20
鲤 鱼	Carp	98.88	97.51	103.12	103.05	97.44	98.26
鲢 鱼	Silver carp			101.68	102.44	102.65	99.44
带 鱼	Hairtail			103.12	99.23	103.29	101.75
大白菜	Chinese cabbage			129.81	104.22	122.87	115.32
黄 瓜	Cucumber			79.93	81.07	89.28	82.71
西红柿	Tomato			75.69	68.93	85.33	83.45
菜 椒	Green bell			64.96	60.27	64.52	69.57
四季豆	Kidney beans			76.69	70.52	77.94	79.90
红富士苹果	Hongfushi apples			96.95	109.58	105.17	114.02
香 蕉	Bananas			84.01	98.19	89.52	103.78
橙 子	Oranges			101.38	110.86	103.48	101.59

3—5 全国农产品集贸市场季度价格走势
Quarterly RMF Prices of the Agricultural Products

（第四季度） (4th quarter)

品　种	Categories	2000	2001	2002	2003	2004	2005
一、价格	Price						
（元/公斤）	(yuan/ kg)						
籼稻	long-grain nonglutinous rice	1.00	1.07	1.03	1.16	1.54	1.46
优质籼稻	High quality long-grain nonglutinous rice	1.18	1.25	1.14	1.35	1.75	1.67
粳稻	Round-grain rice	1.28	1.29	1.11	1.32	1.75	1.77
小麦	Wheat	1.03	1.12	1.04	1.24	1.56	1.46
玉米	Corn	0.93	1.06	1.00	1.23	1.38	1.27
大豆	Soybeans	2.46	2.37	2.46	3.28	3.82	3.47
籼米	Milled long-grain nonglutinous rice			1.62	1.93	2.53	2.47
优质籼米	High quality milled long-grain nonglutinous rice			1.91	2.26	2.94	2.92
粳米	Milled round-grain rice			1.91	2.18	2.92	2.96
面粉	Wheat flour			1.69	1.97	2.41	2.33
棉花	Cotton (unginned cotton)	3.56	3.00	4.05	6.02	4.77	5.54
花生仁	Peanut kernel			4.51	6.13	6.78	6.53
油菜籽	Rapeseeds			2.01	2.75	2.88	2.59
花生油	Peanut oil	8.26	7.82	8.06	10.60	11.12	10.63
菜籽油	Rape oil	6.36	5.81	6.18	7.70	7.80	7.16
豆油	Soybean oil	5.94	5.36	5.91	7.60	7.37	6.67
烤烟	Flue-cured tobacco			7.18	8.69	11.05	12.70
活猪	Hogs	5.77	5.92	5.70	7.10	8.99	7.22
仔猪	Piglet	7.52	7.42	7.32	8.92	13.86	9.85
猪肉	Pork	10.24	10.32	10.00	12.31	14.70	12.44
牛肉	Beef	12.71	13.04	14.31	15.60	16.57	17.60
羊肉	Mutton	14.53	14.76	15.44	16.51	17.27	18.29
活鸡	Live chicken			8.33	9.36	10.61	9.66
鸡蛋	Eggs	5.09	5.39	5.42	5.97	6.76	6.41
草鱼	Grass carp	7.28	7.19	6.93	7.36	9.16	9.19
鲤鱼	Carp	7.57	7.22	6.74	7.17	8.67	8.35
鲢鱼	Silver carp			5.66	5.88	7.04	7.24
带鱼	Hairtail			8.94	9.35	10.29	10.49
大白菜	Chinese cabbage			0.70	0.94	0.75	1.14
黄瓜	Cucumber			2.09	2.38	2.04	2.46
西红柿	Tomato			1.97	2.47	2.09	2.62
菜椒	Green bell			2.15	2.58	2.40	2.95
四季豆	Kidney beans			2.44	2.68	2.60	3.09
红富士苹果	Hongfushi apples			2.80	3.09	3.23	3.59
香蕉	Bananas			2.72	3.27	3.19	3.45
橙子	Oranges			2.78	3.53	3.41	3.32

3—5 续表 continued

品 种 Categories		2000	2001	2002	2003	2004	2005
二、价格变动	Index						
(上季度=100)	(preceding quarter=100)						
籼稻	long-grain nonglutinous rice	103.86	99.64	98.02	110.66	98.64	99.43
优质籼稻	High quality long-grain nonglutinous rice	104.44	100.93	98.27	110.88	97.99	99.73
粳稻	Round-grain rice	99.97	95.61	96.29	112.92	98.13	99.37
小麦	Wheat	106.46	101.50	99.63	114.55	100.95	99.55
玉米	Corn	104.39	93.08	94.26	107.21	94.65	96.79
大豆	Soybeans	94.64	97.48	103.13	111.95	93.96	97.94
籼米	Milled long-grain nonglutinous rice			99.60	109.66	98.09	99.96
优质籼米	High quality milled long-grain nonglutinous rice			99.88	110.81	99.15	100.60
粳米	Milled round-grain rice			98.90	110.40	98.43	100.99
面粉	Wheat flour			98.78	112.56	100.60	99.80
棉花	Cotton (unginned cotton)	103.80	81.34	124.69	131.53	85.57	107.06
花生仁	Peanut kernel			101.17	108.86	98.62	99.33
油菜籽	Rapeseeds			104.61	114.99	99.16	102.63
花生油	Peanut oil	97.61	97.88	101.11	115.57	98.87	99.23
菜籽油	Rape oil	98.89	98.45	106.35	114.70	97.06	98.90
豆油	Soybean oil	96.25	98.69	105.17	116.54	95.70	97.44
烤烟	Flue-cured tobacco			90.18	100.40	107.15	101.64
活猪	Hogs	104.77	102.98	103.54	118.20	100.03	91.14
仔猪	Piglet	101.17	98.42	101.16	114.07	101.72	78.92
猪肉	Pork	104.94	101.94	101.71	116.40	98.57	93.69
牛肉	Beef	100.93	102.73	105.04	104.65	101.25	101.87
羊肉	Mutton	100.05	103.30	103.00	103.49	102.71	102.58
活鸡	Live chicken			99.39	107.62	100.62	91.06
鸡蛋	Eggs	100.69	100.21	99.20	114.14	99.12	94.47
草鱼	Grass carp	97.99	98.78	96.76	101.01	95.09	97.76
鲤鱼	Carp	94.99	96.32	95.76	100.78	92.35	97.06
鲢鱼	Silver carp			96.23	101.69	94.60	97.83
带鱼	Hairtail			98.24	101.47	98.29	98.78
大白菜	Chinese cabbage			69.84	86.43	58.61	77.73
黄瓜	Cucumber			179.59	188.14	141.56	152.90
西红柿	Tomato			147.90	174.22	125.78	136.54
菜椒	Green bell			155.21	159.37	137.66	142.03
四季豆	Kidney beans			137.29	151.16	123.27	128.41
红富士苹果	Hongfushi apples			91.62	82.34	83.61	95.15
香蕉	Bananas			105.08	109.10	92.93	105.99
橙子	Oranges			94.12	96.49	91.77	100.88

3—6 全国农产品集贸市场月度价格走势
Monthly RMF Prices of the Agricultural Products

（1月份） (Jan.)

品 种	Categories	2000	2001	2002	2003	2004	2005
一、价格	Price						
（元/公斤）	(yuan/ kg)						
籼 稻	long-grain nonglutinous rice	1.10	1.02	1.00	1.06	1.23	1.55
优质籼稻	High quality long-grain nonglutinous rice	1.21	1.21	1.13	1.20	1.43	1.75
粳 稻	Round-grain rice	1.32	1.25	1.15	1.12	1.39	1.75
小 麦	Wheat	1.12	1.06	1.08	1.13	1.34	1.56
玉 米	Corn	0.85	0.97	1.00	1.05	1.29	1.31
大 豆	Soybeans	2.37	2.47	2.34	2.72	3.52	3.74
籼 米	Milled long-grain nonglutinous rice			1.58	1.73	2.03	2.53
优质籼米	High quality milled long-grain nonglutinous rice			1.88	2.04	2.40	2.96
粳 米	Milled round-grain rice			1.90	1.97	2.29	2.89
面 粉	Wheat flour			1.73	1.78	2.15	2.39
棉 花	Cotton (unginned cotton)	2.89	3.73	2.89	4.11	5.95	4.66
花生仁	Peanut kernel			4.06	5.02	6.55	6.69
油菜籽	Rapeseeds			2.02	2.24	2.81	2.85
花生油	Peanut oil	8.70	8.10	7.72	8.79	10.99	11.04
菜籽油	Rape oil	7.34	6.17	5.63	6.35	8.04	7.74
豆 油	Soybean oil	6.80	5.52	5.22	6.28	7.76	7.20
烤 烟	Flue-cured tobacco			7.52	7.86	9.33	11.33
活 猪	Hogs	5.51	5.92	5.80	5.91	7.46	8.80
仔 猪	Piglet	6.37	7.59	7.42	7.52	9.22	13.29
猪 肉	Pork	9.30	10.63	10.09	10.20	12.73	14.33
牛 肉	Beef	11.37	13.41	13.35	14.93	16.10	16.95
羊 肉	Mutton	14.20	15.06	15.14	16.42	17.05	18.40
活 鸡	Live chicken			8.35	9.14	10.12	10.51
鸡 蛋	Eggs	4.57	5.16	5.69	5.51	6.18	6.78
草 鱼	Grass carp	6.96	7.34	7.11	7.26	7.70	9.31
鲤 鱼	Carp	7.23	7.80	6.85	7.01	7.60	8.80
鲢 鱼	Silver carp			5.42	5.69	6.26	7.12
带 鱼	Hairtail			8.91	9.66	9.64	10.24
大白菜	Chinese cabbage			0.53	0.81	0.88	0.72
黄 瓜	Cucumber			2.56	3.35	3.53	2.65
西红柿	Tomato			2.48	2.77	3.23	2.49
菜 椒	Green bell			3.14	3.58	3.50	3.11
四季豆	Kidney beans			3.26	3.60	3.66	3.42
红富士苹果	Hongfushi apples			2.66	3.17	3.14	3.24
香 蕉	Bananas			3.06	3.10	3.57	3.24
橙 子	Oranges			2.66	3.28	3.53	3.14

3－6 续表 continued

品　　种	Categories	2000	2001	2002	2003	2004	2005
二、价格变动	Index						
(上月＝100)	(preceding month＝100)						
籼稻	long-grain nonglutinous rice	103.62	101.04	92.80	102.31	101.25	101.06
优质籼稻	High quality long-grain nonglutinous rice		102.10	89.27	105.01	102.42	100.21
粳稻	Round-grain rice	104.26	98.04	90.13	100.15	102.01	100.66
小麦	Wheat	101.34	100.19	95.82	107.39	99.91	100.23
玉米	Corn	91.12	100.67	97.34	102.91	100.91	98.17
大豆	Soybeans	92.43	100.34	100.24	107.81	103.98	99.31
籼米	Milled long-grain nonglutinous rice				105.90	101.37	100.91
优质籼米	High quality milled long-grain nonglutinous rice				105.69	101.09	100.86
粳米	Milled round-grain rice				102.71	102.20	100.26
面粉	Wheat flour				103.94	101.91	99.33
棉花	Cotton (unginned cotton)		103.57	99.53	99.77	101.16	99.92
花生仁	Peanut kernel				108.17	103.44	99.48
油菜籽	Rapeseeds				108.83	98.62	99.13
花生油	Peanut oil		97.59	100.01	107.21	98.96	99.50
菜籽油	Rape oil		99.29	98.74	101.05	101.32	100.27
豆油	Soybean oil		93.85	98.56	101.55	101.13	98.56
烤烟	Flue-cured tobacco				102.66	105.20	98.63
活猪	Hogs		100.69	96.92	102.09	101.65	99.62
仔猪	Piglet		100.39	99.68	102.43	102.16	98.56
猪肉	Pork		104.12	97.66	100.76	101.43	99.57
牛肉	Beef		105.29	101.37	102.28	102.12	102.48
羊肉	Mutton		103.28	101.08	104.09	102.24	104.99
活鸡	Live chicken				108.97	106.83	100.32
鸡蛋	Eggs		101.14	105.74	101.47	101.37	100.58
草鱼	Grass carp		100.90	98.46	105.63	104.80	102.71
鲤鱼	Carp		103.12	95.65	105.89	106.08	101.86
鲢鱼	Silver carp				100.87	106.98	102.25
带鱼	Hairtail				108.06	104.51	100.41
大白菜	Chinese cabbage				113.80	99.34	111.15
黄瓜	Cucumber				127.67	122.41	111.99
西红柿	Tomato				120.29	116.80	115.70
菜椒	Green bell				143.48	122.07	116.45
四季豆	Kidney beans				129.33	118.69	112.92
红富士苹果	Hongfushi apples				109.32	103.43	102.15
香蕉	Bananas				112.15	106.42	101.28
橙子	Oranges				116.00	101.37	96.10

3—7 全国农产品集贸市场月度价格走势
Monthly RMF Prices of the Agricultural Products

(2月份) (Feb.)

品　种	Categories	2000	2001	2002	2003	2004	2005
一、价格	Price						
(元/公斤)	(yuan/ kg)						
籼稻	long-grain nonglutinous rice	1.08	1.02	1.00	1.05	1.28	1.55
优质籼稻	High quality long-grain nonglutinous rice	1.23	1.20	1.13	1.23	1.47	1.77
粳稻	Round-grain rice	1.31	1.27	1.16	1.13	1.44	1.76
小麦	Wheat	1.09	1.06	1.07	1.12	1.35	1.57
玉米	Corn	0.85	1.03	1.01	1.06	1.29	1.31
大豆	Soybeans	2.44	2.49	2.30	2.71	3.56	3.71
籼米	Milled long-grain nonglutinous rice			1.59	1.73	2.09	2.55
优质籼米	High quality milled long-grain nonglutinous rice			1.90	2.03	2.45	3.00
粳米	Milled round-grain rice			1.92	1.98	2.36	2.93
面粉	Wheat flour			1.72	1.80	2.17	2.41
棉花	Cotton (unginned cotton)	2.99	3.76	2.96	4.23	5.99	4.75
花生仁	Peanut kernel			4.09	5.05	6.49	6.71
油菜籽	Rapeseeds			1.90	2.29	2.77	2.84
花生油	Peanut oil	8.64	8.21	7.85	8.88	10.96	11.11
菜籽油	Rape oil	7.32	6.19	5.66	6.35	7.95	7.79
豆油	Soybean oil	6.79	5.67	5.28	6.28	7.78	7.22
烤烟	Flue-cured tobacco			7.51	8.15	9.25	11.87
活猪	Hogs	5.46	5.94	5.81	5.74	7.42	8.80
仔猪	Piglet	6.43	7.88	7.59	7.52	9.37	13.39
猪肉	Pork	9.66	10.31	10.17	10.03	12.49	14.33
牛肉	Beef	12.84	12.95	13.65	14.86	15.96	17.76
羊肉	Mutton	15.08	14.72	15.47	16.34	16.85	19.16
活鸡	Live chicken			8.86	8.70	9.00	11.03
鸡蛋	Eggs	5.32	4.93	5.61	5.29	5.82	6.86
草鱼	Grass carp	6.92	7.15	7.30	7.06	7.89	9.78
鲤鱼	Carp	7.29	7.63	6.79	6.83	7.85	9.23
鲢鱼	Silver carp			5.53	5.41	6.32	7.46
带鱼	Hairtail			9.13	9.46	9.58	10.77
大白菜	Chinese cabbage			0.55	0.88	0.87	0.98
黄瓜	Cucumber			2.82	2.99	2.75	3.71
西红柿	Tomato			2.58	2.87	3.08	2.99
菜椒	Green bell			3.40	3.43	3.36	3.81
四季豆	Kidney beans			3.67	3.81	3.62	4.14
红富士苹果	Hongfushi apples			2.74	3.13	3.11	3.34
香蕉	Bananas			3.32	3.15	3.46	3.40
橙子	Oranges			3.02	3.15	3.42	3.26

3—7 续表 continued

品　种	Categories	2000	2001	2002	2003	2004	2005
二、价格变动	Index						
(上月=100)	(preceding month=100)						
籼 稻	long-grain nonglutinous rice	98.18	100.16	100.16	99.67	104.12	99.97
优质籼稻	High quality long-grain nonglutinous rice	101.65	99.06	100.13	101.97	103.14	101.53
粳 稻	Round-grain rice	99.24	101.78	100.67	101.13	103.86	100.79
小 麦	Wheat	97.32	99.75	99.46	99.15	100.67	100.79
玉 米	Corn	100.00	105.71	100.78	101.03	100.00	100.22
大 豆	Soybeans	102.95	100.84	97.98	99.79	101.30	99.15
籼 米	Milled long-grain nonglutinous rice			100.50	100.08	103.03	100.75
优质籼米	High quality milled long-grain nonglutinous rice			100.75	99.60	102.26	101.51
粳 米	Milled round-grain rice			101.11	100.68	102.77	101.19
面 粉	Wheat flour			99.83	101.19	100.58	100.81
棉 花	Cotton (unginned cotton)	103.42	100.71	102.50	102.90	100.71	101.97
花生仁	Peanut kernel			100.84	100.57	99.09	100.28
油菜籽	Rapeseeds			94.24	102.19	98.67	99.84
花生油	Peanut oil	99.31	101.33	101.62	100.96	99.78	100.63
菜籽油	Rape oil	99.73	100.37	100.54	100.03	98.86	100.65
豆 油	Soybean oil	99.85	102.65	101.30	100.05	100.23	100.37
烤 烟	Flue-cured tobacco			99.90	103.75	99.17	104.74
活 猪	Hogs	99.09	100.38	100.25	97.15	99.43	99.94
仔 猪	Piglet	100.94	103.88	102.35	99.96	101.68	100.73
猪 肉	Pork	103.87	96.97	100.72	98.32	98.07	99.97
牛 肉	Beef	112.93	96.59	102.22	99.51	99.09	104.76
羊 肉	Mutton	106.20	97.73	102.20	99.49	98.81	104.15
活 鸡	Live chicken			106.08	95.19	88.86	104.96
鸡 蛋	Eggs	116.41	95.64	98.57	95.97	94.16	101.22
草 鱼	Grass carp	99.43	97.39	102.59	97.31	102.57	105.05
鲤 鱼	Carp	100.83	97.83	99.07	97.39	103.29	104.85
鲢 鱼	Silver carp			102.15	95.14	101.00	104.85
带 鱼	Hairtail			102.46	97.91	99.37	105.09
大白菜	Chinese cabbage			104.14	109.05	99.07	137.31
黄 瓜	Cucumber			110.13	89.33	78.08	140.21
西红柿	Tomato			104.18	103.66	95.40	120.18
菜 椒	Green bell			108.34	95.81	96.04	122.46
四季豆	Kidney beans			112.30	105.58	98.94	120.84
红富士苹果	Hongfushi apples			103.14	98.60	99.06	103.08
香 蕉	Bananas			108.67	101.33	96.88	105.03
橙 子	Oranges			113.67	95.95	96.92	103.86

3—8 全国农产品集贸市场月度价格走势
Monthly RMF Prices of the Agricultural Products

(3月份) (Mar.)

品　种	Categories	2000	2001	2002	2003	2004	2005
一、价格	Price						
(元/公斤)	(yuan/ kg)						
籼稻	long-grain nonglutinous rice	0.99	1.01	1.05	1.05	1.56	1.56
优质籼稻	High quality long-grain nonglutinous rice	1.23	1.21	1.19	1.23	1.78	1.78
粳稻	Round-grain rice	1.29	1.31	1.19	1.17	1.78	1.78
小麦	Wheat	1.05	1.06	1.08	1.10	1.50	1.57
玉米	Corn	0.84	1.03	1.02	1.08	1.36	1.32
大豆	Soybeans	2.47	2.46	2.28	2.80	3.74	3.71
籼米	Milled long-grain nonglutinous rice			1.63	1.73	2.55	2.57
优质籼米	High quality milled long-grain nonglutinous rice			1.87	2.04	2.91	3.02
粳米	Milled round-grain rice			1.93	1.94	2.84	2.95
面粉	Wheat flour			1.71	1.76	2.34	2.39
棉花	Cotton (unginned cotton)	3.00	3.66	3.07	4.32	6.07	4.91
花生仁	Peanut kernel			4.10	5.25	6.63	6.65
油菜籽	Rapeseeds			1.86	2.14	2.79	2.86
花生油	Peanut oil	8.75	8.27	7.77	8.89	11.05	11.06
菜籽油	Rape oil	7.28	6.15	5.56	6.53	8.04	7.74
豆油	Soybean oil	6.80	5.64	5.24	6.36	7.97	7.17
烤烟	Flue-cured tobacco			7.73	8.56	9.31	11.89
活猪	Hogs	5.47	5.83	5.51	5.67	7.73	8.71
仔猪	Piglet	6.99	7.91	7.68	7.58	10.38	13.90
猪肉	Pork	9.47	10.18	9.78	9.91	12.69	14.03
牛肉	Beef	12.76	12.71	13.34	14.67	15.93	17.37
羊肉	Mutton	14.88	14.61	15.05	16.19	17.04	18.39
活鸡	Live chicken			8.38	8.52	9.21	10.95
鸡蛋	Eggs	5.00	4.93	5.28	5.05	5.79	6.49
草鱼	Grass carp	6.92	7.17	7.13	7.08	8.43	9.58
鲤鱼	Carp	7.42	7.64	6.64	6.73	8.31	8.93
鲢鱼	Silver carp			5.63	5.42	6.55	7.46
带鱼	Hairtail			8.83	9.31	9.59	10.31
大白菜	Chinese cabbage			0.54	1.17	0.94	0.95
黄瓜	Cucumber			2.25	2.84	2.77	3.26
西红柿	Tomato			2.34	3.02	2.79	2.71
菜椒	Green bell			2.89	3.81	3.78	3.66
四季豆	Kidney beans			3.27	4.02	4.11	4.13
红富士苹果	Hongfushi apples			2.77	3.10	3.17	3.29
香蕉	Bananas			3.34	3.15	3.49	3.29
橙子	Oranges			2.94	3.09	3.52	3.25

3—8 续表 continued

品　种	Categories	2000	2001	2002	2003	2004	2005
二、价格变动	Index						
(上月=100)	(preceding month=100)						
籼稻	long-grain nonglutinous rice	91.67	99.26	104.57	99.38	122.46	100.56
优质籼稻	High quality long-grain nonglutinous rice	100.00	100.69	105.37	100.03	121.27	100.28
粳稻	Round-grain rice	98.47	103.57	102.48	104.06	123.49	100.86
小麦	Wheat	96.33	100.20	100.80	97.67	111.50	99.83
玉米	Corn	98.82	100.77	100.60	101.86	105.44	100.35
大豆	Soybeans	101.23	99.08	99.24	103.14	104.96	100.12
籼米	Milled long-grain nonglutinous rice			103.01	100.12	121.98	100.70
优质籼米	High quality milled long-grain nonglutinous rice			98.47	100.49	118.59	100.67
粳米	Milled round-grain rice			100.15	98.18	120.44	100.88
面粉	Wheat flour			99.06	98.20	107.87	99.41
棉花	Cotton (unginned cotton)	100.40	97.51	103.50	102.17	101.17	103.35
花生仁	Peanut kernel			100.23	104.01	102.14	99.15
油菜籽	Rapeseeds			97.92	93.49	100.64	100.48
花生油	Peanut oil	101.27	100.72	98.98	100.17	100.83	99.58
菜籽油	Rape oil	99.45	99.29	98.12	102.86	101.14	99.35
豆油	Soybean oil	100.15	99.42	99.25	101.25	102.44	99.19
烤烟	Flue-cured tobacco			102.94	105.06	100.57	100.17
活猪	Hogs	100.18	98.11	94.88	98.87	104.29	98.98
仔猪	Piglet	108.71	100.37	101.12	100.83	110.75	103.83
猪肉	Pork	98.03	98.72	96.17	98.81	101.64	97.93
牛肉	Beef	99.38	98.08	97.72	98.72	99.83	97.82
羊肉	Mutton	98.67	99.28	97.26	99.12	101.11	96.00
活鸡	Live chicken			94.58	97.87	102.38	99.26
鸡蛋	Eggs	93.98	99.94	94.08	95.58	99.55	94.63
草鱼	Grass carp	100.00	100.26	97.69	100.27	106.76	97.92
鲤鱼	Carp	101.78	100.07	97.83	98.66	105.93	96.81
鲢鱼	Silver carp			101.68	100.22	103.59	99.98
带鱼	Hairtail			96.71	98.41	100.10	95.78
大白菜	Chinese cabbage			97.78	132.44	107.39	96.90
黄瓜	Cucumber			79.76	94.79	100.48	87.89
西红柿	Tomato			90.51	105.33	90.68	90.38
菜椒	Green bell			85.12	111.25	112.31	96.12
四季豆	Kidney beans			89.17	105.54	113.57	99.89
红富士苹果	Hongfushi apples			101.04	99.01	102.08	98.59
香蕉	Bananas			100.61	99.99	101.05	96.68
橙子	Oranges			97.27	98.39	102.76	99.77

3—9 全国农产品集贸市场月度价格走势
Monthly RMF Prices of the Agricultural Products

（4月份） (Apr.)

品 种	Categories	2000	2001	2002	2003	2004	2005
一、价格	Price						
（元/公斤）	(yuan/ kg)						
籼 稻	long-grain nonglutinous rice	1.02	1.04	1.05	1.04	1.58	1.56
优质籼稻	High quality long-grain nonglutinous rice	1.16	1.25	1.19	1.20	1.80	1.77
粳 稻	Round-grain rice	1.22	1.28	1.17	1.18	1.81	1.81
小 麦	Wheat	1.04	1.08	1.07	1.10	1.57	1.58
玉 米	Corn	0.82	1.08	1.01	1.10	1.44	1.33
大 豆	Soybeans	2.57	2.45	2.32	2.87	3.97	3.67
籼 米	Milled long-grain nonglutinous rice			1.59	1.73	2.60	2.56
优质籼米	High quality milled long-grain nonglutinous rice			1.85	2.05	3.01	2.99
粳 米	Milled round-grain rice			1.90	1.98	3.01	2.93
面 粉	Wheat flour			1.71	1.76	2.41	2.39
棉 花	Cotton (unginned cotton)	3.28	3.85	3.24	4.38	6.13	4.75
花生仁	Peanut kernel			4.03	5.41	6.74	6.64
油菜籽	Rapeseeds			1.78	2.12	2.88	2.85
花生油	Peanut oil	8.59	8.16	7.45	9.06	11.30	10.85
菜籽油	Rape oil	6.94	6.19	5.60	6.53	8.11	7.77
豆 油	Soybean oil	6.60	5.74	5.19	6.53	8.04	7.06
烤 烟	Flue-cured tobacco			8.08	8.35	9.47	11.60
活 猪	Hogs	5.38	5.72	5.31	5.63	8.08	8.48
仔 猪	Piglet	7.00	7.96	7.53	7.45	11.19	13.66
猪 肉	Pork	9.22	10.05	9.51	9.87	13.33	13.76
牛 肉	Beef	12.58	12.67	12.99	14.67	15.86	17.08
羊 肉	Mutton	14.55	14.53	15.01	15.97	16.99	17.91
活 鸡	Live chicken			8.41	8.44	9.57	10.70
鸡 蛋	Eggs	4.87	4.95	5.21	5.06	5.92	6.28
草 鱼	Grass carp	7.19	7.25	7.10	7.15	9.22	9.59
鲤 鱼	Carp	7.76	7.73	6.69	6.83	8.92	8.78
鲢 鱼	Silver carp			5.67	5.57	6.88	7.36
带 鱼	Hairtail			8.82	9.36	9.74	10.33
大白菜	Chinese cabbage			0.70	1.36	1.12	1.19
黄 瓜	Cucumber			1.79	2.38	2.11	2.66
西红柿	Tomato			2.11	2.82	2.48	2.85
菜 椒	Green bell			2.62	3.94	3.48	3.95
四季豆	Kidney beans			2.94	3.59	3.48	3.86
红富士苹果	Hongfushi apples			3.02	3.19	3.44	3.23
香 蕉	Bananas			3.32	3.12	3.80	3.22
橙 子	Oranges			2.82	3.22	3.52	3.23

3—9 续表 continued

品　种　Categories		2000	2001	2002	2003	2004	2005
二、价格变动	Index						
(上月=100)	(preceding month=100)						
籼稻	long-grain nonglutinous rice	103.03	102.69	99.86	99.48	100.92	100.10
优质籼稻	High quality long-grain nonglutinous rice	94.31	103.26	99.62	97.72	100.63	99.49
粳稻	Round-grain rice	94.57	97.66	98.52	100.86	101.59	101.63
小麦	Wheat	99.05	101.83	99.05	100.48	104.53	100.40
玉米	Corn	97.62	104.49	99.40	102.01	106.22	100.93
大豆	Soybeans	104.05	99.56	101.96	102.54	106.17	98.93
籼米	Milled long-grain nonglutinous rice			97.19	100.27	101.97	99.79
优质籼米	High quality milled long-grain nonglutinous rice			99.15	100.43	103.39	99.01
粳米	Milled round-grain rice			98.51	101.94	106.12	99.22
面粉	Wheat flour			99.91	99.58	103.09	99.66
棉花	Cotton (unginned cotton)	109.09	104.99	105.63	101.44	101.06	96.63
花生仁	Peanut kernel			98.35	103.08	101.64	99.91
油菜籽	Rapeseeds			95.68	98.79	103.46	99.76
花生油	Peanut oil	98.17	98.65	95.95	101.94	102.17	98.09
菜籽油	Rape oil	95.33	100.60	100.77	99.94	100.85	100.38
豆油	Soybean oil	97.06	101.81	98.96	102.65	100.84	98.54
烤烟	Flue-cured tobacco			104.51	97.55	101.73	97.60
活猪	Hogs	98.35	98.20	96.32	99.22	104.48	97.40
仔猪	Piglet	100.14	100.66	98.04	98.27	107.84	98.25
猪肉	Pork	97.36	98.73	97.26	99.62	105.00	98.08
牛肉	Beef	98.59	99.72	97.35	100.04	99.59	98.34
羊肉	Mutton	97.78	99.44	99.73	98.64	99.71	97.39
活鸡	Live chicken			100.38	99.05	103.88	97.72
鸡蛋	Eggs	97.40	100.32	98.79	100.11	102.32	96.75
草鱼	Grass carp	103.90	101.14	99.66	100.91	109.42	100.12
鲤鱼	Carp	104.58	101.20	100.77	101.45	107.27	98.36
鲢鱼	Silver carp			100.81	102.70	105.04	98.66
带鱼	Hairtail			99.95	100.56	101.58	100.18
大白菜	Chinese cabbage			130.74	116.14	119.68	124.77
黄瓜	Cucumber			79.90	83.93	76.32	81.68
西红柿	Tomato			90.27	93.47	88.64	105.25
菜椒	Green bell			90.48	103.30	92.19	108.01
四季豆	Kidney beans			90.02	89.40	84.53	93.32
红富士苹果	Hongfushi apples			109.18	102.93	108.41	98.15
香蕉	Bananas			99.29	99.31	108.91	97.89
橙子	Oranges			95.81	104.21	100.01	99.33

3—10 全国农产品集贸市场月度价格走势
Monthly RMF Prices of the Agricultural Products

（5月份） (May)

品　　种	Categories	2000	2001	2002	2003	2004	2005
一、价格	Price						
（元/公斤）	(yuan/ kg)						
籼 稻	long-grain nonglutinous rice	1.00	1.08	1.07	1.05	1.58	1.55
优质籼稻	High quality long-grain nonglutinous rice	1.19	1.29	1.20	1.20	1.79	1.76
粳 稻	Round-grain rice	1.23	1.30	1.17	1.15	1.79	1.80
小 麦	Wheat	1.00	1.14	1.07	1.10	1.55	1.55
玉 米	Corn	0.84	1.11	1.04	1.13	1.45	1.32
大 豆	Soybeans	2.63	2.49	2.36	2.91	4.02	3.64
籼 米	Milled long-grain nonglutinous rice			1.62	1.73	2.59	2.54
优质籼米	High quality milled long-grain nonglutinous rice			1.90	2.05	2.97	2.96
粳 米	Milled round-grain rice			1.93	1.97	2.96	2.93
面 粉	Wheat flour			1.73	1.76	2.40	2.38
棉 花	Cotton (unginned cotton)	3.40	3.75	3.04	4.44	6.06	4.91
花生仁	Peanut kernel			4.23	5.54	6.79	6.58
油菜籽	Rapeseeds			1.81	2.26	2.84	2.78
花生油	Peanut oil	8.53	8.11	7.78	9.15	11.24	10.75
菜籽油	Rape oil	6.83	6.00	5.51	6.58	8.17	7.54
豆 油	Soybean oil	6.54	5.53	5.23	6.58	7.94	6.96
烤 烟	Flue-cured tobacco			7.93	8.68	9.72	11.95
活 猪	Hogs	5.27	5.62	5.39	5.56	8.15	8.27
仔 猪	Piglet	7.04	7.72	7.35	7.25	11.26	13.66
猪 肉	Pork	9.20	9.92	9.60	9.82	13.53	13.58
牛 肉	Beef	12.57	12.74	13.35	14.55	15.90	17.19
羊 肉	Mutton	14.52	14.42	15.09	15.74	16.80	17.97
活 鸡	Live chicken			8.26	8.30	9.81	10.78
鸡 蛋	Eggs	4.85	5.02	5.39	4.99	5.91	6.62
草 鱼	Grass carp	7.40	7.20	7.12	7.17	9.65	9.61
鲤 鱼	Carp	8.22	7.60	6.83	6.90	9.72	8.76
鲢 鱼	Silver carp			5.74	5.63	7.24	7.51
带 鱼	Hairtail			8.84	9.33	10.14	10.37
大白菜	Chinese cabbage			0.75	0.96	1.03	1.31
黄 瓜	Cucumber			1.54	1.39	1.60	1.89
西红柿	Tomato			1.80	1.99	1.97	2.42
菜 椒	Green bell			2.33	2.47	2.84	2.97
四季豆	Kidney beans			2.35	2.42	2.77	3.24
红富士苹果	Hongfushi apples			3.05	3.42	3.67	3.27
香 蕉	Bananas			3.12	3.05	3.94	3.14
橙 子	Oranges			2.90	3.21	3.64	3.23

3—10 续表 continued

品 种 Categories		2000	2001	2002	2003	2004	2005
二、价格变动	Index						
（上月＝100）	(preceding month＝100)						
籼 稻	long-grain nonglutinous rice	98.04	103.89	101.93	101.14	99.76	98.96
优质籼稻	High quality long-grain nonglutinous rice	102.59	103.03	100.84	100.34	99.42	99.60
粳 稻	Round-grain rice	100.82	101.23	99.97	97.07	99.06	99.60
小 麦	Wheat	96.15	104.98	100.09	100.15	98.93	98.36
玉 米	Corn	102.44	102.99	102.80	102.97	100.90	99.10
大 豆	Soybeans	102.33	101.66	101.68	101.60	101.25	99.09
籼 米	Milled long-grain nonglutinous rice			101.78	99.87	99.28	99.03
优质籼米	High quality milled long-grain nonglutinous rice			102.60	100.15	98.87	99.08
粳 米	Milled round-grain rice			101.88	99.58	98.20	100.00
面 粉	Wheat flour			101.21	99.94	99.45	99.69
棉 花	Cotton (unginned cotton)	103.75	97.40	93.74	101.37	98.84	103.44
花生仁	Peanut kernel			104.95	102.36	100.71	99.00
油菜籽	Rapeseeds			101.43	106.84	98.51	97.45
花生油	Peanut oil	99.30	99.47	104.35	100.97	99.47	99.09
菜籽油	Rape oil	98.41	96.99	98.36	100.79	100.77	97.04
豆 油	Soybean oil	99.09	96.37	100.71	100.80	98.77	98.55
烤 烟	Flue-cured tobacco			98.22	103.86	102.64	102.95
活 猪	Hogs	97.96	98.24	101.38	98.78	100.88	97.47
仔 猪	Piglet	100.57	96.94	97.61	97.24	100.66	100.01
猪 肉	Pork	99.78	98.71	100.97	99.50	101.50	98.70
牛 肉	Beef	99.92	100.55	102.78	99.14	100.20	100.63
羊 肉	Mutton	99.79	99.23	100.56	98.56	98.88	100.31
活 鸡	Live chicken			98.22	98.36	102.55	100.79
鸡 蛋	Eggs	99.59	101.55	103.32	98.55	99.80	105.39
草 鱼	Grass carp	102.92	99.36	100.28	100.36	104.66	100.20
鲤 鱼	Carp	105.93	98.37	101.97	101.07	109.03	99.75
鲢 鱼	Silver carp			101.22	101.13	105.25	102.03
带 鱼	Hairtail			100.23	99.67	104.11	100.40
大白菜	Chinese cabbage			106.79	70.58	91.80	110.14
黄 瓜	Cucumber			86.12	58.22	75.75	70.80
西红柿	Tomato			85.20	70.49	79.64	85.13
菜 椒	Green bell			89.17	62.78	81.56	75.04
四季豆	Kidney beans			80.01	67.52	79.78	83.92
红富士苹果	Hongfushi apples			100.85	107.23	106.80	101.24
香 蕉	Bananas			93.84	97.77	103.65	97.50
橙 子	Oranges			102.80	99.49	103.61	99.97

3—11 全国农产品集贸市场月度价格走势
Monthly RMF Prices of the Agricultural Products

（6 月份） （Jun.）

品种	Categories	2000	2001	2002	2003	2004	2005
一、价格	Price						
（元/公斤）	(yuan/ kg)						
籼稻	long-grain nonglutinous rice	1.00	1.07	1.07	1.04	1.59	1.49
优质籼稻	High quality long-grain nonglutinous rice	1.22	1.25	1.19	1.22	1.80	1.73
粳稻	Round-grain rice	1.23	1.36	1.18	1.16	1.79	1.80
小麦	Wheat	1.00	1.09	1.03	1.09	1.54	1.48
玉米	Corn	0.87	1.10	1.06	1.14	1.45	1.31
大豆	Soybeans	2.64	2.46	2.37	2.90	4.06	3.60
籼米	Milled long-grain nonglutinous rice			1.63	1.74	2.59	2.51
优质籼米	High quality milled long-grain nonglutinous rice			1.91	2.05	2.97	2.94
粳米	Milled round-grain rice			1.94	1.95	2.94	2.93
面粉	Wheat flour			1.71	1.75	2.39	2.35
棉花	Cotton (unginned cotton)	3.44	3.80	3.14	4.34	5.93	5.02
花生仁	Peanut kernel			4.40	5.60	6.86	6.56
油菜籽	Rapeseeds			1.86	2.28	2.82	2.55
花生油	Peanut oil	8.46	8.19	7.83	9.09	11.12	10.73
菜籽油	Rape oil	6.63	5.96	5.53	6.64	8.13	7.38
豆油	Soybean oil	6.52	5.59	5.26	6.45	7.83	6.94
烤烟	Flue-cured tobacco			8.20	8.83	9.76	12.08
活猪	Hogs	5.16	5.60	5.31	5.53	8.46	8.08
仔猪	Piglet	7.20	7.77	7.22	7.34	11.87	13.28
猪肉	Pork	9.25	9.81	9.60	9.83	14.02	13.45
牛肉	Beef	12.39	12.66	13.52	14.72	15.95	17.26
羊肉	Mutton	14.27	14.39	14.83	15.87	16.76	17.87
活鸡	Live chicken			8.28	8.34	9.96	10.76
鸡蛋	Eggs	4.74	5.08	5.34	4.96	6.41	6.70
草鱼	Grass carp	7.47	7.34	7.09	7.24	9.94	9.52
鲤鱼	Carp	8.20	7.72	6.95	6.96	10.25	8.71
鲢鱼	Silver carp			5.93	5.73	7.63	7.46
带鱼	Hairtail			8.80	9.19	10.53	10.62
大白菜	Chinese cabbage			0.87	0.83	0.98	1.31
黄瓜	Cucumber			1.03	0.92	1.13	1.30
西红柿	Tomato			1.38	1.35	1.39	1.64
菜椒	Green bell			1.46	1.64	1.80	2.03
四季豆	Kidney beans			1.65	1.52	1.86	1.95
红富士苹果	Hongfushi apples			3.38	3.65	3.39	3.43
香蕉	Bananas			2.81	2.98	3.77	3.05
橙子	Oranges			3.02	3.46	3.32	3.27

3－11 续表 continued

品 种 Categories		2000	2001	2002	2003	2004	2005
二、价格变动	Index						
（上月＝100）	(preceding month＝100)						
籼 稻	long-grain nonglutinous rice	100.00	98.94	99.67	99.22	100.69	96.20
优质籼稻	High quality long-grain nonglutinous rice	102.52	97.32	99.01	101.19	100.59	98.14
粳 稻	Round-grain rice	100.00	104.99	100.60	101.08	99.80	99.83
小 麦	Wheat	100.00	95.84	96.43	99.07	99.13	95.49
玉 米	Corn	103.57	99.05	102.47	100.85	99.86	99.55
大 豆	Soybeans	100.38	98.56	100.19	99.52	101.00	99.06
籼 米	Milled long-grain nonglutinous rice			100.72	100.63	100.30	99.01
优质籼米	High quality milled long-grain nonglutinous rice			100.66	99.77	99.84	99.28
粳 米	Milled round-grain rice			100.25	98.85	99.53	99.84
面 粉	Wheat flour			99.27	99.71	99.64	98.80
棉 花	Cotton (unginned cotton)	101.24	101.42	103.35	97.62	97.94	102.31
花生仁	Peanut kernel			103.88	101.07	101.02	99.80
油菜籽	Rapeseeds			103.03	101.02	99.20	91.98
花生油	Peanut oil	99.18	100.91	100.66	99.34	98.95	99.75
菜籽油	Rape oil	97.07	99.27	100.39	100.95	99.47	97.98
豆 油	Soybean oil	99.69	101.07	100.61	98.03	98.66	99.68
烤 烟	Flue-cured tobacco			103.36	101.78	100.43	101.14
活 猪	Hogs	97.91	99.61	98.61	99.47	103.75	97.79
仔 猪	Piglet	102.27	100.60	98.20	101.32	105.39	97.28
猪 肉	Pork	100.54	98.86	99.97	100.11	103.65	99.04
牛 肉	Beef	98.57	99.38	101.34	101.20	100.35	100.39
羊 肉	Mutton	98.28	99.79	98.26	100.83	99.81	99.47
活 鸡	Live chicken			100.25	100.45	101.55	99.76
鸡 蛋	Eggs	97.73	101.17	99.07	99.59	108.46	101.24
草 鱼	Grass carp	100.95	101.82	99.61	100.94	103.02	99.09
鲤 鱼	Carp	99.76	101.55	101.79	100.84	105.46	99.43
鲢 鱼	Silver carp			103.24	101.70	105.44	99.36
带 鱼	Hairtail			99.51	98.50	103.86	102.37
大白菜	Chinese cabbage			115.95	86.29	95.39	99.98
黄 瓜	Cucumber			66.42	66.33	70.77	68.74
西红柿	Tomato			76.49	67.58	70.46	67.48
菜 椒	Green bell			62.52	66.47	63.52	68.41
四季豆	Kidney beans			70.06	62.72	67.03	60.35
红富士苹果	Hongfushi apples			110.81	106.86	105.95	104.88
香 蕉	Bananas			90.29	97.71	95.72	97.20
橙 子	Oranges			104.33	107.93	99.31	101.44

3—12 全国农产品集贸市场月度价格走势
Monthly RMF Prices of the Agricultural Products

（7月份） (Jul.)

品 种	Categories	2000	2001	2002	2003	2004	2005
一、价格	Price						
（元/公斤）	(yuan/ kg)						
籼 稻	long-grain nonglutinous rice	0.95	1.07	1.05	1.04	1.57	1.48
优质籼稻	High quality long-grain nonglutinous rice	1.11	1.26	1.17	1.21	1.80	1.68
粳 稻	Round-grain rice	1.27	1.32	1.16	1.16	1.78	1.79
小 麦	Wheat	0.94	1.09	1.04	1.08	1.53	1.46
玉 米	Corn	0.88	1.15	1.06	1.13	1.46	1.31
大 豆	Soybeans	2.65	2.42	2.37	2.91	4.09	3.56
籼 米	Milled long-grain nonglutinous rice			1.62	1.75	2.59	2.48
优质籼米	High quality milled long-grain nonglutinous rice			1.90	2.04	2.96	2.90
粳 米	Milled round-grain rice			1.92	1.96	2.95	2.92
面 粉	Wheat flour			1.71	1.75	2.39	2.34
棉 花	Cotton (unginned cotton)	3.45	3.89	3.16	4.42	5.75	5.14
花生仁	Peanut kernel			4.40	5.56	6.86	6.54
油菜籽	Rapeseeds			1.93	2.36	2.90	2.50
花生油	Peanut oil	8.51	8.09	7.80	9.12	11.27	10.72
菜籽油	Rape oil	6.60	5.91	5.56	6.68	8.03	7.30
豆 油	Soybean oil	6.21	5.42	5.36	6.49	7.70	6.91
烤 烟	Flue-cured tobacco			8.02	8.79	10.22	12.43
活 猪	Hogs	5.38	5.62	5.35	5.78	8.63	7.97
仔 猪	Piglet	7.32	7.46	7.09	7.51	12.59	12.79
猪 肉	Pork	9.48	9.92	9.60	10.19	14.44	13.33
牛 肉	Beef	12.30	12.72	13.36	14.78	16.13	17.15
羊 肉	Mutton	14.45	14.22	14.72	15.89	16.72	17.75
活 鸡	Live chicken			8.40	8.52	10.20	10.57
鸡 蛋	Eggs	4.71	5.14	5.17	4.93	6.36	6.61
草 鱼	Grass carp	7.60	7.28	7.30	7.30	9.74	9.42
鲤 鱼	Carp	8.28	7.49	7.07	7.05	9.77	8.67
鲢 鱼	Silver carp			5.84	5.72	7.56	7.43
带 鱼	Hairtail			9.19	9.17	10.49	10.57
大白菜	Chinese cabbage			0.97	0.94	1.22	1.50
黄 瓜	Cucumber			0.90	0.89	1.21	1.49
西红柿	Tomato			1.17	1.08	1.34	1.74
菜 椒	Green bell			1.16	1.33	1.58	1.98
四季豆	Kidney beans			1.45	1.37	1.83	2.25
红富士苹果	Hongfushi apples			3.20	3.83	3.99	3.71
香 蕉	Bananas			2.49	2.90	3.51	3.07
橙 子	Oranges			2.91	3.37	3.75	3.30

3—12 续表 continued

品 种 Categories		2000	2001	2002	2003	2004	2005
二、价格变动	Index						
（上月=100）	（preceding month=100）						
籼 稻	long-grain nonglutinous rice	95.00	100.58	98.84	100.00	99.04	99.44
优质籼稻	High quality long-grain nonglutinous rice	90.98	100.44	98.69	99.62	100.18	97.43
粳 稻	Round-grain rice	103.25	97.03	98.25	99.78	99.87	99.50
小 麦	Wheat	94.00	99.95	100.20	98.63	99.20	98.84
玉 米	Corn	101.15	104.26	99.82	99.21	100.61	99.97
大 豆	Soybeans	100.38	98.46	100.10	100.38	100.68	98.73
籼 米	Milled long-grain nonglutinous rice			99.70	100.31	99.73	98.75
优质籼米	High quality milled long-grain nonglutinous rice			99.20	99.64	99.56	98.70
粳 米	Milled round-grain rice			99.07	100.36	100.22	99.62
面 粉	Wheat flour			99.65	100.01	100.06	99.57
棉 花	Cotton (unginned cotton)	100.26	102.34	100.80	101.88	96.89	102.34
花生仁	Peanut kernel			100.10	99.19	100.11	99.64
油菜籽	Rapeseeds			103.90	103.23	103.06	97.87
花生油	Peanut oil	100.59	98.74	99.71	100.33	101.35	99.95
菜籽油	Rape oil	99.55	99.31	100.50	100.49	98.76	98.93
豆 油	Soybean oil	95.25	96.91	101.93	100.65	98.30	99.61
烤 烟	Flue-cured tobacco			97.75	99.52	104.69	102.87
活 猪	Hogs	104.26	100.40	100.76	104.42	102.10	98.64
仔 猪	Piglet	101.67	96.04	98.32	102.26	106.03	96.27
猪 肉	Pork	102.49	101.18	100.06	103.61	102.98	99.08
牛 肉	Beef	99.27	100.47	98.78	100.39	101.10	99.38
羊 肉	Mutton	101.26	98.83	99.29	100.08	99.74	99.29
活 鸡	Live chicken			101.40	102.16	102.35	98.25
鸡 蛋	Eggs	99.37	101.25	96.87	99.21	99.12	98.70
草 鱼	Grass carp	101.74	99.19	102.93	100.82	97.96	98.93
鲤 鱼	Carp	100.98	96.98	101.77	101.19	95.34	99.50
鲢 鱼	Silver carp			98.57	99.83	99.01	99.63
带 鱼	Hairtail			104.47	99.86	99.56	99.59
大白菜	Chinese cabbage			111.16	113.41	123.93	114.26
黄 瓜	Cucumber			87.38	96.50	106.51	114.83
西红柿	Tomato			85.25	79.92	96.37	106.31
菜 椒	Green bell			79.32	80.85	87.73	97.56
四季豆	Kidney beans			87.82	89.85	98.45	115.06
红富士苹果	Hongfushi apples			94.78	104.83	102.55	108.03
香 蕉	Bananas			88.55	97.04	92.90	100.60
橙 子	Oranges			96.27	97.21	103.59	100.80

3—13 全国农产品集贸市场月度价格走势
Monthly RMF Prices of the Agricultural Products

(8月份) (Aug.)

品　种	Categories	2000	2001	2002	2003	2004	2005
一、价格	Price						
(元/公斤)	(yuan/ kg)						
籼 稻	long-grain nonglutinous rice	0.97	1.06	1.04	1.05	1.55	1.46
优质籼稻	High quality long-grain nonglutinous rice	1.15	1.22	1.16	1.21	1.78	1.67
粳 稻	Round-grain rice	1.30	1.34	1.16	1.17	1.77	1.78
小 麦	Wheat	0.98	1.09	1.06	1.08	1.56	1.47
玉 米	Corn	0.89	1.13	1.06	1.15	1.45	1.31
大 豆	Soybeans	2.64	2.41	2.38	2.94	4.08	3.56
籼 米	Milled long-grain nonglutinous rice			1.63	1.75	2.57	2.46
优质籼米	High quality milled long-grain nonglutinous rice			1.92	2.04	2.97	2.89
粳 米	Milled round-grain rice			1.93	1.97	2.96	2.93
面 粉	Wheat flour			1.71	1.75	2.39	2.34
棉 花	Cotton (unginned cotton)	3.50	3.78	3.11	4.46	5.66	5.10
花生仁	Peanut kernel			4.43	5.65	6.90	6.58
油菜籽	Rapeseeds			1.88	2.38	2.89	2.52
花生油	Peanut oil	8.48	7.94	7.87	9.16	11.21	10.76
菜籽油	Rape oil	6.36	5.96	5.77	6.71	8.06	7.22
豆 油	Soybean oil	6.23	5.45	5.62	6.52	7.73	6.85
烤 烟	Flue-cured tobacco			7.96	8.57	10.36	12.55
活 猪	Hogs	5.57	5.74	5.58	6.00	9.01	7.92
仔 猪	Piglet	7.43	7.59	7.33	7.81	13.69	12.50
猪 肉	Pork	9.82	10.13	9.93	10.56	15.01	13.28
牛 肉	Beef	12.66	12.60	13.65	14.90	16.32	17.22
羊 肉	Mutton	14.58	14.41	15.07	15.95	16.77	17.88
活 鸡	Live chicken			8.32	8.70	10.57	10.70
鸡 蛋	Eggs	5.17	5.44	5.59	5.23	6.84	6.77
草 鱼	Grass carp	7.34	7.28	7.08	7.30	9.65	9.39
鲤 鱼	Carp	7.89	7.53	7.03	7.15	9.29	8.55
鲢 鱼	Silver carp			5.98	5.75	7.48	7.35
带 鱼	Hairtail			8.97	9.28	10.45	10.66
大白菜	Chinese cabbage			0.99	1.15	1.34	1.49
黄 瓜	Cucumber			1.23	1.38	1.49	1.64
西红柿	Tomato			1.30	1.45	1.70	1.94
菜 椒	Green bell			1.45	1.59	1.73	2.03
四季豆	Kidney beans			1.90	1.83	2.19	2.42
红富士苹果	Hongfushi apples			3.02	3.86	3.92	3.83
香 蕉	Bananas			2.61	2.95	3.47	3.20
橙 子	Oranges			2.97	3.62	3.70	3.25

3—13 续表 continued

品　种 Categories		2000	2001	2002	2003	2004	2005
二、价格变动	Index						
(上月=100)	(preceding month=100)						
籼 稻	long-grain nonglutinous rice	102.11	99.19	98.52	100.15	98.62	98.83
优质籼稻	High quality long-grain nonglutinous rice	103.60	97.25	98.62	99.95	98.81	99.02
粳 稻	Round-grain rice	102.36	101.29	100.01	100.55	99.43	99.41
小 麦	Wheat	104.26	100.12	101.84	100.55	102.30	100.64
玉 米	Corn	101.14	98.34	99.68	101.49	99.03	100.28
大 豆	Soybeans	99.62	99.82	100.27	100.88	99.90	100.04
籼 米	Milled long-grain nonglutinous rice			100.66	100.34	99.46	99.14
优质籼米	High quality milled long-grain nonglutinous rice			100.93	100.19	100.36	99.69
粳 米	Milled round-grain rice			100.39	100.79	100.24	100.33
面 粉	Wheat flour			100.04	99.79	99.95	99.96
棉 花	Cotton (unginned cotton)	101.39	97.17	98.29	100.89	98.39	99.28
花生仁	Peanut kernel			100.75	101.71	100.47	100.68
油菜籽	Rapeseeds			97.32	101.09	99.50	100.73
花生油	Peanut oil	99.65	98.22	100.90	100.40	99.47	100.38
菜籽油	Rape oil	96.36	100.70	103.82	100.45	100.41	98.88
豆 油	Soybean oil	100.32	100.57	104.76	100.45	100.45	99.22
烤 烟	Flue-cured tobacco			99.31	97.54	101.37	100.96
活 猪	Hogs	103.53	102.06	104.22	103.90	104.41	99.29
仔 猪	Piglet	101.50	101.69	103.32	103.99	108.77	97.71
猪 肉	Pork	103.59	102.09	103.35	103.63	103.93	99.63
牛 肉	Beef	102.93	99.07	102.14	100.82	101.20	100.42
羊 肉	Mutton	100.90	101.33	102.35	100.42	100.30	100.74
活 鸡	Live chicken			99.10	102.14	103.65	101.23
鸡 蛋	Eggs	109.77	105.64	108.19	106.15	107.64	102.37
草 鱼	Grass carp	96.58	100.12	96.88	100.01	99.03	99.74
鲤 鱼	Carp	95.29	100.62	99.45	101.42	95.04	98.58
鲢 鱼	Silver carp			102.29	100.61	98.99	98.92
带 鱼	Hairtail			97.54	101.17	99.69	100.83
大白菜	Chinese cabbage			102.61	122.87	109.53	99.48
黄 瓜	Cucumber			137.54	156.06	123.43	110.03
西红柿	Tomato			111.20	134.77	127.26	111.72
菜 椒	Green bell			125.23	119.54	109.18	102.59
四季豆	Kidney beans			130.85	133.98	119.81	107.66
红富士苹果	Hongfushi apples			94.47	100.72	98.13	103.33
香 蕉	Bananas			104.71	101.90	99.09	104.16
橙 子	Oranges			102.13	107.59	98.79	98.41

3—14 全国农产品集贸市场月度价格走势
Monthly RMF Prices of the Agricultural Products

（9月份） （Sep.）

品　种	Categories	2000	2001	2002	2003	2004	2005
一、价格	Price						
（元/公斤）	（yuan/ kg）						
籼 稻	long-grain nonglutinous rice	0.96	1.07	1.05	1.05	1.57	1.46
优质籼稻	High quality long-grain nonglutinous rice	1.13	1.24	1.16	1.23	1.78	1.67
粳 稻	Round-grain rice	1.26	1.39	1.16	1.18	1.80	1.79
小 麦	Wheat	0.97	1.12	1.05	1.10	1.57	1.47
玉 米	Corn	0.90	1.13	1.05	1.16	1.46	1.32
大 豆	Soybeans	2.51	2.45	2.42	2.94	4.04	3.51
籼 米	Milled long-grain nonglutinous rice			1.63	1.77	2.57	2.47
优质籼米	High quality milled long-grain nonglutinous rice			1.93	2.05	2.98	2.91
粳 米	Milled round-grain rice			1.96	1.98	2.99	2.94
面 粉	Wheat flour			1.72	1.76	2.41	2.33
棉 花	Cotton (unginned cotton)	3.34	3.40	3.48	4.85	5.32	5.28
花生仁	Peanut kernel			4.54	5.67	6.86	6.59
油菜籽	Rapeseeds			1.94	2.44	2.92	2.54
花生油	Peanut oil	8.40	7.93	8.25	9.24	11.28	10.66
菜籽油	Rape oil	6.34	5.85	6.10	6.76	8.02	7.18
豆 油	Soybean oil	6.09	5.42	5.88	6.56	7.68	6.78
烤 烟	Flue-cured tobacco			7.89	8.61	10.36	12.51
活 猪	Hogs	5.58	5.87	5.60	6.25	9.32	7.87
仔 猪	Piglet	7.54	7.58	7.29	8.13	14.59	12.16
猪 肉	Pork	9.98	10.32	9.96	10.98	15.29	13.23
牛 肉	Beef	12.81	12.76	13.85	15.04	16.65	17.44
羊 肉	Mutton	14.54	14.24	15.19	16.02	16.95	17.86
活 鸡	Live chicken			8.42	8.88	10.85	10.57
鸡 蛋	Eggs	5.29	5.54	5.62	5.52	7.27	6.96
草 鱼	Grass carp	7.35	7.27	7.11	7.25	9.52	9.39
鲤 鱼	Carp	7.74	7.46	7.00	7.14	9.09	8.59
鲢 鱼	Silver carp			5.81	5.87	7.29	7.42
带 鱼	Hairtail			9.13	9.20	10.48	10.63
大白菜	Chinese cabbage			1.05	1.19	1.30	1.41
黄 瓜	Cucumber			1.36	1.53	1.63	1.71
西红柿	Tomato			1.52	1.72	1.94	2.08
菜 椒	Green bell			1.56	1.94	1.93	2.21
四季豆	Kidney beans			1.98	2.12	2.30	2.56
红富士苹果	Hongfushi apples			2.93	3.56	3.67	3.79
香 蕉	Bananas			2.67	3.15	3.33	3.50
橙 子	Oranges			2.98	3.98	3.70	3.34

3—14 续表 continued

品 种	Categories	2000	2001	2002	2003	2004	2005
二、价格变动	Index						
(上月=100)	(preceding month=100)						
籼稻	long-grain nonglutinous rice	98.97	100.64	101.22	100.47	101.22	99.60
优质籼稻	High quality long-grain nonglutinous rice	98.26	101.39	100.28	100.97	100.19	100.17
粳稻	Round-grain rice	96.92	103.33	100.03	101.38	101.55	100.62
小麦	Wheat	98.98	103.29	99.11	101.55	100.31	99.62
玉米	Corn	101.12	100.28	99.59	100.44	100.80	100.29
大豆	Soybeans	95.08	101.42	101.91	100.29	98.82	98.49
籼米	Milled long-grain nonglutinous rice			99.54	100.93	99.96	100.60
优质籼米	High quality milled long-grain nonglutinous rice			100.92	100.37	100.33	100.57
粳米	Milled round-grain rice			101.49	100.46	100.98	100.54
面粉	Wheat flour			100.77	100.85	100.76	99.63
棉花	Cotton (unginned cotton)	95.45	89.96	111.78	108.80	94.05	103.47
花生仁	Peanut kernel			102.29	100.37	99.53	100.06
油菜籽	Rapeseeds			103.00	102.56	101.01	101.02
花生油	Peanut oil	99.06	99.82	104.79	100.88	100.66	99.09
菜籽油	Rape oil	99.69	98.16	105.70	100.86	99.57	99.47
豆油	Soybean oil	97.75	99.50	104.67	100.49	99.31	98.98
烤烟	Flue-cured tobacco			99.16	100.44	100.06	99.69
活猪	Hogs	100.18	102.35	100.42	104.20	103.42	99.36
仔猪	Piglet	101.48	99.91	99.50	104.14	106.56	97.30
猪肉	Pork	101.63	101.88	100.38	104.00	101.89	99.63
牛肉	Beef	101.18	101.23	101.52	100.94	102.04	101.26
羊肉	Mutton	99.73	98.82	100.82	100.45	101.05	99.89
活鸡	Live chicken			101.24	102.06	102.69	98.83
鸡蛋	Eggs	102.32	101.97	100.55	105.66	106.21	102.86
草鱼	Grass carp	100.14	99.82	100.54	99.32	98.70	99.93
鲤鱼	Carp	98.10	98.98	99.59	99.92	97.81	100.48
鲢鱼	Silver carp			97.27	102.08	97.41	100.87
带鱼	Hairtail			101.81	99.14	100.23	99.72
大白菜	Chinese cabbage			106.42	102.87	97.45	94.54
黄瓜	Cucumber			110.20	110.32	109.54	104.33
西红柿	Tomato			116.82	118.84	113.73	107.14
菜椒	Green bell			107.43	121.98	111.82	109.03
四季豆	Kidney beans			104.62	115.67	104.74	105.87
红富士苹果	Hongfushi apples			97.04	92.19	93.60	98.97
香蕉	Bananas			102.39	106.75	95.94	109.42
橙子	Oranges			100.14	109.98	100.00	102.75

3—15 全国农产品集贸市场月度价格走势
Monthly RMF Prices of the Agricultural Products

（10月份） （Oct.）

品 种	Categories	2000	2001	2002	2003	2004	2005
一、价格	Price						
（元/公斤）	(yuan/ kg)						
籼 稻	long-grain nonglutinous rice	0.98	1.06	1.02	1.07	1.55	1.45
优质籼稻	High quality long-grain nonglutinous rice	1.16	1.24	1.14	1.25	1.76	1.66
粳 稻	Round-grain rice	1.29	1.32	1.13	1.24	1.78	1.77
小 麦	Wheat	1.00	1.12	1.02	1.14	1.58	1.45
玉 米	Corn	0.90	1.10	0.97	1.16	1.43	1.29
大 豆	Soybeans	2.47	2.40	2.42	3.06	3.93	3.48
籼 米	Milled long-grain nonglutinous rice			1.62	1.80	2.56	2.47
优质籼米	High quality milled long-grain nonglutinous rice			1.91	2.09	2.95	2.92
粳 米	Milled round-grain rice			1.93	2.03	2.96	2.95
面 粉	Wheat flour			1.67	1.80	2.41	2.33
棉 花	Cotton (unginned cotton)	3.50	3.20	3.93	5.90	4.93	5.51
花生仁	Peanut kernel			4.39	5.83	6.85	6.53
油菜籽	Rapeseeds			1.95	2.54	2.89	2.57
花生油	Peanut oil	8.32	7.85	7.86	9.92	11.24	10.61
菜籽油	Rape oil	6.63	5.85	6.10	7.25	7.88	7.17
豆 油	Soybean oil	6.01	5.42	5.72	7.47	7.51	6.70
烤 烟	Flue-cured tobacco			6.95	8.47	10.58	12.64
活 猪	Hogs	5.65	5.85	5.62	6.74	9.26	7.31
仔 猪	Piglet	7.44	7.40	7.36	8.60	14.41	10.55
猪 肉	Pork	10.16	10.30	9.91	11.79	15.07	12.72
牛 肉	Beef	12.77	12.86	14.02	15.30	16.65	17.49
羊 肉	Mutton	14.37	14.70	15.19	16.25	17.13	18.06
活 鸡	Live chicken			8.27	9.08	10.82	10.44
鸡 蛋	Eggs	5.09	5.45	5.44	5.66	6.90	6.66
草 鱼	Grass carp	7.31	7.20	7.00	7.30	9.30	9.29
鲤 鱼	Carp	7.65	7.32	6.87	7.14	8.76	8.47
鲢 鱼	Silver carp			5.69	5.85	7.17	7.35
带 鱼	Hairtail			8.86	9.44	10.37	10.52
大白菜	Chinese cabbage			0.75	1.02	0.90	1.27
黄 瓜	Cucumber			1.52	1.94	1.80	2.19
西红柿	Tomato			1.63	2.14	2.05	2.39
菜 椒	Green bell			1.84	2.24	2.23	2.50
四季豆	Kidney beans			2.03	2.30	2.24	2.78
红富士苹果	Hongfushi apples			2.73	3.16	3.29	3.56
香 蕉	Bananas			2.70	3.15	3.22	3.48
橙 子	Oranges			2.91	3.67	3.57	3.28

3—15 续表 continued

品　种	Categories	2000	2001	2002	2003	2004	2005
二、价格变动	Index						
（上月＝100）	(preceding month＝100)						
籼稻	long-grain nonglutinous rice	102.33	99.03	97.39	101.72	98.94	99.61
优质籼稻	High quality long-grain nonglutinous rice	102.68	100.23	98.56	101.80	98.71	99.39
粳稻	Round-grain rice	102.59	94.94	97.39	105.02	98.84	99.00
小麦	Wheat	103.01	99.47	97.84	103.41	100.67	98.99
玉米	Corn	99.92	97.19	91.89	100.77	98.09	97.87
大豆	Soybeans	98.31	98.17	99.78	103.91	97.33	99.27
籼米	Milled long-grain nonglutinous rice			99.83	101.55	99.42	99.90
优质籼米	High quality milled long-grain nonglutinous rice			98.57	101.87	99.27	100.34
粳米	Milled round-grain rice			98.74	102.58	99.30	100.25
面粉	Wheat flour			97.03	101.95	100.21	100.11
棉花	Cotton (unginned cotton)	104.82	94.19	112.98	121.53	92.64	104.28
花生仁	Peanut kernel			96.76	102.82	99.78	99.16
油菜籽	Rapeseeds			100.41	104.09	99.21	100.94
花生油	Peanut oil	99.10	99.00	95.29	107.41	99.64	99.54
菜籽油	Rape oil	104.57	100.11	99.95	107.17	98.26	99.75
豆油	Soybean oil	98.73	99.97	97.27	113.88	97.82	98.69
烤烟	Flue-cured tobacco			88.05	98.34	102.11	101.07
活猪	Hogs	101.21	99.59	100.39	107.84	99.34	92.94
仔猪	Piglet	98.65	97.60	100.85	105.81	98.78	86.80
猪肉	Pork	101.83	99.83	99.43	107.38	98.58	96.10
牛肉	Beef	99.66	100.83	101.21	101.69	100.02	100.25
羊肉	Mutton	98.86	103.22	99.98	101.42	101.09	101.11
活鸡	Live chicken			98.10	102.28	99.70	98.79
鸡蛋	Eggs	96.16	98.26	96.74	102.46	94.93	95.71
草鱼	Grass carp	99.52	98.96	98.34	100.63	97.74	98.95
鲤鱼	Carp	98.79	98.11	98.08	99.97	96.43	98.59
鲢鱼	Silver carp			97.83	99.62	98.34	99.06
带鱼	Hairtail			97.09	102.62	98.96	98.98
大白菜	Chinese cabbage			71.48	86.37	69.25	90.14
黄瓜	Cucumber			111.79	126.72	110.36	127.96
西红柿	Tomato			107.31	124.40	106.02	114.78
菜椒	Green bell			118.46	115.64	115.44	112.72
四季豆	Kidney beans			102.21	108.65	97.42	108.47
红富士苹果	Hongfushi apples			92.98	88.77	89.67	93.94
香蕉	Bananas			101.20	100.00	96.56	99.44
橙子	Oranges			97.79	92.08	96.40	98.14

3—16 全国农产品集贸市场价格走势

Monthly RMF Prices of the Agricultural Products

（11月份） （Nov.）

品 种	Categories	2000	2001	2002	2003	2004	2005
一、价格	Price						
（元/公斤）	（yuan/ kg）						
籼 稻	long-grain nonglutinous rice	1.00	1.06	1.02	1.19	1.54	1.45
优质籼稻	High quality long-grain nonglutinous rice	1.19	1.25	1.14	1.41	1.75	1.66
粳 稻	Round-grain rice	1.26	1.28	1.10	1.36	1.74	1.76
小 麦	Wheat	1.02	1.11	1.05	1.26	1.56	1.46
玉 米	Corn	0.92	1.05	1.00	1.25	1.37	1.26
大 豆	Soybeans	2.46	2.36	2.46	3.40	3.78	3.46
籼 米	Milled long-grain nonglutinous rice			1.61	1.98	2.52	2.46
优质籼米	High quality milled long-grain nonglutinous rice			1.91	2.33	2.94	2.91
粳 米	Milled round-grain rice			1.90	2.25	2.90	2.95
面 粉	Wheat flour			1.70	2.01	2.41	2.33
棉 花	Cotton (unginned cotton)	3.57	2.90	4.11	6.28	4.72	5.48
花生仁	Peanut kernel			4.50	6.21	6.77	6.53
油菜籽	Rapeseeds			2.01	2.87	2.87	2.58
花生油	Peanut oil	8.16	7.88	8.13	10.78	11.04	10.64
菜籽油	Rape oil	6.24	5.88	6.15	7.93	7.80	7.16
豆 油	Soybean oil	5.94	5.36	5.82	7.67	7.31	6.65
烤 烟	Flue-cured tobacco			6.92	8.74	11.08	12.62
活 猪	Hogs	5.79	5.92	5.70	7.23	8.88	7.09
仔 猪	Piglet	7.56	7.42	7.27	9.12	13.67	9.57
猪 肉	Pork	10.35	10.32	9.97	12.59	14.63	12.27
牛 肉	Beef	12.62	13.08	14.30	15.74	16.51	17.54
羊 肉	Mutton	14.63	14.62	15.37	16.60	17.15	18.18
活 鸡	Live chicken			8.34	9.52	10.52	9.37
鸡 蛋	Eggs	5.09	5.33	5.39	6.14	6.65	6.34
草 鱼	Grass carp	7.25	7.15	6.93	7.43	9.12	9.12
鲤 鱼	Carp	7.50	7.17	6.72	7.20	8.60	8.30
鲢 鱼	Silver carp			5.64	5.93	6.99	7.21
带 鱼	Hairtail			9.01	9.40	10.31	10.48
大白菜	Chinese cabbage			0.64	0.92	0.72	1.04
黄 瓜	Cucumber			2.12	2.33	1.96	2.48
西红柿	Tomato			1.98	2.49	2.06	2.55
菜 椒	Green bell			2.13	2.63	2.31	3.03
四季豆	Kidney beans			2.50	2.65	2.52	3.02
红富士苹果	Hongfushi apples			2.76	3.07	3.22	3.56
香 蕉	Bananas			2.69	3.31	3.17	3.46
橙 子	Oranges			2.60	3.44	3.40	3.32

3—16 续表 continued

品 种	Categories	2000	2001	2002	2003	2004	2005
二、价格变动	Index						
(上月=100)	(preceding month=100)						
籼稻	long-grain nonglutinous rice	102.11	99.52	100.08	111.81	99.05	100.21
优质籼稻	High quality long-grain nonglutinous rice	102.74	100.25	99.55	113.03	99.53	100.17
粳稻	Round-grain rice	97.83	97.38	97.61	109.54	97.66	99.54
小麦	Wheat	101.82	98.83	102.47	110.76	99.15	100.78
玉米	Corn	102.64	95.04	103.69	107.16	95.65	97.91
大豆	Soybeans	99.60	98.00	101.64	111.10	96.15	99.43
籼米	Milled long-grain nonglutinous rice			99.29	110.03	98.52	99.63
优质籼米	High quality milled long-grain nonglutinous rice			100.03	111.72	99.42	99.54
粳米	Milled round-grain rice			98.08	110.70	97.85	100.15
面粉	Wheat flour			101.53	112.01	99.94	99.98
棉花	Cotton (unginned cotton)	102.14	90.43	104.66	106.49	95.75	99.56
花生仁	Peanut kernel			102.45	106.49	98.82	100.01
油菜籽	Rapeseeds			103.47	112.93	99.15	100.63
花生油	Peanut oil	97.99	100.39	103.40	108.63	98.21	100.29
菜籽油	Rape oil	94.17	100.50	100.93	109.33	98.91	99.88
豆油	Soybean oil	98.73	98.93	101.87	102.69	97.24	99.35
烤烟	Flue-cured tobacco			99.59	103.20	104.70	99.79
活猪	Hogs	102.60	101.14	101.46	107.25	95.92	96.94
仔猪	Piglet	101.57	100.37	98.80	106.03	94.87	90.73
猪肉	Pork	101.86	100.18	100.60	106.77	97.04	96.51
牛肉	Beef	98.82	101.70	101.98	102.89	99.14	100.28
羊肉	Mutton	101.79	99.41	101.19	102.16	100.11	100.67
活鸡	Live chicken			100.86	104.87	97.25	89.69
鸡蛋	Eggs	100.04	97.86	99.00	108.51	96.40	95.20
草鱼	Grass carp	99.14	99.31	99.01	101.87	97.98	98.20
鲤鱼	Carp	98.11	97.97	97.88	100.85	98.12	97.99
鲢鱼	Silver carp			99.23	101.42	97.57	98.16
带鱼	Hairtail			101.64	99.50	99.45	99.55
大白菜	Chinese cabbage			84.55	89.76	79.28	81.73
黄瓜	Cucumber			139.74	120.47	108.84	113.54
西红柿	Tomato			121.17	116.33	100.13	106.58
菜椒	Green bell			115.22	117.34	103.77	121.24
四季豆	Kidney beans			123.34	115.07	112.71	108.62
红富士苹果	Hongfushi apples			101.19	97.15	97.95	100.07
香蕉	Bananas			99.68	105.16	98.35	99.28
橙子	Oranges			89.35	93.66	95.31	101.45

3—17 全国农产品集贸市场月度价格走势
Monthly RMF Prices of the Agricultural Products

(12 月份) (Dec.)

品 种	Categories	2000	2001	2002	2003	2004	2005
一、价格	Price						
(元/公斤)	(yuan/ kg)						
籼稻	long-grain nonglutinous rice	1.01	1.08	1.03	1.21	1.54	1.47
优质籼稻	High quality long-grain nonglutinous rice	1.19	1.27	1.15	1.39	1.74	1.69
粳稻	Round-grain rice	1.27	1.28	1.11	1.36	1.74	1.79
小麦	Wheat	1.06	1.13	1.05	1.34	1.56	1.47
玉米	Corn	0.97	1.03	1.02	1.28	1.33	1.26
大豆	Soybeans	2.46	2.34	2.52	3.38	3.77	3.46
籼米	Milled long-grain nonglutinous rice			1.63	2.00	2.51	2.48
优质籼米	High quality milled long-grain nonglutinous rice			1.93	2.37	2.93	2.93
粳米	Milled round-grain rice			1.91	2.24	2.89	2.97
面粉	Wheat flour			1.71	2.11	2.40	2.33
棉花	Cotton (unginned cotton)	3.60	2.91	4.12	5.88	4.66	5.63
花生仁	Peanut kernel			4.64	6.33	6.72	6.51
油菜籽	Rapeseeds			2.06	2.84	2.87	2.61
花生油	Peanut oil	8.30	7.72	8.20	11.10	11.09	10.64
菜籽油	Rape oil	6.21	5.71	6.28	7.94	7.72	7.15
豆油	Soybean oil	5.89	5.29	6.18	7.68	7.30	6.67
烤烟	Flue-cured tobacco			7.65	8.87	11.49	12.84
活猪	Hogs	5.88	5.98	5.79	7.34	8.84	7.25
仔猪	Piglet	7.56	7.44	7.35	9.02	13.48	9.42
猪肉	Pork	10.21	10.34	10.12	12.55	14.40	12.34
牛肉	Beef	12.74	13.17	14.60	15.77	16.54	17.77
羊肉	Mutton	14.58	14.98	15.78	16.68	17.52	18.63
活鸡	Live chicken			8.39	9.48	10.47	9.18
鸡蛋	Eggs	5.10	5.38	5.43	6.09	6.74	6.21
草鱼	Grass carp	7.28	7.22	6.87	7.34	9.07	9.16
鲤鱼	Carp	7.56	7.17	6.62	7.16	8.64	8.28
鲢鱼	Silver carp			5.64	5.85	6.96	7.16
带鱼	Hairtail			8.94	9.22	10.20	10.48
大白菜	Chinese cabbage			0.71	0.89	0.65	1.11
黄瓜	Cucumber			2.62	2.88	2.36	2.72
西红柿	Tomato			2.30	2.76	2.15	2.93
菜椒	Green bell			2.49	2.87	2.67	3.32
四季豆	Kidney beans			2.79	3.08	3.03	3.49
红富士苹果	Hongfushi apples			2.90	3.03	3.17	3.65
香蕉	Bananas			2.77	3.35	3.20	3.42
橙子	Oranges			2.83	3.48	3.26	3.38

3—17 续表 continued

品 种	Categories	2000	2001	2002	2003	2004	2005
二、价格变动	Index						
(上月=100)	(preceding month=100)						
籼稻	long-grain nonglutinous rice	100.26	102.36	100.86	101.43	99.96	101.04
优质籼稻	High quality long-grain nonglutinous rice	99.68	101.65	100.86	98.83	99.57	101.33
粳稻	Round-grain rice	100.58	99.65	101.34	99.97	100.04	101.36
小麦	Wheat	104.23	101.86	100.51	106.15	99.68	100.24
玉米	Corn	104.55	98.22	101.47	102.23	97.45	100.04
大豆	Soybeans	99.95	99.27	102.59	99.52	99.70	100.11
籼米	Milled long-grain nonglutinous rice			100.99	101.41	99.55	100.59
优质籼米	High quality milled long-grain nonglutinous rice			101.13	101.69	99.78	100.90
粳米	Milled round-grain rice			101.02	99.69	99.52	100.50
面粉	Wheat flour			100.75	104.96	99.83	99.91
棉花	Cotton (unginned cotton)	100.79	100.30	100.22	93.73	98.83	102.72
花生仁	Peanut kernel			103.26	101.97	99.33	99.67
油菜籽	Rapeseeds			102.24	99.01	100.06	100.96
花生油	Peanut oil	101.78	97.98	100.86	102.98	100.50	99.92
菜籽油	Rape oil	99.52	97.02	102.15	100.11	98.94	99.84
豆油	Soybean oil	99.15	98.71	106.18	100.16	99.93	100.33
烤烟	Flue-cured tobacco			110.58	101.49	103.71	101.74
活猪	Hogs	101.43	101.13	101.44	101.44	99.45	102.34
仔猪	Piglet	100.04	100.26	101.09	98.87	98.63	98.40
猪肉	Pork	98.65	100.15	101.58	99.70	98.42	100.54
牛肉	Beef	100.98	100.71	102.11	100.19	100.19	101.32
羊肉	Mutton	99.68	102.46	102.64	100.46	102.18	102.50
活鸡	Live chicken			100.65	99.52	99.51	97.97
鸡蛋	Eggs	100.21	101.01	100.82	99.18	101.31	97.88
草鱼	Grass carp	100.34	101.09	99.23	98.79	99.43	100.41
鲤鱼	Carp	100.82	99.97	98.46	99.48	100.47	99.82
鲢鱼	Silver carp			99.89	98.66	99.53	99.32
带鱼	Hairtail			99.21	98.19	98.93	100.03
大白菜	Chinese cabbage			111.73	96.66	90.20	106.91
黄瓜	Cucumber			123.59	123.53	120.72	109.72
西红柿	Tomato			116.15	110.91	104.67	115.21
菜椒	Green bell			117.31	109.06	115.43	109.69
四季豆	Kidney beans			111.47	116.54	120.18	115.51
红富士苹果	Hongfushi apples			105.13	98.95	98.44	102.54
香蕉	Bananas			102.74	101.21	101.12	98.95
橙子	Oranges			108.70	101.40	95.95	101.58

3—18 全国农产品集贸市场月度价格走势(2005 年 1 月)
Monthly RMF Prices of the Agricultural Products(Jan. 2005)

农产品名称	Categories of agricultural products	价格(元/公斤) Price (yuan/ kg)	价格走势 Increase rate 本月比上月上涨 Increase rate over the last month (%)	本月比上年同月上涨 Increase rate over the same month of the preceding year (%)	1—1 月比上年同期上涨 Jan.-Jan. increase rate over the same period of the preceding year (%)
籼稻	Long-grain nonglutinous rice	1.55	1.06	26.52	26.52
优质籼稻	High quality long-grain nonglutinous rice	1.75	0.21	22.36	22.36
粳稻	Round-grain rice	1.75	0.66	26.26	26.26
小麦	Wheat	1.56	0.23	16.80	16.80
玉米	Corn	1.31	−1.83	1.72	1.72
大豆	Soybeans	3.74	−0.69	6.31	6.31
籼米	Milled long-grain nonglutinous rice	2.53	0.91	24.49	24.49
优质籼米	High quality milled long-grain nonglutinous rice	2.96	0.86	23.24	23.24
粳米	Milled round-grain rice	2.89	0.26	26.25	26.25
面粉	Wheat flour	2.39	−0.67	10.92	10.92
棉花(籽棉)	Cotton (unginned cotton)	4.66	−0.08	−21.71	−21.71
花生仁	Peanut kernel	6.69	−0.52	2.08	2.08
油菜籽	Rapeseeds	2.85	−0.87	1.46	1.46
花生油	Peanut oil	11.04	−0.50	0.47	0.47
菜籽油	Rape oil	7.74	0.27	−3.77	−3.77
豆油	Soybean oil	7.20	−1.44	−7.32	−7.32
烤烟	Flue-cured tobacco	11.33	−1.37	21.46	21.46
活猪	Hogs	8.80	−0.38	18.03	18.03
仔猪	Piglet	13.29	−1.44	44.22	44.22
猪肉	Pork	14.33	−0.43	12.57	12.57
牛肉	Beef	16.95	2.48	5.28	5.28
羊肉	Mutton	18.40	4.99	7.90	7.90
活鸡	Live chicken	10.51	0.32	3.78	3.78
鸡蛋	Eggs	6.78	0.58	9.70	9.70
草鱼	Grass carp	9.31	2.71	20.99	20.99
鲤鱼	Carp	8.80	1.86	15.82	15.82
鲢鱼	Silver carp	7.12	2.25	13.69	13.69
带鱼	Hairtail	10.24	0.41	6.25	6.25
大白菜	Chinese cabbage	0.72	11.15	−18.81	−18.81
黄瓜	Cucumber	2.65	11.99	−24.94	−24.94
西红柿	Tomato	2.49	15.70	−22.85	−22.85
菜椒	Green bell	3.11	16.45	−11.16	−11.16
四季豆	Kidney beans	3.42	12.92	−6.50	−6.50
红富士苹果	Hongfushi apples	3.24	2.15	3.20	3.20
香蕉	Bananas	3.24	1.28	−9.14	−9.14
橙子	Oranges	3.14	−3.90	−11.15	−11.15

3—19 全国农产品集贸市场月度价格走势(2005 年 2 月)
Monthly RMF Prices of the Agricultural Products(Feb. 2005)

农产品名称 Categories of agricultural products		价格(元/公斤) Price (yuan/ kg)	价格走势 Increase rate		
			本月比上月上涨 Increase rate over the last month (%)	本月比上年同月上涨 Increase rate over the same month of the preceding year (%)	1—2 月比上年同期上涨 Jan. -Feb. increase rate over the same period of the preceding year (%)
籼稻	Long-grain nonglutinous rice	1.55	—0.03	21.47	23.95
优质籼稻	High quality long-grain nonglutinous rice	1.77	1.53	20.44	21.38
粳稻	Round-grain rice	1.76	0.79	22.53	24.36
小麦	Wheat	1.57	0.79	16.94	16.87
玉米	Corn	1.31	0.22	1.94	1.83
大豆	Soybeans	3.71	—0.85	4.06	5.18
籼米	Milled long-grain nonglutinous rice	2.55	0.75	21.73	23.09
优质籼米	High quality milled long-grain nonglutinous rice	3.00	1.51	22.33	22.78
粳米	Milled round-grain rice	2.93	1.19	24.31	25.27
面粉	Wheat flour	2.41	0.81	11.18	11.05
棉花(籽棉)	Cotton (unginned cotton)	4.75	1.97	—20.73	—21.22
花生仁	Peanut kernel	6.71	0.28	3.31	2.69
油菜籽	Rapeseeds	2.84	—0.16	2.66	2.06
花生油	Peanut oil	11.11	0.63	1.32	0.89
菜籽油	Rape oil	7.79	0.65	—2.03	—2.90
豆油	Soybean oil	7.22	0.37	—7.18	—7.25
烤烟	Flue-cured tobacco	11.87	4.74	28.27	24.85
活猪	Hogs	8.80	—0.06	18.63	18.33
仔猪	Piglet	13.39	0.73	42.87	43.54
猪肉	Pork	14.33	—0.03	14.75	13.65
牛肉	Beef	17.76	4.76	11.30	8.27
羊肉	Mutton	19.16	4.15	13.72	10.79
活鸡	Live chicken	11.03	4.96	22.58	12.62
鸡蛋	Eggs	6.86	1.22	17.92	13.69
草鱼	Grass carp	9.78	5.05	23.91	22.47
鲤鱼	Carp	9.23	4.85	17.58	16.71
鲢鱼	Silver carp	7.46	4.85	18.03	15.87
带鱼	Hairtail	10.77	5.09	12.37	9.30
大白菜	Chinese cabbage	0.98	37.31	12.53	—3.21
黄瓜	Cucumber	3.71	40.21	34.80	1.25
西红柿	Tomato	2.99	20.18	—2.81	—13.06
菜椒	Green bell	3.81	22.46	13.27	0.81
四季豆	Kidney beans	4.14	20.84	14.21	3.80
红富士苹果	Hongfushi apples	3.34	3.08	7.38	5.28
香蕉	Bananas	3.40	5.03	—1.49	—5.38
橙子	Oranges	3.26	3.86	—4.78	—8.01

3—20 全国农产品集贸市场月度价格走势(2005 年 3 月)
Monthly RMF Prices of the Agricultural Products(Mar. 2005)

农产品名称 Categories of agricultural products		价 格(元/公斤) Price (yuan/kg)	价格走势 Increase rate		
			本月比上月上涨 Increase rate over the last month (%)	本月比上年同月上涨 Increase rate over the same month of the preceding year (%)	1—3 月比上年同期上涨 Jan.-Mar. increase rate over the same period of the preceding year (%)
籼 稻	Long-grain nonglutinous rice	1.56	0.56	—0.25	14.64
优质籼稻	High quality long-grain nonglutinous rice	1.78	0.28	—0.40	13.08
粳 稻	Round-grain rice	1.78	0.86	0.07	14.98
小 麦	Wheat	1.57	—0.17	4.71	12.51
玉 米	Corn	1.32	0.35	—2.98	0.17
大 豆	Soybeans	3.71	0.12	—0.74	3.14
籼 米	Milled long-grain nonglutinous rice	2.57	0.70	0.49	14.45
优质籼米	High quality milled long-grain nonglutinous rice	3.02	0.67	3.84	15.68
粳 米	Milled round-grain rice	2.95	0.88	4.12	17.25
面 粉	Wheat flour	2.39	—0.59	2.46	8.03
棉花(籽棉)	Cotton (unginned cotton)	4.91	3.35	—19.03	—20.48
花生仁	Peanut kernel	6.65	—0.85	0.29	1.88
油菜籽	Rapeseeds	2.86	0.48	2.49	2.20
花生油	Peanut oil	11.06	—0.42	0.06	0.61
菜籽油	Rape oil	7.74	—0.65	—3.77	—3.19
豆 油	Soybean oil	7.17	—0.81	—10.12	—8.22
烤 烟	Flue-cured tobacco	11.89	0.17	27.76	25.82
活 猪	Hogs	8.71	—1.02	12.59	16.37
仔 猪	Piglet	13.90	3.83	33.94	40.10
猪 肉	Pork	14.03	—2.07	10.56	12.62
牛 肉	Beef	17.37	—2.18	9.07	8.54
羊 肉	Mutton	18.39	—4.00	7.98	9.85
活 鸡	Live chicken	10.95	—0.74	18.84	14.64
鸡 蛋	Eggs	6.49	—5.37	12.09	13.17
草 鱼	Grass carp	9.58	—2.08	13.65	19.38
鲤 鱼	Carp	8.93	—3.19	7.45	13.47
鲢 鱼	Silver carp	7.46	—0.02	13.92	15.21
带 鱼	Hairtail	10.31	—4.22	7.53	8.71
大白菜	Chinese cabbage	0.95	—3.10	1.54	—1.56
黄 瓜	Cucumber	3.26	—12.11	17.90	6.34
西红柿	Tomato	2.71	—9.62	—3.12	—10.01
菜 椒	Green bell	3.66	—3.88	—3.05	—0.56
四季豆	Kidney beans	4.13	—0.11	0.45	2.59
红富士苹果	Hongfushi apples	3.29	—1.41	3.71	4.75
香 蕉	Bananas	3.29	—3.32	—5.75	—5.50
橙 子	Oranges	3.25	—0.23	—7.55	—7.86

3－21 全国农产品集贸市场月度价格走势(2005 年 4 月)
Monthly RMF Prices of the Agricultural Products(Apr. 2005)

农产品名称 Categories of agricultural products		价 格 (元/公斤) Price (yuan/ kg)	价格走势 Increase rate 本月比上月上涨 Increase rate over the last month (%)	本月比上年同月上涨 Increase rate over the same month of the preceding year (%)	1—4 月比上年同期上涨 Jan. -Apr. increase rate over the same period of the preceding year (%)
籼 稻	Long-grain nonglutinous rice	1.56	0.10	－1.06	10.25
优质籼稻	High quality long-grain nonglutinous rice	1.77	－0.51	－1.52	9.04
粳 稻	Round-grain rice	1.81	1.63	0.11	10.79
小 麦	Wheat	1.58	0.40	0.57	9.25
玉 米	Corn	1.33	0.93	－7.81	－1.97
大 豆	Soybeans	3.67	－1.07	－7.50	0.28
籼 米	Milled long-grain nonglutinous rice	2.56	－0.21	－1.65	9.93
优质籼米	High quality milled long-grain nonglutinous rice	2.99	－0.99	－0.56	11.15
粳 米	Milled round-grain rice	2.93	－0.78	－2.65	11.54
面 粉	Wheat flour	2.39	－0.34	－0.95	5.65
棉花(籽棉)	Cotton (unginned cotton)	4.75	－3.37	－22.58	－21.01
花生仁	Peanut kernel	6.64	－0.09	－1.42	1.04
油菜籽	Rapeseeds	2.85	－0.24	－1.17	1.34
花生油	Peanut oil	10.85	－1.91	－3.94	－0.55
菜籽油	Rape oil	7.77	0.38	－4.22	－3.45
豆 油	Soybean oil	7.06	－1.46	－12.17	－9.23
烤 烟	Flue-cured tobacco	11.60	－2.40	22.57	25.00
活 猪	Hogs	8.48	－2.60	4.97	13.36
仔 猪	Piglet	13.66	－1.75	22.03	35.06
猪 肉	Pork	13.76	－1.92	3.27	10.18
牛 肉	Beef	17.08	－1.66	7.70	8.33
羊 肉	Mutton	17.91	－2.61	5.46	8.75
活 鸡	Live chicken	10.70	－2.28	11.79	13.92
鸡 蛋	Eggs	6.28	－3.25	5.99	11.59
草 鱼	Grass carp	9.59	0.12	3.99	15.11
鲤 鱼	Carp	8.78	－1.64	－1.47	9.40
鲢 鱼	Silver carp	7.36	－1.34	7.00	13.04
带 鱼	Hairtail	10.33	0.18	6.05	8.04
大白菜	Chinese cabbage	1.19	24.77	5.86	0.63
黄 瓜	Cucumber	2.66	－18.32	26.17	10.09
西红柿	Tomato	2.85	5.25	15.03	－4.66
菜 椒	Green bell	3.95	8.01	13.59	2.93
四季豆	Kidney beans	3.86	－6.68	10.90	4.53
红富士苹果	Hongfushi apples	3.23	－1.85	－6.10	1.85
香 蕉	Bananas	3.22	－2.11	－15.29	－8.10
橙 子	Oranges	3.23	－0.67	－8.18	－7.94

3—22 全国农产品集贸市场月度价格走势(2005年5月)
Monthly RMF Prices of the Agricultural Products (May 2005)

农产品名称 Categories of agricultural products		价格(元/公斤) Price (yuan/kg)	价格走势 Increase rate		
			本月比上月上涨 Increase rate over the last month (%)	本月比上年同月上涨 Increase rate over the same month of the preceding year (%)	1—5月比上年同期上涨 Jan.-May. increase rate over the same period of the preceding year (%)
籼稻	Long-grain nonglutinous rice	1.55	−1.04	−1.85	7.62
优质籼稻	High quality long-grain nonglutinous rice	1.76	−0.40	−1.34	6.79
粳稻	Round-grain rice	1.80	−0.40	0.67	8.58
小麦	Wheat	1.55	−1.64	−0.02	7.28
玉米	Corn	1.32	−0.90	−9.45	−3.56
大豆	Soybeans	3.64	−0.91	−9.47	−1.87
籼米	Milled long-grain nonglutinous rice	2.54	−0.97	−1.90	7.36
优质籼米	High quality milled long-grain nonglutinous rice	2.96	−0.92	−0.34	8.66
粳米	Milled round-grain rice	2.93	0.00	−0.87	8.82
面粉	Wheat flour	2.38	−0.31	−0.72	4.32
棉花(籽棉)	Cotton (unginned cotton)	4.91	3.44	−18.97	−20.60
花生仁	Peanut kernel	6.58	−1.00	−3.09	0.19
油菜籽	Rapeseeds	2.78	−2.55	−2.23	0.62
花生油	Peanut oil	10.75	−0.91	−4.30	−1.30
菜籽油	Rape oil	7.54	−2.96	−7.76	−4.32
豆油	Soybean oil	6.96	−1.45	−12.36	−9.86
烤烟	Flue-cured tobacco	11.95	2.95	22.95	24.58
活猪	Hogs	8.27	−2.53	1.42	10.86
仔猪	Piglet	13.66	0.01	21.24	32.03
猪肉	Pork	13.58	−1.30	0.41	8.14
牛肉	Beef	17.19	0.63	8.15	8.29
羊肉	Mutton	17.97	0.31	6.99	8.40
活鸡	Live chicken	10.78	0.79	9.88	13.09
鸡蛋	Eggs	6.62	5.39	11.92	11.49
草鱼	Grass carp	9.61	0.20	−0.45	11.61
鲤鱼	Carp	8.76	−0.25	−9.86	4.98
鲢鱼	Silver carp	7.51	2.03	3.73	11.01
带鱼	Hairtail	10.37	0.40	2.27	6.84
大白菜	Chinese cabbage	1.31	10.14	27.01	6.24
黄瓜	Cucumber	1.89	−29.20	17.93	11.08
西红柿	Tomato	2.42	−14.87	22.97	−0.64
菜椒	Green bell	2.97	−24.96	4.51	3.19
四季豆	Kidney beans	3.24	−16.08	16.66	6.44
红富士苹果	Hongfushi apples	3.27	1.24	−10.98	−1.00
香蕉	Bananas	3.14	−2.50	−20.32	−10.74
橙子	Oranges	3.23	−0.03	−11.40	−8.65

3—23 全国农产品集贸市场月度价格走势(2005年6月)
Monthly RMF Prices of the Agricultural Products(Jun. 2005)

农产品名称 Categories of agricultural products		价格(元/公斤) Price (yuan/kg)	价格走势 Increase rate		
			本月比上月上涨 Increase rate over the last month (%)	本月比上年同月上涨 Increase rate over the same month of the preceding year (%)	1—6月比上年同期上涨 Jan.-Jun. increase rate over the same period of the preceding year (%)
籼稻	Long-grain nonglutinous rice	1.49	−3.80	−6.23	5.12
优质籼稻	High quality long-grain nonglutinous rice	1.73	−1.86	−3.74	4.91
粳稻	Round-grain rice	1.80	−0.17	0.70	7.17
小麦	Wheat	1.48	−4.51	−3.69	5.38
玉米	Corn	1.31	−0.45	−9.73	−4.64
大豆	Soybeans	3.60	−0.94	−11.22	−3.48
籼米	Milled long-grain nonglutinous rice	2.51	−0.99	−3.17	5.47
优质籼米	High quality milled long-grain nonglutinous rice	2.94	−0.72	−0.90	6.96
粳米	Milled round-grain rice	2.93	−0.16	−0.56	7.13
面粉	Wheat flour	2.35	−1.20	−1.56	3.30
棉花(籽棉)	Cotton (unginned cotton)	5.02	2.31	−15.36	−19.74
花生仁	Peanut kernel	6.56	−0.20	−4.26	−0.57
油菜籽	Rapeseeds	2.55	−8.02	−9.35	−1.04
花生油	Peanut oil	10.73	−0.25	−3.52	−1.67
菜籽油	Rape oil	7.38	−2.02	−9.14	−5.13
豆油	Soybean oil	6.94	−0.32	−11.46	−10.12
烤烟	Flue-cured tobacco	12.08	1.14	23.82	24.45
活猪	Hogs	8.08	−2.21	−4.41	8.13
仔猪	Piglet	13.28	−2.72	11.91	28.26
猪肉	Pork	13.45	−0.96	−4.05	5.97
牛肉	Beef	17.26	0.39	8.20	8.28
羊肉	Mutton	17.87	−0.53	6.63	8.11
活鸡	Live chicken	10.76	−0.24	7.94	12.20
鸡蛋	Eggs	6.70	1.24	4.47	10.24
草鱼	Grass carp	9.52	−0.91	−4.25	8.62
鲤鱼	Carp	8.71	−0.57	−15.02	1.09
鲢鱼	Silver carp	7.46	−0.64	−2.25	8.53
带鱼	Hairtail	10.62	2.37	0.80	5.76
大白菜	Chinese cabbage	1.31	−0.02	33.12	10.77
黄瓜	Cucumber	1.30	−31.26	14.54	11.36
西红柿	Tomato	1.64	−32.52	17.77	1.07
菜椒	Green bell	2.03	−31.59	12.55	4.09
四季豆	Kidney beans	1.95	−39.65	5.02	6.30
红富士苹果	Hongfushi apples	3.43	4.88	−11.88	−3.08
香蕉	Bananas	3.05	−2.80	−19.09	−12.17
橙子	Oranges	3.27	1.44	−9.51	−8.80

3－24 全国农产品集贸市场月度价格走势(2005 年 7 月)
Monthly RMF Prices of the Agricultural Products (Jul. 2005)

农产品名称 Categories of agricultural products		价 格 (元/公斤) Price (yuan/ kg)	价格走势 Increase rate		
			本月比上月上涨 Increase rate over the last month (%)	本月比上年同月上涨 Increase rate over the same month of the preceding year (%)	1—7 月比上年同期上涨 Jan. -Jul. increase rate over the same period of the preceding year (%)
籼 稻	Long-grain nonglutinous rice	1.48	－0.56	－5.84	3.46
优质籼稻	High quality long-grain nonglutinous rice	1.68	－2.57	－6.38	3.20
粳 稻	Round-grain rice	1.79	－0.50	0.32	6.13
小 麦	Wheat	1.46	－1.16	－4.03	3.99
玉 米	Corn	1.31	－0.03	－10.30	－5.49
大 豆	Soybeans	3.56	－1.27	－12.94	－4.91
籼 米	Milled long-grain nonglutinous rice	2.48	－1.25	－4.11	4.02
优质籼米	High quality milled long-grain nonglutinous rice	2.90	－1.30	－1.75	5.65
粳 米	Milled round-grain rice	2.92	－0.38	－1.15	5.87
面 粉	Wheat flour	2.34	－0.43	－2.03	2.52
棉花(籽棉)	Cotton (unginned cotton)	5.14	2.34	－10.60	－18.49
花生仁	Peanut kernel	6.54	－0.36	－4.71	－1.18
油菜籽	Rapeseeds	2.50	－2.13	－13.91	－2.93
花生油	Peanut oil	10.72	－0.05	－4.85	－2.13
菜籽油	Rape oil	7.30	－1.07	－8.98	－5.68
豆 油	Soybean oil	6.91	－0.39	－10.28	－10.14
烤 烟	Flue-cured tobacco	12.43	2.87	21.66	24.02
活 猪	Hogs	7.97	－1.36	－7.65	5.69
仔 猪	Piglet	12.79	－3.73	1.61	23.84
猪 肉	Pork	13.33	－0.92	－7.68	3.86
牛 肉	Beef	17.15	－0.62	6.36	8.00
羊 肉	Mutton	17.75	－0.71	6.15	7.83
活 鸡	Live chicken	10.57	－1.75	3.62	10.91
鸡 蛋	Eggs	6.61	－1.30	4.03	9.31
草 鱼	Grass carp	9.42	－1.07	－3.30	6.77
鲤 鱼	Carp	8.67	－0.50	－11.31	－0.86
鲢 鱼	Silver carp	7.43	－0.37	－1.64	6.95
带 鱼	Hairtail	10.57	－0.41	0.83	5.02
大白菜	Chinese cabbage	1.50	14.26	22.73	12.84
黄 瓜	Cucumber	1.49	14.83	23.48	12.33
西红柿	Tomato	1.74	6.31	29.92	3.45
菜 椒	Green bell	1.98	－2.44	25.17	5.73
四季豆	Kidney beans	2.25	15.06	22.74	7.71
红富士苹果	Hongfushi apples	3.71	8.03	－7.18	－3.75
香 蕉	Bananas	3.07	0.60	－12.38	－12.20
橙 子	Oranges	3.30	0.80	－11.95	－9.27

3－25 全国农产品集贸市场月度价格走势(2005年8月)
Monthly RMF Prices of the Agricultural Products(Aug. 2005)

农产品名称 Categories of agricultural products		价格(元/公斤) Price (yuan/kg)	价格走势 Increase rate		
			本月比上月上涨 Increase rate over the last month (%)	本月比上年同月上涨 Increase rate over the same month of the preceding year (%)	1—8月比上年同期上涨 Jan.-Aug. increase rate over the same period of the preceding year (%)
籼稻	Long-grain nonglutinous rice	1.46	−1.17	−5.64	2.28
优质籼稻	High quality long-grain nonglutinous rice	1.67	−0.98	−6.18	1.98
粳稻	Round-grain rice	1.78	−0.59	0.30	5.37
小麦	Wheat	1.47	0.64	−5.59	2.74
玉米	Corn	1.31	0.28	−9.17	−5.97
大豆	Soybeans	3.56	0.04	−12.82	−5.95
籼米	Milled long-grain nonglutinous rice	2.46	−0.86	−4.42	2.91
优质籼米	High quality milled long-grain nonglutinous rice	2.89	−0.31	−2.41	4.59
粳米	Milled round-grain rice	2.93	0.33	−1.06	4.95
面粉	Wheat flour	2.34	−0.04	−2.03	1.94
棉花(籽棉)	Cotton (unginned cotton)	5.10	−0.72	−9.79	−17.45
花生仁	Peanut kernel	6.58	0.68	−4.51	−1.60
油菜籽	Rapeseeds	2.52	0.73	−12.84	−4.19
花生油	Peanut oil	10.76	0.38	−3.98	−2.37
菜籽油	Rape oil	7.22	−1.12	−10.38	−6.27
豆油	Soybean oil	6.85	−0.78	−11.38	−10.30
烤烟	Flue-cured tobacco	12.55	0.96	21.17	23.64
活猪	Hogs	7.92	−0.71	−12.18	3.21
仔猪	Piglet	12.50	−2.29	−8.73	18.86
猪肉	Pork	13.28	−0.37	−11.50	1.73
牛肉	Beef	17.22	0.42	5.55	7.69
羊肉	Mutton	17.88	0.74	6.61	7.68
活鸡	Live chicken	10.70	1.23	1.20	9.60
鸡蛋	Eggs	6.77	2.37	−1.06	7.87
草鱼	Grass carp	9.39	−0.26	−2.61	5.51
鲤鱼	Carp	8.55	−1.42	−8.01	−1.78
鲢鱼	Silver carp	7.35	−1.08	−1.71	5.79
带鱼	Hairtail	10.66	0.83	1.99	4.63
大白菜	Chinese cabbage	1.49	−0.52	11.47	12.62
黄瓜	Cucumber	1.64	10.03	10.08	12.13
西红柿	Tomato	1.94	11.72	14.06	4.45
菜椒	Green bell	2.03	2.59	17.61	6.66
四季豆	Kidney beans	2.42	7.66	10.29	7.95
红富士苹果	Hongfushi apples	3.83	3.33	−2.26	−3.54
香蕉	Bananas	3.20	4.16	−7.90	−11.68
橙子	Oranges	3.25	−1.59	−12.28	−9.66

3—26 全国农产品集贸市场月度价格走势(2005年9月)
Monthly RMF Prices of the Agricultural Products(Sep. 2005)

农产品名称 Categories of agricultural products		价格(元/公斤) Price (yuan/ kg)	价格走势 Increase rate 本月比上月上涨 Increase rate over the last month (%)	本月比上年同月上涨 Increase rate over the same month of the preceding year (%)	1—9月比上年同期上涨 Jan.-Sep. increase rate over the same period of the preceding year (%)
籼稻	Long-grain nonglutinous rice	1.46	−0.40	−7.16	1.18
优质籼稻	High quality long-grain nonglutinous rice	1.67	0.17	−6.20	1.03
粳稻	Round-grain rice	1.79	0.62	−0.62	4.67
小麦	Wheat	1.47	−0.38	−6.24	1.70
玉米	Corn	1.32	0.29	−9.63	−6.39
大豆	Soybeans	3.51	−1.51	−13.11	−6.78
籼米	Milled long-grain nonglutinous rice	2.47	0.60	−3.82	2.13
优质籼米	High quality milled long-grain nonglutinous rice	2.91	0.57	−2.18	3.81
粳米	Milled round-grain rice	2.94	0.54	−1.49	4.19
面粉	Wheat flour	2.33	−0.37	−3.13	1.36
棉花(籽棉)	Cotton (unginned cotton)	5.28	3.47	−0.76	−15.77
花生仁	Peanut kernel	6.59	0.06	−3.99	−1.87
油菜籽	Rapeseeds	2.54	1.02	−12.84	−5.18
花生油	Peanut oil	10.66	−0.91	−5.48	−2.72
菜籽油	Rape oil	7.18	−0.53	−10.46	−6.73
豆油	Soybean oil	6.78	−1.02	−11.68	−10.45
烤烟	Flue-cured tobacco	12.51	−0.31	20.73	23.30
活猪	Hogs	7.87	−0.64	−15.63	0.85
仔猪	Piglet	12.16	−2.70	−16.66	13.89
猪肉	Pork	13.23	−0.37	−13.46	−0.15
牛肉	Beef	17.44	1.26	4.75	7.35
羊肉	Mutton	17.86	−0.11	5.39	7.43
活鸡	Live chicken	10.57	−1.17	−2.60	8.12
鸡蛋	Eggs	6.96	2.86	−4.18	6.32
草鱼	Grass carp	9.39	−0.07	−1.41	4.71
鲤鱼	Carp	8.59	0.48	−5.50	−2.20
鲢鱼	Silver carp	7.42	0.87	1.78	5.33
带鱼	Hairtail	10.63	−0.28	1.47	4.26
大白菜	Chinese cabbage	1.41	−5.46	8.14	12.02
黄瓜	Cucumber	1.71	4.33	4.85	11.47
西红柿	Tomato	2.08	7.14	7.45	4.74
菜椒	Green bell	2.21	9.03	14.67	7.30
四季豆	Kidney beans	2.56	5.87	11.48	8.27
红富士苹果	Hongfushi apples	3.79	−1.03	3.34	−2.75
香蕉	Bananas	3.50	9.42	5.04	−9.96
橙子	Oranges	3.34	2.75	−9.87	−9.68

3—27 全国农产品集贸市场月度价格走势(2005年10月)
Monthly RMF Prices of the Agricultural Products(Oct. 2005)

农产品名称 Categories of agricultural products		价格(元/公斤) Price (yuan/kg)	价格走势 Increase rate		
			本月比上月上涨 Increase rate over the last month (%)	本月比上年同月上涨 Increase rate over the same month of the preceding year (%)	1—10月比上年同期上涨 Jan.-Oct. increase rate over the same period of the preceding year (%)
籼稻	Long-grain nonglutinous rice	1.45	−0.39	−6.54	0.84
优质籼稻	High quality long-grain nonglutinous rice	1.66	−0.61	−5.55	0.77
粳稻	Round-grain rice	1.77	−1.00	−0.45	4.21
小麦	Wheat	1.45	−1.01	−7.80	1.18
玉米	Corn	1.29	−2.13	−9.84	−6.56
大豆	Soybeans	3.48	−0.73	−11.37	−6.85
籼米	Milled long-grain nonglutinous rice	2.47	−0.10	−3.35	1.76
优质籼米	High quality milled long-grain nonglutinous rice	2.92	0.34	−1.13	3.41
粳米	Milled round-grain rice	2.95	0.25	−0.54	3.62
面粉	Wheat flour	2.33	0.11	−3.23	1.04
棉花(籽棉)	Cotton (unginned cotton)	5.51	4.28	11.70	−14.40
花生仁	Peanut kernel	6.53	−0.84	−4.59	−2.03
油菜籽	Rapeseeds	2.57	0.94	−11.32	−5.34
花生油	Peanut oil	10.61	−0.46	−5.57	−2.79
菜籽油	Rape oil	7.17	−0.25	−9.10	−6.53
豆油	Soybean oil	6.70	−1.31	−10.89	−10.09
烤烟	Flue-cured tobacco	12.64	1.07	19.51	22.26
活猪	Hogs	7.31	−7.06	−21.06	−0.37
仔猪	Piglet	10.55	−13.20	−26.77	11.16
猪肉	Pork	12.72	−3.90	−15.64	−1.12
牛肉	Beef	17.49	0.25	4.99	6.97
羊肉	Mutton	18.06	1.11	5.41	7.27
活鸡	Live chicken	10.44	−1.21	−3.49	7.15
鸡蛋	Eggs	6.66	−4.29	−3.39	5.28
草鱼	Grass carp	9.29	−1.05	−0.19	4.45
鲤鱼	Carp	8.47	−1.41	−3.38	−1.97
鲢鱼	Silver carp	7.35	−0.94	2.52	5.11
带鱼	Hairtail	10.52	−1.02	1.49	3.95
大白菜	Chinese cabbage	1.27	−9.86	40.77	13.87
黄瓜	Cucumber	2.19	27.96	21.56	12.73
西红柿	Tomato	2.39	14.78	16.33	5.50
菜椒	Green bell	2.50	12.72	11.97	9.09
四季豆	Kidney beans	2.78	8.47	24.12	10.71
红富士苹果	Hongfushi apples	3.56	−6.06	8.27	−2.01
香蕉	Bananas	3.48	−0.56	8.18	−9.01
橙子	Oranges	3.28	−1.86	−8.25	−9.61

3—28 全国农产品集贸市场月度价格走势(2005 年 11 月)
Monthly RMF Prices of the Agricultural Products (Nov. 2005)

农产品名称 Categories of agricultural products		价格(元/公斤) Price (yuan/kg)	价格走势 Increase rate 本月比上月上涨 Increase rate over the last month (%)	本月比上年同月上涨 Increase rate over the same month of the preceding year (%)	1—11 月比上年同期上涨 Jan.-Nov. increase rate over the same period of the preceding year (%)
籼稻	Long-grain nonglutinous rice	1.45	0.21	−5.45	−0.15
优质籼稻	High quality long-grain nonglutinous rice	1.66	0.17	−4.94	−0.13
粳稻	Round-grain rice	1.76	−0.46	1.46	3.89
小麦	Wheat	1.46	0.78	−6.28	0.05
玉米	Corn	1.26	−2.09	−7.71	−6.83
大豆	Soybeans	3.46	−0.57	−8.35	−7.34
籼米	Milled long-grain nonglutinous rice	2.46	−0.37	−2.26	1.21
优质籼米	High quality milled long-grain nonglutinous rice	2.91	−0.46	−1.01	2.89
粳米	Milled round-grain rice	2.95	0.15	1.80	3.52
面粉	Wheat flour	2.33	−0.02	−3.19	0.51
棉花(籽棉)	Cotton (unginned cotton)	5.48	−0.44	16.15	−11.20
花生仁	Peanut kernel	6.53	0.01	−3.44	−2.27
油菜籽	Rapeseeds	2.58	0.63	−9.99	−6.18
花生油	Peanut oil	10.64	0.29	−3.57	−3.06
菜籽油	Rape oil	7.16	−0.12	−8.21	−7.07
豆油	Soybean oil	6.65	−0.65	−8.96	−10.36
烤烟	Flue-cured tobacco	12.62	−0.21	13.91	21.98
活猪	Hogs	7.09	−3.06	−20.22	−3.37
仔猪	Piglet	9.57	−9.27	−29.97	4.92
猪肉	Pork	12.27	−3.49	−16.09	−3.20
牛肉	Beef	17.54	0.28	6.20	7.02
羊肉	Mutton	18.18	0.67	6.00	7.11
活鸡	Live chicken	9.37	−10.31	−11.00	5.17
鸡蛋	Eggs	6.34	−4.80	−4.58	4.33
草鱼	Grass carp	9.12	−1.80	0.04	3.83
鲤鱼	Carp	8.30	−2.01	−3.52	−2.42
鲢鱼	Silver carp	7.21	−1.84	3.14	4.87
带鱼	Hairtail	10.48	−0.45	1.60	3.76
大白菜	Chinese cabbage	1.04	−18.27	45.13	16.40
黄瓜	Cucumber	2.48	13.54	26.82	13.67
西红柿	Tomato	2.55	6.58	23.82	7.37
菜椒	Green bell	3.03	21.24	30.82	9.58
四季豆	Kidney beans	3.02	8.62	19.62	10.36
红富士苹果	Hongfushi apples	3.56	0.07	10.61	−0.69
香蕉	Bananas	3.46	−0.72	9.20	−6.89
橙子	Oranges	3.32	1.45	−2.34	−8.92

3—29 全国农产品集贸市场月度价格走势(2005 年 12 月)
Monthly RMF Prices of the Agricultural Products(Dec. 2005)

农产品名称 Categories of agricultural products		价格(元/公斤) Price (yuan/kg)	价格走势 Increase rate		
			本月比上月上涨 Increase rate over the last month (%)	本月比上年同月上涨 Increase rate over the same month of the preceding year (%)	1—12 月比上年同期上涨 Jan.-Dec. increase rate over the same period of the preceding year (%)
籼稻	Long-grain nonglutinous rice	1.47	1.04	−4.43	−0.52
优质籼稻	High quality long-grain nonglutinous rice	1.69	1.33	−3.26	−0.39
粳稻	Round-grain rice	1.79	1.36	2.81	3.80
小麦	Wheat	1.47	0.24	−5.75	−0.45
玉米	Corn	1.26	0.04	−5.25	−6.70
大豆	Soybeans	3.46	0.11	−7.98	−7.39
籼米	Milled long-grain nonglutinous rice	2.48	0.59	−1.24	1.00
优质籼米	High quality milled long-grain nonglutinous rice	2.93	0.90	0.10	2.66
粳米	Milled round-grain rice	2.97	0.50	2.79	3.46
面粉	Wheat flour	2.33	−0.09	−3.11	0.20
棉花(籽棉)	Cotton (unginned cotton)	5.63	2.72	20.72	−8.98
花生仁	Peanut kernel	6.51	−0.33	−3.11	−2.34
油菜籽	Rapeseeds	2.61	0.96	−9.17	−6.43
花生油	Peanut oil	10.64	−0.08	−4.12	−3.14
菜籽油	Rape oil	7.15	−0.16	−7.37	−7.10
豆油	Soybean oil	6.67	0.33	−8.59	−10.22
烤烟	Flue-cured tobacco	12.84	1.74	11.74	21.01
活猪	Hogs	7.25	2.34	−17.91	−4.64
仔猪	Piglet	9.42	−1.60	−30.13	1.68
猪肉	Pork	12.34	0.54	−14.28	−4.15
牛肉	Beef	17.77	1.32	7.40	7.06
羊肉	Mutton	18.63	2.50	6.32	7.04
活鸡	Live chicken	9.18	−2.03	−12.38	3.65
鸡蛋	Eggs	6.21	−2.12	−7.81	3.26
草鱼	Grass carp	9.16	0.41	1.03	3.60
鲤鱼	Carp	8.28	−0.18	−4.14	−2.56
鲢鱼	Silver carp	7.16	−0.68	2.91	4.71
带鱼	Hairtail	10.48	0.03	2.72	3.67
大白菜	Chinese cabbage	1.11	6.91	72.01	19.40
黄瓜	Cucumber	2.72	9.72	15.26	13.82
西红柿	Tomato	2.93	15.21	36.29	9.75
菜椒	Green bell	3.32	9.69	24.32	10.84
四季豆	Kidney beans	3.49	15.51	14.98	10.78
红富士苹果	Hongfushi apples	3.65	2.54	15.21	0.52
香蕉	Bananas	3.42	−1.05	6.86	−5.84
橙子	Oranges	3.38	1.58	3.39	−7.98

3－30 2005年各地区农产品集贸市场价格

Annual RMF Prices of Agricultural Products by Region(2005)

单位:元/公斤 Unit:yuan/ kg

地区	Region	粮食 Grain					
		籼稻 long-grain nonglutinous rice	优质籼稻 High quality long-grain nonglutinous rice	粳稻 Round-grain rice	小麦 Wheat	玉米 Corn	大豆 Soybeans
北京	Beijing			2.00	1.60	1.39	3.74
天津	Tianjin	1.67	1.72	1.76	1.58	1.21	3.67
河北	Hebei				1.53	1.13	3.58
山西	Shanxi				1.63	1.07	4.14
内蒙古	Inner Mongolia				1.46	1.07	3.79
辽宁	Liaoning			1.89	1.81	1.03	3.01
吉林	Jilin			1.84		0.93	3.05
黑龙江	Heilongjiang			1.77		0.91	2.70
上海	Shanghai						4.31
江苏	Jiangsu	1.54	1.58	1.78	1.38	1.42	3.27
浙江	Zhejiang	1.75	1.78	1.97	1.76	1.75	4.42
安徽	Anhui	1.44	1.57	1.78	1.36	1.30	3.26
福建	Fujian	1.59	1.82	1.74	1.60	1.60	4.27
江西	Jiangxi	1.43	1.64	1.61	1.24	2.25	3.78
山东	Shandong			1.71	1.44	1.20	3.31
河南	Henan				1.37	1.13	3.34
湖北	Hubei	1.40	1.50	1.53	1.33	1.33	3.51
湖南	Hunan	1.45	1.64	1.75	2.08	1.44	4.09
广东	Guangdong	1.47	1.56	1.42	2.43	3.19	4.81
广西	Guangxi	1.53	1.97	1.86	2.08	1.38	4.12
海南	Hainan	1.67	2.15	1.61		4.09	3.86
重庆	Chongqing	1.43	1.71	2.07	1.39	1.52	3.94
四川	Sichuan	1.45	1.73	1.82	1.44	1.40	3.71
贵州	Guizhou	1.48	1.80	1.54	1.36	1.34	3.63
云南	Yunnan	1.51	2.16	1.79	1.55	1.46	3.62
陕西	Shaanxi				1.39	1.06	3.24
甘肃	Gansu				1.55	1.11	2.91
青海	Qinghai						
宁夏	Ningxia			1.92	1.72	1.08	2.98
新疆	Xinjiang				1.43	1.02	2.49

3—30 续表 1 continued 1

地 区 Region	粮食 Grain				油料 Oil-bearing crops	
	籼 米 Milled long-grain nonglutinous rice	优质籼米 High quality milled long-grain nonglutinous rice	粳 米 Milled round-grain rice	面 粉 Wheat flour	花生仁 Peanut kernel	油菜籽 Rapeseeds
北 京 Beijing			2.80	2.11	6.55	
天 津 Tianjin	2.38	2.55	2.77	2.13	6.66	
河 北 Hebei	2.43	2.83	2.99	2.01	6.38	3.60
山 西 Shanxi			3.14	2.11	6.37	
内蒙古 Inner Mongolia	3.00	3.40	2.61	2.28	6.68	2.78
辽 宁 Liaoning			2.73	2.45	6.48	
吉 林 Jilin			2.62	2.56	6.77	
黑龙江 Heilongjiang	2.80	2.40	2.73	2.34	6.82	
上 海 Shanghai	2.66		3.08	2.70	6.88	
江 苏 Jiangsu	2.52	2.56	2.78	2.24	6.28	2.56
浙 江 Zhejiang	2.48	2.79	2.97	2.43	6.94	2.83
安 徽 Anhui	2.30	2.50	2.80	2.10	6.12	2.43
福 建 Fujian	2.55	3.05	2.99	2.66	7.14	3.47
江 西 Jiangxi	2.39	2.78	2.87	2.70	7.45	2.81
山 东 Shandong			2.94	2.00	5.81	2.95
河 南 Henan	2.58	3.02	3.02	1.85	5.84	2.39
湖 北 Hubei	2.42	2.80	2.70	2.38	6.46	2.25
湖 南 Hunan	2.53	2.98	3.22	2.97	6.64	2.59
广 东 Guangdong	3.13	3.23	3.55	2.72	7.19	
广 西 Guangxi	2.44	3.16	2.93	2.90	6.46	2.90
海 南 Hainan	2.95	3.38	2.61	3.30	7.18	
重 庆 Chongqing	2.39	2.88	3.64	2.80	7.19	2.86
四 川 Sichuan	2.49	3.11	3.08	2.50	6.99	2.54
贵 州 Guizhou	2.33	2.86	2.45	2.34	7.08	2.10
云 南 Yunnan	2.44	3.48	2.83	2.66	7.19	2.67
陕 西 Shaanxi	2.42	2.85	3.11	2.16	6.70	
甘 肃 Gansu	3.00	3.38	3.37	2.13	6.64	3.16
青 海 Qinghai		3.24	3.52	2.34	6.84	
宁 夏 Ningxia		3.23	3.14	2.30	7.19	
新 疆 Xinjiang			3.06	2.10	6.63	2.76

3—30 续表 2 continued 2

地区 Region	棉花（籽棉）Cotton (unginned cotton)	食用油 Edible oil 花生油 Peanut oil	菜籽油 Rape oil	豆油 Soybean oil	烤烟 Flue-cured tobacco
北京 Beijing	5.96	11.64		6.33	12.00
天津 Tianjin	6.19	9.51	7.34	7.18	17.50
河北 Hebei	5.04	11.26	8.19	7.30	
山西 Shanxi	4.71	7.50	7.45	6.02	
内蒙古 Inner Mongolia		12.00	8.45	8.07	6.83
辽宁 Liaoning	6.00	7.57		6.50	15.64
吉林 Jilin				6.66	7.00
黑龙江 Heilongjiang				6.23	11.25
上海 Shanghai	7.00	7.00	7.15	7.14	
江苏 Jiangsu	4.49	9.09	6.97	6.88	13.75
浙江 Zhejiang	4.93	12.01	6.92	7.63	
安徽 Anhui	4.64	9.54	6.89	7.23	9.94
福建 Fujian		9.92	8.91	8.22	10.16
江西 Jiangxi	6.03	11.86	8.31	7.25	
山东 Shandong	5.12	10.92	5.12	6.68	8.92
河南 Henan	5.23	9.20	6.27	6.31	5.08
湖北 Hubei	4.73	9.25	6.53	6.87	
湖南 Hunan	4.55	10.66	8.37	8.33	8.59
广东 Guangdong		12.83	8.63	12.54	23.75
广西 Guangxi		11.99	7.98	9.01	16.14
海南 Hainan		15.50	7.13	8.27	12.00
重庆 Chongqing		12.83	8.02	3.75	
四川 Sichuan	4.80		7.92		8.71
贵州 Guizhou		9.20	6.68	6.60	
云南 Yunnan		10.77	8.10	8.00	18.08
陕西 Shaanxi	4.95	12.99	6.56	7.13	
甘肃 Gansu	5.97	12.74	8.16	9.32	4.67
青海 Qinghai			6.98		
宁夏 Ningxia		8.56	8.09	7.89	
新疆 Xinjiang	4.05		7.00		8.00

3—30 续表 3 continued 3

地区 Region	畜产品 Livestock products						
	活猪 Hogs	仔猪 Piglet	猪肉 Pork	牛肉 Beef	羊肉 Mutton	活鸡 Live chicken	鸡蛋 Eggs
北京 Beijing	9.23	13.91	12.49	15.95	18.36	8.62	5.49
天津 Tianjin	8.48	11.83	13.59	15.00	17.71	6.52	5.32
河北 Hebei	8.09	11.61	13.18	15.53	17.16	8.06	5.43
山西 Shanxi	8.06	18.45	12.60	14.98	16.21	8.82	5.45
内蒙古 Inner Mongolia	8.48	15.23	12.56	14.82	14.90	9.89	5.68
辽宁 Liaoning	7.60	17.08	13.07	16.11	16.61	10.75	5.42
吉林 Jilin	7.87	13.99	12.41	15.02	15.96	8.66	5.55
黑龙江 Heilongjiang	7.66	14.77	11.90	14.40	15.51	7.79	5.27
上海 Shanghai			15.89	21.50	23.00	11.82	6.75
江苏 Jiangsu	7.83	8.82	14.56	18.75	19.16	8.66	6.09
浙江 Zhejiang	8.92	10.12	15.32	26.52	23.73	10.77	6.64
安徽 Anhui	8.71	12.03	14.47	18.53	18.49	9.67	7.14
福建 Fujian	9.75	13.61	14.16	21.81	24.69	16.70	8.59
江西 Jiangxi	8.72	12.00	14.35	18.56	18.56	12.66	8.81
山东 Shandong	7.82	8.97	13.26	16.13	18.65	7.88	5.61
河南 Henan	7.60	13.88	13.17	16.69	18.90	7.81	5.61
湖北 Hubei	7.96	14.45	14.40	16.94	15.17	9.75	6.92
湖南 Hunan	7.90	12.86	13.72	19.21	19.74	12.51	7.66
广东 Guangdong	10.58	9.60	14.36	20.35	20.49	14.38	7.40
广西 Guangxi	7.48	8.68	13.71	20.03	23.04	15.80	7.36
海南 Hainan	9.08	16.52	18.95	20.87	32.92	15.68	7.88
重庆 Chongqing	6.86	8.91	12.63	14.26	13.84	13.89	7.69
四川 Sichuan	6.87	8.85	11.40	15.08	13.24	12.02	8.19
贵州 Guizhou	7.94	10.26	11.47	16.68	17.20	11.38	9.32
云南 Yunnan	7.63	10.62	12.33	19.47	20.70	12.26	8.16
陕西 Shaanxi	7.59	16.64	12.23	17.23	16.98	9.89	5.96
甘肃 Gansu	9.04	20.27	13.67	16.10	14.84	11.38	6.35
青海 Qinghai	8.10	25.60	12.50	16.66	15.46	12.15	6.52
宁夏 Ningxia	9.38	19.91	12.89	16.29	16.46	8.99	5.88
新疆 Xinjiang	8.53	13.39	13.63	16.13	18.55	9.33	5.92

3—30 续表 4 continued 4

地区	Region	水产品 Aquatic products				水果 Fruits		
		草鱼 Grass carp	鲤鱼 Carp	鲢鱼 Silver carp	带鱼 Hairtail	红富士苹果 Hongfushi apples	香蕉 Bananas	橙子 Oranges
北京	Beijing	10.82	8.10	6.50	10.82	2.85	3.12	3.28
天津	Tianjin	7.93	7.18	5.03	7.46	2.39	3.34	2.49
河北	Hebei	9.63	8.65	5.53	9.69	2.20	3.37	2.49
山西	Shanxi	14.18	9.44	7.81	11.37	2.24	3.85	
内蒙古	Inner Mongolia		9.78	6.43	8.49	2.82	3.79	3.33
辽宁	Liaoning	10.23	9.49	7.44	9.91	2.92	4.24	4.03
吉林	Jilin	9.31	9.06	6.86	8.62	3.53	4.35	4.76
黑龙江	Heilongjiang		9.20	6.37	8.58	4.28	4.54	4.94
上海	Shanghai	9.95	8.12	8.99	18.23	4.76	4.29	4.08
江苏	Jiangsu	8.23	7.63	6.27	10.31	3.06	3.15	3.65
浙江	Zhejiang	9.13	8.69	7.08	16.61	4.94	3.12	5.35
安徽	Anhui	8.34	7.85	5.98	10.16	2.71	2.90	2.79
福建	Fujian	10.82	10.24	8.88	11.58	4.52	2.89	4.34
江西	Jiangxi	9.59	7.71	6.19	8.99	3.75	2.63	3.97
山东	Shandong	8.56	8.29	6.27	8.48	2.06	3.15	3.40
河南	Henan	9.05	7.89	5.69	8.36	2.19	2.76	2.35
湖北	Hubei	7.90	6.63	4.80	11.95	3.77	3.58	3.21
湖南	Hunan	9.19	7.34	5.74		4.60	3.04	3.74
广东	Guangdong	10.10	7.66	7.98	12.79	5.58	2.29	3.24
广西	Guangxi	9.56	8.78	5.77	10.60	5.56	2.04	2.57
海南	Hainan	6.38	6.53	7.61	12.45	5.38	1.39	3.37
重庆	Chongqing	9.46	9.87	8.90	11.40	4.45	3.40	2.55
四川	Sichuan	9.23	9.51		10.44	4.15	3.41	2.16
贵州	Guizhou	10.91	10.89		10.44	2.97	2.54	2.28
云南	Yunnan	9.46	10.61	8.67	10.46	3.86	2.03	2.63
陕西	Shaanxi	10.86	9.77	5.57	11.99	2.40	3.45	2.02
甘肃	Gansu	11.31	11.04	9.58	11.97	2.64	4.33	2.99
青海	Qinghai	15.00	10.57	8.49	11.35	4.39	4.64	3.88
宁夏	Ningxia	13.21	9.18	7.23	10.80	2.08	3.87	1.97
新疆	Xinjiang	11.23	8.59	5.42	9.99	3.05	4.42	3.48

3—30 续表 5 continued 5

地 区 Region		蔬菜 Vegetable			
	大白菜 Chinese cabbage	黄 瓜 Cucumber	西红柿 Tomato	菜 椒 Green bell	四季豆 Kidney beans
北 京 Beijing	0.81	2.34	2.20	2.81	3.48
天 津 Tianjin	0.74	2.41	2.24	2.84	3.01
河 北 Hebei	0.71	2.21	1.98	2.91	3.53
山 西 Shanxi	0.91	2.50	2.21	3.16	2.85
内蒙古 Inner Mongolia	0.79	2.30	2.27	3.07	3.78
辽 宁 Liaoning	1.09	2.56	2.40	3.34	3.83
吉 林 Jilin	0.89	2.44	2.52	3.13	3.53
黑龙江 Heilongjiang	0.84	2.58	2.89	3.52	
上 海 Shanghai	1.93	3.32	3.34	4.37	5.68
江 苏 Jiangsu	1.12	2.50	2.47	2.74	3.07
浙 江 Zhejiang	1.66	3.48	3.61	4.17	4.91
安 徽 Anhui	1.20	2.26	2.53	2.54	2.60
福 建 Fujian	1.89	2.36	3.04	3.71	3.43
江 西 Jiangxi	1.28	2.11	2.49	2.62	2.41
山 东 Shandong	0.95	2.20	2.04	2.94	3.40
河 南 Henan	1.11	2.22	2.08	2.33	3.16
湖 北 Hubei	1.57	2.57	2.84	2.90	3.34
湖 南 Hunan	1.50	2.39	2.91	2.82	3.18
广 东 Guangdong	2.15	2.36	2.87	3.30	3.60
广 西 Guangxi	1.74	1.91	2.09	2.46	2.28
海 南 Hainan	2.26	1.50	2.65	2.53	2.41
重 庆 Chongqing	1.19	2.30	2.46	2.53	2.71
四 川 Sichuan	1.14	1.91	2.30	2.50	2.12
贵 州 Guizhou	1.21	1.96	2.12	2.19	2.48
云 南 Yunnan	1.11	1.74	1.71	2.48	1.87
陕 西 Shaanxi	0.81	2.26	2.16	2.74	3.09
甘 肃 Gansu	0.94	2.32	2.29	3.22	3.04
青 海 Qinghai	1.06	2.88	2.46	3.05	3.14
宁 夏 Ningxia	0.83	2.10	1.76	2.93	3.56
新 疆 Xinjiang	0.80	2.15	2.15	2.90	2.98

4

农产品批发市场价格

Prices of the Agricultural Products at the Wholesale Market

4—1 2005年批发市场粮食和油料价格
Prices of Grain and Oil-bearing Crops at the Wholesale Market in 2005

单位:元/公斤 Unit:yuan/kg

农产品名称 Categories of agricultural products	等级 grades	1月 Jan	2月 Feb	3月 Mar
白色硬质小麦 Hard white wheat	三等 Ⅲ	1.72	1.73	1.68
白色软质小麦 Soft white wheat	三等 Ⅲ	—	—	2.00
红色硬质小麦 Hard red wheat	三等 Ⅲ	1.75	1.68	1.74
红色软质小麦 Soft red wheat	三等 Ⅲ	1.80	1.80	1.70
混合小麦 Mixed wheat	三等 Ⅲ	1.60	1.62	1.62
市场销量第一品牌面粉 Wheat flour that sell best at the market	一等 Ⅰ	2.33	2.31	2.37
市场销量第一品牌面粉 Wheat flour that sell best at the market	标准粉 Standard	2.11	2.08	2.09
市场销量第一品牌早籼米 Milled early long-grain nonglutinous rice that sell best at the market	一等 Ⅰ	2.41	2.50	2.50
市场销量第一品牌晚籼米 Milled late long-grain nonglutinous rice that sell best at the market	一等 Ⅰ	2.57	2.58	2.61
市场销量第一品牌早粳米 Milled early medium to short-grain rice that sell best at the market	一等 Ⅰ	2.91	2.57	2.74
市场销量第一品牌晚粳米 Milled late medium to short-grain rice that sell best at the market	一等 Ⅰ	2.82	2.73	2.84
市场销量第一品牌籼糯米 Milled long-grain glutinous rice that sell best at the market	一等 Ⅰ	2.95	2.95	2.95
市场销量第一品牌粳糯米 Milled round-grain glutinous rice that sell best at the market	一等 Ⅰ	2.95	2.98	2.99
黄玉米 Yellow corn	三等 Ⅲ	1.45	1.40	1.44
大豆 Soybeans	合格 Qualified	3.24	3.23	3.29
小米 Millet	合格 Qualified	2.75	2.76	2.84
绿豆 Mung beans	合格 Qualified	5.62	5.64	5.74
红小豆 Small red beans	合格 Qualified	5.70	5.58	5.67
花生仁 Peanut kernel	合格 Qualified	5.72	5.58	5.54
芝麻 Sesame	合格 Qualified	10.89	10.36	10.84
大豆色拉油 Soybean salad oil	合格 Qualified	6.87	6.95	6.81
花生色拉油 Peanut salad oil	合格 Qualified	11.50	10.73	11.01
菜籽色拉油 Rapeseed salad oil	合格 Qualified	6.87	6.96	6.93

4—1 续表 1 continued 1

农产品名称 Categories of agricultural products	国标等级 National grades	4月 Apr	5月 May	6月 Jun
白色硬质小麦 Hard white wheat	三等 Ⅲ	1.74	1.72	1.68
白色软质小麦 Soft white wheat	三等 Ⅲ	1.87	1.87	1.77
红色硬质小麦 Hard red wheat	三等 Ⅲ	1.78	1.75	1.73
红色软质小麦 Soft red wheat	三等 Ⅲ	1.75	1.75	1.70
混合小麦 Mixed wheat	三等 Ⅲ	1.62	1.62	1.50
市场销量第一品牌面粉 Wheat flour that sell best at the market	一等 Ⅰ	2.29	2.28	2.29
市场销量第一品牌面粉 Wheat flour that sell best at the market	标准粉 Standard	2.11	2.09	2.08
市场销量第一品牌早籼米 Milled early long-grain nonglutinous rice that sell best at the market	一等 Ⅰ	2.45	2.41	2.33
市场销量第一品牌晚籼米 Milled late long-grain nonglutinous rice that sell best at the market	一等 Ⅰ	2.54	2.52	2.49
市场销量第一品牌早粳米 Milled early medium to short-grain rice that sell best at the market	一等 Ⅰ	2.62	2.62	2.73
市场销量第一品牌晚粳米 Milled late medium to short-grain rice that sell best at the market	一等 Ⅰ	2.86	2.84	2.86
市场销量第一品牌籼糯米 Milled long-grain glutinous rice that sell best at the market	一等 Ⅰ	2.91	2.87	2.89
市场销量第一品牌粳糯米 Milled round-grain glutinous rice that sell best at the market	一等 Ⅰ	2.90	2.91	2.96
黄玉米 Yellow corn	三等 Ⅲ	1.36	1.37	1.39
大豆 Soybeans	合格 Qualified	3.29	3.37	3.24
小米 Millet	合格 Qualified	2.82	2.86	2.84
绿豆 Mung beans	合格 Qualified	5.83	5.79	5.82
红小豆 Small red beans	合格 Qualified	5.93	5.70	6.01
花生仁 Peanut kernel	合格 Qualified	5.61	5.65	5.68
芝麻 Sesame	合格 Qualified	11.63	10.94	10.79
大豆色拉油 Soybean salad oil	合格 Qualified	6.74	6.70	6.68
花生色拉油 Peanut salad oil	合格 Qualified	11.19	11.22	10.97
菜籽色拉油 Rapeseed salad oil	合格 Qualified	6.99	6.99	6.82

4—1续表2 continued 2

农产品名称 Categories of agricultural products	国标等级 National grades	7月 Jul	8月 Aug	9月 Sep
白色硬质小麦 Hard white wheat	三等 Ⅲ	1.68	1.66	1.61
白色软质小麦 Soft white wheat	三等 Ⅲ	1.80	1.81	1.83
红色硬质小麦 Hard red wheat	三等 Ⅲ	1.72	1.71	1.70
红色软质小麦 Soft red wheat	三等 Ⅲ	1.68	1.69	1.72
混合小麦 Mixed wheat	三等 Ⅲ	1.55	1.54	1.54
市场销量第一品牌面粉 Wheat flour that sell best at the market	一等 Ⅰ	2.31	2.28	2.28
市场销量第一品牌面粉 Wheat flour that sell best at the market	标准粉 Standard	2.10	2.07	2.07
市场销量第一品牌早籼米 Milled early long-grain nonglutinous rice that sell best at the market	一等 Ⅰ	2.27	2.32	2.31
市场销量第一品牌晚籼米 Milled late long-grain nonglutinous rice that sell best at the market	一等 Ⅰ	2.44	2.46	2.45
市场销量第一品牌早粳米 Milled early medium to short-grain rice that sell best at the market	一等 Ⅰ	2.63	2.63	2.63
市场销量第一品牌晚粳米 Milled late medium to short-grain rice that sell best at the market	一等 Ⅰ	2.84	2.94	2.95
市场销量第一品牌籼糯米 Milled long-grain glutinous rice that sell best at the market	一等 Ⅰ	2.90	2.91	2.93
市场销量第一品牌粳糯米 Milled round-grain glutinous rice that sell best at the market	一等 Ⅰ	2.96	2.98	3.07
黄玉米 Yellow corn	三等 Ⅲ	1.43	1.37	1.36
大豆 Soybeans	合格 Qualified	3.31	3.31	3.31
小米 Millet	合格 Qualified	2.87	2.93	2.97
绿豆 Mung beans	合格 Qualified	5.98	5.90	5.81
红小豆 Small red beans	合格 Qualified	6.35	6.00	6.04
花生仁 Peanut kernel	合格 Qualified	5.58	5.89	5.80
芝麻 Sesame	合格 Qualified	10.57	10.50	10.53
大豆色拉油 Soybean salad oil	合格 Qualified	6.54	6.48	6.29
花生色拉油 Peanut salad oil	合格 Qualified	11.27	10.80	10.81
菜籽色拉油 Rapeseed salad oil	合格 Qualified	6.68	6.57	6.52

4—1 续表 3 continued 3

农产品名称 Categories of agricultural products	国标等级 National grades	10 月 Oct	11 月 Nov	12 月 Dec
白色硬质小麦 Hard white wheat	三等 Ⅲ	1.61	1.61	1.61
白色软质小麦 Soft white wheat	三等 Ⅲ	1.84	1.77	1.77
红色硬质小麦 Hard red wheat	三等 Ⅲ	1.70	1.66	1.67
红色软质小麦 Soft red wheat	三等 Ⅲ	1.75	1.70	1.77
混合小麦 Mixed wheat	三等 Ⅲ	1.55	1.53	1.53
市场销量第一品牌面粉 Wheat flour that sell best at the market	一等 Ⅰ	2.27	2.31	2.30
市场销量第一品牌面粉 Wheat flour that sell best at the market	标准粉 Standard	2.03	2.04	2.06
市场销量第一品牌早籼米 Milled early long-grain nonglutinous rice that sell best at the market	一等 Ⅰ	2.33	2.34	2.38
市场销量第一品牌晚籼米 Milled late long-grain nonglutinous rice that sell best at the market	一等 Ⅰ	2.43	2.44	2.45
市场销量第一品牌早粳米 Milled early medium to short-grain rice that sell best at the market	一等 Ⅰ	2.63	2.66	2.65
市场销量第一品牌晚粳米 Milled late medium to short-grain rice that sell best at the market	一等 Ⅰ	2.94	2.92	2.94
市场销量第一品牌籼糯米 Milled long-grain glutinous rice that sell best at the market	一等 Ⅰ	2.93	3.03	3.30
市场销量第一品牌粳糯米 Milled round-grain glutinous rice that sell best at the market	一等 Ⅰ	3.08	3.24	3.30
黄玉米 Yellow corn	三等 Ⅲ	1.33	1.37	1.38
大豆 Soybeans	合格 Qualified	3.14	3.09	3.10
小米 Millet	合格 Qualified	2.92	2.97	2.86
绿豆 Mung beans	合格 Qualified	5.55	5.46	5.43
红小豆 Small red beans	合格 Qualified	5.55	5.06	4.91
花生仁 Peanut kernel	合格 Qualified	5.75	5.89	5.94
芝麻 Sesame	合格 Qualified	10.49	9.88	9.82
大豆色拉油 Soybean salad oil	合格 Qualified	6.29	6.30	6.23
花生色拉油 Peanut salad oil	合格 Qualified	11.23	11.20	11.25
菜籽色拉油 Rapeseed salad oil	合格 Qualified	6.39	6.38	6.31

4—2 2005年批发市场棉花价格
Prices of Cotton at the Wholesale Market in 2005

单位:元/吨 Unit:yuan/ton

月份 Month	129级皮棉 129 grade lint cotton	229级皮棉 229 grade lint cotton	329级皮棉 329 grade lint cotton	328级皮棉 328 grade lint cotton	429级皮棉 429 grade lint cotton	527级皮棉 527 grade lint cotton
1月 Jan	12400	11990	11541	10950	10700	9667
2月 Feb	13500	12370	11788	11500	11025	10613
3月 Mar	13150	12690	12127	11650	11392	10913
4月 Apr	13360	12925	12477	11800	11800	11150
5月 May	13704	13475	12827	12750	12283	11771
6月 Jun	13603	13635	13134	12850	12533	11746
7月 Jul	13850	13644	13264	13200	12640	11930
8月 Aug	14200	13714	13330	13300	12500	12300
9月 Sep	14400	14100	13513	13800	13100	12550
10月 Oct	14900	14200	14188	14133	13650	13150
11月 Nov	15067	14700	14033	14150	13650	12950
12月 Dec	14867	14590	14077	14025	13425	12700

4—3 2005年批发市场果品价格
Prices of Fruit at the Wholesale Market in 2005

单位:元/公斤 Unit:yuan/kg

品种	Commodity	等级 Grade	1月 Jan	2月 Feb	3月 Mar
香蕉	Bananas	中等 Middling	2.70	2.72	2.54
菠萝	Pineapples	中等 Middling	2.68	2.00	2.08
柑	Mandarin oranges	中等 Middling	2.60	2.39	2.16
桔	Tangerines	中等 Middling	2.47	2.64	1.99
橙	Oranges	中等 Middling	2.61	2.73	2.55
柚	Shaddocks	中等 Middling	2.14	2.36	2.66
红富士苹果	Hongfushi apples	中等 Middling	3.17	2.73	2.89
国光苹果	Guoguang apples	中等 Middling	2.04	2.45	2.02
雪花梨	Snowflake pears	中等 Middling	2.78	3.23	2.64
鸭梨	Ya-pears	中等 Middling	1.94	2.68	2.02
荔枝	Litchis	中等 Middling	—	3.00	—
龙眼	Longans	中等 Middling	11.84	12.09	10.90
芒果	Mangos	中等 Middling	23.28	16.40	7.65
西瓜	Watermelons	中等 Middling	2.57	2.33	2.54
甜瓜	Muskmelons	中等 Middling	2.40	8.70	6.32
哈蜜瓜	Hami melons	中等 Middling	5.94	6.00	8.23
草莓	Strawberries	中等 Middling	8.65	7.78	7.92
桃	Peachs	中等 Middling	12.50	—	19.00
杏	Apricots	中等 Middling	—	6.00	5.00
猕猴桃	Yangtaoes	中等 Middling	2.90	3.21	3.90
葡萄	Grapes	中等 Middling	3.41	6.44	4.47
大枣	Chinese dates	中等 Middling	10.54	7.20	6.85
柿子	Persimmons	中等 Middling	3.98	3.50	1.00
山楂	Hawkthorns	中等 Middling	2.95	2.53	2.88
樱桃	Cherries	中等 Middling	—	—	—
圣女果	Little tomatoes	中等 Middling	3.80	3.54	3.29

4—3 续表 1　　continued 1

品种	Commodity	等级 Grade	4月 Apr	5月 May	6月 Jun
香蕉	Bananas	中等 Middling	2.64	2.59	2.47
菠萝	Pineapples	中等 Middling	1.92	2.09	2.07
柑	Mandarin oranges	中等 Middling	2.51	2.67	1.60
桔	Tangerines	中等 Middling	2.37	3.50	
橙	Oranges	中等 Middling	2.69	3.89	1.70
柚	Shaddocks	中等 Middling	2.01	2.26	1.00
红富士苹果	Hongfushi apples	中等 Middling	2.84	2.96	3.09
国光苹果	Guoguang apples	中等 Middling	2.53	2.38	2.00
雪花梨	Snowflake pears	中等 Middling	3.20	3.04	2.00
鸭梨	Ya-pears	中等 Middling	2.13	2.16	2.18
荔枝	Litchis	中等 Middling	16.00	10.41	6.28
龙眼	Longans	中等 Middling	11.68	13.03	11.32
芒果	Mangos	中等 Middling	10.78	7.28	6.66
西瓜	Watermelons	中等 Middling	6.36	2.22	1.35
甜瓜	Muskmelons	中等 Middling	5.28	4.22	1.87
哈蜜瓜	Hami melons	中等 Middling	8.09	5.52	2.90
草莓	Strawberries	中等 Middling	6.00	4.69	5.50
桃	Peachs	中等 Middling	10.30	8.13	4.28
杏	Apricots	中等 Middling	11.75	7.43	2.61
猕猴桃	Yangtaoes	中等 Middling	9.12	6.32	10.51
葡萄	Grapes	中等 Middling	8.14	12.67	7.33
大枣	Chinese dates	中等 Middling	6.40	7.17	6.00
柿子	Persimmons	中等 Middling	3.50		
山楂	Hawkthorns	中等 Middling	3.30	6.75	
樱桃	Cherries	中等 Middling	33.50	20.93	19.63
圣女果	Little tomatoes	中等 Middling	4.04	3.67	2.72

4—3 续表 2 continued 2

品种	Commodity	等级 Grade	7月 Jul	8月 Aug	9月 Sep
香蕉	Bananas	中等 Middling	2.41	2.60	3.07
菠萝	Pineapples	中等 Middling	3.04	3.03	3.59
柑	Mandarin oranges	中等 Middling	4.00	4.00	3.60
桔	Tangerines	中等 Middling	3.60	2.87	2.11
橙	Oranges	中等 Middling	5.43	8.00	7.00
柚	Shaddocks	中等 Middling	3.00	2.95	2.42
红富士苹果	Hongfushi apples	中等 Middling	3.52	3.68	3.53
国光苹果	Guoguang apples	中等 Middling	3.20	2.73	3.24
雪花梨	Snowflake pears	中等 Middling	3.23	2.28	1.80
鸭梨	Ya-pears	中等 Middling	3.18	2.85	2.15
荔枝	Litchis	中等 Middling	6.00	5.20	10.00
龙眼	Longans	中等 Middling	10.80	8.01	10.28
芒果	Mangos	中等 Middling	6.52	6.53	12.72
西瓜	Watermelons	中等 Middling	1.34	1.21	1.78
甜瓜	Muskmelons	中等 Middling	2.13	2.20	2.51
哈蜜瓜	Hami melons	中等 Middling	3.00	2.59	2.70
草莓	Strawberries	中等 Middling			
桃	Peachs	中等 Middling	3.91	2.60	4.85
杏	Apricots	中等 Middling	2.06	3.00	
猕猴桃	Yangtaoes	中等 Middling	7.01	3.19	3.00
葡萄	Grapes	中等 Middling	5.55	3.47	3.81
大枣	Chinese dates	中等 Middling	14.50	5.23	8.29
柿子	Persimmons	中等 Middling	6.00	4.70	2.97
山楂	Hawkthorns	中等 Middling	16.00	16.00	2.55
樱桃	Cherries	中等 Middling	18.00	18.00	
圣女果	Little tomatoes	中等 Middling	2.86	2.96	2.94

4—3 续表 3 continued 3

品种	Commodity	等级 Grade	10 月 Oct	11 月 Nov	12 月 Dec
香蕉	Bananas	中等 Middling	2.98	3.08	2.80
菠萝	Pineapples	中等 Middling	2.62	2.88	2.77
柑	Mandarin oranges	中等 Middling	3.15	3.40	2.70
桔	Tangerines	中等 Middling	2.32	2.39	2.46
橙	Oranges	中等 Middling	4.57	3.79	2.81
柚	Shaddocks	中等 Middling	2.60	2.40	2.97
红富士苹果	Hongfushi apples	中等 Middling	3.48	3.36	3.44
国光苹果	Guoguang apples	中等 Middling	2.58	2.78	3.23
雪花梨	Snowflake pears	中等 Middling	2.33	2.30	3.06
鸭梨	Ya-pears	中等 Middling	2.49	2.46	2.58
荔枝	Litchis	中等 Middling	8.00	12.00	14.00
龙眼	Longans	中等 Middling	11.50	10.65	10.24
芒果	Mangos	中等 Middling	9.23	14.00	25.00
西瓜	Watermelons	中等 Middling	1.94	3.69	3.06
甜瓜	Muskmelons	中等 Middling	3.35	3.73	3.75
哈蜜瓜	Hami melons	中等 Middling	3.01	4.27	4.73
草莓	Strawberries	中等 Middling		12.00	14.71
桃	Peachs	中等 Middling	6.07	7.75	9.53
杏	Apricots	中等 Middling			
猕猴桃	Yangtaoes	中等 Middling	3.22	3.26	3.23
葡萄	Grapes	中等 Middling	4.29	4.45	4.34
大枣	Chinese dates	中等 Middling	7.98	11.33	13.13
柿子	Persimmons	中等 Middling	2.30	2.82	3.62
山楂	Hawkthorns	中等 Middling	2.64	3.80	4.83
樱桃	Cherries	中等 Middling			
圣女果	Little tomatoes	中等 Middling	3.42	3.51	3.84

4—4　2005年批发市场肉、禽、蛋价格
Prices of Meats, Poultries and Eggs at the Wholesale Market in 2005

单位:元/公斤　　Unit:yuan/kg

品种	Commodity	等级 Grade	1月 Jan	2月 Feb	3月 Mar
牛肉(胴体)	Beef carcass	合格 Qualified	14.15	15.48	15.47
羊肉(胴体)	Mutton carcass	合格 Qualified	15.29	17.15	16.26
白条猪(胴体)	Pork carcass	合格 Qualified	12.32	12.10	11.89
后臀尖	Pork hind leg	合格 Qualified	15.20	13.60	13.25
里脊肉	Pork fillet	合格 Qualified	16.54	16.36	16.41
白条鸡(胴体)	Chicken carcass	合格 Qualified	9.73	9.22	9.40
活草鸡(土鸡)	Live local chicken	合格 Qualified	15.47	14.83	15.79
活杂交鸡	Live intercross chicken	合格 Qualified	12.62	13.00	13.40
活三黄鸡	Live sanhuang chicken	合格 Qualified	11.35	11.46	12.54
活乌鸡	Live black chicken	合格 Qualified	16.65	16.32	17.11
活鸭	Live duck	合格 Qualified	12.73	12.83	13.83
鲜鸡蛋	Fresh eggs	合格 Qualified	5.87	5.64	5.12
鲜鸭蛋	Fresh duck eggs	合格 Qualified	8.37	8.16	7.54

4—4续表1　　continued 1

品种	Commodity	等级 Grade	4月 Apr	5月 May	6月 Jun
牛肉(胴体)	Beef carcass	合格 Qualified	15.53	16.22	15.98
羊肉(胴体)	Mutton carcass	合格 Qualified	15.97	15.96	16.40
白条猪(胴体)	Pork carcass	合格 Qualified	11.65	11.39	11.63
后臀尖	Pork hind leg	合格 Qualified	13.80	12.80	13.10
里脊肉	Pork fillet	合格 Qualified	15.86	15.36	15.72
白条鸡(胴体)	Chicken carcass	合格 Qualified	11.19	9.99	10.87
活草鸡(土鸡)	Live local chicken	合格 Qualified	17.23	16.83	17.71
活杂交鸡	Live intercross chicken	合格 Qualified	12.72	13.60	13.60
活三黄鸡	Live sanhuang chicken	合格 Qualified	11.13	12.40	10.87
活乌鸡	Live black chicken	合格 Qualified	17.84	19.20	18.80
活鸭	Live duck	合格 Qualified	13.83	16.60	16.00
鲜鸡蛋	Fresh eggs	合格 Qualified	5.48	6.16	6.09
鲜鸭蛋	Fresh duck eggs	合格 Qualified	8.20	8.46	8.64

4—4 续表 2　　continued 2

品种 Commodity		等级 Grade	7月 Jul	8月 Aug	9月 Sep
牛肉(胴体)	Beef carcass	合格 Qualified	15.85	16.27	16.15
羊肉(胴体)	Mutton carcass	合格 Qualified	15.76	15.89	16.32
白条猪(胴体)	Pork carcass	合格 Qualified	11.24	10.88	10.37
后臀尖	Pork hind leg	合格 Qualified	12.80	12.80	13.12
里脊肉	Pork fillet	合格 Qualified	15.43	15.28	14.77
白条鸡(胴体)	Chicken carcass	合格 Qualified	10.02	10.25	9.55
活草鸡(土鸡)	Live local chicken	合格 Qualified	17.43	17.25	16.02
活杂交鸡	Live intercross chicken	合格 Qualified	13.10	13.00	12.00
活三黄鸡	Live sanhuang chicken	合格 Qualified	10.57	11.21	10.38
活乌鸡	Live black chicken	合格 Qualified	16.82	16.47	16.13
活鸭	Live duck	合格 Qualified	14.42	13.92	13.39
鲜鸡蛋	Fresh eggs	合格 Qualified	6.09	6.13	6.03
鲜鸭蛋	Fresh duck eggs	合格 Qualified	8.26	8.77	8.47

4—4 续表 3　　continued 3

品种 Commodity		等级 Grade	10月 Oct	11月 Nov	12月 Dec
牛肉(胴体)	Beef carcass	合格 Qualified	15.99	16.29	16.82
羊肉(胴体)	Mutton carcass	合格 Qualified	15.10	15.72	16.28
白条猪(胴体)	Pork carcass	合格 Qualified	10.00	9.98	9.98
后臀尖	Pork hind leg	合格 Qualified	12.25	12.02	12.54
里脊肉	Pork fillet	合格 Qualified	15.83	15.33	15.73
白条鸡(胴体)	Chicken carcass	合格 Qualified	9.22	8.15	8.22
活草鸡(土鸡)	Live local chicken	合格 Qualified	16.49	17.15	15.25
活杂交鸡	Live intercross chicken	合格 Qualified	12.25	13.50	11.38
活三黄鸡	Live sanhuang chicken	合格 Qualified	9.64	9.20	9.20
活乌鸡	Live black chicken	合格 Qualified	15.70	15.24	13.86
活鸭	Live duck	合格 Qualified	14.08	15.25	16.13
鲜鸡蛋	Fresh eggs	合格 Qualified	5.56	5.30	5.24
鲜鸭蛋	Fresh duck eggs	合格 Qualified	8.83	8.41	7.83

5

国际市场农产品价格

Prices of the Agricultural Products at the International Market

5—1 2005年美国农产品生产价格
The US Farm Gate Prices of Agricultural Products in 2005

单位:美元　　　　Unit:Dollar

农产品名称	Categories of agricultural products	单位 Unit	1月 Jan	2月 Feb	3月 Mar
大麦	Barley, All	蒲式耳 Bu	2.42	2.37	2.46
饲料用	Feed	蒲式耳 Bu	1.65	1.62	1.68
制麦芽糖用	Malting	蒲式耳 Bu	2.75	2.64	2.74
豆类(干,可食用)	Beans, Dry Edible	英担 Cwt	27.40	27.80	26.60
鹰嘴豆	Chickpeas	英担 Cwt	23.60	28.80	29.30
玉米	Corn	蒲式耳 Bu	2.12	1.95	2.02
棉花	Cotton, Upland	磅 Lb	0.40	0.39	0.42
棉籽	Cottonseed	吨 Ton	112.00	112.00	
亚麻子	Flaxseed	蒲式耳 Bu	8.90	11.00	11.50
干草	Hay	吨 Ton	84.20	84.70	89.10
紫花苜蓿	Alfalfa	吨 Ton	90.90	91.90	96.40
其他	Other	吨 Ton	70.60	70.00	70.40
小扁豆	Lentils	英担 Cwt	14.60	13.90	13.50
燕麦	Oats	蒲式耳 Bu	1.64	1.66	1.74
带壳花生	Peanuts, In-Shell	磅 Lb	0.19	0.19	0.19
豌豆(干,可食用)	Peas, Dry Edible	英担 Cwt	5.87	5.97	5.64
马铃薯	Potatoes	英担 Cwt	5.59	5.76	6.21
糙米	Rice, Rough	英担 Cwt	7.16	6.79	6.88
谷类高粱	Sorghum Grain	英担 Cwt	2.95	2.95	3.04
大豆	Soybeans	蒲式耳 Bu	5.57	5.42	5.95
向日葵	Sunflower	英担 Cwt	13.70	15.10	15.60
烟草	Tobacco	磅 Lb	1.97	1.96	1.47
小麦	Wheat, All	蒲式耳 Bu	3.42	3.36	3.41
冬小麦	Winter	蒲式耳 Bu	3.27	3.27	3.32
硬质小麦	Durum	蒲式耳 Bu	3.62	3.71	3.67
其他春小麦	Other Spring	蒲式耳 Bu	3.60	3.50	3.51
硬红冬小麦	Hard Red Winter	蒲式耳 Bu	3.23	3.25	3.29
软红冬小麦	Soft Red Winter	蒲式耳 Bu	3.12	3.13	3.32
硬红春小麦	Hard Red Spring	蒲式耳 Bu	3.61	3.50	3.51
白小麦	White	蒲式耳 Bu	3.49	3.47	3.50
畜产品	Livestock				
牛腓	Calves	英担 Cwt	125.00	128.00	135.00
牛肉	Cattle, All Beef	英担 Cwt	89.40	89.00	91.30
活猪	Hogs, All	英担 Cwt	53.20	50.70	51.20
山羊	Lambs	英担 Cwt	114.00	114.00	114.00
绵羊	Sheep	英担 Cwt	53.50	51.30	48.20

注:1蒲式耳小麦、大豆=27.216公斤,1蒲式耳玉米、高粱=25.401公斤,1蒲式耳大麦=21.772公斤,1蒲式耳燕麦=14.515公斤,1英担=45.359公斤,1磅=0.454公斤。

Notes:1bu wheat&soybean=27.216kg,1bu corn& sorghum=25.401kg,1bu barley=21.772kg, 1bu oats=14.515kg,1Cwt=45.359kg,1lb=0.454kg.

5－1 续表 1 continued 1

农产品名称 Categories of agricultural products		单位 Unit	4月 Apr	5月 May	6月 Jun
大麦	Barley, All	蒲式耳 Bu	2.32	2.46	2.57
饲料用	Feed	蒲式耳 Bu	1.54	1.71	2.07
制麦芽糖用	Malting	蒲式耳 Bu	2.74	2.90	2.88
豆类(干,可食用)	Beans, Dry Edible	英担 Cwt	28.80	31.90	27.50
鹰嘴豆	Chickpeas	英担 Cwt	22.90	22.30	38.60
玉米	Corn	蒲式耳 Bu	2.00	1.99	2.03
棉花	Cotton, Upland	磅 Lb	0.43	0.42	0.44
棉籽	Cottonseed	吨 Ton			
亚麻子	Flaxseed	蒲式耳 Bu	12.30	11.60	11.20
干草	Hay	吨 Ton	96.90	107.00	102.00
紫花苜蓿	Alfalfa	吨 Ton	103.00	116.00	112.00
其他	Other	吨 Ton	75.40	76.10	73.60
小扁豆	Lentils	英担 Cwt	13.00	12.20	12.00
燕麦	Oats	蒲式耳 Bu	1.65	1.64	1.91
带壳花生	Peanuts, In-Shell	磅 Lb	0.18	0.18	0.18
豌豆(干,可食用)	Peas, Dry Edible	英担 Cwt	5.44	5.26	5.49
马铃薯	Potatoes	英担 Cwt	6.17	6.72	7.66
糙米	Rice, Rough	英担 Cwt	7.06	6.97	6.94
谷类高粱	Sorghum Grain	英担 Cwt	2.96	3.06	3.85
大豆	Soybeans	蒲式耳 Bu	6.03	6.20	6.58
向日葵	Sunflower	英担 Cwt	15.20	15.50	15.60
烟草	Tobacco	磅 Lb			
小麦	Wheat, All	蒲式耳 Bu	3.35	3.31	3.23
冬小麦	Winter	蒲式耳 Bu	3.27	3.23	3.15
硬质小麦	Durum	蒲式耳 Bu	3.63	3.67	3.67
其他春小麦	Other Spring	蒲式耳 Bu	3.39	3.37	3.53
硬红冬小麦	Hard Red Winter	蒲式耳 Bu	3.18	3.17	3.12
软红冬小麦	Soft Red Winter	蒲式耳 Bu	3.16	3.09	3.26
硬红春小麦	Hard Red Spring	蒲式耳 Bu	3.38	3.37	3.53
白小麦	White	蒲式耳 Bu	3.52	3.50	3.48
畜产品	Livestock				
牛腓	Calves	英担 Cwt	140.00	141.00	138.00
牛肉	Cattle, All Beef	英担 Cwt	94.00	92.40	88.50
活猪	Hogs, All	英担 Cwt	51.20	54.90	49.60
山羊	Lambs	英担 Cwt	114.00	115.00	114.00
绵羊	Sheep	英担 Cwt	44.40	44.50	40.90

5—1 续表 2　　continued 2

农产品名称	Categories of agricultural products	单位 Unit	7月 Jul	8月 Aug	9月 Sep
大麦	Barley, All	蒲式耳 Bu	2.38	2.52	2.36
饲料用	Feed	蒲式耳 Bu	1.98	1.79	1.82
制麦芽糖用	Malting	蒲式耳 Bu	2.66	2.88	2.75
豆类(干,可食用)	Beans, Dry Edible	英担 Cwt	25.40	21.30	18.00
鹰嘴豆	Chickpeas	英担 Cwt	27.90	18.60	26.50
玉米	Corn	蒲式耳 Bu	2.11	1.95	1.90
棉花	Cotton, Upland	磅 Lb	0.43	0.42	0.44
棉籽	Cottonseed	吨 Ton		102.00	96.00
亚麻子	Flaxseed	蒲式耳 Bu	10.40	6.28	6.10
干草	Hay	吨 Ton	99.70	99.70	99.00
紫花苜蓿	Alfalfa	吨 Ton	109.00	109.00	107.00
其他	Other	吨 Ton	75.90	74.80	74.60
小扁豆	Lentils	英担 Cwt	11.80	11.80	11.50
燕麦	Oats	蒲式耳 Bu	1.59	1.47	1.54
带壳花生	Peanuts, In-Shell	磅 Lb	0.16	0.17	0.17
豌豆(干,可食用)	Peas, Dry Edible	英担 Cwt	5.21	4.24	4.65
马铃薯	Potatoes	英担 Cwt	8.69	6.84	6.16
糙米	Rice, Rough	英担 Cwt	6.78	6.54	6.95
谷类高粱	Sorghum Grain	英担 Cwt	3.94	3.69	3.41
大豆	Soybeans	蒲式耳 Bu	6.65	6.15	5.77
向日葵	Sunflower	英担 Cwt	15.10	14.20	13.20
烟草	Tobacco	磅 Lb			
小麦	Wheat, All	蒲式耳 Bu	3.20	3.24	3.35
冬小麦	Winter	蒲式耳 Bu	3.15	3.16	3.28
硬质小麦	Durum	蒲式耳 Bu	3.71	3.39	3.40
其他春小麦	Other Spring	蒲式耳 Bu	3.45	3.43	3.50
硬红冬小麦	Hard Red Winter	蒲式耳 Bu	3.13	3.18	3.35
软红冬小麦	Soft Red Winter	蒲式耳 Bu	3.19	3.10	2.95
硬红春小麦	Hard Red Spring	蒲式耳 Bu	3.45	3.46	3.53
白小麦	White	蒲式耳 Bu	3.36	3.12	3.06
畜产品	Livestock				
牛腓	Calves	英担 Cwt	132.00	131.00	133.00
牛肉	Cattle, All Beef	英担 Cwt	85.30	84.50	88.20
活猪	Hogs, All	英担 Cwt	49.80	51.00	49.50
山羊	Lambs	英担 Cwt	109.00	108.00	110.00
绵羊	Sheep	英担 Cwt	40.30	42.30	43.30

5—1 续表 3 continued 3

农产品名称 Categories of agricultural products		单位 Unit	10 月 Oct	11 月 Nov	12 月 Dec
大麦	Barley, All	蒲式耳 Bu	2.41	2.64	2.49
饲料用	Feed	蒲式耳 Bu	1.81	1.77	1.74
制麦芽糖用	Malting	蒲式耳 Bu	2.72	2.93	2.70
豆类(干,可食用)	Beans, Dry Edible	英担 Cwt	18.80	18.30	18.60
鹰嘴豆	Chickpeas	英担 Cwt	27.70	25.40	26.10
玉米	Corn	蒲式耳 Bu	1.82	1.77	1.92
棉花	Cotton, Upland	磅 Lb	0.49	0.49	0.48
棉籽	Cottonseed	吨 Ton	89.40	92.60	95.10
亚麻子	Flaxseed	蒲式耳 Bu	6.05	5.93	5.82
干草	Hay	吨 Ton	97.70	91.70	92.00
紫花苜蓿	Alfalfa	吨 Ton	106.00	97.50	97.70
其他	Other	吨 Ton	76.50	76.30	78.00
小扁豆	Lentils	英担 Cwt	11.80	11.40	12.30
燕麦	Oats	蒲式耳 Bu	1.59	1.63	1.73
带壳花生	Peanuts, In-Shell	磅 Lb	0.18	0.18	0.18
豌豆(干,可食用)	Peas, Dry Edible	英担 Cwt	4.50	4.77	5.04
马铃薯	Potatoes	英担 Cwt	5.54	6.31	6.93
糙米	Rice, Rough	英担 Cwt	6.94	7.44	7.49
谷类高粱	Sorghum Grain	英担 Cwt	2.99	2.82	2.91
大豆	Soybeans	蒲式耳 Bu	5.67	5.62	5.77
向日葵	Sunflower	英担 Cwt	12.80	12.30	11.60
烟草	Tobacco	磅 Lb			
小麦	Wheat, All	蒲式耳 Bu	3.43	3.47	3.54
冬小麦	Winter	蒲式耳 Bu	3.33	3.29	3.46
硬质小麦	Durum	蒲式耳 Bu	3.40	3.25	3.39
其他春小麦	Other Spring	蒲式耳 Bu	3.62	3.73	3.69
硬红冬小麦	Hard Red Winter	蒲式耳 Bu	3.45	3.42	3.56
软红冬小麦	Soft Red Winter	蒲式耳 Bu	2.99	2.81	3.02
硬红春小麦	Hard Red Spring	蒲式耳 Bu	3.68	3.78	3.73
白小麦	White	蒲式耳 Bu	3.14	3.08	3.05
畜产品	Livestock				
牛腓	Calves	英担 Cwt	134.00	133.00	134.00
牛肉	Cattle, All Beef	英担 Cwt	91.10	91.30	93.60
活猪	Hogs, All	英担 Cwt	47.00	43.60	44.30
山羊	Lambs	英担 Cwt	108.00	107.00	102.00
绵羊	Sheep	英担 Cwt	43.70	45.40	46.90

5—2 2005年1月国际市场棉花期货价格
Cotton Future Prices at the International Market (Jan. 2005)

交割日期:2005年3月 单位:美分/磅 Contract month:Mar. 2005 Price quote:US cents/lb

日期 date	最高价 High	最低价 Low	收盘价 Close	平均 Average	交易量 Volume
1—1					
1—2					
1—3	44.90	43.90	44.12	44.40	7081
1—4	44.60	43.41	44.49	44.01	7900
1—5	45.70	44.50	45.62	45.10	19,262
1—6	46.19	45.51	45.81	45.85	17,671
1—7	46.98	45.40	46.56	46.19	18,899
1—8					
1—9					
1—10	47.30	46.10	47.24	46.70	12817
1—11	47.00	45.86	46.20	46.43	12996
1—12	46.70	45.89	46.59	46.30	9,494
1—13	46.45	45.62	46.28	46.04	9,309
1—14	46.30	45.66	46.17	45.98	4,865
1—15					
1—16					
1—17					
1—18	46.80	45.80	46.71	46.30	5550
1—19	48.00	46.65	47.96	47.33	13820
1—20	48.31	47.45	47.58	47.88	10,640
1—21	47.40	46.15	46.97	46.78	10,821
1—22					
1—23					
1—24	46.85	46.05	46.44	46.45	4886
1—25	46.80	45.75	46.78	46.28	8296
1—26	47.35	46.60	46.78	46.98	6,133
1—27	47.10	43.83	43.86	45.47	26,628
1—28	44.25	42.40	43.35	43.33	27,566
1—29					
1—30					
1—31	44.10	43.35	43.76	43.73	9201

注:期货价格为纽约期货交易所(NYBOT)棉花成交价。1吨=2204.6磅。

Notes:The prices of futures are taken as transacted prices of cotton at NYBOT.

1 ton=2204.6 lb.

5—3 2005年2月国际市场棉花期货价格
Cotton Future Prices at the International Market(Feb. 2005)

交割日期:2005年3月 单位:美分/磅 Contract month:Mar. 2005 Price quote:US cents/lb

日期 date	最高价 High	最低价 Low	收盘价 Close	平均 Average	交易量 Volume
2—1	44.35	43.41	43.88	43.88	8192
2—2	44.50	43.75	44.27	44.13	6,094
2—3	44.45	43.10	43.12	43.78	7,459
2—4	43.45	42.81	43.20	43.13	6,720
2—5					
2—6					
2—7	43.75	43.01	43.24	43.38	10,354
2—8	43.15	42.65	42.70	42.90	10,505
2—9	43.70	42.61	43.07	43.16	12,879
2—10	45.00	43.40	44.74	44.20	17,582
2—11	45.30	44.75	44.95	45.03	11,698
2—12					
2—13					
2—14	46.00	45.10	45.56	45.55	11,570
2—15	46.90	45.85	46.28	46.38	15,216
2—16	46.95	45.25	46.20	46.10	7,421
2—17	46.20	45.71	45.98	45.96	6,728
2—18	46.70	45.55	46.54	46.13	5,286
2—19					
2—20					
2—21					
2—22	48.30	46.55	48.25	47.43	1,175
2—23	48.50	47.60	47.90	48.05	275
2—24	47.80	47.00	47.50	47.40	105
2—25	49.25	47.30	49.10	48.28	96
2—26					
2—27					
2—28	50.30	49.80	50.30	50.05	20
2—29					

5—4 2005年3月国际市场棉花期货价格
Cotton Future Prices at the International Market(Mar. 2005)

交割日期:2005年5月 单位:美分/磅 Contract month:May. 2005 Price quote:US cents/lb

日期 date	最高价 High	最低价 Low	收盘价 Close	平均 Average	交易量 Volume
3—1	51.20	49.70	50.59	50.45	10,421
3—2	51.65	49.75	50.19	50.70	12,040
3—3	50.60	49.35	50.52	49.98	6,945
3—4	51.25	50.35	51.23	50.80	4,140
3—5					
3—6					
3—7	51.50	50.40	50.44	50.95	5,851
3—8	51.70	50.55	51.52	51.13	10,249
3—9	52.40	51.25	52.00	51.83	11,508
3—10	53.20	51.65	52.65	52.43	11,766
3—11	53.80	52.15	53.65	52.98	8,830
3—12					
3—13					
3—14	53.20	51.80	53.11	52.50	9,372
3—15	53.70	52.50	53.63	53.10	7,256
3—16	54.20	53.00	53.78	53.60	8,233
3—17	53.25	50.85	51.33	52.05	20,988
3—18	51.75	50.60	50.94	51.18	7,982
3—19					
3—20					
3—21	50.30	49.10	50.12	49.70	18,208
3—22	51.70	50.25	51.38	50.98	7,212
3—23	50.97	49.75	50.58	50.36	6,400
3—24	52.40	50.00	51.59	51.20	6,139
3—25					
3—26					
3—27					
3—28	54.55	52.10	53.96	53.33	12,201
3—29	54.60	53.20	53.58	53.90	8,307
3—30	53.58	52.85	53.38	53.22	6,816
3—31	54.10	52.65	53.03	53.38	10,279

5—5　2005年4月国际市场棉花期货价格
Cotton Future Prices at the International Market (Apr. 2005)

交割日期：2005年5月　单位：美分/磅　　Contract month：May. 2005　Price quote：US cents/lb

日期 date	最高价 High	最低价 Low	收盘价 Close	平均 Average	交易量 Volume
4—1	53.35	50.55	52.80	51.95	19,070
4—2					
4—3					
4—4	53.20	52.30	52.60	52.75	6,978
4—5	52.50	51.95	52.05	52.23	6,728
4—6	52.00	51.25	51.88	51.63	10,094
4—7	53.00	52.10	52.22	52.55	11,795
4—8	53.40	51.52	53.21	52.46	12,424
4—9					
4—10					
4—11	53.70	52.65	53.27	53.18	8,685
4—12	53.30	52.75	53.00	53.03	15,036
4—13	52.60	50.90	51.22	51.75	22,574
4—14	52.50	51.05	52.14	51.78	13,703
4—15	52.35	51.90	52.06	52.13	9,856
4—16					
4—17					
4—18	54.00	51.90	52.78	52.95	12,246
4—19	55.00	53.35	54.18	54.18	8,868
4—20	55.70	53.85	55.54	54.78	9,753
4—21	56.20	54.90	55.70	55.55	9,277
4—22	56.20	54.51	56.15	55.36	7,004
4—23					
4—24					
4—25	60.50	56.30	58.25	58.40	1,461
4—26	58.60	57.45	58.50	58.03	320
4—27	59.00	57.55	57.70	58.28	209
4—28	58.50	56.50	58.40	57.50	158
4—29	58.20	57.80	58.00	58.00	105
4—30					

5—6　2005年5月国际市场棉花期货价格
Cotton Future Prices at the International Market (May 2005)

交割日期:2005年7月　单位:美分/磅　Contract month:Jul. 2005　Price quote:US cents/lb

日期 date	最高价 High	最低价 Low	收盘价 Close	平均 Average	交易量 Volume
5—1					
5—2	57.48	55.90	56.58	56.69	9,611
5—3	56.30	53.91	54.07	55.11	17,442
5—4	54.00	51.80	53.89	52.90	28,418
5—5	54.40	52.60	53.26	53.50	8,682
5—6	53.85	52.75	53.49	53.30	6,010
5—7					
5—8					
5—9	55.20	53.50	55.01	54.35	9,452
5—10	56.00	55.01	55.93	55.51	7,723
5—11	56.90	55.35	56.80	56.13	7,099
5—12	56.15	54.80	55.08	55.48	7,500
5—13	54.90	53.05	53.75	53.98	11,179
5—14					
5—15					
5—16	53.15	52.00	52.01	52.58	12,497
5—17	52.15	50.45	52.06	51.30	18,572
5—18	52.67	51.55	51.80	52.11	8,439
5—19	51.60	50.10	50.15	50.85	19,321
5—20	50.75	49.81	50.05	50.28	10,775
5—21					
5—22					
5—23	51.05	50.10	50.27	50.58	5,877
5—24	50.90	49.61	50.08	50.26	7,543
5—25	50.45	49.87	50.37	50.16	4,626
5—26	50.90	50.35	50.38	50.63	4,689
5—27	50.90	50.28	50.43	50.59	3,029
5—28					
5—29					
5—30					
5—31	49.95	48.50	48.64	49.23	17,079

5—7 2005年6月国际市场棉花期货价格
Cotton Future Prices at the International Market (Jun. 2005)

交割日期:2005年7月 单位:美分/磅 Contract month:Jul. 2005 Price quote:US cents/lb

日期 date	最高价 High	最低价 Low	收盘价 Close	平均 Average	交易量 Volume
6—1	48.70	47.65	48.59	48.18	18,831
6—2	49.21	48.15	48.76	48.68	12,180
6—3	49.10	48.10	48.34	48.60	9,025
6—4					
6—5					
6—6	48.65	47.15	47.37	47.90	11,324
6—7	47.65	46.85	46.94	47.25	14,869
6—8	47.15	46.20	46.89	46.68	14,562
6—9	47.65	46.10	46.29	46.88	17,553
6—10	47.15	46.30	46.96	46.73	13,906
6—11					
6—12					
6—13	47.70	47.25	47.53	47.48	12,646
6—14	47.75	47.25	47.60	47.50	10,711
6—15	47.75	47.00	47.07	47.38	10,148
6—16	47.85	46.55	46.64	47.20	8,314
6—17	47.50	46.80	47.38	47.15	5,844
6—18					
6—19					
6—20	48.55	47.50	48.16	48.03	5,756
6—21	49.00	48.00	48.73	48.50	6,076
6—22	49.25	47.50	47.51	48.38	6,398
6—23	50.05	47.10	49.65	48.58	6,686
6—24	50.30	48.90	50.13	49.60	591
6—25					
6—26					
6—27	50.85	50.05	50.75	50.45	636
6—28	50.70	49.20	49.35	49.95	355
6—29	50.80	49.10	50.80	49.95	172
6—30	52.20	50.50	52.00	51.35	52

5—8 2005年7月国际市场棉花期货价格
Cotton Future Prices at the International Market (Jul. 2005)

交割日期:2005年10月 单位:美分/磅 Contract month:Oct. 2005 Price quote:US cents/lb

日期 date	最高价 High	最低价 Low	收盘价 Close	平均 Average	交易量 Volume
7—1	54.50	53.40	54.40	53.95	401
7—2					
7—3					
7—4					
7—5	55.45	53.95	55.33	54.70	300
7—6	55.10	53.10	53.29	54.10	416
7—7	54.50	53.30	54.15	53.90	253
7—8	54.10	52.90	53.80	53.50	323
7—9					
7—10					
7—11	53.60	52.90	53.15	53.25	165
7—12	51.90	50.15	50.15	51.03	531
7—13	50.00	48.85	49.60	49.43	844
7—14	50.20	49.27	50.20	49.74	477
7—15	50.50	49.50	49.54	50.00	366
7—16					
7—17					
7—18	49.55	48.55	49.09	49.05	457
7—19	48.65	47.95	48.45	48.30	883
7—20	48.90	47.95	48.25	48.43	409
7—21	49.10	48.10	48.90	48.60	344
7—22	50.27	48.65	50.20	49.46	245
7—23					
7—24					
7—25	50.20	49.50	50.20	49.85	214
7—26	51.35	50.00	50.50	50.68	343
7—27	50.30	49.50	50.05	49.90	238
7—28	50.70	49.89	50.11	50.30	149
7—29	51.00	50.15	50.99	50.58	1,761
7—30					
7—31					

5—9 2005年8月国际市场棉花期货价格

Cotton Future Prices at the International Market(Aug. 2005)

交割日期:2005年10月 单位:美分/磅 Contract month:Oct. 2005 Price quote:US cents/lb

日期 date	最高价 High	最低价 Low	收盘价 Close	平均 Average	交易量 Volume
8—1	51.00	50.55	50.70	50.78	210
8—2	51.40	49.80	50.95	50.60	557
8—3	51.35	50.30	50.39	50.83	337
8—4	50.75	50.10	50.60	50.43	143
8—5	50.50	49.60	49.80	50.05	384
8—6					
8—7					
8—8	49.80	49.40	49.42	49.60	230
8—9	49.50	49.15	49.15	49.33	190
8—10	49.11	48.45	48.51	48.78	538
8—11	48.90	47.80	47.88	48.35	666
8—12	48.20	47.00	47.13	47.60	325
8—13					
8—14					
8—15	46.80	46.10	46.15	46.45	467
8—16	46.90	46.25	46.25	46.58	502
8—17	47.10	46.55	47.00	46.83	256
8—18	47.40	46.20	46.26	46.80	326
8—19	46.90	46.00	46.87	46.45	429
8—20					
8—21					
8—22	47.80	46.40	47.30	47.10	960
8—23	47.80	47.10	47.67	47.45	416
8—24	48.05	46.55	47.00	47.30	540
8—25	47.10	46.52	46.52	46.81	175
8—26	46.90	46.70	46.90	46.80	369
8—27					
8—28					
8—29	48.50	46.75	47.63	47.63	321
8—30	49.20	47.70	48.75	48.45	876
8—31	48.95	48.00	48.15	48.48	875

5—10 2005年9月国际市场棉花期货价格
Cotton Future Prices at the International Market (Sep. 2005)

交割日期:2005年10月 单位:美分/磅 Contract month:Oct. 2005 Price quote:US cents/lb

日期 date	最高价 High	最低价 Low	收盘价 Close	平均 Average	交易量 Volume
9—1	48.50	46.40	48.29	47.45	636
9—2	48.80	47.60	48.47	48.20	502
9—3					
9—4					
9—5					
9—6	50.50	48.70	50.45	49.60	1,530
9—7	51.27	50.25	51.25	50.76	1,073
9—8	51.20	50.15	50.37	50.68	962
9—9	50.50	50.05	50.05	50.28	366
9—10					
9—11					
9—12	49.65	48.70	49.60	49.18	293
9—13	49.15	48.00	48.37	48.58	536
9—14	48.80	48.10	48.60	48.45	325
9—15	48.50	48.00	48.04	48.25	241
9—16	48.60	47.85	47.99	48.23	460
9—17					
9—18					
9—19	50.25	48.40	50.17	49.33	533
9—20	49.75	48.65	49.00	49.20	398
9—21	50.30	49.60	50.00	49.95	308
9—22	50.40	48.90	50.00	49.65	701
9—23	50.05	49.00	49.15	49.53	1,767
9—24					
9—25					
9—26	49.50	48.25	49.08	48.88	76
9—27	52.50	49.30	52.00	50.90	32
9—28	53.00	51.85	52.70	52.43	48
9—29	52.20	52.20	53.10	52.20	1
9—30	53.00	52.25	51.50	52.63	2

5—11 2005年10月国际市场棉花期货价格
Cotton Future Prices at the International Market (Oct. 2005)

交割日期:2005年12月 单位:美分/磅 Contract month:Dec. 2005 Price quote:US cents/lb

日期 date	最高价 High	最低价 Low	收盘价 Close	平均 Average	交易量 Volume
10—1					
10—2					
10—3	54.30	53.40	54.24	53.85	8,323
10—4	53.95	53.00	53.05	53.48	5,866
10—5	53.95	52.80	53.91	53.38	5,624
10—6	54.70	53.35	53.75	54.03	10,010
10—7	54.10	53.21	53.63	53.66	3,301
10—8					
10—9					
10—10	56.55	54.50	55.66	55.53	14,852
10—11	55.85	55.10	55.17	55.48	8,335
10—12	56.07	55.27	55.90	55.67	7,460
10—13	57.80	55.80	56.18	56.80	20,244
10—14	57.00	55.10	56.93	56.05	11,038
10—15					
10—16					
10—17	56.93	55.90	56.00	56.42	7,369
10—18	55.75	54.52	55.37	55.14	10,911
10—19	55.00	53.57	54.29	54.29	10,934
10—20	54.90	53.05	53.21	53.98	11,096
10—21	54.60	53.07	54.49	53.84	7,887
10—22					
10—23					
10—24	54.65	53.75	54.03	54.20	6,336
10—25	55.34	54.10	55.23	54.72	8,246
10—26	55.00	54.25	54.76	54.63	5,962
10—27	54.10	52.10	52.13	53.10	20,032
10—28	52.80	51.71	52.52	52.26	13,751
10—29					
10—30					
10—31	52.75	51.57	51.87	52.16	13,809

5—12 2005年11月国际市场棉花期货价格
Cotton Future Prices at the International Market (Nov. 2005)

交割日期:2005年12月 单位:美分/磅 Contract month:Dec. 2005 Price quote:US cents/lb

日期 date	最高价 High	最低价 Low	收盘价 Close	平均 Average	交易量 Volume
11—1	52.70	51.90	52.11	52.30	8,439
11—2	52.35	51.65	52.29	52.00	8,752
11—3	52.99	51.60	51.73	52.30	10,993
11—4	52.15	51.30	51.44	51.73	10,099
11—5					
11—6					
11—7	52.00	51.17	51.26	51.59	15,488
11—8	51.45	50.90	50.96	51.18	17,174
11—9	51.30	50.40	50.41	50.85	16,251
11—10	51.25	49.95	50.20	50.60	19,470
11—11	50.94	50.12	50.72	50.53	15,692
11—12					
11—13					
11—14	51.29	50.61	50.89	50.95	8,987
11—15	51.05	50.26	50.28	50.66	9,960
11—16	50.20	49.30	49.79	49.75	8,921
11—17	50.15	49.26	49.64	49.71	9,295
11—18	49.80	49.25	49.31	49.53	8,939
11—19					
11—20					
11—21	49.55	48.40	48.54	48.98	8,810
11—22	50.50	48.75	49.90	49.63	1,388
11—23	50.10	48.65	48.95	49.38	358
11—24					
11—25					
11—26					
11—27					
11—28	50.50	48.25	48.85	49.38	91
11—29	49.75	49.10	48.98	49.43	119
11—30	49.50	49.00	49.19	49.25	28

5—13　2005年12月国际市场棉花期货价格
Cotton Future Prices at the International Market (Dec. 2005)

交割日期:2006年3月　单位:美分/磅　Contract month: Mar. 2006　Price quote: US cents/lb

日期 date	最高价 High	最低价 Low	收盘价 Close	平均 Average	交易量 Volume
12—1	52.60	51.40	51.53	52.00	14,789
12—2	52.10	51.38	51.77	51.74	5,511
12—3					
12—4					
12—5	52.59	52.00	52.27	52.30	5,998
12—6	52.55	51.95	52.52	52.25	5,403
12—7	52.55	52.20	52.37	52.38	4,369
12—8	53.25	52.30	52.75	52.78	9,852
12—9	52.75	52.17	52.72	52.46	5,348
12—10					
12—11					
12—12	53.60	53.10	53.41	53.35	12,407
12—13	53.75	53.30	53.69	53.53	9,920
12—14	53.60	52.50	53.24	53.05	9,851
12—15	53.35	52.90	53.01	53.13	8,058
12—16	53.45	52.80	53.39	53.13	4,381
12—17					
12—18					
12—19	53.65	53.39	53.63	53.52	4,388
12—20	53.50	53.10	53.22	53.30	4,023
12—21	53.45	52.71	52.85	53.08	6,920
12—22	54.25	53.05	54.14	53.65	15,927
12—23	54.19	53.22	53.54	53.71	6,721
12—24					
12—25					
12—26					
12—27	54.25	53.60	53.80	53.93	5,790
12—28	54.25	53.85	54.07	54.05	5,968
12—29	54.55	53.50	53.65	54.03	10,167
12—30	54.25	53.07	54.19	53.66	10,769
12—31					

6

全国农产品价格调查方案

Programmes for the Price Survey of Agricultural Products

6—1 农产品生产价格调查与指数编报方案

1. 调查目的

农产品生产价格是指农产品生产者第一手(直接)出售其产品时实际获得的单位产品价格。开展农产品生产价格调查是为了全面收集农产品生产价格资料,客观反映全国农产品生产价格水平和结构变动情况,满足农业与国民经济核算需要,为各级政府制定农业保护与农产品流通政策提供决策依据,向社会各界提供优质的农产品价格信息服务。

2. 调查对象

抽选的农业生产经营单位。

3. 调查方式

农产品生产价格调查采取抽样调查和重点调查相结合的调查方法。抽样调查将有农产品出售的农业生产经营单位列为调查对象,采取随机抽样的调查方法;对一些区域性比较强的农产品则采取在主产区主观选样的方法选择农业生产经营单位作为调查对象

4. 调查内容

农产品生产价格调查的内容为被调查单位生产并出售的主要农产品,被调查单位在辅助调查员的指导下将在报告期出售的农产品的名称、出售数量、价格、金额即时记入农产品生产价格调查台帐(台帐表式附后)。

在充分征求部门、地方意见的基础上,根据新的行业分类标准,总队制定了《农产品参考目录》,各地必须执行全国统一的分类标准和代码。

5. 调查周期和数据上报

农产品生产价格调查周期为季度,执行日历年度。

《农产品生产价格基层表》数据由县农调队(统计局)根据住户台帐或住户日记帐数据整理、录入、计算、审核并于季度最后月的 25 日前从网上上报所在省(区、市)农调队。季报表数据应包括农业生产经营单位在报告期出售的农产品的名称、产品代码、计量单位、出售数量、金额、价格以及相应的基期价格。基期价格由县队直接从相应的基期报表中过录。

《农产品生产价格指数表》综合定期报表由各省(区、市)农调队上报国家农调总队,时间为季(年)度最后月的 25 日前。

6. 农产品生产价格的汇总方法

(1)调查单位每种农产品的平均价格(加权算术平均法)

某调查单位在报告期某产品出售金额之和除以报告期该产品出售数量之和。公式为:

$$p_i=\frac{\sum_{j=1}^{n}p_{ij}q_{ij}}{\sum_{j=1}^{n}q_{ij}}$$

式中,p_i 为第 i 个代表品的平均价格,p_{ij} 为第 i 个代表品第 j 次的出售价格,q_{ij} 为第 i 个代表品第 j 次的出售数量。

(2)全国及省(区、市)产品平均价格(加权算术平均法)

全部被调查单位报告期某产品出售金额之和除以报告期该产品出售数量之和。公式为:

$$P_i=\frac{\sum_{j=1}^{n}p_{ij}q_{ij}}{\sum_{j=1}^{n}q_{ij}}$$

式中,P_i 为第 i 个代表品的平均价格,p_{ij} 为第 i 个代表品第 j 个调查单位的出售价格,q_{ij} 为第 i 个代表品第 j 调查单位的出售数量。

7. 农产品代表产品的确定

(1)代表产品选择的原则和要求

①农、林、牧、渔四大类、各中类以及 90%以上的小类均选有代表品,以使价格指数能较好地反映各类别价格变动情况。

②选择对国计民生影响大的产品,一般生产量和销售量大的产品对国计民生影响较大。

③选择稳定性强的产品,因为代表品一经确定,就要连续观察几年。

④选择具有发展前景的新产品作为代表品。

⑤具有地方特色的产品,虽然在全国比重不大,但具有地方特色,也应选为代表品。一些季节性强的产品从全年看比重不大,但在某些季节是当地的主要产品,也要考虑进来,以确保全年和各季

度平均价格及指数的代表性。

代表品一般稳定五年。在五年期间，若产品结构调整较快，以致影响代表性时，可提前进行修订。

(2)国家代表产品的选择

编制农产品生产价格指数是以代表产品(类别)的价格变动来反映全部农产品的价格变化趋势和变动幅度。确定科学、合理的代表品对于编制农产品生产价格指数具有重要意义。如果代表产品过少，会造成代表品不足、价格指数不准确；代表品过多，工作量过大，造成不必要的浪费。根据上述原则，在充分征求部门和地方意见的基础上，国家统计局农调总队制订了全国农产品生产价格调查的代表类别和代表产品。即《农产品参考目录》中用"*"所列示的农、林、牧、渔 4 个大类、14 个中类、30 个小类、180 种代表品。上述代表产品代表的各类别销售额占当年全国农产品销售额的 70%以上，具有足够的代表性。

(3)地方代表产品的选择

各省、自治区、直辖市执行全国统一的分类标准和代码，并根据国家下发的《农产品参考目录》，结合本地实际确定代表产品，包括目录中没有但在当地比较重要的产品。对于各地自行增加的代表品要报总队审定，取得统一编码。

8. 农产品代表品权数的计算

权数是衡量每种产品重要性的指标。由于每种产品在农业经济中的地位和作用不同，其价格变动对全部农产品价格变动的影响也有所不同。所以在计算价格指数时，要科学、合理地确定权数。

(1)权数确定的原则和要求

①只计算代表类别和代表产品的权数(如国家只给农产品参考目录中带※号的类别和产品分配权数)，其他产品不分配权数。

②采用 2000—2002 三年的资料平均计算权数，权数一般五年更换一次。在五年期间，若出现产品更新换代快，以致影响权数代表性的情况时，应及时进行合理修正。

③重点做好大类、中类权数和重要品种权数的审核。对生产量和销售量不大、资料又难以收集的商品，在计算其权数时，可先确定该商品所在类的类值，并确定该类别主要商品的权数，用分摊法将剩余的权数按其比例(重要程度的次序)分配给余下的商品。

④由于农产品生产与出售季节性比较强，为客观、准确地反映农业生产价格变动趋势和变动幅度，要对季度、季度累计和全年分别计算权数。

(2)权数的种类与资料来源

①商品(销售)权数：用于计算农产品生产价格指数

农产品商品(销售)权数主要利用农产品销售额进行计算，各种代表产品的商品(销售)权数合计为 1000。权数资料来源于农村住户和农场的农产品出售金额资料，也可根据农村住户调查季报和帐页资料进行加工整理，或利用农产品产量与商品率资料推算。

②产值权数：用于缩减农业发展速度。

各种代表产品的产值权数合计为 1000。产值权数资料取自农林牧渔业产值统计，或通过重点调查、部门资料进行推算。

9. 农产品生产价格指数的计算方法与步骤

农业生产价格指数是反映一定时期内，农产品生产者出售的农产品价格水平变动趋势及幅度的相对数。生产资料购买价格指数是反映农业生产者购买生产资料价格水平变动趋势及幅度的相对数。

(1)计算每个调查单位每个代表品的价格指数

$$k_{ij}=\frac{P_{ij1}}{P_{ij0}}$$

式中，k_{ij} 为第 j 个调查单位第 i 个代表产品的个体指数，P_{ij1} 为第 j 个调查单位第 i 个代表产品的报告期平均价格，P_{ij0} 为第 j 个调查单位第 i 个代表产品的基期平均价格。

(2)计算代表品的价格指数 K_i

$$K_i=\sqrt[n]{k_1\times k_2\times\cdots\cdots\times k_n}$$

式中，$k_1, k_2, \cdots k_n$ 分别为第 i 个代表产品在第 1 到第 n 个调查单位中的个体指数。

(3)计算小类价格指数

$$K=\frac{\sum K_iW_i}{\sum W_i}$$

其中：K 为该小类指数，K_i 为该小类下第 i 个代表品价格指数，W_i 为第 i 个代表品的产值权数或销售额权数。

(4)计算中类价格指数

$$K=\frac{\sum K_iW_i}{\sum W_i}$$

其中：K 为中类价格指数，K_i 为该中类下第 i 个小类价格指数，W_i 为第 i 个小类的产值权数或销售额权数。

大类及总指数的计算，同中类价格指数计算方法。

(5)季度累计价格指数的计算方法,与分季指数计算方法相同。

(6)国家和省级价格指数的计算方法一致。

10. 有关问题说明

(1)农产品生产价格是农业生产经营单位第一次出售其产品时所获得的价格,因此,所调查的代表品是由被调查单位生产且出售的农产品,外购再出售的农产品不作为调查内容。

(2)如果抽中的调查单位在调查时没有任何销售活动,该记录的各项观测值均为零,在季报时仍应保留该样本,同时上报空记录的个数,并说明情况。如确定该调查户或单位在半年内都不可能有销售活动,则应以样本附近或相似特征的调查对象替换。

(3)县队在数据录入、审核时,如果发现某调查单位某些代表产品报告期与基期价格变动幅度较大,应查询该调查单位出售的该代表品在品种、品质、销售条件等方面是否发生了改变,如果是由于上述非价格变动因素引起的,则应该剔除非价格变动因素,使报告期与基期代表品同质可比;如果新的产品已成为市场主流,则一般应调整基期价格。调整的方法可以相邻农户或地域的同质产品价格代替,如果缺乏相邻农户或地域的同质产品价格,也可以为空。

Programme for the Survey of the Producer Prices of Agricultural Products and for the Calculation of the Price Indices

I. The Purpose of the Survey

The producer prices of agricultural products refer to the actual prices per unit of agricultural products at which the producers of the agricultural products directly sell them. The purpose of conducting the survey of producer prices of agricultural products is to comprehensively collect the data on the producer prices of agricultural products, objectively reflect the situations of the level and structural changes of the producer prices of agricultural products, meet the needs of conducting the agricultural accounts and national accounts, provide the government at different levels with the base data for making the policies of protecting agriculture and circulation of agricultural products and provide the various social circles with the high quality information on the prices of agricultural products.

II. The Respondents of the Survey

The respondents of the survey are the units engaged in the agricultural production and management.

III. The Procedures of the Survey

The method of sample survey combined with the method of key-unit survey is used in the survey of producer prices of agricultural products. In the sample survey, the units engaged in the agricultural production and management are listed as the respondents of the survey and the method of random sample survey is used. For the agricultural products, which grow mainly in certain areas, the respondents of the survey are selected in the major producing areas with the subjective sampling method.

IV. The Contents of the Survey

The contents of the survey of producer prices of agricultural products include the data on the main agricultural products produced and sold by the respondents of the survey. Under the guidance of the auxiliary enumerators, the respondents of the survey should timely keep records on the names, quantities, prices and amount of the agricultural products sold in the reporting period in the accounts of the survey of producer prices of agricultural products or the household journals.

After soliciting the opinions of various departments and regions, the Department of Rural Survey (DRS), National Bureau of Statistics of China (NBS) has worked out the Reference Catalogue of Agricultural Products in accordance with the new Standard Classification of Economic Sectors. The national unified standard classification and their codes should be implemented in different regions.

V. The Cycle of the Survey and the Data Reporting to the Higher Authorities

The cycle of the survey of producer prices of agricultural products is a quarter. The calendar year is implemented.

The data in the Questionnaires of the Grassroots Units on the Producer Prices of Agricultural Products are processed, made entries, calculated and checked by the rural survey organizations of the county bureaus of statistics in accordance with the household accounts or journals. They are finally reported to the rural survey organizations of the concerned bureaus of statistics at the provincial level by means of internets. The quarterly data should include the names, codes, calculation units, quantity sold, amount and prices of the agricultural products sold by the units engaged in the agricultural production and management in the reporting period as well as the concerned prices in the base period. The prices in the base period are directly copied by the county survey organizations from the corresponding questionnaires of the grassroots units.

The periodic tabulated tables on the producer prices of agricultural products and their indices are reported by the rural socio-economic survey organizations of provinces, autonomous regions and municipalities directly under the central government to the Rural Department of Rural Survey, National Bureau of Statistics before 25th in the last month of the quarter.

VI. The method of tabulating the data on the producer prices of agricultural products

(1) The average price of a certain agricultural product in a unit surveyed equals to the sum of money obtained by the unit in selling the agricultural product in the reporting period divided by the total quantity of the agricultural product sold in the same period. (This is the method of weighted arithmetic average). The formula for the calculation is given below:

$$p_i = \frac{\sum_{j=1}^{n} p_{ij} q_{ij}}{\sum_{j=1}^{n} q_{ij}}$$

where p_i stands for the average price of the ith representative product; p_{ij} stands for the selling price of the ith representative product at the jth time and q_{ij} stands for the quantity of the ith representative product. sold at the jth time.

(2) The average price of a certain agricultural product in a certain province (autonomous region or municipality) and in the whole country equals to the sum of money obtained in selling the agricultural product in the reporting period in all the units surveyed divided by the total quantity of the agricultural product sold in the same period. (This is the method of weighted arithmetic average). The formula for the calculation is given below:

$$P_i = \frac{\sum_{i=1}^{n} p_{ij} q_{ij}}{\sum_{j=1}^{n} q_{ij}}$$

where p_i stands for the average price of the ith representative product; p_{ij} stands for the selling price of the ith representative product of the jth unit and q_{ij} stands for the quantity of the ith representative product sold by the jth unit.

VII. The Determination of the Representative Agricultural Products

(1) The principles and requirements for the selection of representative products:

(i) The representative products should be selected from the four major divisions, namely farming, forestry, animal husbandry and fishery, and from the various divisions and more than 90% of the groups, so that the price indices can better reflect the changes of the prices in different categories.

(ii) The products which have great importance to the national economy and people's livelihood should be selected. The products, which have large yields and sales, are generally the products important to the national economy and people's livelihood.

(iii) We should select the products steadily produced, because they should be surveyed continuously for several years after they are selected.

(iv) The new products, which have good prospect for the future development, should be selected.

(v) The products, which have local characteristics, should be selected though their proportion to the total output in the whole country is not large. The products only produced in certain seasons should be selected too, because though not large in the proportion to the annual output, they are main products in certain seasons in the localities. The annual and quarterly average prices and their indices can be representative only when they are included.

The representative products should not changed generally in the period of five years after they are selected. However, if the structure of the products is readjusted quite quickly in the period of five years so that the products formerly selected are no longer representative, the list of representative products can be revised ahead of time.

(2) The selection of the representative products of the whole country

The purpose of the calculation of the indices of the producer prices of agricultural products is to reflect the change trend and change extent of the prices of all agricultural products with the data on the changes of the prices of representative products in different categories. The determination of representative products in a scientific and reasonable way is of great significance to the calculation of the indices of the of producer prices of agricultural products. If the representative products are too few in number, it will result in the insufficiency of the representative products and the inaccuracy of the price indices. But if the representative products are too many in number, it will result in the too heavy workload and unnecessary waste. In accordance with the above-mentioned principles, after fully soliciting the opinions of the concerned departments and regions, the Rural Socio-economic Survey Organization, National Bureau of Statistics of China has worked out the representative categories and the representative products in the national survey of the producer prices of agricultural products. They include the four major divisions, namely farming, forestry, animal husbandry and fishery, 14 divisions, 30 groups and 180 representative products, indicated with the symbol * in the Reference Catalogue of Agricultural Products. The sales of the various categories of the representative products account for more than 70% of the total sales of agricultural products in the whole country in the year. Therfore the categories and agricultural products selected are sufficiently representative.

(3) The selection of the representative products in different regions

The rural survey organizations of provinces, autonomous regions and municipalities determine the representative products in the regions in accordance with the Reference Catalogue of Agricultural Products, in the light of the local actual conditions while implementing the national unified classifications and codes, including those relatively important products in the regions, though they are not included in the national Catalogue. The representative products supplemented by the regions should be reported to the national survey organization for examination, so as to have the unified codes.

VIII. The calculation of the weights of the representative agricultural products

Weights are the indicators measuring the importance of different products. Because each product is different in its position and role in the agricultural economy, the influence of its price change over the price change of all agricultural products is different too. Therefore, we should determine the weights in a scientific and reasonable way in the calculation of price indices.

(1) The principles and requirements in determining the weights

(i) Only the weights of the representative categories and the representative products are calculated. The Rural Socio-economic Survey Organization, National Bureau of Statistics only distributes the weights of the categories and products indicated with the symbol * in the Reference Catalogue of Agricultural Products. As for the other products, no weights are distributed.

(ii) The weights are calculated as averages of the data of the three years 2000 — 2002. The weights are generally changed once in every five years. If the old products are quickly renewed or upgraded by the new ones in the five years so that the formerly determined weights are no longer representative, the weights should be timely revised in a reasonable way.

(iii) Attention should be mainly paid to the examination of the weights of the major divisions and divisions as well as the weights of important products. As for the commodity, which is not large in its yield and sales and is difficult to collect the data, we can firstly determine the weight of the category, to which the commodity belongs, secondly determine the weights of the main commodities in that category and finally distribute the remainder of the weight of the category to the other commodities in that category in a proportional way, namely in the order of their importance.

(iv) Because the agricultural products are generally produced and sold in different seasons, we should calculate the weights for the quarter, for the accumulative data from the beginning of the year to the quarter and for the whole year respectively, so as to objectively and accurately reflect the change trend and change extent of the producer prices of agricultural products.

(2)Kinds of weights and data sources

(i) Weights of sales of the commodities: They are used to calculate the indices of the producer prices of agricultural products.

The weights of sales of the commodities are calculated mainly on the basis of the data on the sales of agricultural products. The sum of the weights of sales of the various representative agricultural products equals to 100. The data sources for the calculation are the data on the sales of agricultural products of the rural households and farms. We can also process the data on the basis of the quarterly report of the survey of rural households and the concerned accounts or estimate on the basis of the data on the yields of agricultural products and their commodity rate.

(ii) Weights of output value. They are used to deflate the agricultural growth rate.

The sum of the output values of various representative products equals to 100. The data sources for the calculation of weights of output value are the statistical data on the output value of farming, forestry, animal husbandry and fishery. We can also estimate on the basis of the data of key-unit survey or the data from the concerned departments.

IX. The Methods and Steps for the Calculation of the Indices of the Producer Prices of Agricultural Products

The indices of the producer prices of agricultural products are relative numbers, which reflect the trends and extents of the changes of the producer prices of agricultural products sold by the producers in a certain period.

(1) The calculation of the price index of each product in each unit surveyed

$$k_{ij}=\frac{P_{ij1}}{P_{ij0}}$$

whereK_y*stands for the individual price index of the ith representative product in the jth unit surveyed*; P_{y1} *stands for the average price of the ith representative product in the jth unit surveyed in the reporting period and* P_{y0} *stands for the average price of the ith representative product in the jth unit surveyed in the base period.*

(2) *The calculation of the price index of the representative product* K_i

$$K_i=\sqrt[n]{k_1\times k_2\times\cdots\cdots\times k_n}$$

where K_1, K_2, K_n *stands respectively for the individual price index of the ith representative product in the first, the second the. nth unit surveyed.*

(3) *The calculation of the price index of the group*

$$K=\frac{\sum K_iW_i}{\sum W_i}$$

where K stands for the price index of the group, K_i *stands for the price index of the ith representative product in the group and* W_i *stands for the weight of output value or the weight of sales of the ith representative product.*

(4) *The calculation of the price index of the division*

$$K=\frac{\sum K_iW_i}{\sum W_i}$$

where K stands for the price index of the division, K_i*stands for the price index of the ith group in the division and* W_i *stands for the weight of output value or the weight of sales of the ith group.*

The calculation of the price index of the division and the calculation of the general price index are similar as that of the division.

(5) *The method for the calculation of the price index in the period from the beginning of the year to the end of the quarter is similar to the*

calculation of the quarterly price index.

(6) *The method for the calculation of the national price index is similar to the calculation of the provincial price index.*

X. The Treatment of Some Problems

(1) The producer prices of agricultural products are the prices at which the units engaged in the agricultural production and management sell the products for the first time. Therefore the representative product surveyed refers to the agricultural product produced and sold by the unit surveyed. The agricultural product purchased from other units and resold should not be included in the survey.

(2) If the selected unit in the sample survey has no activities of sales, the observed value on sales is zero, the data of the sample unit should be still included in the quarterly report and the situations should be reported to the higher authorities. If the selected household or unit in the sample survey will definitely have no activities of sales in the future half year, the household or unit should be replaced by the household or unit in the nearby areas or other respondent, which has the similar characteristics.

(3) In the course of making data-entries and examination and verifying data, if the statisticians in the county survey organization find that the change extents of the prices of certain representative products in a certain unit surveyed between the reporting period and the base period are relatively large, they should inquire if there is any change in the variety, quality or selling condition of the representative product. If the change is caused by non-price factors, the non-price factors should be removed, so as to make the representative product in the reporting period comparable with that in the base period. If the new product represents the main trend in the market, its price in the base period should be readjusted. In the readjustment, the price of the product of the same quality in the neighboring agricultural household or the neighboring area can take its place. If no price of the product of the same quality in the neighboring agricultural household or the neighboring area can be found, the data in the base period can be blank.

6—2 农产品集贸市场价格调查方案

1. 调查目的

农产品集贸市场价格是指全国农产品主产区集贸市场主要农产品的成交价格。开展农产品集贸市场价格调查旨在收集农产品集贸市场价格资料,准确把握全国大宗农产品在主产区的价格走势,为提高我国农产品主产区的区域优势和市场竞争力服务。

2. 调查内容

农产品集贸市场价格调查内容包括农牧渔业36种主要产品的集贸市场价格(调查品种见《农产品集贸价格调查表》)。

3. 调查对象

农产品集贸市场价格调查的统计范围为全国选中的农产品主产县。

4. 调查周期与数据上报

(1)农产品集贸市场价格调查周期为月报。

(2)采价时间为每月20日左右,即每月19—21日内任一工作日。

(3)数据上报时间:价格资料由各省(区、市)农调队每月25日前上报总队。

5. 采价办法

(1)各省(区、市)对调查品种要统一口径,不得随意变换。所有调查品种的采价范围都是指一般普通商品、中等规格。经过加工,带有品牌包装的商品不在调查之列;经过分拣后加入精美包装作为礼品出售的农产品也不在调查之内。

(2)对于固定采价集市上没有的品种(如稻谷、活猪和籽棉等),为了保证调查数据的完整性,可采取以下几种办法:(1)可到其他有出售的市场取得价格;(2)仅在调查日当天无出售的产品,可根据上一日的情况采价;(3)原粮和籽棉可用市场上的大米和皮棉按当地的折算比率取得或到大米和籽棉加工点取得;(4)活猪价格可到农户或屠宰场取得;(5)当地不生产、也不从外地调入的产品价格就空缺。

(3)对同一品种不同等级价格的采价不好把握时,可用交易量较大的三个以上摊位价格的简单平均价作为该产品的价格。对同一品种、同一摊位、同一等级成交价格不一致时,用交易量较大的成交价作为该摊位、该产品的价格。

(4)食用油:采普通散装油价格。

(5)猪、牛、羊肉如市场上出售的是带骨肉,采价时需按当地比率折成去骨价。

(6)水产品:淡水鱼要求是采活鱼价格;带鱼可采死鱼价(包括每条规格在0.5—1公斤重的冷冻带鱼段)。

(7)蔬菜:采新鲜蔬菜价格。

(8)水果:采新鲜水果价格。

6. 填报说明

(1)农产品集贸市场价格调查表由省、自治区、直辖市农调队报送。

(2)产品代码与计量单位:产品代码按M405表规定填报;单价单位为元/公斤(如采价时为“元/斤”应换算为元/公斤)。

(3)价格数据保留两位小数。

(4)如部分产品缺项,单价项应空缺(不要补“0”)。

(5)各省(区、市)农调队对农产品集贸市场价格调查数据不作汇总处理,通过农调内网直接上报以调查县为单位的集贸市场价格原始数据。

(6)严格数据审核。当月单价与上月或上年同月相比增减幅度较大时应进行认真核实、确认,并随《农产品集贸市场价格调查上报表》报送文字说明。

(7)开展农产品市场价格专题分析,有关农副产品价格的重大信息与研究报告,及时报送文字材料。

(8)年度价格走势分析与调查数据质量评估报告随12月价格报表一同报送。

7. 指标解释

(1)籼稻:水稻的一种,茎秆较高较软,叶子黄绿色,稻穗上的籽粒较稀,稻粒长而细。

(2)优质籼稻:经过杂交育种改良后的籼稻。

(3)粳稻:水稻的一种,茎秆较矮,叶子较窄,深绿色,稻粒短而粗。

(4)玉米:一年生草本植物,茎高二、三米,叶子长而大，子实比黄豆稍大。

(5)籼米：籼稻碾出的米，黏性小。

(6)优质籼米：优质籼稻碾出的米。

(7)粳米：粳稻碾出的米，黏性较大。

(8)面粉：小麦磨成的粉，调查规格品是普通标准粉。

(9)籽棉：是指棉农从棉枝上摘下的、未经轧花加工除籽的棉花。籽棉经过加工后去掉棉籽的棉花叫皮棉。籽棉加工成皮棉的比例一般是 10:3，即 10 公斤籽棉可加工成 3 公斤皮棉。

(10)花生仁：去壳的生花生。

(11)活猪：待宰的肥猪(也称毛猪，一般在 65 公斤以上)。

(12)仔猪：待育肥的普通小猪(一般指 10 公斤以下刚断奶的猪)。

(13)草鱼：身体圆筒形，微绿色，生活在淡水中，吃水草。

(14)鲤鱼：身体侧扁，背部苍黑色，腹部黄白色，嘴边有须一对，淡水鱼。

(15)鲢鱼：身体侧扁，鳞细，背部青黑色，腹部白色，淡水鱼。

(16)菜椒：也称柿子椒。

(17)四季豆：部分地区也称扁豆。

(18)中等：产品规格栏的“中等”有两种含义。原粮的“中等”是指国家规定的中准级，其他品种的“中等”是指市场实际交易数量较多的质量等级。

Programme for the Survey of the Prices of Agricultural Products at the Rural Market Fairs

I. The Purpose of the Survey

The prices of agricultural products at the rural market fairs refer to the unit prices of main agricultural products, which have been stricken bargains at the rural market fairs in major producing areas in China. The purpose of conducting the survey of the prices of agricultural products at the rural market fairs is to collect the data on the prices of agricultural products at the rural market fairs, accurately keep abreast of the change trend of the prices of the staple agricultural products in the major producing areas in the whole country and serve for the purpose of improving the regional superiority and competitive power at the market of the major producing areas of agricultural products in China and their competitive power at the market.

II. The contents of the survey

The contents of the survey of the prices of agricultural products at the rural market fairs include prices of 36 main agricultural products of farming, forestry, animal husbandry and the fishery at the rural market fairs (As for the variety surveyed, see the questionnaires used in the survey of the prices of agricultural products at the rural market fairs).

III. Respondents of the survey

The statistical coverage of the survey of the prices of agricultural products at the rural market fairs includes the major producing counties of agricultural products selected in the sample survey in the whole country.

IV. Cycle of the Survey and Data Reporting

(1) The cycle of the survey of the prices of agricultural products at the rural market fairs is a month.

(2) The date for collecting the price data is about the 20th of every month, namely any working day in the period 19th — 21th.

(3) The date for reporting data: The price data are reported by the rural socio-economic survey organizations of provinces, autonomous regions and municipalities under the central government to the national rural survey organization before the 25th of every month.

V. Methods for Collecting the Data on Prices

(1) The rural survey organizations at the provincial level should pay attention that the specifications of the varieties surveyed should be unified in different time and should not be changed at will. All the varieties listed for collecting their prices refer to the ordinary commodities with medium standard. Those commodities, which have been processed and packaged with brands, are not to be surveyed. The agricultural products, which have been picked out, beautifully packaged and sold as gifts, are also not to be surveyed.

(2) For the varieties (such as paddy, live pig and unginned cotton, etc.) not sold at the specified rural market fairs for collecting price data, the following methods can be adopted so as to ensure the complete data coverage: (i) The price data can be collected from the other market fairs, at which these varieties are sold; (ii) For the varieties, which are not sold only on the day for the survey, the data on their prices on the preceding day can be collected; (iii) The data on the prices of the unhusked rice and unginned cotton can be converted on the basis of the data on the prices of husked rice and ginned cotton at the market with the local conversion rate or can be collected from the spots where the unhusked rice or unginned cotton are processed into husked rice or ginned

cotton; (iv) The data on the price of live pig can be collected from the rural households or slaughter house; (v) For the products neither produced in the locality nor transported from other places, their price data can be blank.

(3) When it is not easy to make decision for collecting the price data of the same variety with different grades, the simple average of the prices of more than three vendor's stands which have relatively bigger sales volumes can be taken as the price of that variety. When the prices at which the bargains are stricken are not the same for the same grade, same variety at the same vendor's stand, the price at which the bargain is stricken with the biggest sales volume can be taken as the price of that variety at that vendor's stand.

(4) For edible vegetable oil, the price in bulk and in ordinary grade can be collected.

(5) For pork, beef and mutton, if they are sold with bones, their prices without bones can be estimated with the local conversion rate.

(6) For aquatic products, the prices of live fish should be taken for the freshwater fish while the price of dead fish can be taken for the hairtail, including the frozen hairtail segments with the weight of 0.5—1 kg for each hairtail.

(7) For vegetable, the prices of fresh vegetable should be collected.

(8) For fruits, the prices of fresh fruits should be collected.

VI. Instructions

(1) The questionnaires for the survey of the prices of agricultural products at the rural market fairs should be reported by the rural rural socio-economic survey organizations of provinces, autonomous regions and municipalities under the central government.

(2) Codes of products and units of calculation: The codes of products should be filled out in accordance with the stipulations for Table M405. The unit for calculation of the unit price is yuan / kg.

(3) Two decimals are required to be kept in price data.

(4) If the data of parts of products are unavailable, the item on unit price should be blank.

(5) The rural socio-economic survey organizations of provinces, autonomous regions and municipalities should not tabulate the survey data on the prices of agricultural products at the rural market fairs, but should directly report the original data on the prices of agricultural products at the rural market fairs in every county by the means of the internet.

(6) The data should be strictly examined and verified. When the unit price of the month increases or decreases by a quite big margin as compared with the previous month or the same month in the previous year, it should be seriously checked and confirmed.

(7) The annual analysis report on the change trend of prices and appraisal report on the quality of survey data should be reported along with the price questionnaires of December.

VII. Explanatory Notes on Indicators

(1) long-grain nonglutinous rice: a kind of paddy rice with quite tall and soft stem and its leaves are yellowish-green. The grains are sparsely grown in the ears of rice. The grains of rice are long and thin.

(2) High quality long-grain nonglutinous rice: The improved nonglutinous rice after crossbreeding.

(3) Round-grain rice: a kind of paddy rice. Its stalk is comparatively low. Its leaves are comparatively narrow and deep green. The grains of rice are short and wide.

(4) Maize: an annual herb. Its stalk is 2—3 meter tall. Its leaves are long and large. Its grains are a little larger than soybeans.

(5) Milled long-grain nonglutinous rice: rice husked from the long-grain nonglutinous rice. It has little stickiness.

(6) High quality Milled long-grain nonglutinous rice: rice husked from the high quality long-grain nonglutinous rice.

(7) Milled round-grain rice: rice husked from the round-grain rice. It has comparatively

high stickiness.

(8) Wheat flour: powder husked from wheat. The specification for the survey is the ordinary standard flour.

(9) Unginned cotton: refers to the cotton picked down by the cotton farmers from the cotton branches and unginned. When the unginned cotton is ginned and the seeds are removed, it is called ginned cotton. 10 kg of unginned cotton can be generally processed into 3 kg of ginned cotton.

(10) Peanut kernel: refers to the shelled peanut.

(11) Live pig: refers to the grown pig to be slaughtered. Its weight is generally greater than 65 kg.

(12) Piglet: refers to the ordinary young pig to be fattened up. It generally refers to the newly weanned pig. Its weight is generally less than 10 kg.

(13) Grass carp: Its body is shaped like a cylinder and is greenish. It lives in freshwater and takes waterweeds as its food.

(14) Carp: Its body is squad shaped. Its back is black and its belly is yellowish white. It has a pair of beard near its mouth. It is a kind of freshwater fish.

(15) Silver carp: Its body is squad shaped. It has thin scales. Its back is greenish black and its belly is white. It is a kind of freshwater fish.

(16) Sweetbell: It is called shizijiao or caijiao in China.

(17) Kidney beans: It is called sijidou or biandou in different regions in China.

(18) Medium grade: There are two meanings. The medium grade of raw grain refers to the middle grade stipulated by the government. The medium grade of other products refers to the quality grade at which the bargain of a large quantity of products strike.

6—3　农产品批发价格调查方案

1. 调查目的

农产品批发价格是指全国大中型农产品批发市场或从事农产品批发交易的经营单位进行农产品批发交易的成交价格。开展农产品批发价格调查旨在收集农产品批发价格资料，准确把握全国主要农产品价格走势与供求状况，满足各级政府和宏观决策部门研究制定农村经济政策的需要，为提高我国农产品市场竞争力服务。

2. 调查内容

农产品批发价格调查内容为农林牧渔业主要农产品的批发交易价格，调查品种分为粮油、棉花、蔬菜、果品、花卉、肉禽蛋、水产品和木材共八个类别。

3. 调查对象

农产品批发价格调查的对象为农产品批发市场或从事农产品批发交易的经营单位。调查网点根据交易品种和成交量综合确定，全国共调查 100 家农产品批发市场和经营单位。

4. 调查周期与上报日期

农产品批发价格调查周期为月报，批发价格上报日期为每月 25 日。

粮油、蔬菜、果品、花卉、肉禽蛋和水产品价格的采价日期为上报日的前一个工作日。棉花和木材价格的报告期为上月 25 日至当月 24 日。遇法定节假日，采价和上报日期顺延，按实际采价日期填报。

5. 调查方式

(1)粮油、蔬菜、果品、花卉、肉禽蛋和水产品的批发价格以市场内该种农产品最大批发商(摊位、商家或商号)单笔最大交易为准。最大交易量前三家为批发商调查样本，一般优先选择交易量最大的批发商作为采价对象，并在一年内保持相对稳定。

批发价格为采价日单笔最大交易量的成交价格。价格资料由调查员在采价日对批发商进行现场访问取得。

(2)棉花和木材批发价格按被抽中市场或经营单位在报告期内批发交易的全部成交情况填报。

批发价格为批发交易的加权平均价格。价格资料由被调查单位对报告期内相关产品的全部销售情况逐一分类登记，并定期整理、报送价格数据。

(3)实行全国统一的统计分类标准和编码。各地可根据需要适当增加调查指标，但不得改变指标排列顺序和编码。

6. 数据报送与汇总

(1)各省(区、市)农调队通过国家统计系统内部信息传输系统(Openmail)直接报送批发市场和经营单位的价格资料。

(2)数据上报采用规定的 EXCEL 模板格式，价格保留两位小数。缺省指标可不予填报，但不得改变指标顺序和数据格式。

(3)批发价格数据汇总工作由国家统计局农村司负责。

Programme for the Survey of the Prices of Agricultural Products at the Wholesale Market

I. The Purpose of the Survey

The wholesale prices of agricultural products refer to the prices at which the bargain of the wholesale trade of agricultural products are stricken at the large and medium-sized wholesale market of agricultural products or at the units engaged in the wholesale trade of agricultural products. The purpose of conducting the survey of wholesale prices of agricultural products is to collect the data on the wholesale prices of agricultural products, accurately keep abreast of the change trend of prices of main agricultural products and the situation of their supply and demand in the whole country, so as to meet the needs of the government at different levels and the departments of macro-economic decision-making for formulating the rural economic policies.

II. The Contents of the Survey

The contents of the survey of wholesale prices of agricultural products include the prices of the main agricultural products in farming, forestry, livestock and fishery in the wholesale trade. The varieties surveyed are classified into the following eight categories: (1) grain and edible oil, (2) cotton, (3) vegetable, (4) fruits, (5) flowers, (6) meat, poultry and eggs, (7) aquatic products and (8) wood.

III. Respondents

The respondents of the survey of wholesale prices of agricultural products are the wholesale markets of agricultural products or the units engaged in the wholesale trade of agricultural products. The units to be surveyed are determined on the basis of the trade varieties and sales volume. A total of 100 wholesale markets of agricultural products and the units engaged in the wholesale trade of agricultural products are surveyed in the whole country.

IV. Survey Cycle and Reporting Date

The cycle of the survey of wholesale prices of agricultural products is a month. The date for reporting the wholesale prices is the 25th of every month.

The date for collecting the data on grain, edible oil, cotton, vegetable, fruits, flowers, meat, poultry, eggs and aquatic products is the working day preceding the reporting date. The period for reporting the data on the prices of cotton and wood is the period from the 25th of the previous month to the 24th of this month. When it happens to be a national festival or holiday, the date for collecting or reporting the price data is postponed correspondingly. The actual date for collecting the price data is to be reported.

V. Procedures of the Survey

(1) For the wholesale prices of grain, edible oil, cotton, vegetable, fruits, flowers, meat, poultry, eggs and aquatic products, the data on the price of the product of the largest individual trade at the largest vendor's stand, store or shop in the market are to be collected. The first three largest vendor's stands, stores and (or) shops are the sample units. The largest vendor's stand, store or shop in the market is generally to be selected to be the respondents. The respondents should be stable in a year.

The wholesale price refers to the price of the product of the largest individual trade on the day for collecting price data. The price data are collected by the enumerator from the wholesale vendor's stand, store or shop in the interview on the day for collecting price data.

(2) For the wholesale prices of cotton and wood, the price data should be filled out in the

light of the actual conditions of the wholesale trade of the selected market or the unit engaged in the trade in the reporting period.

The wholesale prices are the weighted average prices in the wholesale trade. The price data on the wholesale of the concerned products should be recorded one by one by the respondents in a classified way and should be periodically processed and reported.

(3) The national unified standard statistical classification and codes are implemented. The survey indicators can be implemented by the different regions in the light of their needs, but no changes should be made in the order and codes of the indicators.

VI. Data Reporting and Tabulation

(1) The rural survey organizations in different regions should directly report the price data of the wholesale markets and the units engaged in the wholesale trade by means of the Open mail 1, an internal system of information transmission in the national statistical system.

(2) The stipulated format EXELL should be used in reporting data. Two decimals should be kept in the price data. The unavailable data can be left out but no changes should be made in the order of indicators and data format.

(3) The Departmeut of Rural Survey of the National Bureau of Statistics is responsible for the work of tabulation of the data on the wholesale prices.

附录　农产品参考目录

Appendix　Reference Catalogue of Agricultural Products

附录 农产品参考目录
Appendix Reference Catalogue of Agricultural Products

农产品类别与品名	Agricultural Products	生产价格代表产品 Representative Products for Producer Price of Agricultural Products	计量单位 Unit
一、农业产品	I. Farming products	*	
1. 谷物及其他作物	1. Cereal and other crops	*	
1. 1 谷物(原粮)	1. 1. Cereal (unprocessed food grains)	*	公斤 Kg
1. 1. 1 小 麦	1. 1. 1. Wheat	*	公斤 Kg
硬粒小麦	Hard wheat	*	公斤 Kg
软粒小麦	Soft wheat	*	公斤 Kg
混合小麦	Mixed wheat	*	公斤 Kg
其他小麦	Other wheat	*	公斤 Kg
1. 1. 2 稻 谷	1. 1. 2. Paddy	*	公斤 Kg
早籼稻	Early long- grain nonglutinous rice	*	公斤 Kg
晚籼稻	Late long-grain nonglutinous rice	*	公斤 Kg
粳稻	Round-grain rice	*	公斤 Kg
其他稻谷	Other paddy	*	公斤 Kg
1. 1. 3 玉 米	1. 1. 3. Maize (corn)	*	公斤 Kg
黄玉米	Yellow maize	*	公斤 Kg
白玉米	White maize	*	公斤 Kg
混合玉米	Mixed maize	*	公斤 Kg
其他玉米	Other maize		公斤 Kg
1. 1. 4 杂 粮	1. 1. 4. Coarse cereals		公斤 Kg
谷子	Millet		公斤 Kg
高粱	Chinese sorghum		公斤 Kg
大麦	Barley		公斤 Kg
荞麦	Buckwheat		公斤 Kg
元麦	Hull-less Barley		公斤 Kg
青稞	Highland barley		公斤 Kg
莜麦	Naked oats		公斤 Kg
燕麦	Oats		公斤 Kg
其他杂粮	Other coarse cereals		公斤 Kg
1. 1. 5 谷物副产品	1. 1. 5. By-products of cereals		公斤 Kg
小麦秸	Wheat straw		公斤 Kg
稻草	Rice straw		公斤 Kg
玉米杆	Corn stover		公斤 Kg
大麦杆	Barley straw		公斤 Kg
谷子杆	Millet stalk		公斤 Kg
高粱杆	Chinese sorghum stalk		公斤 Kg
1. 2 薯 类	1. 2. Potato	*	公斤 Kg
红薯	Sweet potato	*	公斤 Kg
马铃薯	White Potato	*	公斤 Kg
其他薯类	Other potatoes		公斤 Kg
薯藤	Potato vines		公斤 Kg

续表 1 continued 1

农产品类别与品名	Agricultural Products	生产价格代表产品 Representative Products for Producer Price of Agricultural Products	计量单位 Unit
1.3 油 料	1.3. Oil-bearing crops		公斤 Kg
花生	Peanut		公斤 Kg
油菜籽	Rapeseeds		公斤 Kg
芝麻	Sesame		公斤 Kg
向日葵	Sunflower		公斤 Kg
胡麻籽	Flaxseeds		公斤 Kg
苏籽	Perillaseeds		公斤 Kg
其他油料作物	Other oil-bearing crops		公斤 Kg
花生蔓	Peanut vine		公斤 Kg
油菜籽杆	Rapeseed stalk		公斤 Kg
芝麻杆	Sesame stalk		公斤 Kg
向日葵杆	Sunflower stalk		公斤 Kg
胡麻籽杆	Flaxseed stalk		公斤 Kg
1.4 豆 类	1.4. Beans	*	公斤 Kg
大豆	Soybeans	*	公斤 Kg
绿豆	Mung beans	*	公斤 Kg
红小豆	Small red beans	*	公斤 Kg
蚕豆	Broad beans		公斤 Kg
豌豆	Peas		公斤 Kg
芸豆	Kidney beans		公斤 Kg
其他杂豆	Other beans		公斤 Kg
豆秸	Beanstalk		公斤 Kg
1.5 棉 花(籽棉)	1.5. Cotton (unginned cotton)	*	公斤 Kg
细绒棉	Thin-staple cotton	*	公斤 Kg
长绒棉	Long-staple cotton	*	公斤 Kg
棉籽	Cottonseeds		公斤 Kg
棉花杆	Cotton stalk		公斤 Kg
1.6 麻 类	1.6. Fiber crops	*	公斤 Kg
黄红麻	Jute and blueish dogbane	*	公斤 Kg
亚麻	Flax	*	公斤 Kg
苎麻	Ramie	*	公斤 Kg
线麻	Hamp		公斤 Kg
苘麻	Abutilon fibre		公斤 Kg
剑麻	Steel hemp		公斤 Kg
其他麻类	Other fiber crops		公斤 Kg
麻杆	Stalks of fiber crops		公斤 Kg
1.7 糖 类	1.7. Sugar crops	*	公斤 Kg
甘蔗	Sugarcane	*	公斤 Kg
甜菜	Beet	*	公斤 Kg
其他糖料	Other sugar crops		公斤 Kg
蔗尾	Top of sugarcane		公斤 Kg
甜叶菜	Beet leaves		公斤 Kg

续表 2

continued 2

农产品类别与品名	Agricultural Products	生产价格代表产品 Representative Products for Producer Price of Agricultural Products	计量单位 Unit
1.8 烟 草	1.8. Tobacco	*	公斤 Kg
烤烟叶	Flue-cured tobacco	*	公斤 Kg
晒烟叶	Sun-cured tobacco	*	公斤 Kg
白肋烟	Whiteerib tobacco		公斤 Kg
香料烟	Perfume tobacco		公斤 Kg
其他烟叶	Other tobacco		公斤 Kg
烟杆	Tobacco stalk		公斤 Kg
1.9 其他农作物	1.9. Other agricultural crops		公斤 Kg
青饲料	Greenfeed		公斤 Kg
牧草	Herbage		公斤 Kg
绿肥	Green manure		公斤 Kg
桑叶	Mulberry leaves		公斤 Kg
席草	Lepironia articulata.		公斤 Kg
蓖麻籽	Castor beans		公斤 Kg
除虫菊	Pyrethrum		公斤 Kg
薄荷油	Peppermint oil		公斤 Kg
莲子	Lotus seed		公斤 Kg
菖蒲	Calamus		公斤 Kg
苇子	Reed		公斤 Kg
菱角	Water caltrop		公斤 Kg
红黑瓜子	Red and black melon seed		公斤 Kg
龙须草	Agrimony		公斤 Kg
木薯	Tapioca		公斤 Kg
糜子	Mizi		公斤 Kg
黍子	Millet		公斤 Kg
蕉芋	Canna edulis Ker		公斤 Kg
野生植物的采集	Gathering of wild plants		公斤 Kg
未列明的其他农作物	Other agricultural crops		公斤 Kg
2.蔬菜、园艺作物	2. Vegetable and Horticulture crops	*	
2.1 蔬菜	2.1. Vegetable	*	
2.1.1 叶菜类	2.1.1. Leaf vegetable	*	公斤 Kg
菠菜	Spinach	*	公斤 Kg
芹菜	Celery	*	公斤 Kg
大白菜	Chinese cabbage	*	公斤 Kg
元白菜	Cabbage	*	公斤 Kg
甘蓝	Wild cabbage	*	公斤 Kg
花椰菜	Cauliflower	*	公斤 Kg
莴笋	Asparagus lettuce	*	公斤 Kg
油菜	Rape	*	公斤 Kg
其他叶菜	Other leaf vegetable		公斤 Kg
2.1.2 瓜菜类	2.1.2. Gourd vegetable	*	公斤 Kg
黄瓜	Cucumber	*	公斤 Kg

续表 3 continued 3

农产品类别与品名	Agricultural Products	生产价格代表产品 Representative Products for Producer Price of Agricultural Products	计量单位 Unit
冬瓜	White gourd	*	公斤 Kg
西葫芦	Summer squash	*	公斤 Kg
苦瓜	Balsam pear	*	公斤 Kg
丝瓜	Towed gourd	*	公斤 Kg
南瓜	Pumpkin	*	公斤 Kg
打瓜	Citrullus lanatus		公斤 Kg
瓠子	Bottle gourd		公斤 Kg
其他瓜菜	Other gourd vegetable		公斤 Kg
2.1.3 块根、块茎菜类	2.1.3 Root and tuber vegetable	*	公斤 Kg
萝卜	Radish	*	公斤 Kg
胡萝卜	Carrot	*	公斤 Kg
生姜	Ginger	*	公斤 Kg
芋头	Eddo		公斤 Kg
苔干	Tribute vegetable		公斤 Kg
百合(根)	Lily (root)		公斤 Kg
芋艿	Taro		公斤 Kg
山药	Chinese yam		公斤 Kg
其他块根、块茎菜	Other root and tuber vegetable		公斤 Kg
2.1.4 茄果菜类	2.1.4. Eggplant, tomato and chili, etc.	*	公斤 Kg
茄子	Eggplant	*	公斤 Kg
西红柿	Tomato	*	公斤 Kg
辣椒	Chili	*	公斤 Kg
青椒	Sweetbell	*	公斤 Kg
其他茄果菜类	Others		公斤 Kg
2.1.5 葱蒜类	2.1.5 Onion and Garlic	*	公斤 Kg
大葱	Scallion	*	公斤 Kg
蒜苔	Garlic stalk	*	公斤 Kg
蒜头	Garlic head	*	公斤 Kg
洋葱	Onion		公斤 Kg
蒜苗	Garlic bolt		公斤 Kg
小葱	Shallot		公斤 Kg
韭菜	Fragrant-flowered garlic		公斤 Kg
其他葱蒜类	Others		公斤 Kg
2.1.6 菜用豆类	2.1.6. Garden beans	*	公斤 Kg
四季豆	Kidney beans	*	公斤 Kg
豇豆	Cowpeas	*	公斤 Kg
其他菜用豆	Other garden beans		公斤 Kg
2.1.7 水生菜类	2.1.7. Water vegetable	*	公斤 Kg
莲藕	Lotus root	*	公斤 Kg
茭白	Wild ruice stem	*	公斤 Kg
荸荠	Water chestnut		公斤 Kg
其他水生菜	Other water vegetable		公斤 Kg

续表 4 continued 4

农产品类别与品名	Agricultural Products	生产价格代表产品 Representative Products for Producer Price of Agricultural Products	计量单位 Unit
2.1.8 食用菌(干鲜混合)	2.1.8. Mushroom	*	公斤 Kg
香菇(干品)	Mushroom (dried)	*	公斤 Kg
蘑菇(鲜品)	Mushroom (fresh)	*	公斤 Kg
黑木耳(干品)	Black edible fungus (dried)	*	公斤 Kg
白木耳(干品)	Tremella (dried)	*	公斤 Kg
金针菇(鲜品)	Golden mushroom		公斤 Kg
猴头菌(干品)	Bearded tooth(dried)		公斤 Kg
平菇(鲜品)	Oyster mushroom		公斤 Kg
花菇(干品)	Black forest mushroom		公斤 Kg
其他食用菌	Other edible mushrooms		公斤 Kg
2.1.9 其他蔬菜	2.1.9. Other vegetable		公斤 Kg
椿芽	Chinese cedrela sprouts		公斤 Kg
黄花菜	Other vegetable		公斤 Kg
空心菜	Mater convolvulus		公斤 Kg
荷兰豆	Snow pea		公斤 Kg
芥菜	Mustard		公斤 Kg
莜麦菜	Naked oats		公斤 Kg
生菜	Lettuce		公斤 Kg
苋菜	Amaranth vegetable		公斤 Kg
未列明的其他蔬菜	Other vegetables		公斤 Kg
2.2 花卉	2.2. Flowers	*	
2.2.1 鲜切花	2.2.1. Fresh flowers	*	枝 Branch
百合花	Lily	*	枝 Branch
康乃馨	Carnation	*	枝 Branch
满天星	June snow (serissa)	*	枝 Branch
勿忘我	Forgetmenot		枝 Branch
非洲菊	Flameray Gerbera	*	枝 Branch
玫瑰	Rugosa rose	*	枝 Branch
郁金香	Tulip		枝 Branch
情人草	Myosotis		枝 Branch
其他鲜切花	Other fresh flowers		枝 Branch
2.3 其他园艺作物	2.3. Other horticulture crops		
2.3.1 盆栽植物	2.3.1. Potted plant		盆 Pot
杜鹃	Cuckoo	*	盆 Pot
兰草	Orchid		盆 Pot
水仙	Asphodel		盆 Pot
菊	Chrysanthemum		盆 Pot
月季	China rose		盆 Pot
茉莉	Jasmine		盆 Pot
仙人掌(球)	Cacti		盆 Pot
夜来香	Evening primrose		盆 Pot
2.2.3 观赏苗木	2.2.3. Ornamental	*	株 Individual

续表 5　　continued 5

农产品类别与品名	Agricultural Products	生产价格代表产品 Representative Products for Producer Price of Agricultural Products	计量单位 Unit
香樟	Fragrant camphor		株 Individual
松柏	Coniferae		株 Individual
银杏	Gingkgo		株 Individual
茶花	Camellia		株 Individual
玉兰	Yulan		株 Individual
2.3.3 草坪草皮	2.3.3. Sod for lawn	*	平方米 Sq. m
2.3.9 其他园艺作物	2.3.9. Other horticulture crops		平方米 Sq. m
3. 水果、坚果、饮料和香料	3. Fruit, nut, beverage and perfume	*	
3.1 水果、坚果	3.1. Fruits and nuts	*	公斤 Kg
3.1.1 园林水果	3.1.1. Garden fruits		公斤 Kg
苹果	Apples	*	公斤 Kg
红富士苹果	Hongfushi apples	*	公斤 Kg
国光苹果	Guoguang apples	*	公斤 Kg
秦冠苹果	Qinguan apples	*	公斤 Kg
香蕉苹果	Banana apples		公斤 Kg
金冠苹果	Jinguan apples		公斤 Kg
元帅苹果	Yuanshuai (Marshal) apples		公斤 Kg
新红星苹果	New Hongxing apples		公斤 Kg
其他苹果	Other apples		公斤 Kg
梨	Pears	*	公斤 Kg
雪花梨	Snowflake pears	*	公斤 Kg
鸭梨	Ya-pear:Chinese white pears	*	公斤 Kg
酥梨	Soft-pear:a kind of pears	*	公斤 Kg
香梨	Bergamot pears		公斤 Kg
苹果梨	Apple pears		公斤 Kg
冬果梨	Dongguo pears		公斤 Kg
其他梨	Other pears		公斤 Kg
柑桔	Citrus	*	公斤 Kg
柑	Mandarin oranges	*	公斤 Kg
桔	Tangerines	*	公斤 Kg
橙	Oranges	*	公斤 Kg
柚	Shaddocks		公斤 Kg
其他柑桔	Others		公斤 Kg
其他水果	Other fruits	*	公斤 Kg
香蕉	Bananas	*	公斤 Kg
菠萝	Pineapples	*	公斤 Kg
荔枝	Litchis	*	公斤 Kg
龙眼	Longans	*	公斤 Kg
芒果	Mangoes		公斤 Kg
木瓜	Papayas		公斤 Kg
橄榄	Chinese olives		公斤 Kg
桃	Peachs		公斤 Kg

续表 6 continued 6

农产品类别与品名	Agricultural Products	生产价格代表产品 Representative Products for Producer Price of Agricultural Products	计量单位 Unit
杏	Apricots		公斤 Kg
杨梅	Waxberries		公斤 Kg
猕猴桃	Chinese goosebeeres		公斤 Kg
葡萄	Grapes	*	公斤 Kg
红枣	Red Chinese dates	*	公斤 Kg
柿子	Persimmons		公斤 Kg
沙果	Sand fruits		公斤 Kg
李子	Plums		公斤 Kg
番石榴	Guavas		公斤 Kg
枇杷	Loquats		公斤 Kg
青枣	Green Chinese dates		公斤 Kg
青梅	Greengages		公斤 Kg
其他园林水果	Other garden fruits		公斤 Kg
3.1.2 瓜果类	3.1.2. Melons	*	公斤 Kg
西瓜	Watermelons	*	公斤 Kg
甜瓜	Cucumis meloes	*	公斤 Kg
哈密瓜	Hami melons	*	公斤 Kg
香瓜	Musk melons		公斤 Kg
伊丽莎白瓜	Elizabeth melons		公斤 Kg
华莱士	Wallace melons		公斤 Kg
草莓	Strawberries		公斤 Kg
其他瓜果	Others		公斤 Kg
3.1.3 坚果类	3.1.3. Nuts	*	公斤 Kg
椰子	Coconut		公斤 Kg
腰果	Cashew		公斤 Kg
杏仁	Apricot kernel		公斤 Kg
槟榔	Areca		公斤 Kg
沙棘果	Seabuck thorn		公斤 Kg
其他坚果	Other nuts		公斤 Kg
3.2 茶及其他饮料(干品)	3.2. Tea and other beverages (dried)	*	
3.2.1 茶	3.2.1. Tea	*	
红毛茶	Black tea	*	公斤 Kg
宰毛茶	Green tea	*	公斤 Kg
乌龙茶	Oolong tea	*	公斤 Kg
紧压茶原料	Raw material for pressed tea		公斤 Kg
其他茶	Others		公斤 Kg
3.2.2 可可和咖啡	3.2.2. Cocoa and Coffee		公斤 Kg
咖啡豆	Coffee bean		公斤 Kg
可可豆	Cocoa bean		公斤 Kg
3.2.3 其他饮料(干品)	3.2.3. Other beverages (dried)		公斤 Kg
3.3 香料作物	3.3. Perfume crops		公斤 Kg
月桂	Laurel		公斤 Kg

续表 7 continued 7

农产品类别与品名	Agricultural Products	生产价格代表产品 Representative Products for Producer Price of Agricultural Products	计量单位 Unit
丁香	Clove		公斤 Kg
茴香	Fennel		公斤 Kg
香茅草	Citronella		公斤 Kg
留兰香	Spearmint		公斤 Kg
薰衣草	English lavander		公斤 Kg
百里香	Chinese thyme		公斤 Kg
茉莉花	Jasmine		公斤 Kg
其他	Others		公斤 Kg
4. 中药材	3. Traditional Chinese medicinal materials	*	公斤 Kg
茯苓	Fuling (poris cocos)	*	公斤 Kg
党参	Tangshen (pilose asiabell)	*	公斤 Kg
当归	Chinese angelica	*	公斤 Kg
黄芪	Root of membranous milk vetch	*	公斤 Kg
金银花	Honeysuckle	*	公斤 Kg
人参	Ginseng	*	公斤 Kg
黄连	Rhizome of Chinese goldthread	*	公斤 Kg
甘草	Licorice root	*	公斤 Kg
贝母	Bulb of fritillary	*	公斤 Kg
红花	Safflower	*	公斤 Kg
元胡	Amur corydalis	*	公斤 Kg
枸杞	Fruit of Chinese wolfberry	*	公斤 Kg
砂仁	Villous amomum	*	公斤 Kg
菊花	Chrysanthemu	*	公斤 Kg
白术	Largehead atractyldes	*	公斤 Kg
半夏	Tuber of pinelia	*	公斤 Kg
麦冬	Tuber of dwarf lilyturf		公斤 Kg
三七	Pseudo-ginseng		公斤 Kg
西洋参	American ginseng		公斤 Kg
麻黄参	Chinese ephedra		公斤 Kg
玄参	Root of Zhejiang figwort		公斤 Kg
肉桂	Cinnamon		公斤 Kg
生地	Dried rhizome of rehmannia		公斤 Kg
厚朴	Bark of official magnolia		公斤 Kg
杜仲	Bark of eucommia		公斤 Kg
薄荷	Peppermint		公斤 Kg
枳壳	Trifoliate-orange		公斤 Kg
田七	Notoginseng		公斤 Kg
两面针	Shinleaf pricklyash		公斤 Kg
板蓝根	Root of common baphicacanthus		公斤 Kg
苦丁茶	Kudin crotoxylum (bitter tea tree)		公斤 Kg
罗汉果	Siraitia		公斤 Kg
藿香	Ageratum		公斤 Kg

续表 8 continued 8

农产品类别与品名	Agricultural Products	生产价格代表产品 Representative Products for Producer Price of Agricultural Products	计量单位 Unit
天麻	Tuber of elevated gastrodia		公斤 Kg
灵芝	Glossy ganoderma		公斤 Kg
穿心莲	Creat		公斤 Kg
桔梗	Rampion		公斤 Kg
白芍	Root of herbaceous peony		公斤 Kg
地黄	Glutinous rehmannia		公斤 Kg
干姜	Dried ginger		公斤 Kg
桂枝	Cassia twig		公斤 Kg
丹参	Root of red-rooted salvia		公斤 Kg
大青叶	Common conehead		公斤 Kg
白芷	Root of Dahurian angelica		公斤 Kg
川芎	Ligusticum wallichii		公斤 Kg
泽泻	Water-plaintain		公斤 Kg
附子	Monkshood		公斤 Kg
云木香	Common Aucklandia Root		公斤 Kg
牛夕	Root of bidentate achyranthes		公斤 Kg
凡皮	Fanpi：a kind of traditional chinese medicine		公斤 Kg
玉金	Yujin：a kind of traditional chinese medicine		公斤 Kg
牛膝	Twotooth achyranthes		公斤 Kg
虫草	Chinese caterpillar fungus		公斤 Kg
黄姜	Yellow ginger		公斤 Kg
太子参	Pseudostellaria heterphylla		公斤 Kg
其他药材	Other medicinal materials		公斤 Kg
二、林业产品	II. Forest products	*	
2.1 林木的培育和种植	2.1. Cultivation and planting of forest trees		
2.1.1 育种育苗	2.1.1. Breeding and growing seedings		亩 mu
育苗面积	Growing seeding areas		亩 mu
2.1.2 造林	2.1.2. Afforestation		亩 mu
人工造林	Manual afforestation		亩 mu
飞机播种造林	Afforestation by airplane		亩 mu
2.1.3 抚育和管理	2.1.3 Breeding and administration		
零星植树	Sporadic tree planting		株 Individual
迹地更新	Slash regeneration		亩 mu
幼林抚育	Breeding of forest of young growth		亩 mu
成林抚育	Breeding of grown forest		亩 mu
2.2 竹木采运	2.2 Felling and transport of bamboo and wood	*	
2.2.1 木材采运	2.2.1 Felling and transport of wood	*	立方米 Stere
2.2.1.1 原木	2.2.1.1 Log	*	立方米 Stere
红松	Korean pine	*	立方米 Stere
落叶松	Larch	*	立方米 Stere
马尾松	Masson pine	*	立方米 Stere
杉木	China fir	*	立方米 Stere

续表 9 continued 9

农产品类别与品名	Agricultural Products	生产价格代表产品 Representative Products for Producer Price of Agricultural Products	计量单位 Unit
云南松	Yunnan pine	*	立方米 Stere
杨木	Poplar		立方米 Stere
桐木	Tung		立方米 Stere
油木	Youmu		立方米 Stere
桦木	Birch		立方米 Stere
2. 2. 1. 2 薪材	2. 2. 1. 2. Firewood		根 Bar
2. 2. 2 竹木采运	2. 2. 2. Felling and transport of bamboo	*	根 Bar
水竹	Water bamboo		根 Bar
斑竹	Mottled bamboo		根 Bar
毛竹(楠竹)	Mao bamboo	*	根 Bar
蒿竹	Hao Bamboo	*	根 Bar
淡竹	Henon bamboo		根 Bar
小杂竹	Small mixed bamboo		根 Bar
其他竹材	Other bamboo		根 Bar
2. 3 林产品的采集	2. 3 Gathering of forest products	*	
2. 3. 1 天然和人工林的果实	2. 3. 1. Products of natural and artificial forest	*	公斤 Kg
橡胶	Rubber	*	公斤 Kg
生漆	Raw lacquer	*	公斤 Kg
紫胶	Shellac	*	公斤 Kg
白蜡	White wax		公斤 Kg
油桐籽	Seeds of tung oil tree	*	公斤 Kg
油棕籽	Fruits of oil palm		公斤 Kg
乌桕籽	Seeds of Chinese tallow tree	*	公斤 Kg
山苍籽	Seeds of mountain spicy tree		公斤 Kg
五倍籽	Chinese gall (gall nut)	*	公斤 Kg
油茶籽	Seeds of tea-oil tree	*	公斤 Kg
棕片	Palm fibre	*	公斤 Kg
松脂	Rosin		公斤 Kg
栲胶	Tannin extract	*	公斤 Kg
核桃	Walnut	*	公斤 Kg
板栗	Chinese chestnut	*	公斤 Kg
白果	Ginkgo	*	公斤 Kg
松子	Pine nut	*	公斤 Kg
花椒	Chinese prickly ash	*	公斤 Kg
八角	Anise	*	公斤 Kg
桂皮	Cassia bark	*	公斤 Kg
胡椒	Pepper		公斤 Kg
茴油	Fennel oil		公斤 Kg
桂油	Cassia oil		公斤 Kg
其他果实	Other products		公斤 Kg
2. 3. 2 其他林产品采集	2. 3. 2. Gathering of other wild plants		公斤 Kg
柳条	Willow twigs		公斤 Kg

续表 10 continued 10

农产品类别与品名	Agricultural Products	生产价格代表产品 Representative Products for Producer Price of Agricultural Products	计量单位 Unit
藤条	Rattan		公斤 Kg
竹笋干	Dried bamboo shoots		公斤 Kg
桉树叶	Eucalyptus leaves		公斤 Kg
葵叶	Mallow leaves		公斤 Kg
黄柏	Yellow cypress		公斤 KS
茅草	Couch grass		公斤 Kg
未列明的其他林产品采集	Gathering of other wild plants		公斤 Kg
三、牧业产品（畜产品）	III. Animal products	*	
3.1 牲畜的饲养	3. 1. Livestock raising	*	
3.1.1 牛的饲养	3. 1. 1. Cattle raising	*	公斤 K8
活牛(毛重)	Live cattle(grossweight)	*	公斤 Kg
牛肉	Beef	*	公斤 KS
3.1.2 羊的饲养	3. 1. 2. Sheep raising	*	公斤 K8
活羊(毛重)	Live sheep	*	公斤 KS
羊肉	Mutton	*	公斤 Kg
3.1.3 其他牲畜饲养	3. 1. 3. Other livestock raising		公斤 KS
马	Horse		公斤 Kg
驴	Donkey		公斤 KS
骡	Mule		公斤 KS
骆驼	Camel		公斤 Kg
其他未列明的牲畜饲养	Other livestock raising		公斤 KS
3.1.4 奶产品	3. 1. 4. milk products		公斤 Ke
牛奶	Cow milk	*	公斤 Kg
羊奶	Sheep milk	*	公斤 K8
其他奶类	Other milk		公斤 KS
3.1.5 毛绒产品	3. 1. 5 Hair and down products		公斤 Kg
山羊毛	Goat's wool		公斤 Kg
绵羊毛	Sheep's wool		公斤 KS
山羊绒	Cashmere		公斤 KS
绵羊绒	Sheep's down		公斤 Kg
牦牛毛	Yak hair		公斤 KS
牦牛绒	Yak down		公斤 Kg
骆驼绒	Camel hair cloth		公斤 Kg
马鬃	Horse's mane		公斤 Kg
马尾	Horse's tail		公斤 Kg
其他毛绒产品	Other Hair and down products		公斤 KS
3.1.6 其他牲畜产品	3. 1. 6. 0 Other animal products		公斤 KS
3.2 猪的饲养	3. 2. Hog raising	*	公斤 KS
活猪(毛重)	Hog (gross weight)	*	公斤 Kg
猪肉	Pork	*	公斤 Kg
猪鬃	Bristles		公斤 K8
3.3 家禽	3. 3. Poultry	*	—公斤监

续表 11 continued 11

农产品类别与品名	Agricultural Products	生产价格代表产品 Representative Products for Producer Price of Agricultural Products	计量单位 Unit
3.3.1 肉禽(毛重)	3.3.1. Poultry (gross weight)		公斤 Kg
鸡	Chicken	*	公斤 Kg
鸭	Duck	*	公斤 Kg
鹅	Goose	*	公斤 Kg
鹌鹑	Quail		公斤 Kg
其他家禽	Other poultry		公斤 Kg
3.3.2 禽蛋	3.3.2. Eggs		公斤 Kg
鸡蛋	Chicken's eggs	*	公斤 Kg
鸭蛋	Duck 's eggs	*	公斤 Kg
鹅蛋	Goose' s eggs	*	公斤 Kg
鹌鹑蛋	Quail 's eggs		公斤 Kg
其他蛋	Other eggs		公斤 Kg
3.3.3 羽绒	3.3.3.. Eider down		公斤 Kg
鸭绒	Duck 's down		公斤 Kg
其他羽绒	Other down		公斤 Kg
3.4 狩猎和扑捉动物	3.4. Hunting and catching animals		张 Sheet
兽皮	Furs		张 Sheet
未列明的动物皮张	Furs not identified		张 Sheet
3.9 其他畜牧业	3.9. Other livestock products		
3.9.1 各种鸟类	3.9.1. Birds		公斤 Kg
鸽子	Pigeon		公斤 Kg
火鸡	Turkey		公斤 Kg
山鸡	Pheasant		公斤 Kg
鸵鸟	Ostrich		公斤 Kg
其他鸟类	Other birds		公斤 Kg
3.9.2 家养动物	3.9.2. Domestic animals		公斤 Kg
兔	Rabbit		公斤 Kg
兔毛	Rabbit hair	*	公斤 Kg
狗	Dog		公斤 Kg
猫	Cat		只 Individual
其他家养动物	Other domestic animals		头 Individual
3.9.3 珍贵动物	3.9.3. Rare animals		头 Individual
鹿	Deer		头 Individual
熊	Bear		头 Individual
獐	Roe		头 Individual
狐狸	River deer		公斤 Kg
水貂	Fox		头 Individual
蛇	Marten		公斤 Kg
其他珍贵动物	Other Rare animals		公斤 Kg
3.9.4 虫类	3.9.4. Worms		公斤 Kg
蚯蚓	Earthworm		公斤 Kg
蝎子	Bristles		公斤 Kg

续表 12 continued 12

农产品类别与品名	Agricultural Products	生产价格代表产品 Representative Products for Producer Price of Agricultural Products	计量单位 Unit
其他虫类	Other Worms		公斤 Kg
3.9.5 活的家畜产品	3.9.5. Live poultry products		
蚕茧	Silkworm cocoon		公斤 Kg
蜂蜜	Honey		公斤 Kg
蜂蜡	Beeswax		公斤 Kg
麝香	Musk		公斤 Kg
鹿茸	Pilose antler		公斤 Kg
其他活的家畜产品	Other live poultry products		
3.9.6 毛皮的生产	3.9.6. Production of furs		
动物皮张	Animals' furs		张 Sheet
其他毛皮的生产	Other furs		公斤 Kg
四、渔业产品	IV. Fishery products	*	
4.1 海水水产品	4.1. Seawater aquatic products	*	公斤 Kg
4.1.1 鱼类	4.1.1. Fish	*	公斤 Kg
大黄鱼	Large yellow croaker	*	公斤 Kg
小黄鱼	Small yellow croaker	*	公斤 Kg
带鱼	Hairtail	*	公斤 Kg
鲈鱼	Perch	*	公斤 Kg
沙丁鱼	Sardine	*	公斤 Kg
鳕鱼	Cod	*	公斤 Kg
石斑鱼	Grouper	*	公斤 Kg
醍鱼	Anchovy		公斤 Kg
梭鱼	Barracuda		公斤 Kg
金枪鱼	Tuna		公斤 Kg
鲳鱼	Silvery pomfret	*	公斤 Kg
海鳗	Moray		公斤 Kg
鲅鱼	Spanish mackerel	*	公斤 Kg
鲐鱼	Chub mackerel		公斤 Kg
马面鱼	Black scraper		公斤 Kg
黄姑鱼	Spotted maigre		公斤 Kg
鳓鱼	Chinese herring		公斤 Kg
马鲛	Japanese Spanish mackerel		公斤 Kg
鲱鱼	Herring		公斤 Kg
梅童鱼	Baby croaker		公斤 Kg
鲻鱼	Mullet		公斤 Kg
蓝圆	Blue scad		公斤 Kg
远东拟沙丁鱼	Far East imitation sardine		公斤 Kg
太平洋鲱	Pacific herring		公斤 Kg
鲆鲽	Left-eyed flounder		公斤 Kg
舌鳎	Tonguefish		公斤 Kg
其他海水鱼类	Other seawater fish		公斤 Kg
4.1.2 海水甲壳蟹类	4.1.2. Seawater shrimp and crab	*	公斤 Kg

续表 13 continued 13

农产品类别与品名	Agricultural Products	生产价格代表产品 Representative Products for Producer Price of Agricultural Products	计量单位 Unit
对虾	Prawn	*	公斤 Kg
毛虾	Shrimp	*	公斤 Kg
爬虾	Mantis shrimp		公斤 Kg
脊尾白虾	Exopataemom carimicauda		公斤 Kg
鹰爪虾	Trachypemaeus curvirostris		公斤 Kg
梭子蟹	Swimming crab	*	公斤 Kg
锯缘青蟹	A kind of seawater crab		公斤 Kg
其他海水甲壳类	Other seawater shrimps and crabs		公斤 Kg
4.1.3 海水贝类	4.1.3. Seawater shellfish	*	公斤 Kg
贻贝	Mussel	*	公斤 Kg
扇贝	Scallop	*	公斤 Kg
牡蛎	Oyster	*	公斤 Kg
鲍鱼	Abalone		公斤 Kg
海水珍珠	Seawater pearl		公斤 Kg
蛤	Clam	*	公斤 Kg
蚶	Blood clam		公斤 Kg
海螺	Conch		公斤 Kg
蛏	Razor clam	*	公斤 Kg
其他海水贝类	Other seawater shellfish		公斤 Kg
4.1.4 藻类	4.1.4. Seaweeds	*	公斤 Kg
海带	Kelp	*	公斤 Kg
紫菜	Laver	*	公斤 Kg
其他藻类	Other seaweeds		公斤 Kg
4.1.5 其他海水产品	4.1.5. Other seawater products		公斤 Kg
墨鱼	Inkfish		公斤 Kg
鱿鱼	Squid		公斤 Kg
章鱼	Octopus		公斤 Kg
海蜇	Jellyfish		公斤 Kg
海参	Sea cucumber		公斤 Kg
其他未列明的海水产品	Other seawater products		公斤 Kg
4.2 内陆水域水产品	4.2. Aquatic products in inland water areas	*	公斤 Kg
4.2.1 淡水鱼类	4.2.1. Freshwater fish	*	公斤 Kg
青鱼	Black carp	*	公斤 Kg
草鱼	Grass carp	*	公斤 Kg
鲤鱼	Carp	*	公斤 Kg
鲢鱼	Silver carp	*	公斤 Kg
鲫鱼	Crucian carp	*	公斤 Kg
罗非鱼	Tilapia	*	公斤 Kg
虹鳟鱼	Rainbow trout	*	公斤 Kg
白鱼	Whitefish		公斤 Kg
鳜鱼	Mandarin fish		公斤 Kg
白鲳鱼	Round spadefish		公斤 Kg

续表 14 continued 14

农产品类别与品名	Agricultural Products	生产价格代表产品 Representative Products for Producer Price of Agricultural Products	计量单位 Unit
黑鱼	Snakeheaded fish		公斤 Kg
鲶鱼	Oriental sheatfish		公斤 Kg
武昌鱼	Blunt-snout bream		公斤 Kg
鳙鱼	Variegated carp		公斤 Kg
鲮鱼	Dace		公斤 Kg
鳊	Bream		公斤 Kg
鲂	John dory		公斤 Kg
黄颡鱼	Yellowcat fish		公斤 Kg
银鱼	Whitebait		公斤 Kg
淡水鲈	Freshwater perch		公斤 Kg
大马哈鱼	Chum salmon		公斤 Kg
乌鳢	Snakehead mullet		公斤 Kg
淡水鳗	Freshwater ell		公斤 Kg
其他淡水鱼类	Other freshwater fish		公斤 Kg
4.2.2 淡水甲壳类	4.2.2. Freshwater shrimps and crabs		公斤 Kg
龙虾	Lobster	*	公斤 Kg
罗氏沼虾	M. rosenbergii	*	公斤 Kg
青虾	Freshwater shirimp		公斤 Kg
克氏螯虾	Red Swamp crayfish		公斤 Kg
基围虾	Greasyback shrimp	*	
红螯螯虾	Red clow		
大闸蟹	Steamed crab		公斤 Kg
其他淡水甲壳类	Other freshwater shrimp and crab		公斤 Kg
4.2.3 淡水贝类	4.2.3. Freshwater shellfish	*	公斤 Kg
淡水珍珠	Freshwater pearl		公斤 Kg
螺蛳	Spiral shell		公斤 Kg
河蚌	Freshwater mussel		公斤 Kg
其他淡水贝类	Other freshwater shellfish		公斤 Kg
4.2.4 其他淡水养殖产品	4.2.4. Other freshwater breeding products		公斤 Kg
河鳗	River eel		公斤 Kg
牛蛙	Bullfrog		公斤 Kg
甲鱼	Soft-shelled turtle		公斤 Kg
黄鳝	Ricefield eel		公斤 Kg
泥鳅	Loach		公斤 Kg
龟	Tortoise		公斤 Kg
蛙	frog		公斤 Kg
未列明的其他淡水养殖产品	Other freshwater breeding products		公斤 Kg